"FIVE HUNDRED YEARS AGO OR MORE": p. 198

ULSTER SCOTS
AND
BLANDFORD
[MASSACHUSETTS]
SCOUTS

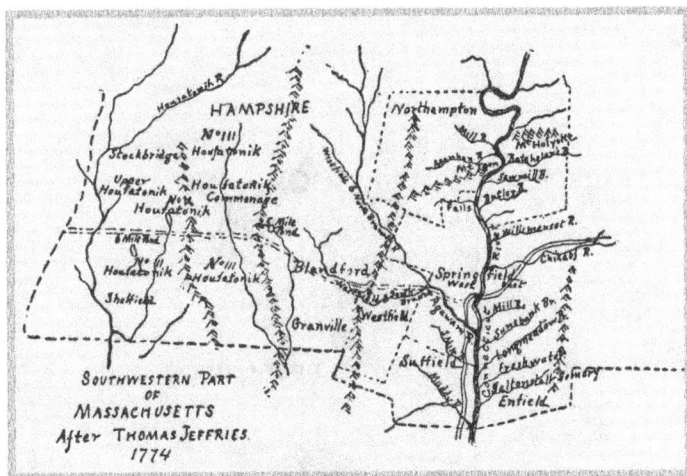

Sumner Gilbert Wood

Author of *The Taverns and Turnpikes of Blandford, 1733–1833*

HERITAGE BOOKS
2010

HERITAGE BOOKS

AN IMPRINT OF HERITAGE BOOKS, INC.

Books, CDs, and more—Worldwide

For our listing of thousands of titles see our website
at
www.HeritageBooks.com

A Facsimile Reprint
Published 2010 by
HERITAGE BOOKS, INC.
Publishing Division
100 Railroad Ave. #104
Westminster, Maryland 21157

International Standard Book Numbers
Paperbound: 978-0-7884-0632-4
Clothbound: 978-0-7884-8423-0

FOREWORD

THE early chapters of this present writing are devoted largely to an interpretation of the habits of mind and soul of the Ulster Scots and their immediate descendants. Said a daughter of one of this doughty race to a friend who had opened her eyes to some of the stirring history of this people, "Now I understand my father." Permanent and mighty forces of the spirit operated through the century-long residence of the migrant Scots in Ulster. Their careers and the significance of their contribution to American history must be in large degree a closed book to their own descendants unless these things are understood.

I fondly hope that those who read these pages will find here the prophecy and the philosophy of the old Blandford not only, but of every other New England community whose history was begun or largely moulded by these people.

A score of years ago I promised to write upon "The Homes and Habits of Ancient Blandford." Hitherto I have been prevented by professional duties outside of this town of my one-time residence and work. This book is the fulfilment of that promise, in part. Further fulfilment depends on the success of this venture. "Small erections may be finished by their first architects; grand ones, true ones, ever leave the copestone to posterity. God keep me from ever finishing anything. This whole book is but a draft. Oh, Time, Strength, Cash and Patience!"

My thanks are due, and hereby expressed, to many, including the Blandford Town Improvement Committee, the editor of the *Springfield Republican,* and many others, among whom are many of my closest personal friends.

SUMNER GILBERT WOOD.

West Medway, Massachusetts.
September, 1928.

"A PEOPLE WHICH TAKES NO PRIDE
IN THE ACHIEVEMENTS OF REMOTE
ANCESTORS WILL NEVER ACHIEVE
ANYTHING WORTHY TO BE REMEM-
BERED BY REMOTE DESCENDANTS."

Thomas Babington Macaulay.

TABLE OF CONTENTS

LIST OF ILLUSTRATIONS

Note: Of the illustrations, Nos. 1 and 7 are from photographs taken by Miss Helen Hinsdale. Nos. 2, 9, 13, 22 and 23 are from pen and ink sketches by Mrs. Wood. No. 21 is from an old photograph of the Lloyd family. The rest, except reproductions of ancient documents, are from photographs taken by the author.

CHAPTER I

The Settlement of Scots in Ulster Under Elizabeth and James:

Dragons' Teeth and Armed Men

The great migration from the North of Ireland which began in the year 1718 brought into being not less than two-score settlements in four New England states before the first half of the century had closed. Nearly half of these were in Maine, while New Hampshire and Massachusetts received in about equal numbers nearly all the rest, Connecticut coming in for two. In thirty years beginning with 1751 the number of new settlements from this source in these same states with the addition of Vermont was nearly or quite double that of the earlier period. In practically all of them churches were organized after the order of the Scotch Presbyterian church. These widely scattered settlements maintained intercommunication with one another in intimate ways growing out of a common history of stress and strain, an intercommunication which was powerfully augmented by the ecclesiastical organization of their ancestral church. Professor Perry has happily called this the Presbyterian circuit. It reached out long arms to embrace other like communities in the Middle states.

In old Hampshire county, Massachusetts, a lonely trail had been blazed between Springfield and the West. Now and then a traveler followed the long bridle path on horseback, or perchance afoot. He was a messenger of state; or he carried letters; or he was a landed proprietor, or a surveyor, or an adventurer. A few miles out from Springfield was the village of Westfield, on the river of that name. Thence westward it was mountain and wilderness to the valley of the Housatonic. In the midst, in 1733, a rude tavern, known as Pixley's,* offered the tired and hungry wayfarer food and drink and repose. This primeval caravansary stood on the westernmost edge of Blandford, as the tract came to be known. Two years later a settlement was begun a half-dozen miles eastward of the solitary inn. A rugged country it is, and rugged folk were they who first scaled these hills to open the forests to the light of day.

For the most part they were Scots from the North of Ireland, and they entered Blandford in a body; not scatteringly; not by way of some happy convenience or good fortune. Of purpose they came; with principle and conviction solid as the rocks of those templed hills, with a common history behind them, and common hopes surging in their militant breasts. They were from Ulster, in North Ireland. That we may know something of the real genius of their homes and habits, and of the homes and habits of all the Ulster Scots, to Ulster we go, into whose soil they struck deep the roots of their adventurous life. For, be it known, ours is to be a tale of wanderings, of strangers and pilgrims on earth. Old Pixley's is a true if ghostly symbol of it all. Adventurers from Ulster who settled Blandford and scores of other towns had the germs of wanderlust in their veins. They were for ever seeking a country of their own and never finding it. Their land was a land of visions, their voyage of life an adventure of Argonauts, their past a dream, their future an ideal. Once in Blandford, or wherever, and well settled, like birds of passage they scattered over the vast reaches of the West. From their wanderings their children's children still send back

---

* The story of this is told in "The Taverns and Turnpikes of Blandford, 1733-1833."

to their fond homes in the New England wilderness their "All hail, and farewell!"

It does not belong to the purpose of this book to trace out any considerable history of these people previous to their settlements in Ireland. But some rather intimate jottings may fittingly occupy a few paragraphs. The subject is a recondite one, and this brief sketch is suggestive rather than exhaustive.

The Ulster settlements were composed of a mixture of Lowland and Highland Scots. "The Scottish Highlanders are the remnant of the great Celtic race which remained untouched by the Roman and Saxon invasions on the south, and the Danes on the east and west, of the country, and they were the last to oppose with perfect success the otherwise conquering arms of Rome." *

For a little while then we are in Ireland. The North Channel is narrow, and over across there were Scots, quite ready to leave their poor homes for better, if such they might perchance find. Passage to and fro was always easy. And always and everywhere there are those whose roots strike but a little way down into the soil, especially when life is hard, where rewards of living are poor and every tomorrow is like every yesterday, gray and hopeless, or mayhap adventurous and irresponsible.

So it happened that when the higher powers had emptied out many a home of sorry Ireland by the will of kings and queens who recked not overmuch of justice and mercy, the Emerald Isle saw strange hearthfires lighted where its native fires had been put out, in many a fertile vale and along many a grassy mead.

Irish chieftains and demigods were a buccaneering folk no doubt, and the underlings of the land found

---

* "The Scottish Clans and their Tartans."

living hard and hazardous at best. But there was in these hearts a fierce loyalty to Irish traditions and masters. In the checkered history of the English crown the soil of Ireland became a sort of plaything, and the confiscation of lands was a game of war, convenience and greed. Dishonor and massacre, forsooth, seemed not to be crimes when committed upon a barbarous people. Elizabeth's lord deputy in Ireland was challenged with remonstrance for his bloody deeds, and replied, "By the sword I have won these lands, and by the sword will I keep them."

What Elizabeth had begun James I proceeded to accomplish more completely. English and Scottish settlers were invited to occupy Irish lands confiscated by the divine right of kings and queens for the use and behoof of their favorite subjects. "The fruitful plains of Armagh, the deep pastoral glens that lie between the sheltering hills of Donegal, the undulating meadow lands stretching by the noble lakes and rivers of Fermanagh, passed from the race which had possessed them since before the redemption of mankind. . . . The alluvial lands were given to English courtiers whom the Scotch king found it necessary to placate, and to Scotch partisans whom he dared not reward in England. The peasants driven out of the tribal lands to burrow in the hills or bogs were not treated according to any law known among civilized men." *

The king indeed considered his Ulster policy his masterpiece of statesmanship, and often boasted of it. It must be allowed that his attempted transformations of economic and civic customs in Ireland were ideally far in advance of anything which the island had known. There had been no fixture of land titles and therefore no

---

* C. G. Duffy, quoted in Larned's History for Ready Reference, old edition, Vol. 3, p. 1764.

incentive to individuals to improve the land. Official lawlessness had known no let nor hindrance. In the place of such a condition James instituted English law in Ireland. To the natives he awarded citizenship, and set up a small standing army to preserve order.

But the native Irish preferred to remain barbarian, and were deeply averse to James's civilizing regulations. Besides, they could never forget that the lands which were to benefit most by these reforms had been taken from them by violence, so that the very reforms were laid upon foundations of injustice which cried to heaven for vengeance. "Your sheriff," said Maguire to the new lord deputy, "shall be welcome to me; but let me know beforehand his eric, or the price of his head, that, if my people cut it off, I may levy the money upon the county."* That was a characteristic and prophetic answer of Ireland to the representative of a power which was saying, "Peace, peace, when there was no peace." And this was bound to be until memory should melt into oblivion, or hope be lost in despair. No wonder James had plenty of occupation for his little standing army in Ireland.

It was not altogether a peace-loving folk, either, whom the English royalty was transporting into Ulster.

The Campbell clan was the most powerful and warlike in Scotland. They occupied the country of Argyll, and were divided into several lines, or houses. The Fergusons were inclined to peace. David, John, James, Robert, William were characteristic names in this clan. The Kerrs were Highlanders, also the Lindsays and Maxwells and Scotts, of which last named clan was the famous Sir Walter. There were Blairs from Ayrshire. Then there were the Stuarts, Stewarts, Steuarts, or Stewards, the name having been derived from the office

---

* Hume, IV, 422.

of Lord High Steward of Scotland, which they held for nearly two centuries before they came to the throne.*

Five centuries of intimate Scottish history centered around the distinguished personages of this royal family. Great numbers from Ayre, Galloway, Dumfries, Dumbarton, Renfrew, and notably from Argyle, were in the Ulster migration. They were as sharply diverse from the English as were the Irish. "They were un-English in all their ideas, hating the institutions of England, civil and ecclesiastical, with a bitterness elsewhere unknown, to which the Revolution (i.e., the American) gave full vent." †

> "Wha wadna join our noble chief,
>   The Drummond and Glengarry,
> McGregor, Murray, Rollo, Keith,
>   Panmure and gallant Harry?
>   Macdonald's men,
>   Mackenzie's men,
>   Macgilvery's men,
>   Strathallan's men,
>   The Lowlan' men,
>   Of Callander and Airly." ‡

There were other and later movements of population from Scotland into Ireland. Cromwell the Protector swept vast acres of the Irishry and imported more Scots, especially of the soldiery, for the purposes of peace and justice as he saw it. Finally, a century or thereabout after the first Scots entered Ulster for purposes of settlement, William III, that most enlightened monarch, yet followed in the footsteps of his illustrious royal predecessors in respect of peopling Ireland by ousting the natives of the land. The sovereigns of England seemed

* "The Scottish Clans and their Tartans."
† Douglas Campbell.
‡ Alexander Laing.

not to be aware that they were scattering dragons' teeth all over that luckless island. But the laws of the universe did not forget that for every such poisoned tooth thus sown an armed man would arise to bathe his sword in the blood of the unnatural succession. The very genius of caprice, oppression, uncertainty of title, and menace to the peace of the whole land was injected into the veins of Irishmen and Irish politics. At all times the children and children's children of the dispossessed were diligently taught lessons of reprisal and revenge. So it was by no accident that twice in a half century Protestants in Ireland saturated the soil with their blood or wept over their fire-swept cottages and church buildings ravaged by the unforgetting and "despairing Irishes."

In these scattering settlements of English and Scotch, the latter greatly outnumbered, or came to outnumber, the rest. They were hardier and took more kindly to the climate of the new country. Cromwell noticed the difference among his soldiery. Some English remained. Londonderry took its name from English proprietors and colonists. But our present interest is with the Scots, whose holdings came to be largely in the north and east of Ulster. By 1610 most of the new settlers in Ulster were Scots. Clearings, settlements and general construction went on apace, not, however, without difficulty. "Bands of irreclaimable natives" still occupied the woods and fastnesses, and made good their inherited right of plunder, even as the disinherited children of the East in the olden time did to the Hebrew squatters in Palestine. Detailed descriptions of the country in or about 1610 are accessible, only one of which will serve us for an example here:

"How exceedingly well standeth Ardmath (i.e., Armagh), better rich soil there cannot be, but so poor, as I do verily think, all the household stuff in that city is not worth 20 pounds. Yet it is the primate of all Ireland, and, as they say, for antiquity, one of the most ancient in all Europe. It is also of so small power as forty resolute men may rob, rifle and burn it. Were it a defenced corporation, it would soon be rich and religious, and security would make one acre more worth than twenty now be."* In addition, "the woolfe and the wood-kerne within culiver shot of his fort" made necessary to the planter the driving in of his cattle at night. Here, in truth, were dragons' teeth already coming up out of the very soil.

Two-thirds of the North of Ireland thus became occupied. This section grew to be the most prosperous in the island, when undisturbed, and has so remained. "Farms and homesteads, churches and mills, rose fast amid the desolate hills of Tyrone.† . . . The evicted natives withdrew sullenly to the lands which had been left them by the spoiler; but all faith in English justice had been torn from the minds of the Irish, and the seed had been sown of that fatal harvest of distrust and disaffection which was to be reaped through tyranny and massacre in the time to come." With such a historic background, of what avail would the introduction of "The Reformation" be by Henry VIII., and Edward VI., and Elizabeth, and James I., "the wisest fool in Europe," however benevolently intended?

I now proceed to give a condensed account of the early settlements, particularly by the Scots, drawn from the story of Rev. Andrew Stewart, minister of Donaghadee from 1645 to 1671. This writer was son of the Rev. A. Stewart, of Donegore. The historian is able to tell of events which his own eyes saw, and of which he might truly have said himself was "a part." The

---

* Quoted from ancient MSS. by Reid, I, 79.
† Green, Shorter History, Chap. VII, Sec. viii.

manuscript is cited somewhat at length by Reid, in his "History of the Presbyterian Church in Ireland," and it is from the pages of this careful and conscientious historian that I make the following sketch.

As has already been said, Londonderry was chiefly an English interest, and so was Coleraine. "Sir Hugh Clotworthy obtains the lands of Antrim, both fruitful and good." Chichester was given an estate therein, which he improved, built the "prosperous mart Belfast," and erected "a stately palace" in Carrickfergus. Conway built Lisnegarvy, and Moses Hill cleared the woodlands of Hills, building a town called Hillsborough. These were all originally English settlements, made in places "where formerly had been nothing but robbing, treason and rebellion." Of the Scots nation, there was a family of Balfours, of the Forbeses, of the Grahames, two of the Stewarts, and not a few of the Hamiltons. The Macdonnells founded the earldom of Antrim by King James's gift, the Hamiltons the earldoms of Strabane and Clanbrassil, and there were besides several knights of that name, Sir Frederick, Sir George, Sir Francis, Sir Charles his son, and Sir Hans, all Hamiltons; for they prospered above all others in this country after the first admittance of the Scots into it. This little story already uncovers the Irish roots of several Blandford families.

In the county of Down, the Hamilton and Montgomery families "proved the most successful promoters of the Scottish plantation, and were intimately connected with the subsequent vicissitudes of the Presbyterian Church in Ulster"—also, we may add, in Blandford. Con O'Neill, an Irishman having vast land possessions, "being rebellious,"—forsooth—"and his land falling to the king, was imprisoned" awaiting the time of "an ignominious death." We will not stop to meditate upon this Irishman's sins, venial or mortal, considering that, to be just, we should be obliged to make quite a catalogue of James's also, and that would be too long a story. Suffice it to say that Con's wife was a lady of large resource, who most wisely consulted with "Mr. Hugh Montgomery, of Broadstone, in Scotland, a man sober, kind, humane, and trusty, to whom she revealed her husband's case and her own desire, saying, if Mr. Montgomery would be at pains and charge to purchase from the king her husband's life and liberty, with a third part of the estate for him and her to live on, the said Montgomery should, with their great good will, have the other two parts, to be purchased by the king's grant." Thereupon follows such a story of Con's escape from prison, of bribing the king for a pardon for the same, through the intermediation of James Hamilton, and the promise that Montgomery should turn over half of his two parts to Hamilton for the job, as, in all its intricacies and adventures might worthily go along with the stories of Robin Hood. Hamilton thought it worth his while to relinquish his fellowship in the University of Dublin for this business, and took with him Sir James Fullerton, who was "in high favor at the English court." As a result, "Con has his life and a third part, Montgomery has a third part, and Mr. James Hamilton has a third part of Con O'Neill's estate in Down. Hugh and James were made knights, and later lords, Montgomery, of Ards, and Hamilton, of Claneboy." Glory enough, one might think.

But there were some by-products: James got hold of most of the land, while Hugh received chief honor as favorite of the king; and the two working together in this business of land-grabbing, succeeded in developing not a few jealousies and squabbles, the which were also bequeathed as an abundant inheritance to the generations following. The date of this business was 1605.

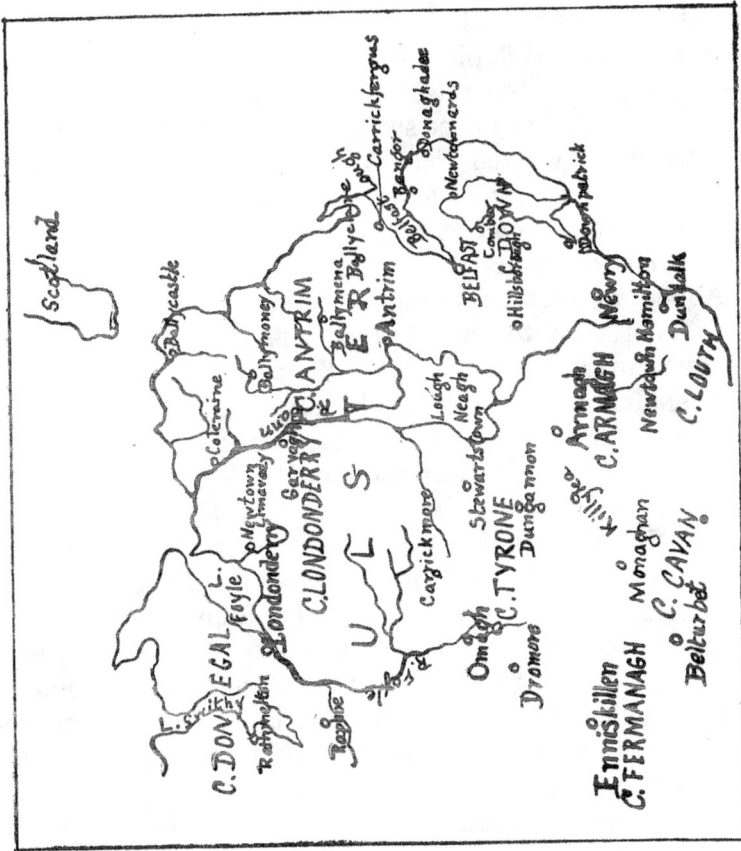

A PART OF ULSTER

Now "land without inhabitants is a burden without relief," remarks our Stewart historian. "The Irish were gone, the ground was desolate, rent must be paid to the king, tenants were none to pay them." Right here the Montgomery manuscripts afford us a realistic picture of passing scenes: "Let us pause awhile, and we shall wonder how this plantation advanced itself, especially in and about the towns of Donaghadee and Newton; considering that in the spring-time, 1606, those parishes were more wasted than America when the Spaniards landed there; for in all these three parishes aforesaid, thirty cabins could not be found, nor any stone-walls; but ruined, roofless churches, and a few vaults at Grey-Abbey, and a stump of an old castle in Newton."

We return to the Stewart source: The two lordly adventurers made some of their friends sharers and freeholders under them. Several farmers, gentlemen from Scotland, came across: Shaws, Calderwoods, Boyds and Keiths from the North. Towns and incorporations were laid: Newton, Donaghadee, Comber, Old and New Grey Abbey. Many of the Hamiltons followed Sir James,—his brothers and other farmers: Maxwells, Rosses, Moors, Bayleys. And he founded towns and incorporations: Bangor, Holywood, Killileagh where he built a strong castle, and Ballywater. "These foundations being laid, the Scots came hither apace, and became tenants willingly and sub-tenants to their countrymen (whose manner and way they knew), so that in a short time the country began again to be inhabited." The Montgomery manuscripts add, concerning the settlements made under that name and favor: Sir Hugh "considered that the contentions which too frequently happen concerning tythes, might breed dislike between the people and minister. Therefore he gave unto the incumbents salaries, with glebes and perquisites for marriages, christenings, burials, and Easter offerings; the clerk and sexton also had their share of fees; and the people of those days resorted to Church, and submitted to its censures, and paid willingly their ecclesiastical dues; and so were in no hazard of suits in ecclesiastical courts." Sir James Hamilton did likewise. Thus far (and no farther) the Stewart manuscript, with the few amendments as noted.

There were other amalgamations, and they carry us far back into the early history of Britain. The Fergusons, for example, derive their name from Fergus, son of Eric, first king of the British Scots. He left Ireland in 503, and settled on the coast of Argyle or the adjacent islands. The royal coronation stone, the Stone of Scone, it should be remembered, was brought from Ireland, and has served for centuries its traditional use for the sovereigns of the United Kingdom. The two separated portions of Ancient Scotia had much to do with each other in the early centuries, Ireland being then, of the two, much farther advanced in the arts of civilization.

The Cochrans, it is contended, were from Clan Armond, now Tipperary, in Munster, but the claim is challenged. Morrison, in like manner, it is asserted, harks back to the McMurroughs, sons of Murrough, or Murroughsons, of Leinster, while by still others the origin is traced from the Teutonic Morhs, or the wilds of Germania.

The Cochrans and Moors, or Mooars, according to Professor Perry* settled about Ballymoney, Kilrea and Colraine, in the valley of the Bann in the reign of James II. The McKinstrys came from the vicinity of Edinburgh and went to Brode parish in Antrim. William Knox, father of John, William and Adam, is said to have been born in Glasgow, whence he went to Ireland.

---

* "The Scotch-Irish" etc.

John Thompson, who joined the Blandford group some little time after the settlement there, was born in St. Michael's parish, Dublin. Jane Wallace, wife of James, first saw the light in Belturbet, County Cavan. Their bones lie in the old Blandford burying ground, under the pines. The Provins (Provan, Provin, Provence, Provance, etc.), in particular William and Mercy (or Marcy, or Mary) passed from Scotland to Ulster not very long before the migration to America. They were very early comers to Blandford, though not the very first.

In the counties of Down and Antrim, there appear on the rent rolls of the years 1681 and 1688, as holding farms of the Hamilton estates, such names as these, so familiar in the early life of Blandford: Alexander, Anderson, Black, Browne, Campbell, Carr (Kerr), Cochran, Ferguson, Gilmore, Hamilton, Henry, How, Lindsay, Maxwell, Mitchel, Montgomery, Moore, Patterson, Read, Scott, Stewart, Thompson, Watson, White, Wilson, Young.* Other residents in these two counties bore the names of Johnson, Millar, Robinson, Smith. "Along the shores of Down and Antrim, and by the banks of the Six-Mile Water and the Main, the colonists were almost wholly from the Lowlands of Scotland." †

The result of the various migrations was an amalgamation pretty compact in respect of character and manners. Withal a good deal of Irish accent in speech clung to them like a burr. They spelled as they pronounced, with an airiness and eclat most refreshing. All sorts of documents bear witness to the fact. Cromwell's

---

* Charles A. Hanna.

† Ibid., quoting from J. S. MacIntosh, "The Making of the Ulstermen." Students of the subject interested to learn in more minute detail about the issuance of grants in 1610 to Scottish undertakers, may do well to consult the treatise of Charles A. Hanna.

soldiers were more thoroughgoing mixers than any of the rest. However, these were a very minor influence in Ulster history. In general, stout contenders for racial distinctions may not rightly ignore the fact that time mixes races and classes.

King James had ordained that the rising settlements should be made in orderly fashion on this wise: Three kinds of allotments were to be made by three grades of operators respectively. First, British undertakers were to lay out allotments of two thousand acres each. Next were certain official servitors of the crown who should divide their territories into allotments of fifteen hundred acres. And last, certain trusty natives were to make divisions of one-thousand acres. The first class were bound, within four years, to build a castle and bawn,* and to plant on their estates forty-eight men, eighteen years old or upwards. The house or castle was built within this fortification, sufficient to secure the denizens and their cattle from the incursions of the marauding Irish. We shall see whether they did or not. The second class must within two years build a strong stone or brick house and bawn; and a third a bawn. There were provisions requiring sufficient settlers, and the houses were to be adequately provided with military arms.† This did not look much like peace. One-quarter of the whole territory was designated for public uses, as church, school and corporation.

By way of illustration of the more prosperous estates one may cite the enterprise of Sir William Stewart, who in or about 1622 built "a fair castle" and gathered a plantation of a hundred or more families of "British," meaning British subjects including Scotch, the hundred

---

* A bawn was a walled enclosure, with towers usually surmounting each at the corners.

† Reid, I, 75f.

houses being "in the midst of the parish." This knight
had obtained lands in 1610. By 1618 he had erected at
Ramelton, "a large and strong tower, 80 feet square,
16 feet high, with four flankers; and a fair strong castle,
being three stories and a half high; and had made a
large town, consisting of 45 houses, in which there are
57 families, all British,"—again meaning English or
Scotch. "He hath also begun a church of lime and stone,
which is built to the setting on of the roof. There is also
a water mill for corn. It is a market-town, and standeth
very well for the good of the country and the king's
service." *

All this in general outline leaves us the task of finding
out our friends whose homes and habits we are seeking.
As has been already intimated, these were not lords and
knights and their ladies, albeit some of these same lords
and knights and ladies were progenitors of the homely
folk whose homes and habits we are seeking out. And
the descendants unraveled some of the problems of life
beyond the fortune and ability of the aforesaid lords,
knights and ladies. Or if not progenitors, some of these
men and women of title, as also we have discerned, were
kin more or less remote and landlords of the men,
women and children about whose faces and souls we
want to know as much as possible.

These last, be it remembered, were the tenantry. The
condition of tenants was all much complicated by the
admixture of ancient Irish institutions and traditions of
yearly tenant rights and the regulations of the English
crown. Whatever the system, always implying hardship
even at best, and at worst becoming tragedy, rents
entered as an undying first lien on the renter's right and
home. There was first of all a large financial obligation
due from the proprietor to the king, for "even the king

---

* Reid, I, 111f, note.

is served by the field." The landlord in sooth felt that he must live, and, of course, he must live better than his tenant, else why be a landlord? In Londonderry, for example, there were the Merchant Tailors' Company, the Fishmongers' Company, the Vintners' Company, the Worshipful Company of Grocers. "Worshipful," no doubt; enterprising and genial gentlemen among themselves, but worshipful among their tenants; not without generous instincts, nor lacking consciousness of their superiority. Who that knows Irish history can doubt the aptness of the historian Duffy's irony in the observation: "The companies of Skinners, Fishmongers, Haberdashers, Vintners and the like thereupon became Absentee Proprietors, and have guzzled Irish rents in city feasts and holiday excursions to Ireland from that day to this." * While he was speaking of the native Irish in particular, and even though Ulster in the hands of the Scots became the most flourishing part of the island, the essential facts about tenantry must remain true of the Ulstermen also. Set it down in memory, these were the poor of the land.

Holding in mind the facts above cited, we should hardly expect to find that the better sort even of the poor of Scotland came over to build and occupy the humble cottages of Ulster. On the contrary, to use a phrase of Cromwell, they were "the rogue-and-vagabond species of Scotland." † We might supplement this with the emphatic and highly picturesque epithets of John Milton in 1649 who speaks of them as "a generation of highland thieves and redshanks." ‡

Dr. Reid, historian, so often cited in these pages, himself bone of their bone, characterizes the new tide of

---

* History for Ready Reference, article "Ireland."
† Cromwell's Letters and Speeches. Carlyle, II, 198.
‡ Quoted by Reid, II, 177n.

immigrants into Ulster as lawless, godless, disorderly and violent, the scum both of England and Scotland, "hoping to be without fear of man's justice, in a land where there was nothing, or but little as yet, of the fear of God." They came in such swarms, these fugitives from debt and justice, that the northern counties of Ulster were soon swarming with them. Atheism, drinking, fighting, murder and adultery became the order of the day, and the example of the ministers was not above the practices of their flocks. "For their carriage," remarks this careful historian, "made them abhorred at home in their native land, insomuch that 'Going to Ireland' was looked on as a miserable mark of a deplorable person. Yea, it was turned into a proverb; and one of the worst expressions of disdain that could be invented was, to tell him that 'Ireland would be his hinder end.'"

The counties of Antrim and Down made much more rapid progress than the rest. The other counties — Derry, Donegal, Tyrone, Armagh, Fermanagh and Cavan,—comprising a total of more than two million acres, included but 400,000 acres of forfeited lands. The rest was wilderness and land still held by native proprietors. The cream had been wrested from the native Irish. Of the forfeited acres one-quarter was held for church, school and corporation. By 1618 less than a fourth part of the land was fully inhabited, though 8,000 men able to bear arms had gone thither, all of British (including Scotch) descent. There were 107 castles with bawns, 19 castles without bawns, 42 bawns without castles or houses, and 1,897 dwelling houses of stone and timber.

We have been picturing in our minds great walls, bawns, castles and refuges. What is going to tame the unsocial and anarchic forces already admitted? It is not well to become blind because one has had to see ugliness. Our quest just now is truth. We are going to New England presently, and we shall find that there one of the first things they did was to erect a church and look for a godly minister. Moreover, to survey the pit from which we were digged and the hole of the rock whence we were hewn is a most wholesome pursuit. It is not well to forget the question once asked of men who overmuch esteemed pride of blood and race,—"Know ye not that of these stones God can raise up seed to Abraham?" So in fact it proved in those early days in Ulster.

CHAPTER II

The Ulster Homes and Habits: The Kirk

Edgar Guest sings,

"It takes a heap o' livin' in a house to make it home."

and a nation or people is composed of homes. By the time a people can sing with all their hearts,

"My country, 'tis of thee,
Sweet land of liberty,"

a big "heap o' livin'" has been done. When these people sailed away from Northern Ulster to Boston in 1718, the chief furniture they took with them was the sentimental and spiritual furniture of generations. Neither Blandford nor any other town, taken in possession and opened to the world *en masse* by a company of immigrants from one community across seas, can for one moment be supposed to have accomplished that colossal act without such impalpable but most real and germinant furnishings. Antiques from Ulster or early New England may be curious and valued witnesses to the past and a joy of the present, but the most priceless antiquities, even as the present most significant realities, are such as our own Lowell has put into immortal and familiar verse:

"We live in deeds, not years,
In thoughts, not breaths,
In feelings, not in figures on a dial."

A few little facts catalogued in the formal content of a printed page or two cannot adequately introduce these folk to us as we knock at their doors. Homes and habits mean much. They are not mere phenomena, but both roots and fruit, forces vital and formative. I have wanted to live with these people in North Ireland, and I have wanted that my readers should live with them, or their homes and habits over here will be darkened by mystery.

Having made this little digression, we will continue with the story, resorting to the same authority for our facts. Many of the ministers, before leaving Scotland, had been both ignorant and profane, and had left their country for their country's good. But a gracious leaven came down upon them like the blessed dews of heaven, so that by the year 1630 a radical change had transpired. Their numbers were augmented, they achieved prosperity, and became in large numbers worthy ministers of the people. The opening of new fields along with new opportunities and increasing responsibilities helped to sober them. Being a new sect transplanted into new soil, and the fear that these ministers might be removed by the resident bishops, of the Church of England, served as a stimulus to the spirit of loyalty on the part of the people. The meetings became crowded, and were often long protracted.

The change was not alone religious and moral, but social and far-reaching. As has just been intimated, the outward pressure of the established ecclesiasticism, accentuated by the inherited tyranny of a Stuart king, cemented the loyalty of the Presbyterian Scots to their church and minister. James was for making his church, and the people's church, serve his high political purposes, and the battle became joined forthwith.

What Patrick Adamson had said in 1574 remained true for generations: "There were three sorts of bishops: my lord bishop, my lord's bishop, and the Lord's bishop. My lord bishop was in the papistrie; my lord's bishop is now, when my lord gets the benefice, and the bishop serves for nothing but to make his title sure; and the

Lord's bishop is the true minister of the gospel." * This witty saying may serve for our understanding of the condition ecclesiastical for many years.

The work of reformation, which was of several years' duration, spread beyond the bounds of Antrim and Down to the skirts of neighboring counties. It centered in the country of the Bann, and its passing into history is the secret of the inoculation of a new energy into the life sources of the Irish Scots of New England some generations later.

Some of the early apostles of this revival are eminently worthy of mention by name. They were James Hamilton, Edward Bruce, Mr. Hubbard, James Glendenning, John Ridge, Robert Cunningham and Robert Blair. These were the seven angels of the churches, and Blandford folk long afterward bore the names of some of them. There were others. Robert Blair had been a professor in the University of Glasgow, and was driven out in 1625 by the persecuting policy of James I. He became minister of the church in Bangor, where he exerted a mighty influence not confined to his parish or town. The fame of this religious and moral transformation spread over England and Scotland and across the sea to America. But for these men the whole history of North Ireland would have lacked much of the lustre which it has had.

This new life impulse upon a population in Ireland whose beginnings were so lowly and ill-savored, constrained a bitter hater of all things Presbyterian to tell of his amazement, almost his admiration. This was Leslie, bishop of the church of England in these parts. We shall have sundry occasions to cultivate his acquaintance. He preached and published a sermon which he dedicated to Wentworth, that apostle of tyranny and

---

* Hetherington, 76.

repression. This was in 1636. In this sermon the bishop paid his respects to the prodigious growth the Presbyterians were making in his diocese, which comprised the counties of Down and Connor, a progress so meaningful that he felt he must report it to his liege lord. He took particular pains to explain the causes of it, among which he enumerated the exemplary holiness of the ministers, their diligence in preaching, and their fidelity in rebuking the vices of the great. We are here beginning to uncover more of the principal facts and developments of our quest, the homes and habits of ancient Blandford, as these germinated in the homes and habits of ancient Ulster.

To resume our perusal of the bishop's sermon. He proceeded in some choice paragraphs to pay his compliments to the women of the Presbyterian churches, speaking of them as the "weaker sexe, in whom there is least ability of judgment." Then followed tearful reference to the seduction of Adam by Eve, of Samson by Delilah, and of persecutors of Paul by "certaine devout and honorable women" of the Jews. The prelate proceeded: "These new Gospellers make use of such instruments to oppose the Church, and for the most part their proselytes are of that sexe, as if their generative virtue were so weake that they could beget none but daughters. Now to search a little into the cause of this: Besides the weaknesse of their judgment to discern between truth and error, and the naturall inclination which is in women to pitty; two things especially make them in love with that religion; one is, it is naturall unto the daughters of Eve to desire knowledge, and those men puff them up with an opinion of science, inabling them to prattle of matters of divinity, which they and their teachers understand much alike: insomuch that albeit Paul hath forbidden women to speake in the church, yet they speake of Church-matters more than comes to their share. The other is, a desire of liberty and freedome from subjection; for these teachers allow them to be at least Quarter-masters to their husbands, insomuch that I have not learned that faction to prevaile but where husbands have learned to obey their wives, and where will and affection weare the breeches. There is a civill constitution in the authentickes against women who would not receive the holy and adorable communion, that they should lose their douries or jointures; which if it were in force in this kingdome, I think some of our ladies would not be so stiff-kneed, choosing rather to goe without that blessed sacrament than to receive it kneeling." *

So little am I able to make record in this narrative of the distinctive activities of women that I am glad to insert this delicious and informing bit of prelatical irony. Indeed, I feel personally indebted to the right reverend bishop for a little glimpse, not only into the churches of these Irish Scots, but into their homes as well. The women, it appears, had become "quarter-masters to their husbands." That is, they managed the domestic affairs of the household in such a way that "their husbands could safely trust in them;" all of which means that they were many degrees above incompetent managers or underlings. The bishop expressly mentions that this had come about through a good understanding: "will and affection weare the breeches;" and this, more-over, in respect of those fine arts of the cottage home wherein the discerning husbands have wisely and affec-tionately accorded to the queen of the house that "liberty and freedome" which are her right. We thank thee, O learned and observant bishop, for this flash-light picture of the Scottish cotter and his helpmate!

* Reid.

Furthermore, the bishop has told us of this early rise of the women in the church. They have already in this second quarter of the seventeenth century come to understand thoroughly the genius of the Presbyterian church, so that they "prattle of matters of divinity," not as novices and bunglers, but as accomplished confessors of a faith wherein "they and their teachers understand much alike;" and this, furthermore, not in private conversation only, but speaking "in the church," which "Paul hath forbidden women" to do; and further still, these "daughters of Eve," absorbing knowledge to impart it again to the rest in hearing "more than comes to their share." Again, O bishop, we are grateful to thee for having thus added much to our fund of knowledge, and we begin to question thy judgment of the "weake generative virtue" of "these new Gospellers."

In this story of the development of the Ulstermen's church life, there is rich store for our information regarding the habits of thinking of the Irish Scots; and more, of their character, their personality, and withal of the whole manhood, all of which is far more to our purpose than just an inventory of their daily chores, their implements and their physical toil, their little homes and farms, and their neighborhoods, much as we would prize all this. The children's children of these men and women emerged on Blandford farms and streets the same kind of men and women, and we mean to greet them there on those rugged hills and slopes not as strangers to us, but old and loved friends, "warts and all."

We are getting little glimpses here and there into the homes and habits we so much want to know about. Here is one more, from the terrorizing rule of the infamous Wentworth, later earl of Strafford. This precious sectary was trying by hook and crook and all the arts of repression so well known to him, to root out nonconformity.

He had given certain instructions to Leslie, who returned answer to his lord to the effect that threat of excommunication failed to bring these lowly cotters to obedience, since "they know well that they will not be apprehended, in regard of the liberty the lords have of excluding all sheriffs." Thus is indicated a kind of paternal protection of the peasantry by their landlords, which, however, did not always avail, as most of the landlords were prelatic. The lord deputy aforesaid promptly informed the lord bishop that he would nevertheless see to it that his "pursuivants" would get them just the same.* This was in 1638. Once more Leslie averred that the matter was not so simple as it appeared to his lord. Thereupon followed mention of matters ecclesiastical and religious which do not specially concern our present narrative. But it has its intimate social inferences bearing on the subject now in review.

Leslie again wrote: "As for those who contemn my process and oppose my jurisdiction, they are more in number than would fill all the gaols in Ireland; but the church-wardens are the deepest in that guilt, who will present none, who are disobedient to the government, and to that purpose they are chosen. As in Scotland they are entered into a bond to defend one another by arms, so it seems that in my diocese they are joined to defend one another by their oaths. I have therefore in obedience to your lordship's commands, sent a list of these church wardens, extracted out of my registry: if it may so please your good lordship to make all of them examples, it will strike terror into the rest of that faction."† Would that we had the roster of those doughty wardens! Presbyterianism was a mighty bond

---

* Reid, I, 222f.
† Ibid., 226.

of union, even to the last extremity. We shall have further evidence.

Still again, in another letter to Wentworth, the bishop continued to complain bitterly of the church wardens, against whom he had "a double complaint," since they were "set to look upon the fabrick of the Church," yet keep the greatest part of their temples "no better than hog-styes;" that "it is one of the mysteries of their religion, that God is most purely served, when he is worshipped slovenly in a poor and homely cottage, and that any cost is too much to be bestowed upon God's service." One may easily discount something of Leslie's scorn of their temples "no better than hog-styes" and be duly thankful to the lordly prelate for this little peep through the door of the "humble houses" of these poor, with their sod fires and hard scrabble to rebuild a devastated land.

Devastated it was indeed. The historian Reid spreads on his pages in monotonous detail a catalogue of the ecclesiastical ruins of the country in town and village: "all the churches ruined"; "church decayed"; occasionally a church rebuilt, or building. It was like a land swept by earthquake and volcano, just beginning to struggle back to human occupancy.

Within their humble cottages, in close proximity doubtless to the barnyards and with too little distinction between the habits of cows and pigs and of human beings, learning habits of industry and thrift so far as cruel conditions would allow, lived these people. They were ever under the stimulus and discipline of a religion inherently intellectual and spiritual. If their habits were uncleanly, as every historical evidence too abundantly proves, at least let it be remembered that their origins had been bad, their conditions were hard, and the age at its best preceded by generations any general

knowledge and practice of eugenics. Professor Perry
has elaborated in detail upon detail the uncleanly ways
of these people of the Bann valley. Mr. Bolton has
contributed a liberal paragraph or two. If Bishop Leslie
found bitter fault with them for the untidiness of their
churches, it should be considered that this was but a
reflection upon their home life, not rightly a slant upon
their religion or their respect for the house of God.

No doubt their use of water was illiberal both upon
their persons and in all their home life. No doubt, as
Professor Perry has written,* this thing had "ill consequences . . . in diseases and mortality of children; in a
disgust felt for uncleanly old people; in an intolerable
stench arising from crowded religious assemblies, often
prolonged for hours and hours; and in a prejudice and
mockery on the part of neighbors trained in and accustomed to more cleanly personal habits . . . —barns and
pig-pens were in close proximity to the houses, and the
two were scarcely discriminated from each other; the
methods of farming were to the last degree uncleanly
and unwholesome and disgusting. . . . Their company
was more or less avoided by the English on this account,
and their rights doubtless less respected; the intermar-
riages that took place for two generations were for the
most part with the lowest and poorest of the low and
poor English; and with the major part of this class of
people in New England the steps upward to the daily
bath and the decent water-closet have been unreasonably slow and interrupted."

Professor Perry was intimately acquainted with the
Scotch Irish in New England, they being his own kith
and kin. The conditions he describes must have been
an importation of habit and inheritance. Further em-
bellishment of the subject is afforded in several para-

---

* "The Scotch-Irish" etc.

graphs of Mr. Bolton's interesting story of this same people.

One longs to know more than is yet revealed about the homes and home life of these early Scotch settlers in Ireland. It would seem one might assuredly assume that the spirit of enterprise and thrift would become engrafted upon country and village life there. The influences of church and ministry which so marvellously developed even in the earliest years took care of that. History abundantly proves it to have been true of Ulster as a whole. Certain survivals of cottage architecture of the very early period of this settlement are definite and grateful witnesses to the fact. Doubtless these survivals should be conceded to be of the best. The poorer sort of homes would perish. The horrid and wholesale fires of Ireland's history in periods of rebellion and war would leave only the most substantial.

One of the most important towns in the presbytery of Coleraine was Aghadowey. There David Blair came to live, in 1610, leaving his native Ayrshire home; David, great-grandfather of Matthew who became one of Blandford's first citizens. He became the progenitor of a widely scattered clan in America. This village of Aghadowey grew into a thrifty and tidy community with thatched cottages lining its main street.

It should not be forgotten that in many of the years nothing was safe from hostile men and raving wild beasts unless enclosed. Flocks and herds had to be driven in at night. What Dr. Gaius Glenn Atkins so finely says* of the English countryside must be true everywhere under the given conditions: "A barnyard is an ancient and honorable institution, being the shelter into which a man gathered his cattle, his gear, and his

---

* In an article contributed to "The Congregationalist," June 3, 1926: "The Greensward Road."

crops directly he began to dig himself into the soil. The student of human institutions might maintain with considerable force that the barnyard is the primitive hearthstone of society, and that any civilization may be tested by its barnyards. If the house is part of the barn, as in a deal of rural France, you have a habit which continues the tradition of a time when the barnyard was a fortress in a war-cursed land. If the barnyard is slovenly and its buildings open to the wind, agriculture is only an expedient to exploit the soil and the farmer in spirit at least a squatter on his land."

By necessity these people were, and remained, for the most part, close to the soil. After James I. entered upon his imperial policy, it was seen to that the motherland should not be seriously incommoded by competition or trade on the part of subjects residing and operating abroad. Manufacture and commerce were ruinously hampered in Ireland. Agriculture itself was unreasonably and cruelly limited for the enrichment of the landlord and the consequent impoverishment of his tenant. In the reign of Charles II. exportation to England of cattle, sheep and pigs, salt beef and bacon, and butter and cheese, was prohibited. Further ban upon the exportation of woolen manufactures provoked the sheep-raisers of Ireland to the profitable if hazardous business of smuggling. The tenant farmer was forced to keep his plow off many a rich meadow or upland to afford his landlord grazing land for this illicit enterprise.

Potatoes became the staple food of Ireland after their introduction by Raleigh. Milk and butter varied the diet. The cultivation of potatoes extended with extraordinary rapidity. They were easy to raise. One man could grow enough to feed forty people. They were quite apt to be allowed to remain in the soil; for the climate of Ireland is mild, raiding armies would not stop to dig up these vegetables, and after the too frequent invaders had passed on, the farmer could go out and dig a dinner for his family. But for a perpetual staple with no sufficient alternative the potato is not an ideal article of diet, and, as the world knows, sometimes that one crop failed. Then there was starvation. No wonder Ireland once upon a time paid its compliments to Raleigh by a parade of men bearing potatoes stuck on poles and raised high in air. This vegetable continued to be a staple crop with the Irish Scots after the New England migration.

We pass to the drinking habits of these people. No account of them could be adequate or just without mention of this in some detail, even as no description of the people of the United States in the first quarter of the twentieth century could be complete or even fair without the story of the eighteenth amendment, moonshining, bootlegging, rumrunning and hi-jacking. Professor Perry says, "They discriminated against water, in their estimate of beverages. Account for it as we may, high altitude, Celtic restlessness, strenuous poverty, aspiration above realization, cheap whiskey, what not, the Scotch of whatever origin and whatever residence grasp and hold too much stimulus *per capita* of the population. It was always so. It is so now. It is not because they are *canny*, and it is not because they are Presbyterians. *I do not know the reason why!*" (The Italics are his.) If Prof. Perry could not find the reason, it would be presumptuous for me to assume to explain. They were poor; they were sometimes ill fed; they lived for ever under the harrow of persecution, repression, danger, temptation. Hard conditions do become an initial temptation to drink with many, and an irritant to others who already have the appetite. "Give strong drink unto him that is ready to perish, and wine unto the bitter in soul: let him drink, and forget his poverty, and remember his misery no more." So wrote King Lemuel.*

The English in Ireland were prone to the ravages of what was known as the flux, called in Ireland "the country disease," induced by the marshiness and fogginess of the island. But it was not Ireland altogether. Perhaps it was the Scottish nature as a peculiar variety of human nature.† A certain carpenter was about to work for an old lady in Glasgow. She offered him a dram, and asked him whether he would have it then or wait till his work was done. "Indeed, mem," he replied, "there's been sic a power o' sudden deaths lately that I'll just tak it now."‡

> "Inspirin' bauld John Barleycorn,
> What dangers canst thou make us scorn!
> Wi' tippeny we fear nae evil;
> Wi' usquebae we'll face the devil."

So sings Bobbie Burns in Tam O' Shanter.

> "Whilst all the Hibernian kerns, in multitudes,
> Did feast with Dhamerags stew'd in usquebaugh,"

sings another.

The subject demands some further attention, and we may give to it the more heed as one of serious importance, not unmixed with satisfaction from the fact that the Blandford descendants of these people so nobly responded to the tragic need of reform.§ The judicious Reid gives us once and again glimpses into this rather lurid aspect of Scotch Irish life. Here is this little significant incident, of date 1643, during "the cessation,"

---

* Proverbs 31:5, 6.

† I have dwelt upon this at length in my earlier writing, "The Taverns and Turnpikes" etc.

‡ This story is vouched for as true by Dean Ramsay.

§ I have told of this also in detail in my "Taverns and Turnpikes of Blandford."

when the Scottish forces in Ulster were in desperate condition and garrisons were emptied. There was a garrison at Newry which was compelled to make a truce with the rebels in order to get supplies. Naturally it was a very delicate and doubtful procedure wherein resort was had to the traditional characteristic of Irish bargain-making. The garrison was in "extreme want of all manner of provisions, both for back and belly." Reid acknowledges his source to be Turner's Memoirs: "For this reason, by Monroe's toleration, I had a meeting with an Irish colonel, one Thulough O'Neill, sent by Sir Philemy. We met at Lirioter (Pointz Pass) each of us with twenty horse: and after an hour's discourse and the drinking of some healths in aqua vitae and Irish Usquebaugh, we concluded a cessation of arms with them for our own garrison."

Another historical note, illuminating from several different angles, may here be appended, of date 1655, in the period of the Protectorate. It was a sorry time for persistent and stubborn Jacobites like these doughty Scotchmen. Few Presbyterian ministers were left in Ireland, and the few who were there "had nothing allowed them now for full five years (from 1649 to 1654) except what the people under the burdens and oppressions of strangers could out of their poverty spare them." * The matter was under negotiation through friendly mediation, and had been already summarized some months before in these terms as given in a letter by Fleetwood of Dublin to secretary Thurloe: "The other business which I shall mention is about tythes, which I understand is endeavored by some to be continued in the old way. And though in my owne judgment I little scruple the payment thereof, yet knowing that it hath bine a bone of contention, I could wish it

_____
* Reid, II, 291.

might be otherwise settled here—besides, if it should be continued as formerly, it wil be a meanes to keep in many a wicked man in severall parishes who must, where the tythes are but small, (as before) keep an ale-house. But if wee may have libertie to collect the tythes and bring them into one tresurye, as now wee doe, we shall be able to maintane a gospel-ministry in Ireland; and by this means they having dependence on the state for their maintenance, we shall be able to restraine some troublesome spirits, which may bee to apt to give disturbances to the publique peace, of which there have bine sad experience in the North; and 'tis doubted that most of them continue their old bitter spirits."

Records of church discipline allow us intimate insight into the grapple of the presbytery—and therefore of the hearts of the more earnest people—with this besetting sin which invaded even the ministry, and from which the Presbyterian church strove gallantly to cleanse itself. We read:* A strong commission of "ministers, and ruling elders, persons of knowledge and quality" were sent, who "did, in an orderly way, call before them divers who had been received as ministers in these parts before, there being divers scandals proved before and upon them, they were deposed. These were Mr. Robert Barclay for trading in a way inconsistent with the ministry, for cursing and swearing, profaning the Sabbath, intruding on a neighboring parish, and for frequent drunkenness; Mr. Brown for drunkenness, swearing, and railing against authority; Mr. James Baxter for drunkenness, swearing, baptizing and marrying promiscuously, and for railing against the professors of godliness; Mr. Robert Young for known debauchery; Mr. Archibald Glasgow for drunkenness, swearing, and railing against religion; Mr. George Hamilton for tippling,

* Reid, II, 145.

and sometimes inveighing against professors of godliness; and Mr. Major for profaning the Sabbath, and
promiscuous baptizing, &c. &c. In all which the president did concur with the presbytery's commission, and
a letter of thanks was returned to him for his zeal."
What reactions of moral judgment this searching and
drastic housecleaning of the church of God in that
troubled and war-stricken land must have produced
needs little imagination to picture.

Let the reader of these pages consider with what
almost frenzied earnestness the following catalog of ills
gripped the Ulster church in the middle of the seventeenth century:

"It is enacted by the session of Templepatrick: First,
that all complaints come into the Session by way of bill:
the complaintive is to put in one shilling with his bill,
and if he proves not his point, his shilling forfeits to the
session-book. This is done to prevent groundless scandal.
Second, That all beersellers that sell the best beer,
especially in the night-time, till people be drunk, shall
be censured. Third, That if parents let their children
vague or play on the Lord's-day, they shall be censured
as profaners of the Sabbath. Fourth, That all persons,
standing in the public place of repentance, shall pay the
church officer one groat. Fifth, that no children be baptized till the parents who present them come to some of
the elders and get their children's names registered, that
the elders may testify of them to their minister." A
later meeting further enacted: "That if there be any mis-
demeanor, as drunkenness or squabbling at bridals, besides the censures the persons themselves come under
who commit the abuse, the persons married shall forfeit
their privileges." The discerning will draw certain
inferences from these church statutes altogether illuminating of some of the ways of human society in Ulster

nearly three hundred years ago, and compare it with the same period in New England.

The first censure on record, following these enactments, is, "That John Cowan shall stand opposite the pulpit, and confess his sin, in the face of the public, of beating his wife on the Lord's day." One wishes to know what the punishment might have been had the beating been inflicted on a week-day. The probability seems to be that John had taken "a drap too much."

The ministry, too, then as now, were not all perfect. In Mr. Bolton's book already cited I find the statement that in 1700 the clergy were censured by the Synod because they, their wives and children, were "gaudy and vain," in their manner of dress. They were cautioned to avoid "powderings, vain cravats, half shirts and the like," as well as "sumptuous, prodigal dinners" at ordinations. McGregor and Boyd withstood the allurements of fashion, but were found wanting in other virtues. McGregor, having taken several cans of ale at Coleraine, where, as he said, "less might have served," was in 1704 after a vote of "not proven," nevertheless severely admonished before the whole synod of Ulster. Thus did the church through the years discipline the consciences and habits of these people in respect of self control and self respect, as well as of frugality and the nurture of home life.

The culture of flax was a somewhat limited industry before the Elizabethan era, after which it developed in Ulster by rapid strides. Before the middle of the seventeenth century this valuable product of the soil had become the most important commercial commodity of the island, and paid the major part of the May rents. English merchants bought it in Ulster and transported it to Lancashire, where one-hundred pounds of it were

A Real Ulster Flax Wheel — Double Wheel and Treadle

Flax-Spinning

The spinner is wearing a silk dress much more than a century old. The patch of paper behind the wheel is a scrap of old wall paper in the parsonage.

known to be bought and sold in a day.* Following the potato crop the small Ulster farms were sown to flax. The season-long and elaborate processes of bleaching, drying, and working into yarn kept busy hands at work all winter long, much as in rural New England in a former generation woolen yarn was worked by the winter fireside into stockings and ornamented mittens.† Much has been made of Wentworth's encouragement of the linen enterprise; but that arch-manager of a kingdom looked out sharply for himself first, last and all the time, and did not a little to thwart the interests of the humble producers on the farms. The products of this industry went into cloaks, head-dresses for women and shrouds; the latter were always white.

> "Oh, sweet is the sound of the shuttle and the loom,
>   As the weaver plies his trade;
> And fair is the flicker of the sunlight in the room
>   By the swinging lattice made.
> But naught to the weaver are the light and merry din:
>   He works with his head down bowed.
> And dulled are his senses and his soul is dark within,
>   For he weaves his darling's shroud."

Salmon fishing on the Bann and the Foyle came in its season, a lively and interesting incident in the laborious and grinding life of the cotter. A little flashlight of history reveals to us how much this annual fishing season meant to the dwellers on the Bann and the Foyle. The Rebellion of 1641 had just swept through Ulster. Coleraine was "almost famished," and some Ulstermen went to its relief. They "marched down to Dungiven castle, one of the king's houses, which was kept by Colonel Manus MacGuy Ballagh MacRichard O'Kane. He, upon parley, delivered up the castle. Hence we marched

---

* Reid, I, 200n.
† For interesting details of this Ulster home industry, v. Bolton, 44ff.

to Coleraine, every regiment bestowed some (of their plunder) upon the town; the soldiers at easy rates sold some of the rest, but such as were delivered to the right owners. At Castle Roe, a mile from Coleraine, were lodged seven colors of the enemy to secure the Bann fishing to themselves. We took the colors, put many to the sword; and the town of Coleraine hath a garrison there now, and enjoys the fishing to themselves, being the greatest salmon fishing in Christendom." *

The discipline of poverty must have been a provocation to adventure and an aid to resource. Artizanship was necessary. There were other things to do and to learn than the soil immediately invited, or the market provided for people as poor as these. Anticipating our story a bit, not long after the Ulster emigration to New England, a large company settled for a time in Worcester, Massachusetts. With them was a scattering of the future Blandford pioneers. Of this settlement of Irish Scots, the historian † of Worcester says: They "were frugal, and peaceful, contributing to the prosperity of the province, by the example of diligence and the introduction of the useful arts." This is valuable and welcome testimony.

In the ecclesiastical controversies of the closing decade of the seventeenth century, Rev. John McBride, minister for twenty years in Belfast, wrote: "The people we plead for are not the idle and consuming caterpillars of the nation, but industrious laborers, ingenious artists, and honest traders," etc.‡ The "ingenious artists" we may assume were not devotees of the Muses, but artisans of brain and brawn.

It is a fact not to be glossed over by mere passing

* Reid, I, 348, quoting Col. Mervyn's "Exact Relation."
† Lincoln.
‡ Reid, III, 60.

mention that these people, forbears of Blandford and
other Scotch Irish towns in America, were stanch sup-
porters of a learned ministry. This was not imposed
upon them from above, but was the policy of their own
vision, ordered and provided out of deep convictions,
and pursued with studied carefulness. It was looked
after by acts and resolves of their presbyteries, assemblies and synods and paid for through their hard econo-
mies made possible by the toil of the men and the wifely
"Quartermasters of their husbands." These things were
looked to year by year with a jealous zeal. Persecution
only served to spur them on to greater carefulness and
zeal to educate their young candidates. In 1690, during
the reign of Charles II., Dr. Reid bears witness:
"Though for a long time they were prohibited, in most
parts of the province, from erecting places of worship,
from holding presbyteries, ordaining ministers, and even
from preaching in public, yet the great body of Presbyterians adhered steadfastly to their principles; ordinances were secretly administered among them, new
ministers were ordained by stealth in private houses,
and even two 'philosophical schools' (as schools of theology were called) were established, in the counties of
Antrim and Down, for the education of intending ministers." * At the half-yearly meeting of Synod, held in
Belfast in 1691, notwithstanding many pulpit vacancies
—so shortly following the tragic events of 1689—and
the consequent urgent demand for ministers to fill the
numerous vacancies, that body unanimously "agreed
and concluded, that none enter into the ministry without
laureation," that is, without having gone through a regular course of education, and taken the degree of Master
of Arts in one of the Scottish universities.† This dif-

---

* Reid, III, 12.
† Ibid., 19.

ficulty persisted into the early years of the succeeding
century, especially as the number of congregations increased. The church, however, never relaxed her efforts
to secure the services of pious and educated men.*

All this produced its legitimate fruits in the minds of
the people, who, as they demanded a thinking and educated ministry, were themselves the more stimulated to
thinking.

In the services of the church the sermon was exalted
to high dignity; so much so that it excited the reproof
of the established authorities. Our old friend Bishop
Leslie found bitter fault with the Presbyterian pastors
for neglecting the prayers and catechism of the prayer
book, albeit they were most scrupulous in the use of
prayers and a catechism of their own. As for the sermon,
that prelate complained: "Preaching amongst you is
grown to that esteem that it has shuffled out of the
Church both the publique prayers which is the immediate worship of God, and this duty of catechising; and
is now accounted the sole and onely service of God, the
very *consummatum est* of all Christianity, as if all religion consisted in the hearing of a sermon. Unto whom I
may say in the words of the apostle, 'What? is all hearing? Is the whole body an eare?' Or, tell you in the
words of a most reverend prelate, 'That if you be the
sheep of Christ, you have no mark of his sheep, but the
eare-mark.'" This was in 1638; in that "dead, dark
world of the seventeenth century," to use an apt phras-
ing of Carlyle, wherein men, "unfortunate mortals, were
a set of mimetic creatures, rather than men; without
heart-insight as to this Universe, and its Heights, and
its Abysses; without conviction or belief of their own
regarding it at all;—who walked merely by hearsays,
traditionary cants, black and white surplices, and inane

* Reid, 90.

confusions;—whose sole existence was therefore a grimace."

It was very much more than a grimace among these Presbyterians of Ireland. Lacking as they may have been in aesthetic expressions of worship, they were trained to think, and trained to utter their thoughts, whether in church or neighborhood or before magnates and kings. They were trained, moreover, in the moral values of life and the elements of stalwart convictions and appropriate choices. And they were hard to beat. The laymen had come to their own in the Presbyterian church both in Scotland and Ireland. The Presbyterians of Scotland had begun to undergo the most hideous persecutions for their faith: impoverishing penal assessments and robberies, imprisonments, selling into slavery beyond seas, tortures the most fiendish, and deaths oft, and this on an increasing scale for more than a score of years. While Ireland had not to suffer in just these ways, the peoples of the two countries were close together in the fellowship of suffering, and there was much passing to and fro between them. While Leslie was chiding his nonconforming proteges in Ulster for their independent and provoking manners, the same things precisely were going on in the Presbyterian churches of Scotland. It was a thoroughgoing reforming movement. Hetherington* informs us that in Scotland there was no small withdrawal of Presbyterians "during the operation of the prelatic party" into private meetings, where they engaged in reading the Scriptures, exhortation and prayer, "for their mutual edification." He adds the information that several joined these assemblies who had been in Ireland and other countries for a considerable time.

It all was no small education for the time when they

* p. 180.

lived: education in religion, in self assertion and self control, in democracy; in short, in the whole of manhood and womanhood. The children imbibed it, and they in turn "told it to their children." The Presbyterian church was just come to its "second reformation" in old Scotland and all along the yeast of democracy had been powerfully at work in both kingdoms. It liberated the minds of the people. It enriched and enlivened the life of cottagers who walked the humble ways of society and the high ways of human souls gripping realities in the midst of repression and persecution. Trouble always starts question, question provokes discussion and agitation, while these get men close to reality. By necessity the fireside talk partook of the elemental principles of human living, of liberty and society, of church and state, of right and wrong, justice and injustice, character and destiny. The women who milked the cows, the girls and boys who fed the pigs and chickens, the granddames who spun the flax and made linen garments, the men who did their small business and got together after meeting, were forward in helping to make New England, to make Blandford, to open and shape the great West that was to be. These were the middle classes of society, the great mass of the people, in Scotland and in Ulster. When these were suppressed, or oppressed, beyond the point of endurance in the ways of industry and thrift, as came to be the case both in Scotland and North Ireland, then the whole of society was prone; the very life of the nation was dying.

A group of a half-dozen of the "prelatical clergy" was selected in 1670 in the interests of the English Church, to travel over the western counties of Scotland for purposes of propaganda among the Presbyterians. The selection was made by Bishop Leighton of Dunblane. Gilbert Burnet, celebrated author of "The His-

tory of Our Own Times," was one of the six. This prelate
was honest enough to tell the truth of what he saw and
heard on this memorable tour among a people who had
for decades been furnishing the world with some of the
most heroic martyrs of history. "We were indeed
amazed," he wrote, "to see a poor commonalty so capable to argue upon points of government, and on the
bounds to be set to the power of princes in matters of
religion. Upon all these topics they had texts at hand,
and were ready with their answers to anything that was
said to them. This measure of knowledge was spread
even among the meanest of them, their cottagers and
their servants."*

Now here is a lifelike picture of "our own folks."
Some of them came from these very western counties,
and communication, as I have already said, was close.
What was true of the west counties of Scotland was true
of the north counties of Ireland. A few years before
this, that same prelatic historian set out to portray the
shady and ragged character of the clergy whom the
Stuart regime had installed in livings of the ousted
Presbyterians, as "very worthless persons . . . who had
little learning, less piety, and no sort of discretion, . . .
mean and despicable in all respects, . . . the worst
preachers I ever heard; they were ignorant to a reproach." The Presbyterians of Ulster knew this same
sort too well, and that is why they refused to hear them.
Burnet, having thus finished with the clerical favorites
of the Stuart king, proceeded to characterize the Presbyterian ministers whom these wretched clerics had displaced. "The former incumbents," he wrote, "who were
for the most part Protesters, were a grave, solemn sort
of people. Their spirits were eager, and their tempers
sour; but they had an appearance that created respect.

* Quoted by Hetherington, 239.

They were related to the chief families in the country either by blood or marriage, and had lived in so decent a manner that the gentry paid great respect to them. They used to visit their parishes much, and were so full of the Scriptures, and so ready at extempore prayer, that from that they grew to practice extempore sermons. By these means they had a comprehension of matters of religion greater than I have seen among people of that sort anywhere. As they (i.e., the ministers) lived in great familiarity with their people, and used to pray and to talk oft with them in private, so it can hardly be imagined to what a degree they were loved and reverenced by them." *

We seem to be back again on the same ground with our old friend Leslie, but in an atmosphere of larger fairness and comprehension. Remember, there were no railroads, and neither were there any newspapers in Ulster. Reid says † that as late as 1721, three years after the great migration to New England, there "was not a single newspaper in the province" of Ulster. So important an event as the succession of George III. to the throne, was not learned by this people until eleven days after. The people's resources and recreations were in themselves. Their churches fed mind and heart; not infrequently, indeed, the body too, for doles to the poor were many. They were what they were by reason of their religion flowering and fruiting in their churches, and nurtured by their learned and beloved pastors. This was their life. They were a people of one book, but many ideas, and mighty convictions, readers and expounders of the Bible as it came to be drawn up in the confession and the shorter catechism of the Westminster Assembly; a people whose genius produced John

---

* Quoted by Hetherington, 220.
† III, 293.

Knox and Andrew Melville, and many another worthy follower.*

In all these years of the Stuart kings and of Cromwell, a powerful yeast was at work in all the three kingdoms. England emerged into wild and threatening ferment. There was the Puritan revolt everywhere. The Pilgrims had gone to Plymouth almost a generation before the Protector came to the kingdom. Englishmen were swarming by many thousands to Massachusetts Bay. Back in the old country Independents and Baptists or Anabaptists, Levellers and what-not, good and bad, sensible and fanatic, were rising in swarms, an army of men to reckon with, challenging all the wit and wisdom of Oliver Cromwell, the greatest personage of the age, one of the greatest personages of any age. By and by liberalism crept into the old orthodox churches themselves; into Scottish Presbyterian churches; into the churches of like faith in Ulster, a persistent and irrepressible uprising. When Carlyle affirms that the Presbyterians were bound to the letter, he seems to slight this most pregnant fact. Liberalism, Arminianism, Pelagianism, forecastings of "New Theology," were tremendously rife in Ulster, culminating indeed after our people left for Boston; but the effects of it entered into Blandford life, and into the troubled life of Blandford pioneers, to make them the very pioneers they became, and then to shadow them for a generation in the ministry of one of the most picturesque clerics that old Hampshire town ever harbored, himself an Ulsterite

---

* Charles A. Hanna says, p. 505: "For many years the history of Ulster, as far as it has a separate history, is chiefly ecclesiastical. It must be so; for this is a story of Scotsmen and of the first half of the seventeenth century, and at that time the history of Scotland is the history of the Scottish Church. Church polity, Church observance, Church discipline, fill all the chronicles, and must have formed the public life of the people." The writer need not have confined the remark to the first half of the seventeenth century.

indeed, the Rev. James Morton. We are here in these old times in the very roots of things which made Blandford what it was to become for a full century. 'Twas "an age on ages telling; To be living" was "sublime." But the sublimity of it lay not on the surface. In Ulster there was little opportunity for stagnation in any respect. Everywhere and always there were irritants enough to keep the blood warm and stirring.

By the middle of the seventeenth century half the population of all Ireland was Protestant, and half the people of Ulster were Scotch Presbyterians. Calvin was their spiritual father and John Knox was their godfather. Calvinism, whatever its faults — and it had many — at least brought democracy into being, for it put every man alone in the presence of his Maker and Judge to answer for his own soul. It has never been for such men to fear the face of man. The Scottish people were practically without parliaments until John Knox make the Kirk a popular assembly. "If," says Green in his Larger History, "its government by ministers gave it the outer look of an ecclesiastical despotism, no church constitution had proved so democratic as that of Scotland. Its influence in raising the nation to the consciousness of its power was shown by a change that passed from the moment of its establishment over the face of Scotch history."

"John Knox! John Knox is come! he is come! he slept last night in Edinburgh!" Thus was Greyfriars monastery roused to consternation by the hysterical announcement of one of its monks in 1559. And Scotland and the rest of the world have never forgotten it. Babies born that year had a little more than passed their majority when a respectful protest was read in the presence of Monarchy, a protest by Scotch Presbyterians because their inherent liberties were violated by his majesty. "Who dares subscribe these treasonable articles?" roared the clerk of Royalty. "We dare!" exclaimed Andrew Melville; and stepped unfalteringly forward to sign, a group of other commissioners following to take up the same pen to the same paper — to dare a King. Fourteen years later still, this same Andrew Melville, by the grace of God his head yet on his shoulders, pulled the king's sleeve and called him "God's silly vassall." Silly, indeed, because he had forgotten what this redoubtable Scotch Presbyterian proceeded forthwith to tell that same James VI.: "Sir, as divers times before I have told you, so now again I must tell you, there are two kings and two kingdoms in Scotland. There is Jesus Christ the king, and his kingdom the Kirk, whose subject James VI. is, and of whose kingdom not a king, nor a lord, nor a head, but a member. And they whom Christ hath called to watch over his kirk and govern his spiritual kingdom have sufficient power so to do both together and severally." No wonder King James aforesaid, in one of his furious outbreaks of devilish passion, cried, "A Scottish presbytery agreeth as well with a monarchy as God with the Devil." History has inscribed on her imperishable tablets that at least this which a King said is for ever true — of the kind of monarchy which King James represented.

CHAPTER III

"Universal Misery and Blood and Bluster" *:
Dragons' Teeth and Armed Men

In Rome's institutional world the memory of what had been done in Ireland in the time of the English and Scotch settlements was diligently kept green. The sowing of dragons' teeth had been by England's monarchs. Their diligent cultivation was left to the care of Rome and the Irish. Silently and with purpose it was done, and it was done unremittingly.

Roger Moore was the particular and immediate apostle of revenge and reprisal. By almost miraculous secrecy and ingenuity, by letters, by emissaries, by every artifice of savage propaganda, he incited the mass of Irishmen in the whole kingdom to revolt and butchery. Moore stressed the fact that the Irish were everywhere more numerous than the supplanters of the lands and hearthfires of their fathers. A certain date was fixed, and though on the very eve of it some warning leaked out, the silent and scattered army of the insurgents found little impediment.

The children and children's children of Tyrone and Tyrconnel had been well taught. Byron's immortal poem on the destruction of Sennacherib's host might be recalled in this connection:
"The Assyrian came down like the wolf on the fold."
But that which the poet so eloquently wrote concerning the fate of Assyria's host—
"That host on the morrow lay withered and strewn"—
could not be said concerning the Irish raid. The dis-

---

* Carlyle.

possessed Irish and their religious sympathizers struck
with an impact so sudden and so furious as to make
defence for a time almost impossible. It came upon the
Protestants of Ireland like a lightning stroke out of the
blue. It shocked the whole empire and carried terror to
the capital itself.

The time was opportune. Charles I. was running his
mad course of tyranny, upsetting the civic order and
throwing everything into uncertainty and confusion.
The plan of the Irish was to wipe out the Protestants
and establish the old order, incidentally recovering one
hundred and ten thousand pounds of revenue to the
church of Rome.

The pent-up passions of a whole generation broke
forth in this rebellion of 1641—race hatred, religious
frenzy, revenge of ancient extermination and robbery,
all diligently fanned to white heat. Castles, houses,
goods of every description were seized in the orgy of
violence and passionate abandon. Then followed massacre—indiscriminate, unpitying, infernal. Slow murders
were prolonged through indescribable horrors of torture.
Old-time neighbors who had lived with the new-comers
in seeming good will suddenly turned to fiends of
slaughter. Little children taking lessons from infuriated
mothers put forth their tiny hands in horrid co-operation. The island became desert.

Undoubtedly the main target of reprisal and vengeance was the episcopacy. But once passions of the
mob were let loose together with all the dogs of war,
the Presbyterians of Ulster could not by any means
escape. To say that these suffered less than the rest of
Protestant Ireland, and there drop the matter, as some
historians have done, is to garble history. Destruction
and butchery among the Presbyterian Scots were slight

only by comparison with the greater sufferings of the English.

Derry, Carrickfergus and Newry were allotted for capture and their inhabitants for imprisonment with as little violence as possible. As the raids proceeded these castles fell in succession: Claremont, Moneymore, Mountjoy, Newry — where fifteen townspeople were hanged — then Monaghan, Castleblaney, Carrickmacross, Clougheter, Fermanagh and the open towns of Derry and Donegal. Enniskillen, Derry and Newtonlimavady were saved, also Coleraine. Armagh and Carrickfergus were made safe. This latter was the only fortified town on the east coast of Ulster. "On the Sabbath day, the Protestants from the surrounding districts rushed into the town in considerable numbers in a state of great consternation, most of them equipped with no better arms than pitchforks, and attended with crowds of affrighted women and children."* Ballingplace, Lisburn in Down, Antrim and Templepatrick were defended. Much of the lower part of Antrim county was saved under the leadership of Archibald Stewart with eight hundred men whom he himself raised, while Robert Lawson by extraordinary bravery and despatch rescued Belfast and Lisburn.

During these operations the Scottish inhabitants had been pretty generally spared. The more influential among their ministers had already fled to Scotland from the persecutions of Strafford, and the principal part of their gentry had done likewise. The persons of those who remained were at first unmolested.

Remembering the boast of some historians that Ulster was largely let alone in this Irish rebellion, we will for a moment turn our attention to the county of Antrim. Our informant shall be Reid, whom Macaulay acknowl-

---
* Reid.

edges to be one of his chief and most trusty authorities. Reid cites an original manuscript, admitting probability of some exaggeration, but claiming truth for the general picture: "The Lord sent a pestilential fever which swept away innumerable people; insomuch that in Coleraine there died in four months by computation six thousand; in Carrickfergus, two thousand five hundred; in Belfast and Malone, above two thousand; in Lisnegarvey, eight hundred; and in Antrim and other places, a proportionable number." Another cited witness states that the mortality in Coleraine "was such, and so great, as many thousands died there in two days; and that the living, though scarce able to do it, laid the carcases of those dead persons in great ranks, into vast and wide holes, laying them so close and thick as if they had packed up herrings together."

The passing over of the Presbyterian population in Ulster by the rebels led to some degree of confidence for a time, but that confidence was ruthlessly violated. Irish neighbors of Robert Stewart of Irry in the county of Tyrone, who had gathered an armed force of six hundred men, persuaded Stewart to disband his troops with the assurance that there was no need for them, with the consequence that most of them were murdered on the very night of the disbandment. There were other similar instances. The fury of passion developing in power and extent by virtue of its own exercise led at last to a religious war which was in large measure indiscriminate. Sir Phelim O'Neill, who led a force of four thousand men, reduced the castle of Lurgan which William Brownlow had defended for a fortnight. Brownlow at last capitulated, and was given pledge of immunity for his family and property. Upon the surrender, "Sir William, his lady, and children, were cast into prison, his house was rifled, his servants were stripped, and plundered, and many of them inhumanly butchered, while the inhabitants of the town were treated with similar unprovoked cruelty." Sir Phelim had already taken the town and castle of Strabane, taking Lady Strabane as a prize of war, and later marrying her. To her he said, "he would never leave off the work he had begun until mass should be sung or said in every church in Ireland; and that a Protestant should not live in Ireland, be he of what nation he would."*

Upon this there followed the civil wars, the rise of Cromwell and the restoration of the Stuart dynasty. The purpose of this chapter does not at all depend upon a detailed story of this period, though acquaintance with it will immensely help to an intelligent and sympathetic understanding of the place in history which the Ulster Scots filled, and the temper of their life and career. I know not how I can do better than to transfer to these pages one short, lurid pen-picture of the whole era from the discerning and trenchant Carlyle†: "The history of the Irish War is, and for the present must continue, very dark and indecipherable to us. Ireland, ever since the Irish Rebellion broke out and changed itself into an Irish Massacre, in the end of 1641, has been a scene of distracted controversies, plunderings, excommunications, treacheries, conflagrations, of universal misery and blood and bluster, such as the world before or since has never seen. The History of it does not form itself into a picture; but remains only as a huge blot, an

---

* I have drawn practically all this story of the rebellion from Reid, Vol. I, Chapter VII. I have given but a bit here and a bit there of this historian's account, which is careful and conservative. He rejects many exaggerated stories, carefully weighs evidence, and refuses to commit himself to the absolute accuracy of figures, even of contemporaries of the war. He is careful to relate some cruel reprisals in the counter attacks which I have thought it not necessary to reproduce. He also is careful to accord to the Roman Catholic side the credit of certain judicial acknowledgments of the horrors of the campaign.

† I, 374.

indiscriminate blackness; which the human memory cannot willingly charge itself with! There are Parties on the back of Parties; at war with the world and with each other. There are Catholics of the Pale, demanding freedom of religion; under my Lord This and my Lord That. There are Old Irish Catholics, under Pope's Nuncios, under Abbas O'Teague of the excommunications, and Owen Roe O'Neal;—demanding not religious freedom only, but what we now call 'Repeal of the Union;' and unable to agree with the Catholics of the English Pale. Then there are Ormond Royalists, of the Episcopalian and mixed creeds, strong for King without Covenant; Ulster and other Presbyterians, strong for King *and* Covenant: lastly, Michael Jones and the Commonwealth of England, who want neither King nor Covenant. All these plunging and tumbling, in huge discord, for the last eight years, and have made of Ireland and its affairs the black unutterable blot we speak of."

Such were the confusing and terrifying experiences of the Ulster Scots in a period of signal, perhaps up to that time unparalleled, controversies and turmoils. It all was for a storehouse of tradition for the whole generation of children to be born in a decade, the inheritance of lurid memories, like an age-long nightmare. As old homes were rebuilt or regathered, churches reorganized, and communities re-established, fireside counsels and talk would enter into the warp and woof of little lives, the near ancestors of future refugees across the sea. There were sad vacancies which only the slow passing of time could fill, as the daily treadmill of toil should be resumed amid the hardship of poverty attenuated by all which had happened. For this was the unchanging lot of most.

In the utter chaos which was abroad in Ireland from

end to end, Cromwell was at his wits' end to know what
to do. He said to Parliament, September 4, 1654: "You
have great works upon your hands. You have Ireland
to look to. There is not much done to the planting
thereof, though some things leading and preparing for
it are. It is a great business to settle the Government
of that Nation upon fit terms, such as will bear that
work through:" which Carlyle interprets to mean, "Of
planting Ireland with persons who will plough and
pray, instead of quarrel and blarney!" The great Protector thereupon proceeded to make some incisive references to "those afflicted people who forsook their inheritances and estates here . . . to go into a waste howling wilderness in New England . . . for Liberty's sake,"
which thing was now ever and anon most searchingly
before the minds of these Ulster Scots. The very next
year a thousand Irish girls went to Jamaica besides a
mass of riff-raff from Scotland. Softly open the cot-
tager's door a crack, and hear them talking it all over
around the family hearth!

It must be said that, considering the general turmoil,
the Presbyterian churches in Ireland prospered marvellously during much of the period covered by the Protectorate. In 1653 there were twenty-four resident Presbyterian ministers in Ulster. Soon after there were
eighty, and the territory so covered had become widely
extended into counties not strongly held before. Nonconformity became politically triumphant, and for a
time was properly no longer nonconformity at all.
Episcopacy in Ulster was practically gone, and many
former Episcopalians sought and obtained entrance into
the churches of the Scots. There was a re-migration back
into Ireland of the original settlers and their children.
By June, 1642, the first regularly constituted presbytery
in Ireland sat at Carrickfergus, when this body pro-

ceeded at once to take measures for the rehabilitation of their ministry.

In 1643 England became Presbyterian,—the England of James and of Charles—the England of Laud who maintained that the Presbyterians had no religion at all! The English parliament signed the Scots' Solemn League and Covenant, as if drawn up by an angel from heaven. At St. Margaret's it was, in the chancel, where one by one the members lifted up their hands in solemn oath, and put their names to the parchment. Oliver Cromwell signed. Young Sir Harry Vane signed. "The whole Parliamentary Party, down to the lowest constable or drummer in their pay, gradually signed." *

"We all, and every one of us underwritten, do protest, that after long and due examination of our own consciences in matters of true and false religion, are now thoroughly resolved of the truth, by word and spirit of God; and therefore we believe with our hearts, confess with our mouths, subscribe with our hands, and constantly affirm before God and the whole world, that this is the only true Christian faith and religion," etc. So reads the weighty instrument. It had already been embraced by the Presbyterians with satisfaction and eagerness. In Scotland, five years before, the essence of it had been taken with the most solemn imaginable earnestness and reverence, at Greyfriars. The crowded churchful signed. Then it was removed into the churchyard, spread out on a level gravestone and signed by a multitude outside. As space in the parchment filled up, initials were crowded into every available spot. Some wept; some shouted; some opened a vein and signed in blood; some added the words, "till death."

It was Scotland's condition of entering the war against Charles and "the malignants," that England

* Carlyle.

should sign too. And it was done throughout the length and breadth of Britain, pledging all to the doctrine and discipline of the word of God as interpreted by the Scottish church.

David Hume, sceptic and Puritan-hater that he was, describes the situation as a "passion which seized the nation for Presbyterian discipline," and "a wild enthusiasm which at that time accompanied it." He declares, "all orders of men had drunk deep of the intoxicating poison," namely, of checking the traditional ecclesiastical authority.*

In the inevitable reaction the Solemn League and Covenant presently became a crime in the three kingdoms. So much for allowing religion to become the football of politics. It had to be. When Independency gripped the souls of the people Cromwell himself changed, for he was one of them. The real heart of the Scots clung to the Stuarts. Hateful and brutal as these monarchs were to their own race, casting law and decency to the winds, treading down whomsoever stood in their way, the Scots nevertheless would forgive them to the last. Independents of whatever complexion were, in the eyes of the Covenanters, schismatics, sectaries, anabaptists, blasphemers. Days of fasting and prayer were numerous. The stanch old Covenanters prayed as they believed and felt; prayed, therefore, like seeming traitors to the government. Cromwell had to restrain them. Killing a king, especially a Stuart king, no matter how black his crimes, was to the Scots an unforgivable sin. Cromwell could not allow such propaganda, even in the implications of a prayer, however veiled the phrases.

There was the war with Spain. When the fasts and thanksgivings were proclaimed throughout the kingdoms, for defeats or successes, "the brethren" of the

* V, 189.

Presbyterian churches, "never judging themselves to be incorporated with them, durst not espouse their course, especialy these solemn appearances before God; knowing that this, though now flourishing and pretending some owning of religion, yet was iniquity at bottom."* Were not the men of the government Independents? Had they not killed a king? The Protector was as gentle with them as he could be considering what an inextricable jumble political and military affairs were in during the civil wars. ". . . the unhappy Irish are again excommunicating one another," writes the sympathetic Carlyle concerning the events of 1650; "the Supreme Council of Kilkenny is again one wide howl."

Under Henry Cromwell's mild administration the Presbyterians were protected but he felt the necessity of watching them, and proscribing some of their political or semi-political activities, particularly in Derry, Coleraine, Carrickfergus and Belfast. By 1660, the year that Charles II. came to the throne, they numbered something like a hundred thousand souls, and were said to be able to raise an army of forty thousand fighting men.

---

* Quoted from Adair, by Reid, III, 309.

CHAPTER IV

Siege of the Kirk; Siege of Londonderry:
Still, Dragons' Teeth and Armed Men

From this time on, these Presbyterians had to look carefully to their steps. Charles was a hater of their sect, as of nearly all else good, and he presently appointed the learned and eloquent Jeremy Taylor bishop of Down, our old friend Leslie having gone back to England. Taylor was a thoroughgoing prelatist, esteeming Presbyterians to be "the greatest enemies to monarchy and most disobedient to kings." True to his convictions, he presently declared thirty-six of their churches vacant (1661), because the ministers refused to take the Test, and forthwith put priests and curates in their places. The sorry consequences of this action of the bishop shall be related in the words of Adair: "The old enemies became bitter and triumphed, and kept a searching and severe eye over the outed ministers that they might get some advantage of them. For generally they did reside in some places of their parishes, being excluded not only from their maintenance, but from their houses that the parishes had built for ministers; except those houses that were built by themselves and were their own property. They did also, as the danger and difficulty of that time allowed, visit the people from house to house; and sometimes had small meetings of them by parcels in several places of the parish in the night-time, which were narrowly pried into and sometimes gotten knowledge of, and by these observers and ministers called in question. Yet Providence brought them off again. Besides, there were some who had been once of the brethren by profession and ordained by them, who now, turning with the times, became more dangerous than others." * The example set by Jeremy Taylor was soon followed by other prelates in Ulster. Episcopal reordination, offered to these ejected ministers, was for the most part declined. Sixty-one Ulster ministers were thus deposed and ejected. Of all the ministers challenged only seven conformed. In the midst of it all, orders went forth to the magistrates that the hangmen in the various communities should publicly burn the Solemn League and Covenant.

Thus were these people made to drink the bitter dregs of the cup, in grief, humiliation and confusion. Their ministers were made outcasts. Most of these chose the way of peace and soberness, like true priests set for the cure of souls doing what they could for the quiet nurture of their flocks. Some few young and ambitious bloods went about from place to place stirring up the spirit of contention. Some went to "the hills." Adair relates that after a time the people became more of one mind, choosing the way of the quieter leaders, becoming convinced of "the imprudence of the one, and the true prudence and courage of the other, in sticking to them under difficulties and discouragements around them. They were convinced of this more and more when that way the prudenter ministers took, did, by degrees and insensibly without much observation of the magistrate, make way for the more public exercise of their ministry, as afterward it proved. And it is to be observed that the faithful ministers of Ireland, the first planters of the gospel in these bounds, when they were put from the public exercise of their ministry by the bishops, did not use that way of gathering the people to the fields. But they dwelt privately in their houses, and received as

* Quoted by Reid, II, 348.

many as came to them of their own parishes; though
they had greater provocations to do so, because they
got not the same liberty, but were shortly after chased
out of the country by pursuivants from Dublin." *

Hereon hang several historical situations. The last
reference in the citation is to events which had occurred
about twenty-five years before. The phrase "the way of
gathering the people to the fields" seems to be a veiled
reference to what the churches in Scotland were doing,
possibly to similar policies here and there in Ireland
itself. The Presbyterians in Scotland were more militant, trod more the way of the martyrs, than the pru-
dential way Adair relates the Presbyterians of Ireland
were taking. These churchmen of Scotland defied the
orders of the crown and his bishops; maintained that
as Scotland had the constitutional right of religious freedom, therefore the king was acting unconstitutionally
and should not be obeyed. So when nothing else was left
to them, if they were to worship together at all, they
resorted in great masses to the fastnesses of the High-
lands, or concealed places in the borders of the bogs,
and there held their worship. Sometimes they went
armed, and there were bloody encounters, and martyr-
doms that were holocausts, or even insurgent bodies
going out to muster an army. The Irish churches on the
other hand, tried what might come by way of non-
resistance, or by appeal and quieter ways of evading the
official injunctions, so that martyrdom in its extremities
was well nigh unknown in Ireland.

Much depended, further, on the temper of the lord
deputy, or the bishop, or other authority. Some of these
were extremely lenient, some more severe. So one
extreme followed another, with intervening gradients
varying according to conditions. It sometimes happened

---

* Reid, quoting Adair, II, 363.

that Irish law conflicted with English law, in which case the latter was the last word in the event of appeal. Then too, and this was particularly true under the reign of King William, the king may have sincerely wanted to favor the Scots, but parliament might be of a different mind, or the exigencies of politics might stand in the way. For William had not the way of the Stuarts, to rule or ruin.

So, in these particulars, Ireland and Scotland were two countries differing from each other sometimes as much in policy as in geography, though fundamentally their faith and discipline were identical. It must be said that while Ulster Scots got out from under the heel of despotism in many instances, on the whole the iron heel was there, and they were under it until they fled West. The see-saw continued. Sometimes the ministers were obliged to choose between banishment or prison. Sometimes no gatherings were allowed, and everybody was disarmed. Again, even ordinations were allowed, and fines and other hindrances to assemblies were dropped. In 1665 The Five-Mile Acts passed the English Parliament, forbidding all non-conforming ministers who should refuse to take the oath of passive obedience and non-resistance, to reside within five miles of any city, borough or corporate town, or any place where they had previlously officiated. Again, in 1672, young ministers flocked from Scotland to Ireland, and there was some little embarrassment on that account.

Writing of conditions in Ulster in 1670, Reid observes concerning the Ulster Scots: "They generally were of an humble extraction and sort of people, yet Providence ordered their liberty and quiet when others, more deserving and who had greater ground of expectation, were deprived of it. Thus the ministers with the people, having by the wonderful providence of God an open

door given them, continued the exercise of their ministry; and their assemblies daily grew so that within a
while every congregation erected a house for their meeting together, and began to celebrate the sacrament in
their public assemblies." *

The whole thing was a tragic jumble, alternating with
periods of insecure calm. In a general survey like this,
dates are of secondary concern. Let us look back a
moment over a period of ten years. The Duke of Ormond
was lord lieutenant and general governor of Ireland. A
deputy of his, Lord Orrery, found it difficult to hold an
even hand, and expressed his embarrassment to his over-
lord on this wise: "The thing is very weighty in its consequences, and difficult in the resolution; and therefore
your grace's judgment, which I humbly beg, is most
requisite for our guidance. If the laws be fully put
into execution, ten parts of eleven of the people will be
dissatisfied; if they be not put in execution, the church†
will be dissatisfied and sects and heresies continued, I
doubt not, for ever; and if any of the sects be indulged,
it will be partiality not to indulge to all; if none be
favored it may be unsafe. This is to me a short state
of the case, and too true a one. If England and Scotland
fall roundly upon the papists and non-conformists, and
we do not, Ireland will be the sink to receive them all
If they are fallen upon equally in the three kingdoms,
may they not all unite to disturb the peace?" ‡

The burning focus of all the wrongs inflicted upon
this people thus hunted and driven was The Test, so
known. The Test Act became a law of the realm in
1673, but the spirit of it was an active force many long
years before that. The Act required the taking of the

* II, 408.
† I.e., the Establishment.
‡ Reid, II, 365.

oath of allegiance and supremacy and receiving the sacrament of the Supper in accordance with the usage of the Church of England, and rendered all ineligible to any kind of civil office who refused to subscribe to The Test. It was not repealed until long after the people we are interested in left Ireland. Other indignities sorely stung and crippled these people, but The Test was the abomination of desolation.

The Presbyterians held it to be idolatry to partake of the holy Supper kneeling. They positively refused to do it. The Church of England authorities, on the other hand, looked upon this refusal as meticulous, silly and stubborn, and erected such refusal into monstrous irreligion, nigh to blasphemy. All Puritanism of the time revolted in this particular, as did the Presbyterians. The early Christian confessor, haled to the judgment of pagan Rome, was demanded to give but a sign, a mere motion of the body, to indicate his worship of the Emperor. This the faithful refused to do, and suffered martyrdom. Even so the loyal Scot took his ground respecting kneeling when receiving the sacrament. Some of the most delicious argumentations between bishop and minister were exhibited in public debate at the time of the trial of Presbyterian ministers under Leslie; microscopical points of refined logic, "kittle pints" so dear to the Scotchman; and because these ministers could not be persuaded, they were deposed. It must needs be borne in mind that to the Scot of the seventeenth century — yes, and of the eighteenth too — all this was tragedy, the way of life or death, of peace or storm. In short, it became the way of choice between Ulster and New England, between the waters of the Bann and the wildernesses of Maine, or New Hampshire, or Massachusetts. It is worthy of a little pause.

These Presbyterians held that the genius of this holy

Communion inhered in what they called "a table gesture." It was a meal, that is; holy, indeed, but a meal.
The Twelve were grouped about the Lord as at a meal.
To the mind of the Scot that could mean nothing but a
table. When a table was spread, they sat at the table.
Whether right or not, that was the idea. And heaven
and earth could not move them from it. It must be "a
table gesture."

The rebellion had been a cruel blow to the Ulster
people. But cataclysmic as it was, the experience of
it was less damaging and less painful to these self-
respecting and high-spirited people than the age-long
disabilities and shameful indignities they were compelled to endure by legal enactments. Just before the
outbreak of the rebellion an address had been prepared
and presented to the Long Parliament in the person of
their steadfast friend, Sir John Clotworthy. It contained
a list of grievances and a petition for the relief of the
same, and was drawn out in thirty-one numbered sections. The House was deeply impressed, and the Presbyterians were relieved. Even the Irish parliament
became Puritan. But as in a few years, when the Stuart
house regained the throne, the whole situation was reversed, and all the troubles of the past were renewed
and increased, it will not be any solecism to make record
herewith of the pith of these complaints.

The instrument just referred to was entitled, "The
humble Petition of some of the Protestant Inhabitants
of the Counties of Antrim, Downe, Derry, Tyrone, &c.,
part of the Province of Ulster, in the Kingdom of Ireland, Humbly representeth" etc.

The introduction to this address contains these clauses
by way of general description of the plight of these
people:—"partly by the cruel severity and arbitrary
proceedings of the civil magistrate; but principally

through the unblest way of the prelacy with their faction, our souls are starved, our estates undone, our families impoverished, and many among us cut off and destroyed.

"The prelates have their canons of late, their fines, fees and imprisonments at their pleasure; their silencing, suspending, banishing and excommunicating of our learned and conscionable ministers; their obtruding upon us ignorant, erroneous and profane persons to be our teachers; their censuring of many hundreds, even to excommunication, for matters acknowledged by all to be indifferent and not necessary. . . . These our cruel taskmasters have made of us who were once a people, to become, as it were, no people, an astonishment to ourselves, the object of pity and amazement to others, and hopeless of remedy unless" Parliament intervenes. They pray "for reparation in some measure, of our unutterable damages; your petitioners settled in a way whereby their persecuted ministers may have leave to return from exile . . . and an open door continued unto us, for provision of a powerful and able ministry, the only best way to promote plantation, and settle the kingdom in the possession and practice of true religion," etc.

Some of the numbered counts are these: the absolute prohibition of the "weekly lectures;" the sacramental test applied to schoolmasters; Papists given liberty to teach where Protestants are prohibited; slanderous and libellous propaganda against the Presbyterians officially encouraged; Star Chamber indignities to the perversion of justice; corruption of church privileges for purposes of graft; unreasonable fees and punishments for those who transgress oppressive enactments; buying and selling the sacraments, and charges impossible to pay for marriages and burials; gross corruption of the High Commission Court; brutal treatment of "women and maids," with excruciating details; the seizing of private lands to the impoverishment of many.

Five loyal and courageous Presbyterian ministers were on trial before our old friend Bishop Leslie. As a result of the trial, these men were deposed. They were Mr. Brice of Broadisland, Mr. Ridge of Antrim, Mr. Cunningham of Holywood, Mr. Colvert of Oldstone, and Mr. Hamilton of Ballywater. The bishop preached a discourse on the occasion, published and dedicated to Wentworth in the year following the trial, which was 1636. In it he argued that if the Presbyterians stood out upon the importance of "the table gesture" in the celebration of the Supper, they were logically bound to introduce all the other peculiarities of an ordinary feast: "Then why doe yee not receive the Sacrament in your dyning-roomes? for the Church is not a fit place to eate and drinke in. Why doe you not salute and welcome one another before you sit downe, as the manner is at civill feasts? Why doe you not use trenchers, napkins, knives, as well as stooles? Why doe you not eate a full meale, feede heartily, drinke oftener than once, and pledge one another? For all these doe belong to a liberal and honorable intertainment, and the prerogative of guests, to receive but one bit of bread, and one drop of wine, as it is eyther to stand or to kneele. Why doe you not intertaine discourse with one another? And especially why doe you not keepe on your hats, as at other feasts, that so you may bee, jacke-fellow-like with Christ in your social communions? I am afraid it will come to this at last, by that time your people have learned all the mysteries of your religion." Thus once more has this interesting bishop handed down to us an intimate photograph of the manners and customs we want to know about, in addition to illuminating the special matter in hand.

The observance of this sacramental meal was infrequent for a variety of reasons. There was the opposition of the Episcopal authorities, who were, be it observed, officers of the state. Penalties were likely to follow. There was lacking in many of the communities any suitable place for the meal, celebrated as they were bound to celebrate. The elements of the Supper were hard to get also. In the old session book of the congregation of Burt, near Derry, is an entry which is instructive in this respect. The session resolved on the observance of the Supper, and sent a messenger all the way to Belfast to make the necessary purchases. These included "thirty-six pottles of claret." Two other persons were authorized to provide the wheat and get it ground and baked. The expense of this business amounted to above six guineas, a large sum in those days. The following are the items: wine, four pounds seventeen shillings six pence; carriage, twelve shillings; wheat, eight shillings; grinding, one shilling two pence; baking, two shillings six pence; cask (!), two shillings eight pence; tickets, three shillings six pence;—total, six pounds seven shillings ten pence. The reader will draw his own conclusions from these little incidents as to many hardships of life in general among Blandford forbears in Ulster. In Londonderry, New Hampshire, tokens or tickets were used in the admission of communicants. I have no evidence that this custom prevailed in Blandford.

Another realistic picture of a local Communion service is one of date July 2, 1704, at Killileague, where the service began about seven o'clock in the morning. Seven tables were set. The Sunday following there was a similar service at Cumber, where there were ten and a half tables. The service there began at eight.*

---

* Reid, III, 91.

It is not necessary for us to keep very closely to the succession of calendar dates in our review of sacramental observances and the Sacramental Test. The Test was not removed from the statute book of Great Britain and Ireland until after the migrations were in process. It was in essentials the same old story from generation to generation. Differences were in detail only. Invariably, in their formal appeals to the imperial government for relief from oppression, the religious situation is the one most strongly pressed.

In a sermon preached by Bishop King and printed and circulated "in private" in 1693, the Presbyterians of Ulster were charged with neglecting public religious functions. In the course of the sermon the bishop made the following statement: "Lastly, never see anybody offer to administer, or desire to receive the food of life in the Lord's Supper." The discourse finally being very widely circulated, the Rev. Joseph Boyse, of Dublin, a scholar and dialectician of great power, made reply, which was soon followed by another from the pen of the venerable Robert Craighead, Presbyterian minister of Derry. The latter informs the bishop that the one and only obstacle to their doing as the bishop would have them do is the intolerance of their Episcopal oppressors themselves: "It's rare to celebrate it more than once a year in any congregation of our communion, where the congregations are brought to any tolerable settlement. I grant the time was, that the people of our persuasion, both ministers and others, were so pursued by bishops' courts, because of their meeting together, and adhering to their sound principles, that some were imprisoned, many excommunicated, and their families broken, others hunted as partridges on the mountains, and especially, if they were found celebrating the Lord's

Supper."* Before he concluded, he averred he was "weary of these empty debates."

The year that Charles II. died, general discussions were passing between the presbyteries, led by the ministers of Derry and Donegal, on the question of removal to America. The result was some actual settlement on these shores, though not in New England. The renowned Francis Mackemie took up his abode in Virginia, the first Presbyterian minister to settle in North America. He with some others organized the first presbytery regularly organized in the New World.†

These Presbyterian Scots had tried to do their part toward healing the wounds of Ireland. They were industrious, they were resourceful, they lived simply and honestly, they pursued a career calculated to build up a friendly Christian society. They endeavored to make peace with their neighbors. But certain provocations intensified native tendencies to clannishness; and their faith, while it marvelously stimulated the mind and laid firm and broad foundations of a liberty-loving state, yet embodied also some elements of intolerance and opened some doors of pride and prejudice. It was their misfortune more than their fault that they were domesticated on the soil of Ireland by virtue of initial violence and wholesale reprisal which the aboriginal inhabitant could never forget or forgive. The wealthy and lordly among them, to whom they paid rent and in whose power lay the worldly fortunes of these humble folk, had not the habit nor had they pursued the policies, of genuine fellowship with the Irish. Their manners toward these were haughty and aloof. The dispossessed Hibernian was for ever reminded that he was an underling and outcast. He was indeed indolent and barbarous and

---

* Reid, III, 32.
† Ibid., II, 425.

wished to remain so. All, or almost all, that had been done for him was unwelcome and abhorred. He had no way to cope with the situation except by a wholesale rising which should extinguish the entire system. Antagonisms of race, of taste and habit, or religion and social condition, rankled and burned and waited for a day of retribution which should not fail as failed the rebellion of 1641.

That is why, on the day of their secret and desperate revolt — December 9, 1688 — they flung their flag to the breeze in Dublin so that all might read on its folds the flaming legend, "Now or Never, Now and For Ever!" They chose well their opportunity. Sometime before, James II., Papist as he was, had deliberately turned over the reins of government, in Ireland, both civil and military, to the Irish Catholics. With a secrecy profound and long continued, by warlike preparations which covered the island and pased over no cottage among the humble faithful, by diligent propaganda which turned over every smithy and every home among their number into a manufactory or a storehouse of murderous and destructive instruments, by priestly exhortations and by laws or official commands, the great day of reckoning was set apart. As time passed and plottings ripened, the Protestants were disarmed or threatened, and encircled by awful menaces of dire evil to come. Thousands meantime fled the country in terror.

When the storm of fury broke, it was a raid of indiscriminate and awful ruin. The regular army, which in three months came to number something like one hundred thousand armed men, was followed by an unorganized and demonized horde of pillagers. Nothing was sacred in their eyes. Property of every description was seized or desolated. Cattle and sheep by the hundreds of thousands were slain, and the slayers became like starving beasts in possession of their prey. Multitudes of the people were stripped of their clothing and driven out stark naked to go whither they might.

Why continue the detail? Let the reader seek the general histories. Particularly to be commended is the twelfth chapter of Macaulay's History of England. There one may find eloquently told this melancholy yet thrilling tale of Ireland's horrors, the immortal epic of Enniskillen and Londonderry, and the final rout of the armies of the besiegers. We here take leave of Enniskillen only because our present particular interest is with Londonderry. Enniskillen was made glorious in her day of desperate defence. To Londonderry fled those people of the Bann waters who might be able to reach that city of refuge. Her heroic stand is the story of the fathers and mothers of the New Hampshire Londonderry, of Blandford, and of many another New England village. Nothing in all history surpasses it in heroism — not Thermopylae, not Rheims.

The story of all this — of the wonderful discipline of the little city, its heart-breaking weeks of slow starvation and deaths as the citizens and refugees watched far down the bay the ships sent from England for their relief and daring not to come nearer; the daily resort of the people to the cathedral to listen to the cheer of their chaplain and mayor, Walker, and to pray; their refusal to capitulate to the vastly overwhelming forces of the besieging enemy; the bravery of the women who passed out food and ammunition to the fighting men halting through utter exhaustion; the silent burying of their dead; the pestilence that was worse than missiles from musket or cannon; the final relief, and the sullen departure of the besiegers from before a wretchd town wall which human courage to desperation had alone made impregnable;— all this and much more in thrilling de-

tails is the story of Londondery during its famous siege.
Well has Macaulay written: "A PEOPLE WHICH
TAKES NO PRIDE IN THE ACHIEVEMENTS OF
REMOTE ANCESTORS WILL NEVER ACHIEVE
ANYTHING WORTHY TO BE REMEMBERED
BY REMOTE DESCENDANTS."

I have omitted much of this gruesome and awful history of reprisal and revenge. The Act of Settlement was
repealed by the Irish Parliament, thus transferring all
property to Celtic landlords. Pursuant to this a great
Act of Attainder was passed, "a law without a parallel
in the history of civilized countries." The list of the
attainted was kept secret, so that death might be visited
at any time on any victim anywhere that he might be
found, without any kind of warning. And the country
was dragged for victims.

If, as Macaulay justly observes, both parties in this
horrid strife, "had been placed, by a fate for which
neither was answerable, in such situation that, human
nature being what it is, they could not but regard each
other with enmity," it is also true, which this same historian takes pains to observe, that no doubt can exist
as to which party most cruelly abused its day of power.

I wish I might here display the roster of the men and
women who, later climbing the hills of New Glasgow
and building their log houses there, had been crowded
behind the bulwarks of that famous "City of Refuge."
A few who were probably there may be named. For the
most part the book is sealed. I have carefully looked for
them among the time-worn stones of the old burying
ground under the pines of Blandford hill. I have
searched in the old Murrayfield cemetery beside the
river. In both these ancient and quiet resting-places are
old rough moss-covered markers from which the stroke
of hammer and chisel never resounded — no date, often

not even an initial. In the Blandford ground at least not a few graves of the settlers have become entirely obliterated.* But some remain. The following eight, all from the cemetery on the hill, are all the names I am able to muster in this connection: Mrs. Hannah Stewart, wife of Charles, died Feb. 14, 175-. If, as would appear, the date is 1751, as she died in her 78th year, she was sixteen years old the year of the revolution. Margaret Crooks, wife of James, dying March 17, 1741, in her 85th year, was thirty-three. Hugh Hamilton died Feb. 20, 1763 in his 90th year; he was sixteen. Anne Boies, wife of David, born 1683, died August 25, 1766; she was six. David her husband first saw the light the very year of the outbreak and died Dec. 15, 1752. James Wilson died in 1759 at 81; so he was eleven. Samuel Crooks was born the year of the siege, dying at 87 in 1776. Robert Wilson was a year old, dying at 80 March 21, 1768. Thus are a few of the secrets of the long past delivered up, and we have presented to our imagination a little group of boys and girls, infants in arms or about to be born, and one woman of 33, most of whom, probably, and possibly all, were in that besieged city-fortress during those terrible days. Some of them would remember it and tell the thrilling expeience to the next generation. If, because of imperfect record, there were shut up in Londonderry, of Blandford's forbears, a much larger number than eight,—whatever the number may have been, the story of it became a Blandford tradition, a living link with the old aerie of Ulster's rocky history.

---

* The late Enos W. Boise, Esq., who was intimately acquainted with the town's early history, told me that the highway had encroached on some of the ancient graves. It once became my duty to select a suitable spot for a new grave in one of the largest lots there. I studied the spot closely. I took counsel with others who were wiser than I in such matters, finally selecting a location which seemed to all least likely to interfere with any possible earlier interments. By the time the grave was well opened small vestiges of human skulls and other bones nearly gone back to mother earth were found.

Among Blandford's first settlers were several families of the name of Anderson. The matron of one of these families bore witness, after the removal to Blandford, that she had "seen a house and barn filled with Protestants set on fire and all burned together." * It would seem almost certain that Mrs. Anderson, and not improbably her family, had also found refuge in Londonderry.

William Caldwell was in Londonderry during the siege, as was Adam Blair;† or, according to another authority,‡ Abraham Blair. These men so distinguished themselves for bravery that they were relieved from taxation anywhere in the British provinces. After coming to this country they occupied "exempt farms" for a time in Worcester.§

---

* I have this testimony from Mrs. Mary W. Morrison, of Ashtabula, Ohio, quoting from a letter of date, Feb. 11, 1865, written by her mother, Mrs. Walton, who wrote that she remembered her great-grandmother Anderson, who handed down this reminiscence.

† Lincoln's History of Worcester.

‡ The Scotch Irish in America, by Samuel Swett Green.

§ I am unaware of the immediate connection, if any, between the early Blairs and Caldwells of Blandford and these heroes. Adam Blair was an early Blandford name.

CHAPTER V

THE DILEMMA: BOND OR FREE?

The British government had extraordinary occasion to remember with gratitude the Scots of Ulster. They stood in the gap and filled it with their bodies as a rampart against the forces of the revolution. Because of them William of Orange had time to gather his forces and bring the conflict to a speedy end. Then William became King. Among all Scotchmen and all Protestants the joy was great, and expectation bright. The battle of the Boyne was hailed as the dawning of a new era, for William of Orange was one of the most liberal-minded men of his time, and he thought well of the Presbyterians.

But William's reign was a keen disappointment. The king could not by any means do in all respects as he would. The controversies and parties of half a century gone had left their certain inheritance of division. Jacobites were plotting to restore the Stuarts. Tories and churchmen in England had to be reckoned with. William tried to take a middle course and pleased nobody. Embroilments and fears and political devices to meet uncomfortable social, religious or industrial emergencies bred a cesspool of rotten jobberies and broken promises. Whatever profit might arise from such business materialized in the rise of English favorites to place and power, even in the church, and all of it was at the expense of Ireland.

Following the war the churches in Scotland were bursting, since Ulstermen had fled thither in numbers. Ulster was left with the Presbyterians in vast preponderance. The church buildings were not large enough to accommodate the worshippers and gatherings of thousands covered the fields. Bishop Leslie wrote to the king that the Episcopalians were not one in fifty.* Roman Catholics were of course now under the ban. What then? What cheer for the hunted Scots? had their day come at last? The Test Act was still in force and year by year was being carried out and on to its logical conclusions. Presbyterians were excluded from all public offices, the prohibition extending to the army and navy. It barred the teachers from teaching and the preachers from marrying and from burying the dead unless by use of the Episcopal ritual. This regime extended into the reign of Queen Anne.

In 1705 Daniel DeFoe, writing in Newgate prison, defended the cause of the Presbyterians in these bitter terms: "It seems somewhat hard, and savours of the most scandalous ingratitude, that the very people who drank deepest of the Popish fury, and were the most vigorous to show both their zeal and their courage in opposing tyranny and Popery, and on the foot of whose forwardness and valour the Church of Ireland recovered herself from her low condition, should now be requited with so injurious a treatment as to be linked with those very papists they fought against." This very thing was being proposed at the time in Parliament, in a bill to prevent the growth of Popery. De Foe proceeds: "This will certainly be no encouragement to the dissenters to join with their brethren the next time the Papists shall please to take arms and attempt their throats. Not but they may perhaps be fools enough, as they always were, to stand in the gap; (and as they continued to do) but if ever the crisis should arise, would not all the world call them fools to do anything again that merits to be 'remembered to their honour?' If this be the Church's

* Reid, III, 13.

method of 'remembering' favours, if this be their returns of gratitude, let them fight for them next time that dare trust their temper. . . . If these are Church of Ireland politics, for shame, gentlemen, never reproach the native Irish for winking when they shoot; for never marksman took such aim as this. 'Tis such a tale of a tub, the very Irish themselves must laugh at it; for what could be of more service to the Popish interest in that kingdom than to see the Protestants thus divided and persecuting each other?"

Year after year the Presbyterians petitioned parliament for relief, but in vain. They took such reprisals as they could. If we may believe the charge of one of the bishops — King, of Derry — they took no apprentices that would not engage to go to meeting with them; employed none nor traded with any that were "not of their own sort," if they could avoid it; planted their land with the help of such; and on all juries and other occasions favored such "more than justice." * Just before the year of the emigration, an election in the county of Antrim put in office an elder of the Presbyterian church, his opponent being a tory and pledged to uphold The Test. This tory subsequently complained that "This project, it must be presumed, had been the subject of their deliberations in presbyteries and synods, as it afterwards became matter of their popular harangues even from the pulpit; insomuch that matters are come to that pass in several parts of Ulster, that the gentlemen of the Church, even in their own towns and estates, are obliged to apply to dissenting teachers and elders for the interest and voices of their own tenants." †

So far as conditions could be made use of it was

* Reid, III, 85.
† Ibid., 196.

becoming a game of give and take. Sometimes a sense of humor relieved an embarrassing situation. The Rev. Gilbert Kennedy, minister in Tullylish, in the county of Down, wrote to a friend October 5, 1716: "Our prelates are violent where I live. Four of my flock have been lately delivered to Satan for being married by me; I question if they'll take as many from him these two days as they delivered in one." *

A delicious story of an elopement is told by Mr. Bolton.† It was in 1715, three years before the New England migration. Apparently wanting to escape Episcopal condemnation attaching to Presbyterian marriage rites, Hugh Montgomery, with his fiance Miss Jane Cargill of Ballymoney, betook himself to Ballymena, where there was a curate, Robert Donald, of the established church. There they were married, and the marriage was duly recorded by the curate, and sworn to by John Freeland and William Hodge. There could be no contradiction of that, and no challenge of it by the constituted authorities. Jane belonged to an influential family, and our historian suggests that perhaps Hugh had found some difficulty in getting within the choice circle. But trouble came just the same, for the session of Hugh's home church would not by any means concede that such procedure was necessary, or even allowable. Rather was it to be condemned, and they told him so. Whereupon the young groom meekly confessed *"the disorder of his marriage"* and "his sorrow for it." ‡

Details of Ulster's troubles might be drawn out to greater length than these pages have recorded. It is time, however, to pass on. Rentals increasing beyond endurance, privileges of church and civic life narrowing,

---

* Reid, III, 209.
† P. 127.
‡ This Hugh Montgomery came to New England. There was one of that name, a first settler in Blandford.

laws tightening to a strangle hold, Ireland as a whole bled white in order to render her helpless for further rebellions or further revivals of any kind whatever, she had sunk already in 1709 to the condition pictured by Dean Swift, famous as churchman and writer: "We look upon the Papists to be altogether as inconsiderable as women and children. Their lands are almost entirely taken away from them, and they are rendered incapable of purchasing any more; for the little that remains, provision is made by the late Act against Popery that it will daily crumble away. To prevent which, some of the most considerable among them are already turned Protestants, and so in all probability will many more. Then, the Popish priests are all registered, and without permission (which I hope will not be granted) they can have no successors; so that the Protestant clergy will find it perhaps no difficult matter to bring great numbers over to the Church; and in the meantime the common people, without leaders, without discipline, or natural courage, being little better than hewers of wood and drawers of water, are out of all capacity of doing any mischief, if they were ever so well inclined." Next, the learned and satiric dean, dipping his pen in gall.and wormwood, excoriated the Presbyterians: "'Tis agreed among naturalists that a lion is a larger, a stronger, and more dangerous enemy than a cat. Yet if a man were to have his choice, either a lion at his foot, bound fast with three or four chains, his teeth drawn out, and his claws pared to the quick, or an angry cat in full liberty at his throat, he would take no long time to determine." *

At last, as the great historians assure us, Ireland lay prone, and remained so for a century, suffering "the most terrible legal tyranny under which a nation has

* Quoted by Reid, III, 126f.

ever groaned." * Mr. Bolton most aptly remarks, in his book to which I have made repeated reference,† "A Scot might starve in Ireland as peaceably as he was likely to do in a strange land beyond the sea, but to be thwarted in his views of right and of heaven stirred him to action." The laws and the administration of the empire had created a desert and called it a peace.

Some of us used to sing this old-time Irish song, beginning:

"O Paddy dear, and did you hear the news that's going round?
The shamrock is forbid by law to grow on Irish ground;

. . . .

They're hanging men and women there for wearin' of the green."

The historic intervals in Ireland were short when some race, or sect, or class were not "forbid by law" to do some innocent thing, from the time of Henry VIII. to well into the last century.

We sing, "The land of the free and the home of the brave." The land of the free is a free land. The home of the brave is freed from bondage by brave, free men.

"They love their land, because it is their own,
And scorn to give aught other reason why;
Would shake hands with a king upon this throne.
And think it kindness to his majesty."

Such a people may lift up their eyes to heaven and thank God that they are not under bondage to any man except to love one another.

In my study of Blandford and her beginnings, I have pored over the scrawled and yellowed manuscripts of the sires; I have regaled myself in the midst of their almost utter freedom from orthographic rules, observing only the aim to drive straight for the sound of the words; and in the midst I have discerned an almost

---

* Green, Shorter History, Chap. 9, Sec. 8.
† P. 43.

FACSIMILE OF CERTAIN BLANDFORD SIGNATURES, 1757

FACSIMILE OF CERTAIN BLANDFORD SIGNATURES, 1757

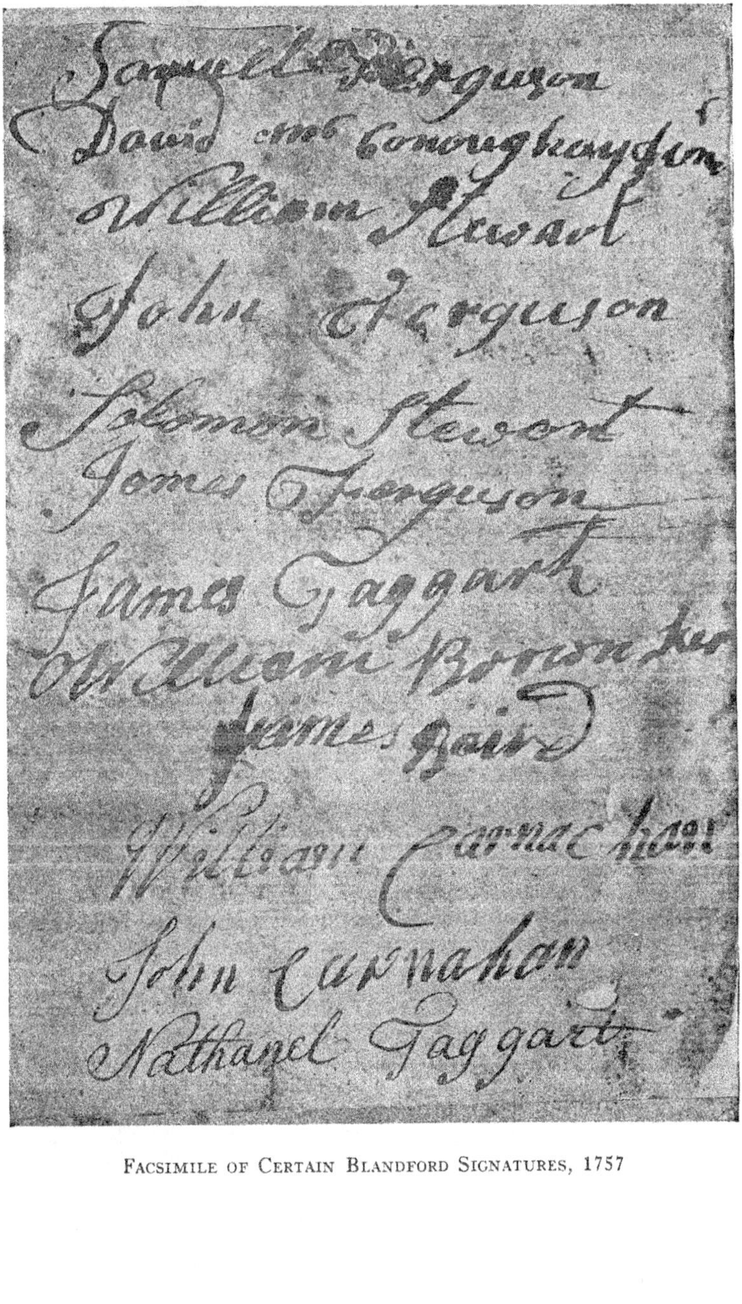
Samuel Ferguson
William Stewart
John Ferguson
Solomon Stewart
James Ferguson
James Taggart
James Baird
John Carnahan
Nathanel Taggart

Facsimile of Certain Blandford Signatures, 1757

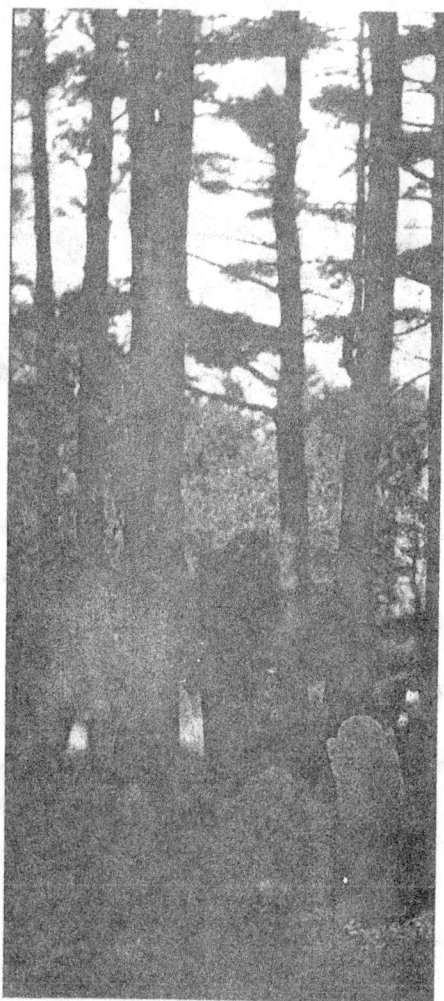

"THE TIME-WORN STONES:" p. 80

invariable obedience to one rule, namely this: that the omnipresent, puissant fact, the thing on which home and meeting house and school and the feet of man and beast must rest, that out of which food for both must come, and down into which at last the tired, worn body of each is laid to rest, is adorned and saluted with a capital initial. I have observed on these records, one name after another, of men of dignity, men wearing wigs and carrying titles, which titles and names aforesaid were taken lightly by being writ small. But I have so seldom seen that mystic word, *land*, so entered upon the written page, that I have been led to think the writer dreaming when, in a moment of lapse, he fails to dignify this word with its usual capital initial. I have seen the surname of "Freeland," of which there were several representatives, familiar in the records of the early days in Blandford — degraded to the place of a common noun, thus: "freeland"; and I have seen it separated in the middle and made two words, the one headed with the small, or lower case, "f," and the other adorned with a capital — "free Land," in order that this meaningful and historic presence, second only to the presence of the Deity who created it — LAND — be given its sentimental significance. I make this record here because it became an inheritance of the soul, a vision of power and beauty and right and inexpressible satisfaction. And the Ulster home burned the thing deep into the dreams and visions of the Ulster Scots.*

* Prof. Max Farrand writing of early incentives to American immigration, mentions land as among the first: "Yet, after all, the greatest attraction was probably that of land. In a world whose political and social structure was based upon land-holding, and at a time when in older communities land was difficult, if not impossible, to obtain, it may readily be appreciated how dazzling the chance appeared when a continent was to be given away." Again, on p. 19, "If the land were not freely given the impatient colonists seized it." He cites conditions in Pennsylvania in 1725.

CHAPTER VI

Good-bye, Ireland!

Human influences and motives, like chemical elements, are most often far from simple and are hard to analyze. Professor Max Farrand, already quoted in the last chapter, affirms that "the primary interest of Englishmen, as well as of Europeans, in planting colonies, was a commercial interest. . . . The first necessity with which they were confronted was that of supporting life." But what is life? Ask the martyr; ask the Pilgrim of Plymouth; ask the Scotchman of Ulster. The writer just quoted allows that religion was "at times the greatest incentive of all," a large admission for one writing history from the view-point that economics explains pretty nearly all that requires explanation.

The Scots of Ulster, like their kinsmen of old Scotland, put mighty emphasis on religion. Invariably, in their formal appeals to the imperial government for relief from oppression, the religious situation was the one chiefly urged, when economically their situation was becoming desperate. In 1712—to add one more example to many already contained in these pages—a committee of synod, Mr. Iredell, was despatched with a petition for relief addressed to her majesty, Queen Anne.

The petition alludes to the false statements which have gone up to the throne through her majesty's civil or ecclesiastical governors to the intent that the petitioners had not of late been disturbed in the exercise of religious worship where they had settled congregations, and cites these facts: "We beg leave to acquaint your majesty that of late years the renewal of leases is refused to divers Presbyterian lessees; and in many leases

90

of church and college lands there are clauses inserted prohibiting under great penalties the building or continuing of meeting-houses, and that Presbyterian inhabitants should dwell upon the premises; some whereof have been severely executed already to the great prejudice and expense of many of your faithful subjects, and will ruin divers of our settled congregations, unless your majesty shall see it meet in your great clemency to divert the severity of these proceedings."* In the next year Mr. Iredell and two others had an interview with the new lord-lieutenant in respect of these same or similar conditions, assuring him that "the melancholy apprehensions of these things have put several of us upon thoughts of transplanting ourselves into America, that we may there in a wilderness enjoy, by the blessing of God, that ease and quiet to our consciences, persons and families, which is denied us in our native country."†

Nearly four-score years later, when, in the midst of profound and protracted troubles in their church in Blandford, "William Boies and John Hamilton, Commete of the aggrieved Bretherin of the Church in Blandford," presenting their grievances to their presbytery, declared that "the faithfull preaching of the word & the ordinances of God and the Church" were esteemed by them "Dearer than all worldly concerns," spoke out of deep conviction, and were following scrupulously and characteristically in the steps of their progenitors in generation after generation.

One may like their religion, or dislike it: that is an entirely irrelevant matter. The part which the student of their history has to play is to discover and recognize the facts. And the facts are that in their own souls

"Religion is the chief concern
     Of mortals here below,"

* Reid, III, 151.
† Ibid., 173.

as one of the old hymns has it. It became still more emphatically true to their consciousness in inverse proportion to their deprivations by arbitrary authority and insane prejudice.

The migration which began in 1718, to New England, was the first migration of Presbyterians in any considerable number. A good many Quakers had come, settling mostly in the more southerly parts of the country. The early eighteenth-century exodus had no commercial significance whatsoever. There was no commerce between Ulster and New England. The ships which took the fugitives from Ulster across carried the persons and their individual effects. It was an emigration, not an exportation. They had nothing to bring but their persons, their almost negligible domestic goods, and their incalculable freight of sentimental and spiritual inheritance. The emigrants of 1718 were only a vanguard. Alarmed, the imperial government presently took measures to make life a little less intolerable for the Scots in Ireland. But lacking vision to do this with any degree of heart or thoroughness, the surge began again and continued, still further impelled by famine and poverty.

In the spring of this year, 1718, a minister in Ulster wrote to a friend in Scotland thus: "There is like to be a great desolation in the northern parts of this kingdom by the removal of several of our brethren to the American plantations. No less than six ministers have demitted their congregations, and great numbers of their people go with them; so that we are daily alarmed with both ministers and people going off." * A dozen years later it was spoken of as a "humour," "a contagious distemper." Many went to the West Indies. New England received a constant stream of new recruits to the earlier

---

* Reid, III, 340.

settlements or to later ones. Upon those who remained in Ireland the effect of all this was most depressing.

A biographical incident of highest significance in this connection attaches to the story of Blandford, and is illustrative of this peculiar people in a large and general way. It has to do with David Boies, who first saw the light in the year of the Londonderry siege. In course of time David with Anne his wife, after some wanderings turned their faces westward to the new "Glasgow," which a few years later became incorporated under the name of Blandford. Presently David was made ruling elder in the church. No office of greater dignity could be placed in his trust. Side by side in "the city under the hill" stand to this day the two monuments of this elder and his esteemed consort. This mature couple had settled in the main street of the town not without some earnest thoughts upon the great subject of home-choosing for the soul as for the body. David, and doubtless his faithful spouse, took full appraisal of the time as one of the great turning movements of their life together. He would set it down in writing; would give it perspective; would bear overt witness for his posterity to read.

"Eternal, Jehovah," the document begins, "I desier to Com unto thee a poor Wretched sinner a miserabl Cretur who am full of sin and of iniquity Defiled in all the powrs and facquilties of both soul and body by reason of original Sin and actual transgression and am justly Liable unto thy wrath and Displeasur not only in this World but also in that which is to Come," etc. Whereupon he humbly confesses his utter inability to help himself or get help anywhere except through the "Blessed word" revealed through "Jesus Christ," whom he promises to follow "trough good report and Bad report and to Continue faithfull unto lifes end." In re-iterated sentences he lingers upon his conviction that his right even to plead for mercy is derived only from the prescriptive invitation divine "to invit me poor sinfull miserabl me to Com and Enter into Covenant with" God, which invitation he heartily embraces: "Let it be a Bargain Lord I Belive help my unbelif . . . and o Lord God let not my failings make void this Covenant."

"Dated the 18th of Apriel: 1738   David Boies"

A reverent descendant, the late esteemed Enos W. Boies, for long years town clerk of Blandford, rescued this family inheritance and reproduced it in copper plate fac simile. The document is written in a firm, rather ornate hand entirely representative of the virility of the writer. It is a voice out of the long, long past. Its conceptions and phraseology are antique. Nevertheless, it is the voice of a true, strong man of his time. Wonder as one may at a system of theology and discipline of faith which could so belittle humanity, and caricature— in some respects—the Christian revelation of the Father in heaven, the breath of the religion of the time was in it. It reveals the warp and woof of the confessor's soul, and of the souls of his fellow believers, such men and women as made Blandford, and Londonderry, and any other typical community in the Presbyterian circuit. The old eagle's nest might be torn to pieces. But such eaglets as these defy the elements. The ocean is but a pond; the wilderness is an abode deliberately chosen, not the abode of cagelings, but the home of the freeborn.

Such was the faith of these people going down to the sea and confronting the great Atlantic. Columbus had conquered it; the Pilgrims had weathered it; the Puritans of Massachusetts Bay had subdued a fringe of coast. Nevertheless, to these would-be adventurers of the early eighteenth century, America, even New England, was "wilderness." They were not to settle down in Boston, or Salem, or Plymouth, but were going out

into the wilds. They were to be scouts, pioneers. That
was the understanding. It certainly was so among the
informed on this side of the Atlantic. Before they actually left it must have been burned into their own
souls too. They had endured hardness: they were to
endure more hardness. They knew perfectly well from
what they were going. None but the most shallow and
flippant could or would ignore that to which they were
going. They pondered it long. It was no new spasm of
enthusiasm. For decades the vision had appeared, and
reappeared, and appeared again. It meant physical
danger, the breaking up of home, separation of dearest
friends, severing of racial associations; a challenge of
every kind of resource; risk of health, of fortune, cer-
tainty of hardship; prizes to be won at cost of untold
risk; weariness, loneliness, unrest; success to the hard-
iest and bravest.

Naturally as the time approached, many withdrew.
There were discussions in the family circle, at the
church, among little knots of neighbors, in the great representative assemblies. Pastors talked it all over with
their flocks. Ministers and others wrote about it to one
another, or to leading citiezns abroad. Sea captains were
consulted. The thing got abroad. There was not only a
door to be shut, but a door to be opened. Agitation increased and broadened. Boston had not yet become
accustomed to immigrations except of its own kind. The
New England coast had been for centuries a resort of
ambitious and hardy adventurers. There were land
speculations, land proprietorships, prospectings for
settlers and settlements. There was the comprehensive
interest, not to say rivalry, of statecraft. Frontiers were
not established, nor where they fortified, except feebly
or uncertainly. And the North American Indian had

kept the knowledge of the fact for ever alive with bloody incident.

The influence of the Mathers in New England history in this period and that immediately preceding was very extensive. They were men of prodigious learning, great piety, and large acquaintance with affairs, both in New England and Great Britain. Nonconformists all of them, by reason of which the elder men had removed to New England, they at once rose to the highest positions. In one person or another the family carried weight in England, Scotland and Ireland, at the universities and at court; and equally in New England, at Harvard University, in pulpit oratory, in the most prolific publications of books, and in affairs generally. Cotton Mather was for a long time colleague with his father, Increase, in the pastorate of the North Church, Boston. It was one of the favorite schemes of the Rev. Cotton Mather to buttress the dangerous frontiers of New England with a fringe of sturdy Scotch settlers. For years he interested himself in this scheme by correspondence and propaganda generally. His vision swept along the western and northern fringes of New England beginning with his own Massachusetts, stretching across mountains, plains and rivers to Eastern Maine. Nor did his dreams end there, for he would fain also grasp Nova Scotia. The personality and writing of this unique man commanded the attention and respect of Benjamin Franklin. Undoubtedly we must recognize Cotton Mather to be among the foremost apostles of the Scots of Ireland as desirable emigrants to New England.

When Mr. Mather preached his "Boston Lecture" of Dec. 27, 1698, on "The History of Ten years, Rouled Away Under the Great Calamities of a War with Indian Salvages," it may not have been given with the view to direct incentive to any future Scotch pioneers coming over. It might serve, however, as inducement to New England adventurers opening this back door to that people. The lecture is of prodigious length, and I shall make no extensive citation from it. But students of this history will find herein some lurid glimpses of what these hardy and long-suffering folk were about to come to as they weighed in the balances of their canny judgment the choice between the old-world persecutor and the new-world "salvage." To the "Boston Lecture" then, in the North Church, at seven o'clock, of date as above* we betake ourselves.

The text of the lecture is from the Book of Judges, vi. 3,5,6: "The children of the east came up against them; and they entered into the land to destroy it; and Israel was greatly impoverished:"—"No less than ten years have rouled away since we have been plunged into the distresses of war with a barbarous enemy. In this war we have seen the 'fruitful land' of almost one whole province, and another whole county, 'turned into barrenness;' . . . I am to lead you this day through a spacious country, which has been on many accounts the most charming part of New England; and I must herewithal say, 'Come, behold the works of the Lord, what desolations he hath made in that land.' . . . Two of our MAGISTRATES have been barbarously killed by the Indian murderers. . . . Two of our MINISTERS have been struck down into the earth by the Indian *dragon*. There have been some *rich men*, that were finely scituated, and 'had all things richly to enjoy:' but this war has reduced them to such necessity, that within less than one year they have come to *beg their bread!* Little boys and girls, even these little *chickens*, have been seized by the Indian *vultures* . . . And our little ones have been hideously

---

* Cotton Mather's "Magnalia," the Seventh Book, Appendix: 24 solid pages of large octavo.

whipt unto death by those merciless tygres, whose 'tender mercies are cruelty.' . . . Several hundreds of our neighbors, first and last, have been carried into captivity by the most beastly and bloody things that ever wore the shape of men in the world . . . While they have seen their nearest relations torn in pieces alive before their eyes, and yet those eyes afraid of dropping a tear at the mournful sight: Yea, when they have even looked when they should be themselves roasted alive to make a *feast* and a *sport* for the horrid *cannibals!* . . . Moreover, is it not a very *humbling* thing, that when about an *hundred* Indians durst begin a war upon all these populous colonies, an army of a *thousand* English raised must not kill one of them all; but instead thereof, more of our *soldiers* perish by sickness and hardship than we had *enemies* then in the world? . . . Is it not a very *humbling* thing, that we should have 'evil pursuing of us' at such a rate, that in other lands afar off, and on the Exchange in London, strangers have made this reflection: 'Doubtless New England is a country in ill terms with Heaven?' . . . Is it not a very *humbling* thing, that when peace is restored unto the whole English nation, and when peace is enjoyed by all America, poor New England should be the *only land* still embroil'd in war?"

This is what our migrating people were to be offered an open door to. This is the secret, on this side the ocean, of their welcome. These were to be their wide acres, their open lands. When the Pilgrims came over, they had some degree of opportunity of peaceable arrangements with the aborigines; not much, but some. But what were these poor sheep to have? And the fact became not so very far different from the prospect. Yet these people came, knowing at least in some measure to what they were coming; came, also, with smarting, blistering memories of what they were leaving. Doubtless, too, the spirit of wanderlust and of adventure was not lacking.

Before the summer of 1718 had begun there came to Governor Shute of Massachusetts Bay, one bearing a parchment containing three hundred and eighteen signatures to this address: "We whose names are underwritten, Inhabitants of ye North of Ireland, Doe in our own names, and in the names of many others, our Neighbors, Gentlemen, Ministers, Farmers, and Tradesmen, Commissionate and appoint our trusty and well beloved friend, the Reverend Mr. William Boyd, of Macasky, to his Excellency, the Right Honorable Collonel Samuel Suitte, Governor of New England, and to assure His Excellency of our sincere and hearty Inclination to Transport ourselves to that very excellent and renowned Plantation upon our obtaining from His Excellency suitable incouragement. And further to act and Doe in our Names as his prudence shall direct. Given under our hands this 26th day of March, Anno Dom. 1718."

Mr. Boyd himself did not sign, nor did he come to remain. His military title was won in war for King William, and the confidence which the signers placed in him was achieved as á faithful pastor among these people. The original parchment hangs upon the wall of the Historical Society in Concord, New Hampshire. The signers all registered their own original autographs except thirteen. Professor Perry observes: "It may well be questioned, whether in any other part of the United Kingdom at that time, . . . in England or Wales, or Scotland or Ireland, so large a proportion as ninety-six per cent of promiscuous householders in the common walks of life could have written their own names."

This parchment has been so thoroughly investigated by students of the movement that I have not considered it needful to do other than adopt the conclusions of these men. It has been copied into many books. There is before me the list as given in Bolton's "Scotch Irish Pioneers," also as transcribed by Temple in his History of Palmer. The former of these two writers states that while four ministers signed the address, not one of them came to live in New England. He pronounces it a puzzling list, seeming to have been prepared in some haste somewhere in the Bann valley, perhaps at a meeting of presbytery. He adds, "All of the names doubtless looked impressive to Governor Shute, even if upon us the significance of many of them is lost. And perhaps both the Governor and Cotton Mather were no wiser than we are." * It should be recognized that the list by no means represents in any accurate way the names of householders who actually came over that following summer in "the five ships."

The encouragement which the Rev. Mr. Boyd received on his presentation of the address of would-be settlers in New England from the valleys of the Bann and the Foyle, was, I will not say, academic. It was sufficiently significant to indicate a hearty welcome. Really, it was a welcome to these people to come over here and get out to the frontiers where they would stand between the old settlements and the fire of the Indians. There was no kind of contract, verbal or written. It might be said, there was an understanding. The rest should be left for later negotiation. So far as any definite homes were concerned, they were to go out not knowing whither they went. Consider it: they were a brave people!

Boyd was not the only agent or commissioner in this business. Two other ministers, for example, Robert Homes and Thomas Craighead, men of consequence and

* P. 104f.

education, had long been in the field; brothers-in-law, both Edinburgh University men, both warmly welcomed by Samuel Sewall. Both, after considerable professional service over here, did not a little in the encouragement of the spirit of migration among our people of Ulster. Cotton Mather was behind them too, and the influence of all these men opened long reaches of coast to the thoughts of the Ulsterites along the New England coasts, the Jerseys and Pennsylvania.

The coast of Maine offered great attractions to not a few ambitious men. One of these was Robert Temple, an Englishman of high degree. By letters of introduction from Nathaniel White, his uncle, a merchant in the New England Plymouth, he enlisted the interest of some of the prominent men of affairs of Massachusetts Bay — Belcher, Hutchinson, Oliver, Pepperell — in land proprietorships. After some considerable pioneering along the coast, he determined to see what he could do in the Kennebec country, particularly to the east of that river, where was a large territory belonging to Colonel Hutchinson and the Plymouth company, with whom he entered into contract with the view to settlements, and finally brought several hundred families thither on the shores of the Kennebec, in 1719 and 1720. This enterprise was sadly disturbed by Indian raids, many of the settlements were broken up, and the inhabitants scattered.

Another extensive series of settlements, largely peopled by Ulster Scots, was made in another section of the Maine seaboard under the leadership of the resourceful and ambitious Samuel Waldo. This enterprise was undertaken in connection with the "Muscungus Patent," granted by the Plymouth Council in 1629, later divided among the "Ten Proprietors," and extended again to include the "twenty Associates," three of whom were Jonathan Waldo, his son Samuel, and a cousin, Cornelius. Samuel was, or became, a personage of great power, both here and in old England. He finally achieved possession of a tract of a half million acres which became known as the "Waldo Patent." The land lay between the Penobscot and St. George rivers, and comprised the whole or major part of the present Knox and Waldo counties, with more or less of Penobscot county. While this land enterprise might seem at first blush to take us rather far afield from our main search, there is yet a very vital connection. The first settlers whom Waldo selected for his new communities were the Irish Scots, some of them of recent immigration in 1735, but others who had been in the country from the first arrival in 1718. He had seen their quality, and valued it for its sterling worth.*

I have diverged a little from our main quest because it would be quite impossible to keep within the local or personal limits of Blandford settlement and Blandford settlers and at the same time give any adequate story of Blandford at all. The previous few paragraphs may serve to suggest, in part, and following pages will indicate more fully, what Professor Perry felicitously called the Presbyterian circuit. Necessarily these people were more or less in a state of flux. Perilous conditions of the times and the locations brought it about. Racial characteristics intensified it. To a degree, and in not a few instances to a very large degree, identical family names appear and reappear in the early years throughout all these settlements, in all New England, in New York, in Pennsylvania. They were going and coming, marrying and giving in marriage, intermingling family contacts

---

* For the extremely condensed, or rather, selected, facts here given in this paragraph, I am indebted in large degree to a valuable article by Wm. Willis in the Collections of the Maine Historical Society, Vol. VI., and to the "Waldo Genealogy," by Lincoln.

and racial interests for many years. Subsequent material in these pages will verify this in some detail.

The exact number of passengers which "the five ships" of tradition brought over is not known. It has been variously estimated, from a thousand down to six or seven hundred. The number of families appears to have been about one hundred and twenty. An average of five to a family would fix the total at about seven hundred and fifty souls and this seems a moderate estimate. Seven hundred and fifty immigrants, landed on Long Wharf, Boston, in one short season, some hundreds of them at one time together, was a prodigious and fateful affair. Others were to follow. There was no public provision made for them. Immigration laws and accommodations were not yet. The "freedom of the city" was by no means theirs. Where should they go? What should they do? How should they be fed and lodged? It was a serious problem. No wonder there was excitement in Boston town. Who were there to meet them? With what sensations did these sea-farers step on shore, and begin to think of "a home within the wilderness"? Surely, Cotton Mather must have been there, and with him some little company of well-wishers, backed by a growing crowd of curious, suspicious and speculative folk whose welcome would hardly hearten either the lonely or the adventurous. Mather at once assumed the attitude of the friend who felt his own responsibility in the enterprise, and was ready with measures of thoughtfulness, neighborly assistance and professional service.*

Probably many stayed on shipboard for a little. Some found friends in town or in the vicinage. Most of them were not so poor that they could not provide for themselves. Many doubtless were ready to work. The leaders

* See footnote on next page.

would begin at once to seek for suitable openings for settlement. Altogether, one must admire the courage of these men and women, for they had burned their bridges and were not disposed to look back. Landed proprietors were there with their suggestions and offers of farms and opportunities of home-building. Governor Shute's henchmen were doubtless there to point out the way, "Westward, ho!" or "Northward!" and there were weighing of these offers and careful bargainings, and consultations with the more influential among the various companies. There was more or less of segregation among the immigrants. The company that built Nutfield, New Hampshire, later called Londonderry, kept together, trying out Casco Bay at first, but spending only one winter there. Some stayed in and around Boston, while others went north as far as Andover, Massachusetts, and settled there. Still others scattered along the Merrimac river. The company which interests us chiefly, and which comprised at first something like fifty families, went to Worcester.

As our story of their past amply proves, these were a self-respecting, self-reliant, intelligent and forceful people. They had become inured to difficulties and troubles, by conditions cruelly hard, and were not

---

* "Scotch-Irish Pioneers," by Charles Knowles Bolton, 1910, is the only book, to that date, giving any specific details of the "five ships." This author says there is but one source for these facts, namely, the "News Letter," the only paper of the day in New England. His account is of great interest. I must refer my readers to it. Briefly, the main bare facts are these: (1) An unnamed ship from Londonderry, John Wilson, master, arrived July 28, with emigrants. (2) Another, the brigantine "Robert," James Ferguson, master, from Glasgow and Belfast, bringing the future settlers of the New Hampshire Londonderry. (3) Same day, "William," Archibald Hunter, arrived from Coleraine. (4) The "Mary Anne," Andrew Watt, arrived from Dublin, apparently about the same time, also probably without any of our company. (5) Another ship from Dublin about a month later, the "Dolphin," John Mackay, with but few Scotch Irish. (6) Sept. 1, "Maccallum," James Law, from Londonderry, bringing more than twenty families. There are many details of interest in these pages of Mr. Bolton's book, but there would appear to be no way in which to determine in which of the above named vessels the Worcester contingent came over.

ground down by them. The spirit of independence, of democracy and of a great faith came with them across the seas. They had a purpose firm and they were hard to beat. The fact that some of them were warned to leave because they seemed to lack resources sufficient to keep them "off the town" was no more than the carrying out by the local authorities of a universal custom. It is what they themselves habitually did once they became established as a community. Indeed, somewhat softened and diluted, there still exists the operation of certain poor-laws by the shrewd officials of the New England country town, by virtue of which some poor wretch is ever and anon shunted from one town to another. It is a double game, on the one hand, of outwitting a neighboring board of overseers of the poor, and on the other, of guarding the local treasury. No doubt Boston authorities may have had some reason for carefulness in respect of certain among this large inrush of immigrants. At best the town was hard put to it to take care that the markets should be able to feed so many mouths at reasonable prices on a spot-cash basis.

CHAPTER VII

1718: New England, Ho!

In the province of Massachusetts Bay in that autumn of 1718, there was very much more in the wind than just a commissariat problem. Witness, for example, an Act of the Great and General Court in the year 1720, two years after the incident of "the five ships." This legislative body, finding that after so long a time certain of the companies "recently arrived from Ireland, and others from this Province," were in no hurry to depart, "ordered that the said people be warned to move off within the space of seven months," on penalty of prosecution "by suits of trespass and ejectment." Whether or not this enactment was aimed at certain stray tarriers of the 1718 immigration, or later arrivals, or both, it illustrates, together with certain other indications of suspicion and dislike, the presence in court quarters and in popular sentiment of a prejudice against this kind of neighbors except as buffers out on the dangerous frontiers.

It is not well that we should be too hard in our judgments of Boston or of Massachusetts in this instance or in similar matters generally. Human nature has intolerant germs ready to grow bitter fruit almost any time, anywhere. I have in a former work on Blandford shown how our own people did their share of exclusion on occasion. On the whole we carry "the white man's burden" rather poorly. We like "our own sort" best. The "ins" and the "outs" are not usually distinguished either justly or kindly.

A measure of self-satisfaction and intolerance inhered in these same Scotch Presbyterians of North Ireland.

They were positive beyond challenge that their system, alike of doctrine and of ecclesiastical discipline, was by revelation through the Holy Scriptures. Could they not cite chapter and verse? Could anything be clearer than that all came down to their fathers from God out of heaven? Therefore were all other systems false in large measure or altogether. Prelacy was idolatry. Independency, all forms of Congregational government, were chaos, even anarchy. Episcopacy they did not like, but Independency was far worse. Wherever they were in the new country, they ran up against one or the other with an aversion which provoked strong resentment.

This explains much of their history. It explains Worcester; it explains Hopkinton; it explains Londonderry; it explains them altogether as the stormy petrels of New England. This might seem enough, but it must not be forgotten that other strains of Puritanism had their convictions too, and some rough corners or sharp edges. Long decades of persecution and the stiffening of resistance, whether passive or aggressive, hardened them as steel in the fires. Added to all this were the peculiarities of race or condition within their little bailiwick, all intensified by reason of their enforced isolation, their poverty the result of oppression which amounted to robbery. How else than clannish, peculiar, ofttimes provoking could they be, until such time as a kind Providence should enlarge their hearts and soften the prejudices and proud asperities of other Puritans or Prelatists? Meantime, the sterling qualities of their essential manhood developed them into the most substantial of citizens, the most unconquerable of patriots, the most resourceful of pioneers.

The fact that certain families of the new immigration chose to remain in or about Boston, content with the society which they found there on their disembarkation, would seem a pleasing indication that the spirit of camaraderie was not altogether lacking among them. Scotch Irish names appear to some extent in the vital records of Boston at this time, and in the church records. There, or in the near vicinity, appear such Blandford family names as Blair, Black, Campbell, Carr or Karr (often spelled in Blandford records as Ker), Duncan, Kennedy, Lindsay, Moor, Smith, Taggart. Of those who left for one or another of the frontiers, not all could go forthwith. For a few weeks or even months population would be congested, and the food supply became matter of careful calculation on the part of town authorities, to say nothing of individual householders. But all such matters found adjustment, even the uncomfortable number and popularity of the taverns in the Hub!

Meantime, embarrassments and discomforts, or even racial prejudice, found some agreeable easement in one profitable industry which the newcomers had imported with them. As matter of course they had brought over seas their varied implements for the culture of flax and the manufacture of linen. Spinning wheels and other paraphernalia connected with the art were articles of common household furniture. These things were unknown in New England until these strange people appeared with them. The Londonderry people excelled in the making of linen, but all knew and practised it. The appearance of the industry at once created a sensation. The small wheels (often with double treadle) worked by the women and propelled by foot, turning out beautiful and useful products, created a new want among Bostonians.

The Scotch Irish women gave an exhibition on Boston common in the spring of 1719, and prizes were awarded to the most skillful. For four years the ardor continued in Boston, and ten years after, state prizes were paid in Bristol County for the best pieces of linen cloth made in that county. Produced under this initiative it found ready sale at good prices in Springfield and all the older towns. By the time another generation had arisen, this art was made compulsory by legislative action, a provincial law of 1756 requiring the selectmen of the various towns to "assess" the families under their several jurisdictions "according to their skills and abilitic" "at one or more spinners," or even fractions thereof. The stint was to extend over thirty weeks in the year, at "three pounds pr. weeke of linin, cotton, or woollen" under penalties for non-fulfilment.

Blandford was full of these little wheels, which were known as foot wheels. They turned out a finer product than the large wheel for spinning wool, common in New England. We have in our home a towel of linen spun and woven on Beech Hill (which is partly in Blandford and in larger part in Granville) the flax for which was grown and prepared right there. Almost all kinds of garments and some articles of domestic furnishings were made of this cloth in Blandford.

Some years after the group of people which this historical survey is especially following had left the vicinity, the Irish Scots in Boston organized a Presbyterian church on Federal Street, then known as Long Lane. Its first minister was the Rev. John Moorehead. This was the first Presbyterian church in New England. It maintained close relation with the Synod in Ireland. In 1739, uniting with other scattered members of that persuasion, they established the first presbytery in New England, called the presbytery of Boston. With this the Blandford church became connected.

The town of Boston which the eyes of this company looked out upon was as yet the remotest prophecy of what it has since become. Its population was around ten thousand. William Wood's famous "true, lively, and experimentall description of that part of America, commonly called New England" published in 1634* locates Boston as "two miles north-east of Roxberry." Wood's account runs thus: "This neck of land is not above four miles in compass; in form almost square, having on the south side, at one corner, a great broad hill, whereon is planted a fort, which can command any ship as she sails into any harbour within the still bay.† On the north side is another hill, equal in bigness, whereon stands a windmill. To the north-west, is a high mountain, with three little rising hills on the top of it; wherefore it is called THE TRAMOUNT. From the top of this mountain a man may overlook all the islands which lie before the bay, and descry such ships as are upon the sea-coast. This town, although it be neither the greatest nor the richest, is yet the most noted and frequented" etc.

The "great broad hill," originally called Corn Hill, later received the name of Fort Hill, which name it still bears. The hill on which was the windmill is the modern Copp's Hill. Originally it rose fifty feet above sea level. Of the "Tramount" the editor of the "Chronicles" says: "The top of this beautiful hill, which was in the rear of the State House, was 138 feet above the level of the sea. With its two adjoining eminences it occupied about 100 acres of ground. The easternmost hill was where Pemberton Square now stands, and the westernmost occupied what is now called Mount Vernon, near Louisburgh Square. The central elevation received the name of Sentry and afterwards Beacon Hill, from the Beacon which was placed on its summit to alarm the country in case of invasion, by setting fire to a tar-barrel fixed on

---

* Incorporated in Young's Chronicles, 391ff.

† Blandford soldiers were quartered here while Washington was besieging the British in Boston.

the top of it. The beacon was blown down by the wind in Nov. 1789. The wood-cut represents the three hills as they appeared when seen from Charlestown." This description will be sufficiently intelligible to modern readers. Captain John Bonner's map of 1722* displays the rounded top of Beacon hill as an abrupt cone. Opposite Copp's hill a ferry connected the town with Charlestown. Opposite the present North station were the "Mill Pond" and "Mill Damm," the latter locating the famous "Mill-dam road" of later generations. The wind mill "on the north side" is noted on the map, on what was then called "Snow Hill." It was brought down from Watertown in 1632 "because it would not grind but with a westerly wind." North of Beacon hill there were several rope walks, and another windmill in the midst, while to the west were the "Powder House," the "Watch House," and a "garden" in the rear of two houses. The old Granary burying ground is there, but not so called. The "COMMON" is designated but not definitely enclosed. Three trees stand on the area, two of them together just northwest of the "Burying Place," one of them being designated as "Bridewell," grewsome indication of the fact that it was there where criminals were publicly hanged.

As the map above named was issued only four years after the landing of our company of Scots, it represents essentially the town as they came to know it. It will not be out of place to indicate certain general features and spots of particular interest. The water front bristles with wharves and shipping, "Long Wharfe" running farthest into the harbor. King street, now State, runs thence directly up to the "Town House," later known as the "Old State House," but not the building which we know. This street continues westerly under the name

---

* Boston Post Road.

of Queen street, as far as "Treamont" (which was so called, as far as to Beacon street,—then "Common" street southerly from that point). Beyond the "Burying Place" it disappears in the open "COMMON" which is bordered westerly by "West Hill," "Fox Hill," and "Roxbury Flats." This area was a cow pasture open to all who desired to use it as such.

Our present Washington street bore three several names. From the present Adams square southward as far as to Milk street, this thoroughfare was known as Cornhill, thence to Essex it was called Newbury, and beyond that southward to the Neck, Orange. At the narrowest point there was a fortification. This way our pilgrims may have taken for their wilderness homes. On the map, just inside the "fortification" is the notation, "From Town H. One Mile."

Returning to Essex street, and turning down thither, at the farther end is "Hills Wharf," where South street crosses at right angles, running into "Cow Lane" at the foot of Summer. Here is the present South station, where Federal and Summer streets terminate. At this lower end of Long lane the Presbyterian church of a later date chose the site for their building, a resort which came to mean much to all the Scots of New England. This was also the distillery district of the town. There were not a few of these enterprises which turned out "New England Rum." "Cow Lane" ran along about a quarter of a mile to "Fort Hill" and "Battery March." Turning to the left we enter Milk street, so known then as now, at the westerly end of which is the "Old South," so indicated on the map. This was a wooden building, not the historic one of brick with the beautiful spire and Revolutionary associations. It had stood there since 1669, on the spot which had once been Governor Winthrop's garden. Our friends would not then appreciate the significance of the fact that in this house, twelve years before, a Boston boy named Benjamin Franklin was baptized.

School street was so named for the Boston Latin school whose building then stood just behind the "Chh. of England,"—not the stone structure we now know as King's Chapel, but a wooden one. Our company would look upon the one with loving eyes and upon the other with loathing. Not far away was the "Brattle St. Church," a wooden building, while down at the foot of Summer, near where the Presbyterian church was to be, stood the "New South," a flourishing church of liberal principles. The Quakers were on Leverett's lane, right in the heart of the town. Over at the North end stood the "Old North" church which was to become so historic, and a couple of blocks away the "New North," erected in 1714. In that same section of town, over against the "Mill Pond," was the "Baptist Meeting," or "Anabaptist,"—for both names are given to it,—an object which would provoke in our Scotch company the intensest scorn. It would have been hard for them to find an acceptable church anywhere. Not improbably many of these people had found temporary abodes thereabout.

We will retrace our steps to the vicinity of the town hall, the fashionable residential district of the town. Nearly opposite the Old South was the "Governours House," later known as the "Old Province House," the most elegant and costly dwelling in town, built of brick, three stories in height, with a magnificent doorway and an imposing cupola, in the midst of a handsome and beautifully shaded lawn.

The Old Corner Bookstore had recently been built. It would attract our company much less, probably, than some of the taverns, of which there were two on the very wharf on which they had landed. The Crown Coffee House was on Long wharf, kept by Thomas Selby.* The Bunch of Grapes stood at the head of Long wharf, and the tide flowed nearly up to the tavern door. It became one of the most famous of all Boston taverns, particularly in Revolutionary times, as the resort of local Revolutionary heroes. The Green Dragon, "by far the most popular of all Boston resorts," † stood near Hanover and Union streets. Its sign of hammered metal was a replica of one belonging to a tavern of the same name in London. The old site is still marked by a tablet carrying a similar emblem. Its habitues "represented the muscle of the Revolution." ‡ There were many others.

I have not mentioned among the churches The Old Church, first among them all, opposite King street. Opposite that stood the whipping post and the stocks. Dock square was just at the head of the Town Dock, a salt inlet which has since been filled in and built over. Captain John Bonner noted, in a corner of his map, these interesting items: "Streets 42   Lanes 36   Alleys 22 Houses near 3000. 1000 Brick rest Timber Near 12000 people."

After all the above might be added the Alms House, on Beacon street, almost or perhaps exactly covering the spot where now stands the impressive Shaw monument. These migrant Scots from Ireland as little wanted to land there as the town of Boston cared to have them.

---

* Drake.
† Mann.
‡ Drake.

CHAPTER VIII

Scouting Through the New England Wilderness

It has already been noted that our pioneer companies cherished the somewhat nebulous thought of settling down in "the wilderness" of New England. This thought never left them. They knew themselves as frontiersmen. Of the three groups,—the "Nutfield" or Londonderry, group, the Maine group, and those who were left, the last named adopted the idea of reinforcing the unstable settlement in Worcester. This they proceeded to do, it is supposed, sometime in the fall of 1718. It was in well-nigh desperate need. Well endowed by nature, with good soil, an abundance of water and pleasing landscapes, it needed nothing more to insure growth and prosperity than a sufficient start against fearful odds which recent events had presented. Incorporated in 1684, it was too weak even now to hold any town meeting, and had never had one. The early settlers were of English extraction. They had gathered there into a settlement called at first Quinsigamond— an Indian name still adhering to the beautiful lake within its boundaries. Far out as it was on the frontier, albeit but fifty miles from Boston, the settlement had been twice begun and abandoned, the last time following an Indian attack in 1709. By 1718 there were something like two hundred souls there, sheltered in fifty-odd log dwellings, and protected by several garrison houses, one of which was a block-house, or fort, of the conventional type. There they were making a determined stand under the forceful leadership of Jonas Rice, the first permanent settler in the community. Professor Perry, who made a careful study of the movements of the Scotch Irish pioneers, estimates that "at least fifty families—large families—went straight from Boston to Worcester that autumn, and that the population of the place was thus more than doubled at one stroke."

One had not to go very far west from Boston without getting out into wild nature. King Philip's War had pretty thoroughly reduced the province except the eastern fringe of settlements and those along the Connecticut river to a state of utter desolation. Brookfield had been wiped out. There was no village between it and Springfield. From Worcester to Marlborough it was a waste. Following the ravages of Philip's warriors for half a century or the better part of it there were sporadic attacks upon all frontiers in New England and New York. Many were fleeing the Kennebec country which was in a chronic state of panic. The famous Hannah Dustin incident occurred in Haverhill in 1697. Groton had been visited only a little before. Garrisons were a common recourse. There were officers on the watch everywhere. Pioneering was for men and women of courage. There were Indian tribes all over the province, and the whole country was crossed by Indian trails and a few English bridle paths.

Anything which might by courtesy be called a road, except as connecting the villages and towns near the coast soon vanished into a narrow path or trail still in a state of nature. Wagons were not conveyances for popular use, for the roads would not accommodate them. Just one year before "the five ships" arrived at Long wharf, the Connecticut colony granted a monopolistic privilege to run a wagon from Hartford to New Haven. Travel and transporation were preferably by water, if possible, however roundabout it might be. Streams were crossed at fords where fords were, and paths were worn to and from them as connecting links. Where fords could not be found and necessity required, foot bridges were made by felling large trees across the streams. A horse bridge was made by two split trunks with perhaps a rail for a guard. At the time of our Scotch Irishmen's first treks these were the transportation privileges. Even a cart could not venture much to the westward of Boston. Baggage must be carried on the person or strapped to horses.

The paths followed largely the trails made by the aborigines. These soft-footed and light-stepping folk left the lightest kind of impression on the soil. The booted British or European following on made the first hard-trodden path. Then the mounted post rider or settler developed it by slow stages a grade nearer to a road.

The famous Old Bay Path developed in this way out of many units originally separate. It was laid out in 1673. "At a county court holden in Charlestown, December 23, 1673, John Stone, Sen., of Sudbury, John Woods of Marlborough, and Thomas Eams of Framingham, . . . were appointed and impowered to lay out an highway for the use of the country leading from the house of John Livermore in Watertown, to a Horse Bridge (then being) near the house of Daniel Stone, Jun., and thence the nearest and best way to Marlborough, and thence to Quaboag." * What this road was like is eloquently set forth by a petition of certain leading citizens of Brookfield to the General Court, in 1700:

"To his Excellency, Richard, Earl of Bellomont:

"Wee the subscribers being very senceable of the inconveniencys that may happen in as much as the

---

* I.e., Brookfield. This citation is copied from Temple's North Brookfield.

stated Road to Conitticot especially Betwixt Wooster and Brookfield is verry much incumbered with Trees ffallen & many Rocky Swamps & other impassable Obstructions to Travellers, Drovers & others, & hazzarding life or limb of both men and Horses & other Creatures to great Losses & Damages, Humbly propose that there bee a Suteable allowance Granted to repaire & amend s^d Road, at least to the sum of ——— pounds Out of the Publique Treasurie of this Province, which we Humbly leave to consideration, & Subscribe:" etc. The General Court appropriated five pounds and put it into the hands of the petitioners to make the road "passable." There is little reason to suppose the road east of "Wooster" was much if any better.

Imagine the earnest plans, the sundry and anxious negotiations, the fateful land deals, the slowly developing groups of migrants, the selection of routes, the procuring of horses, the arrangement of personal baggage, of farming and other implements and household effects, the motley and picturesque appearances of these groups as they started off in one direction or another for their new homes amid risks and dangers unseen and practically omnipresent; the talk of the travelers, the wide-eyed curiosity of the little children and the chatter of the older ones as the shadows of the vales, the open landscapes of the high divides, and the crossings of the streams, all filled the days and the passing hours with study, or pageantry, and kaleidoscopic experience.

Egress from Boston was possible by either of two ways. Across the Neck into Brookline there was the road to Newton, and the horse bridge, known as the Mill bridge over the Charles into Watertown. That bridge was at the head of tide-water. There has been a bridge there ever since. At the Watertown end of the present one is an inscription reading thus: "A bridge

Crossed near here as Early as A. D. 1641. Here by the Mill Bridges were built A. D. 1647, 1667 and 1719." Along this route went Pynchon and the other settlers of the Roxbury group to set up the nucleus of Springfield on the Connecticut.

Pynchon's company pursued the way of the Old Connecticut Path. It ran from Cambridge along the river Charles, through Watertown, where connection with it was had from the other side the river by the Mill bridge. Thence it ran through Waltham to Framingham, at the north end of Cochituate pond, thence to Hopkinton, Grafton, Dudley, etc., to Hartford. Six years before Pynchon's exodus, the chief of the Wabbaquassetts, in Woodstock, with a company of Indians, transported on their backs to Boston a large quantity of Indian corn, and sold it there to the people who were suffering want. This was the beginning of the history of this famous highway, so far as concerns the English. John Oldham followed this trail in 1633, lodging at Indian towns all the way. Connecticut pioneers used it, carrying their household goods and driving their cattle. Mrs. Hooker, wife of the famous Thomas Hooker, minister and founder of Hartford, was borne along this lonely trail upon a horse litter.* This path, or trail, the Indians had traversed since time out of mind.

In 1662 the "Great Bridge" spanning the Charles between Cambridge and Brighton was erected. "For one hundred and thirty years, or until the opening of the West Boston-Cambridge bridge, the 'Great Bridge' was the principal way for traffic across the river to the north and west."† This may have been the bridge Blandford forbears crossed.

The old Connecticut road was hilly. A new way was

---

* Dr. Temple's History of North Brookfield.
† Stephen Jenkins, 392.

opened in 1648 which avoided the hills in large measure, and was called the "Nashaway Path." Diverging from the former road at Weston, the town next westerly beyond Waltham, it ran through Sudbury Centre, Stow, Lancaster (Nashaway), Princeton, south part of Barre, north part of New Braintree, West Brookfield, and thence to Springfield. "From Weston to Lancaster, this was an English highway; but westerly from Lancaster it evidently followed old Indian trails." * This path left the Old Connecticut Path at "Happy Hollow in Wayland, and ran through North Framingham, Marlborough and Worcester to Quaboag, or Brookfield. This last named town was the converging point of all the above thoroughfares. Thence they diverged again.

Besides these long trails there were many cross-ways and by-ways, quite analogous to the intersecting links of all countrysides. Post riders traveled all the main paths or trails until the days of the stage coach. The first mail in the country was carried thus from New York to Boston the very year that the Bay Path was opened, passing through Brookfield, Worcester and Cambridge.†

Of peculiar interest to all Blandford lovers should be the story of Levi Pease, of whose Blandford career I have written in "The Taverns and Turnpikes of Blandford, 1733-1833," ‡ the pioneer in stage coach and turnpike history, who became a figure of national reputation, operating over some of these very paths just outlined. Josiah Quincy was his passenger going to New York in 1784, and wrote of his experience on this wise: "I set out from Boston on the line of stage lately established by an enterprising Yankee, Pease by name, which

* Temple's North Brookfield.
† Jenkins.
‡ Chapter Two.

at that day was considered a method of transportation of wonderful expedition. The journey to New York took up a week."* Little did any one of our traveling company from Boston to the westward in search of a home along these trails, imagine what mighty influences were germinal among them for opening this great commonwealth to the traffic and enterprise of the republic.

The curtain is quite too closely drawn over this whole page of Blandford pioneers' thrilling epic of home-seeking along their westward way. It must have been preceded by not a little individual prospecting for homesteading. The exact date of the march is not recorded. Hanna puts it in 1719,—not, as Perry and Bolton, 1718. If fifty families were all, they were speedily increased in number, if at least we take into our purview the neighboring towns, as neighbors then were located—often many miles apart. If the sojourn of most of them in Worcester was to be stormy and brief, they were blissfully, or mayhap doggedly, ignorant or unmindful of it. They were dead in earnest, and they met each day's adventure as travelers who "sought a city."

The appropriate leader of this company was a minister, the Rev. Edward Fitzgerald of Londonderry. They did not go as an organized church, but they proposed to organize, and the pivotal forces which acted, and were to act, as primary considerations in their life, were religious, and continued to be such. In 1722 town organization was effected, and the Scots seem to have had their share in the offices assigned. They formed a religious society and not infrequently worshipped by themselves, under the ministrations of Rev. Edward Fitzgerald and Rev. William Johnston, although not

* This letter, including much more than I have here quoted, is copied into Jenkins's "The Old Boston Post Road," p. 24. The later career of this Blandford innkeeper and influential citizen may be found interestingly described in this same treatise, pages 33, 301, 348ff, 351f, 418.

abandoning the church on the common which had been functioning before their arrival. The two congregations were not very unequal, but their tastes and habits were wide apart. Considerable history was enacted in the very early years of the combined settlements having relation to impossible church adjustments. Details might be given at length, but these need not detain us inasmuch as the families which finally settled Blandford, so far as they came from Worcester at all, broke away so early as to make this chapter in Worcester life for the most part irrelevant to our story.

Religious and racial antipodes were there facing one another. The Coleraine company split off in 1736. A contingent going out to settle in "The Elbows," or Palmer, had already left in 1730, while more than ten years before the last named date the company which by and by were to plant Blandford, first called New Glasgow, had begun to foregather in Hopkinton—that is to say, before these folk had been in Worcester a single year. The first mal-contents thus emerge as the subjects of this present treatise. Worcester for them was but

"A sleep, a dream, a story,
   By strangers quickly told,
An unremaining glory
   Of things that soon are old."

The transition is somewhat recondite. Tradition insists that the stages of Blandford beginnings are, on this side of the water, Boston, Worcester, Hopkinton, New Glasgow or Blandford. In truth the matter is not by any means so simple. Let us look into it a little.

The Hopkinton and Upton Land Records* bear witness that at least two future Blandford citizens invested in real estate in Hopkinton, March 25, 1720. These

* Vol. I, Cambridge Registry.

were "Samuel Crooks of Hopkinton" and James Montgomery. The instruments conveying these estates were indentures of lease made out on this pattern: between his Excellency William Burnett, the Hon. William Dummer and the Hon. William Taylor, Esq., etc., all inhabitants of Massachusetts Bay, trustees of the Hopkins Charity (as the following chapter will explain), and the aforesaid Samuel Crooks; which indenture conveys to the said Crooks the possession of a farm of ninety-four acres for ninety-nine years, subject to a yearly rental of twenty-three shillings and six pence, the same to be paid in semi-annual instalments, September 25 and March 25. The lessee is obligated therein to erect, or cause to be erected, "a suitable farm house eighteen foot in Length at the Least & Sixteen foot in Breadth and Seven foot between joynts, within two years and a Barn Twenty foot Square within four years and fence in with a good Sufficient fence according to law" etc. A memorandum follows to this effect: The residue of the land over and above twelve thousand five hundred acres, comprising "the Cedar Swamps in that part of the Township," shall remain in common among the tenants, each to have his proportionate right and privilege in the same; and those signing leases within three years from March 25 last may cut cedar and pine "for covering, flooring & furnishing the Houses & Barns" etc., but not for purposes of sale. James Montgomery's lease was for ninety-five acres, and was similar to that of Crooks. On this same date Robert Huston was apparently with the Hopkinton newcomers, as he then witnessed a signature for Jacob Gibbs. Crooks purchased his lease for the sum of six hundred pounds, the witness to his signature being John Wood.

John and Robert Hambleton early went to Rutland, where Hugh bought land in 1721. John not improbably went with him, for on June 7 of the following year Jacob Stevens of Stow granted him a deed conveying fifty acres in that town in payment for "living and Settling a Lot of Land . . . to the Satisfaction of the Committee." This was to be located on that part of Stevens' "second Division of Upland" yet to be "drawn and laid out" as the grantor's lot. Hugh is designated in the deed as "Laborer," and thus he demonstrated his own ability to become a homesteader in New Glasgow some years later. Six and one-half years passed before this deed was recorded in Cambridge, for Worcester was then in Middlesex county. It was no half day's picnic to make that little business trip in this perilous year. At this time the settlements along the coast of Maine were being raided by Indians, and Irish Scots who had gone there were fleeing the country, some to Worcester and vicinity, some to Londonderry, some as far south as to Pennsylvania. Hamiltons (including John), Cochrans, Fergusons, Montgomerys and Youngs, all first or very early settlers of Blandford, were among these refugees.

A deed of date Nov. 14, 1726, is on file in Cambridge conveying to "Armour Hamilton of Hopkinton" an undesignated one third of a tract in that town containing two hundred and fifty acres yet to be delimited "by any Committee or Proprietors agreement had made and concluded upon," "the cedar swamp therein excepted to him the said Armour Hamilton." William Boyce was one of the witnesses to the signing of the deed, which was not recorded until March, 1730. Contemporary with these Hamiltons in and about Worcester were other Hamiltons—John Senior, John Junior, Amor and others, becoming a numerous family or clan. Amor is always so spelled, whereas in the other locations the name is

Armor. John of Brookfield—John Junior at any rate, was a large dealer in land. Not so the Blandford settler.

"Daniel Ston of Hopkinston" acquired April 19, 1726, a similar lease which he sold three years later. Samuel Ferguson of Westborough obtained one Oct. 27, 1732. David Boies took out one near the time of the removal of all this Scotch Irish group to Blandford. The previous habitat of not a few of these families it is impossible to learn from the deeds they took out, for nearly always they designate their residence as in the locality they are adopting as their future home. They were foot free as it were. Whatever personal goods and implements they had could be strapped on the back of an animal or two, so that "wherever they hung their hat" was "home, sweet home" to them. Not that they lacked the home instinct; they had it mightily, only for the time then being they looked not back, but "nightly pitched their moving tent a day's march nearer home." Hopkinton vital records early show births in resident families bearing the names of Blandford pioneers: to Hugh and Elizabeth Black, 1720; William and Elizabeth Donaghy (Dunakey, Donahoe), 1720-1; Walter and Grisel Stewart, 1722-3; James and —— Beard, 1727; Israel and Mary Gibbs, 1727-8; Armour and Agnes Hambleton, 1728; John and Mary Wood, 1727; Daniel and Mary Stone, 1726; Mathew and Mary Blare, 1728; James and Elizabeth Wark, 1731; Samuel (and, probably, Mary) Crook, 1731; James Montgomery, 1733; Robert and Jeney Black, 1733-4.

The "orthodox church" of Worcester has left for posterity to read the lists of those assigned sittings in their house of worship in the years 1724 and 1733. There are many Scotch Irish names there, but not one of any first settler of Blandford except James Hambleton. Mr. Bolton has inscribed a list of thirty-four names of "chief

Worcester Scotch Irish settlers," * and not one of them
became an original Blandford settler. This does not at
all mean, of course, that no Blandford men were there;
but it may mean that they were not there long enough
to "leave a rack behind."

Samuel Ferguson appears to have been among early
refugees from Casco Bay. He took up home lots with
the first in 1737. John and William Ferguson together
bought two the next year, when the first trading in
these lots began. They were "both of Grafton." John
Stuart appears to have come from Londonderry, N. H.,
he and Walter both getting to Blandford via Boxford
and Hopkinton. Samuel, however, made an interme-
diate lodgment in Westborough, where he was living
when he took up land in Hopkinton. Adam Knox too
went thither from Boxford. Samuel Cook moved from
Cambridge to Hopkinton. Robert Cook was a charter
member of the Hopkinton church, 1724, as were William Donaghoi, Robert Hambleton, Robert Huston,
Samuel Wark and John Wood. Hugh Black and his
wife joined the next year. Josiah Rice, born in Framingham in 1701, also married the widow of (Capt.)
John Wood in that same town in 1728. There were
Blairs, Gibbses, Hows, Rices, Stones, Wilsons and
Woods in Framingham in the first quarter of the 18th
century. These are all names connected with Blandford's earliest history.

The Cochrans were settlers in Worcester, but not un-
till after living a somewhat wandering life, perhaps in
Londonderry, perhaps in Andover, possibly in both.
Hugh Maxwell represents the sorrowful story of Crom-

---

* P. 188.

well's prisoners, sent across to New England.* He was a first settler, going first to Woburn, then Hopkinton. He did not remain long in Blandford. The Montgomerys, Hustons and Campbells were first in Pemaquid. These were important families in Blandford's early history† though the Campbells were not first comers. Daniel How came to Hopkinton from Framingham. He was a carpenter. Samuel Cook was of Mendon. David Boyce, "Taylor," came late to Hopkinton, perhaps just for the purpose of joining the great emigration thence. This is he of the "Covenant with God." The name of Boyce does not appear on the church records of Hopkinton. Matthew Blair joined it in 1728. There were sundry Blairs in Worcester. Israel Gibbs and his wife Mary joined the Hopkinton church in 1731.

English Gibbses were in the colonies as early as the Massachusetts Bay settlements. Among these was Matthew, who settled in Sudbury. The Hopkinton and Blandford Israel was grandson of Matthew. Marrying Mary Hamilton, he became to all intents and purposes a patriarch of Scotch Irish stock, succeeding generations intermingling and intermarrying with old Ulster families. Israel was thirty and Mary was twenty-eight at the time of the emigration from Hopkinton, and their son Israel was the first male child born in the new settlement. A family tradition has it that Israel and his wife spent a night in Brookfield with the Glasgow company.‡

Robert Henry was in Lunenburg as late as 1735. There were three Freelands, Joseph, James and James,

---

* In the "Old South Leaflet" No. 93, the statement is made that "in the time of Cromwell, several thousand Irish men and women had been shipped to the British colonies in North America, many of them—550 in 1653—coming to New England, practically as slaves." Maxwell may not have been the only one of such a group—or their descendants—in the Blandford settlement.

† v. Wood, *passim.*

‡ I gather these facts from The Gibbs Family Bulletin, Number Two, Published by Dr. Howard Gibbs, who is writing a history of the Gibbs clan.

Jr. During the inevitable readjustments following the first allotments of home lots in Blandford, readjustments the more urgent because the locations in both divisions were settled by lot rather than by choice, James Freeland sold both his original lots to William Brown "Living on Land Called the Gore Lying Between Worcester and Oxford in the County of Worcester," early in 1739. And about that same time Alexander Osburn, Weaver, original settler, parted with both his home lots to "Robert Young of Glascow." Thus were the Youngs early introduced into Blandford story. They were of the Worcester contingent.

Before "New Glasgow" became an incorporated town by the name of Blandford — in 1641 — other changes in land ownership and citizenship took place. Several came from Boston: James Henry, Laborer, James Caldwell, Laborer, Henry Caswell, Merchant; Robert Wilson, Jr., from Malden, Robert Wilson (perhaps the "Jr.'s" father), from "Lin," Thomas Reid and Andrew Graham, from Worcester.

The foregoing rather tedious enumeration seems to have been necessary to establish the conclusion that Blandford settlers had little to do vitally with Worcester. That famous frontier settlement was indeed an important influence in many ways. It served as a sort of distributing center, a social clearing house for new population movements. It would seem from all the scattered evidences that it was actually home to comparatively few future Blandford families, and to most of them for only a very short time. There quickly emerged, in Worcester, a violent religious division between the two racial factors.

Now these Presbyterian Scots from Ireland had it in their souls to go and to remain where they could build the whole social and religious fabric according to the

desires of their own heart. That was the secret of the
Londonderry (N. H.) settlement.* It came to be the
corner stone of the Pelham upbuilding, and of Coleraine.
It was, before either of the latter, the vision of the
scattered seed of the Blandford church and town. They
wanted virgin soil. They did not find it in Worcester.
They thought they would find it in Hopkinton, for they
began to enter there early enough, as they fondly hoped,
to possess the land. When, after a dozen years or so of
diligent homesteading, sweeping the whole of New England for a compact and doughty nucleus to be planted
there, they found the old New England blood and the
old Orthodox faith and practice again besting them, and
after a furious contest, they once more packed up, bag
and baggage, uniting into one mighty band of sixty
families, under contract, (and others, scattering) and
captured a new, virgin soil beyond the Connecticut,
where, until they came, the only inhabitants were the
wolves and other creatures of the forest save one lonely
caravansary near the edge of the township, a half dozen
miles away. Here is the genius of the whole story. Here
is the thread which if not lost will reveal the secret
alleys of the whole labyrinth.

Pity their narrowness if you will. Laugh at their castle
in the air if you must. Set it down that if even in this
they were ultimately defeated, that they never saw the
day when they were at peace; that the years as they
passed opened doors to the great wide world; that their
Presbyterian church became Congregational by the end
of the century; that when into the bounding West there
poured forth a certain colony to form a church and a

---

* The Rev. James MacGregor stated the reasons thus succintly: "1. To
avoid oppression and cruel bondage; 2. To shun persecution and designed
ruin; 3. To withdraw from the communion of idolaters; 4. To have an
opportunity of worshipping God according to the dictates of conscience
and the rules of his inspired Word."

town and a school which should be Episcopalian by virtue of its own contract, that colony, planted in the great
Ohio, should find its chief funds, one of its first pioneers
and not a few of its members in the town once fondly
named by ardent Scotch Presbyterians "New Glasgow,"
— set it down that they were hard to beat, and that, all
in all, they showed to the New World some real vision of

> "God's plan
> And measure of a stalwart man,
> Limbed like the old heroic breeds,
> Who stands self-poised on manhood's solid earth,
> Not forced to frame excuses for his birth,
> Fed from within with all the strength he needs."

CHAPTER IX

Hopkinton: Pitching Tents and Striking Tents

We come now to focus our attention upon Hopkinton, fifteen miles southeasterly from Worcester as the crow flies. Hopkins was a London merchant who came to America in 1637, and for many years was governor of Connecticut. In his will he left five hundred pounds for "upholding and promoting the kingdom of the Lord Jesus Christ" in New England. This fund finally passed over to the benefit of Harvard College; and in 1715 the trustees of the fund obtained permission of the General Court to purchase of the Indians of Natick the lands commonly known by the name of Magunkaquog. This tract, first known as the Hopkins Donation, was afterward called Hopkinton, and the trustees were empowered to grant leases of the land for a term not to exceed ninety-nine years. These leases ran from March 25, 1723, at an annual rental of three pence per acre, until 1742, when the terms were changed. The town was established December 13, 1715.

Towns are seldom made in a day, but Blandford came about as near to it as possible. By the time Blandford was incorporated a township, the Irish Scots of Worcester, reinforced every now and then from every whither, had scattered to the four winds of heaven, with only a pitiful remnant left to weep over the charred timbers of their temple. Spencer, Stow, the Elbows, Pelham, Western, Coleraine, Hopkinton, Unadilla in New York on the banks of the Susquehanna, picked up the scattering fragments which gathered to themselves still other fragments from the "Presbyterian Circuit," chiefly of New England. But Hopkinton was foremost.

We have seen something like fifty families going from Boston to Worcester. Seventy-eight families were to emigrate, mostly from Hopkinton, to New Glasgow.* But now the pilgrims were hurrying into Hopkinton as their gathering place fondly hoping that at last they might therein find their altars and their fires secure.

The town is rich in story and romance. Writers of our colonial history and tradition have perpetuated the weird tale of Sir Charles and Lady Frankland. Mrs. Stowe's story of the Dench house and of the two little waifs who strayed in there and set up housekeeping for a little time is deeply graven in New England fantasy and sentiment. It is a story aside from our particular quest, but its aroma must have lingered as a reminiscence among those who continued to have more or less to do with the old town of Hopkinton. The tale and its gathered legends, Mrs. Stowe bears witness, formed the topic of many an excited hour of childhood days in those parts, was crooned over by different story-telling gossips, and "had, in its structure and arrangements, the evident impress of days nevermore to be reproduced in New England."

But of more significance than grewsome statues which looked at little children with eyes that followed them wherever they went, of more importance than romances that smacked of a life which the New England conscience and religion had come to its hour to reform and make pure, besides being of absorbing interest, is the story of those pilgrims, not having yet attained, neither

---

* In the subsequent development of this story various and sundry figures will be cited from one and another document among our sources, as to the number of families required to settle the new township finally called Blandford. This will occur over and over again. These strange discrepancies are almost inexplicable. The final appeal must be to the legislative enactments. These give, invariably, sixty families afterwards increased by eighteen on account of Lawton's fraudulent survey. It is to be definitely noted, furthermore, that the actual census of the named families of first settlers bears out the actuality of this amazing number.

already perfect, who were pressing toward their mark, forging their notable and worthy links in the history of our nation.

If it is not given to us to open the doors of the first log houses set up in Hopkinton in the earliest years of her settlement — except as the deed or two already cited in the foregoing chapter may allow the real seer to do — an incident or two in Hopkinton's infancy may yet lead us to something palpable and significant.

The Wood family came to Hopkinton early. Benjamin, son of Captain John, was one of the original contractors for home lots in New Glasgow, and in the year of the migration thither was married in Hopkinton. The father was an original member of the Hopkinton church. A private journal of a Framingham resident contains this item: "John Hood, fence viewer, 1712, dismissed to found a Church in Hopkinton, Aug. 22, 1725." The name was Wood, not Hood. Sometimes it was called "Whood" by people who probably had not yet lost a certain English peculiarity of pronunciation. Just when Capt. John went to Hopkinton is not written. He died there in 1725, and his widow married Josiah Rice, who also took up two homelots with the original settlers of our town. Captain John Wood built "a mansion house" in Hopkinton, and in it ran a tavern business.*

In the merry month of May, 1723, a young minister was about to settle in Westborough. Like every well-ordered clergyman of his day, Rev. Mr. Parkman kept a diary. He was returning from Westborough to Watertown, after having secured his call, and wrote in his diary this soul-stirring entry: "I stopped in Hopkinton at Mr. Wood's, where I fared sumptuously on roast goose, roast pea hen, baked stuffed venison, beef, pork,

---

* While Benjamin Wood did not become a permanent resident in Blandford, it is a satisfaction to me, their descendant, to know that my forbears bore a vital part in the history which I am writing.

&c." The bill of fare at this dinner indicates that the settlers in that yet unsubdued country were not generally suffering the pangs of unsatisfied hunger. "We smoked a pipe," the diary goes on to narrate, "and read Gov. Shute's 'Memorial to the King.'" Why should they be interested in Governor Shute's Memorial to the King? When they recorded a deed of purchase of land for a home, did not these subjects of the king write it down with the date at the foot thereof phrased on this wise: done "on this..........day of..........In ye*..........Year of our Sovereign Lord George ye First of Great Britain France and Ireland King Anno Domini One Thousand Seven hundred and Twenty..........."? In those weighty phrases the passing kings of the isles and provinces were named before the King of all the earth.

There were some special and particular reasons why just then "Governor Shute's Memorial to the King" should be under discussion in the wayside caravansaries of growing New England, and particularly in this one in the town of Hopkinton. In the previous year a troupe of Indians visited Merry Meeting Bay and ran off with nine families of prisoners. This was followed by the burning of Brunswick and the proclamation of war known in history as Lovell's war. The flight of Scotch Irish from all these parts has already been referred to, and it is entirely possible some of the refugees were already coming to Hopkinton and near-by towns. But that was not all. The royal Governor was of course for taking suitable care of these ravaged coasts, but it must be done in his own way. The General Court was taking hold of the matter vigorously, and it and the governor clashed in the matter of procedure and prerogative. So it became a matter of protection against the Indians on the one hand, and on the other against the govern-

---

* Wherever an italic letter appears on the end of a word it denotes an elevated letter in the Original Document.

A TABLE OF OLD DISHES

The three plain round dishes, the large plain cup (or flip mug), and the teapot are of pewter, brought by early settlers from the old country. The candlesticks are of brass. The cloth covering the table was woven of flax grown on Beech Hill, more than a century ago.

mental invasion of the liberties of a province which had begun to love the rule of kings and their minions not any too well. The Governor had betaken himself to the king in person with his "memorial," and was still over there when Captain John Wood and the Rev. Mr. Parkman had their smoke talk together.* They had already suffered enough, the people thought, from the abuse of royal prerogatives and the divine right of kings falsely so called, and being carried toward a climax which was already preparing the way for '76. Governor Shute was a master hand at the interpretation of such royal prerogatives, and had been in chronic quarrel with the General Court. This little glimpse into Hopkinton life tells us what the people were thinking about and of what they were talking at the taverns. They were, and were going to be, troublesome proteges of a governor who thought more of the king than of the people.

It was in this same month of May, 1723, "In a meeting of the biger part of the Inhabitants of Hopkinton," before the settlement had become organized, that the people voted, first, "The Indevering for a minister to preach with us constantly on Sabath days." Like the apostolic church of old, before a mature organization had developed, or a permanent roof covered them, they met for divine worship in the house of one of their number, John How. It was a large square building with gambrel roof and stone chimney. They had already been meeting thus for something like a year, before the titles to their land were securely in hand. At this meeting it was further voted "To levi a tax of an half peny upon the acre upon all the lots that are either taken or picked upon by gentlemen that they will take them, for the support of a minister, . . . that they will every man bring in his propotion to said tax to John How by the last day

---

* Barry.

of June next insuing"; that they would "have a contribution every Sabath, and that every man paper his money and write his name upon the paper, and set the sum that he puts in." It was furthermore "Voted, That Mr. Hustone—[the Robert Hustone, or Houstin, etc., later in Blandford]—and Mr. Wood shall receive said contrebution and take account of what it is, and deliver it to the aforesaid John How, and take care of said papers that none of them be lost. 6. Voted, That Mr. Wood and John How take care that we are constantly provided with a minister to preach with us on Sabath days. 7. Voted, to meet at John How's house on Sabath days at present."

Three quarters of a century before this, Edward Johnson, in his since famous "Wonder-working Providence of Zion's Saviour in New England," describing a company as "ready to swarm and settle on the building of another town," says, "They gather into a church at their first settling; for indeed, as this was their chief errand, so was it the first thing they ordinarily minded, to pitch their tabernacles near the Lord's tent." Thus did these pilgrims and strangers, not for the first time, nor for the last.

The first town meeting in Hopkinton was convened March 26, 1724. Five years later the town was "yet unsettled in great measure." There is testimony to this in a petition of the citizens, and a legislative Act following thereon in 1729, granting extended permission to tax unimproved lands. By this time there was a large number of former Ulstermen there, and of future Blandford citizens. The latter are to be reckoned as among the real builders of two towns.

At this first town meeting, John How was moderator, and was elected town clerk and first selectman. John Wood was second selectman, dying before his term was completed. "Mr. Robert Hambleton" and "Mr. Robert Huston" were chosen "Tying men." Benjamin Wood, son of John, was selectman several times in the early years. Robert Houston served in that office in 1725-6, and again in 1727-8, also as constable in 1734. Samuel Wark was selectman one term, and was school committee in 1729, as well as being constable and committee on building the meeting house. In 1728 Robert Cook was school committee, and in 1731 and 1732, constable. The latter dignity was conferred on Daniel How and Thomas Reed in 1728, in which year also William Doneghy was a highway "Survair." When a new highway was projected, in 1729, a committee of six were charged with the responsible duty, and half that number were men on whom Blandford town was later to rely for frequent public services: Hugh Hambleton, Israel Gibbs and William Doneghy. John Osborn was highway surveyor in 1731, and selectman the next year. Robert Black was field driver in 1731. James Freeland was chosen to keep good order and peace in the town in the year 1737, while, to complete the list, Daniel Stone and John Hambleton had performed the onerous duties of hog reeves two years earlier.

I have mentioned that Robert Huston was constable in 1734. That this office was no sinecure while as yet the settlement was scattered and the community in need of scrupulous watch and care, a bit of judicial record bears witness. It was not unusual in those days for an offender, when he perceived his case to be perilous, to go to the justice of the peace and enter complaint against himself, in the hope thereby to get off with a lighter punishment than to fall involuntary prey to the officers of the law. I have seen in the manuscript records of Hopkinton the entries of several such complaints and the accompanying judgments. It happened that in this

year of grace 1734, one John Galloway stole a sheep
from John Wood, eldest son of Captain John, deceased.
A smiting conscience, or perhaps more probably, a quak-
ing fear of constable Huston or some compeer of that
worthy officer, sent Galloway with heavy feet to make
voluntary confession of his crime to the judge. One
wonders what hard fate might have befallen this poor
sinner had he waited for the more lagging movements
of the officers of the law, when one reads this entry:

"Octr 7th: 1734

Middlesex Ss:

John Galloway of Hopkinston in the
County of Middlesex

Before John Jones Esqr did own
himself gilty of Stealing a Sheep that appeared to be
Insign John Wood

and is therefore sentenced to pay sd Wood 20 shillings damage & three-fould, & to be whipt 15 Lashes
on his naked Back & to pay Cost & to Stand committed
till Sentence be performed

John Jones Justice of the Peace."

In those days the way of the transgressor was hard.
One sheep gone astray meant loss in itself besides portending ill to the whole flock, especially when the lost
sheep went not on its own legs. Society must be protected and property made secure. These little incidents
are ephemeral, many of the offices held were petty, and
this whole chapter is writ of the day of small things
which, however, it is well not to despise. It was the day
of beginnings, and everything stands out individualized.
The whole is not little. When a new road was opened,
it was an event of consequence. By and by it would
become a thoroughfare for a people, and even then it

was an avenue for the significant development of the
homes and habits—habits of mind, soul, character—of
an integral member of a State. Where the road was to
go was virgin forest and swamp. The wolves howled
there. It was a land of darkness and of the shadow of
death, and where the light thereof was as darkness.
When a meeting house was to be erected, it meant what
a cathedral across the seas in lands already bristling
with architectural splendors meant to the hungering,
aspiring hearts of mankind. These humbler buildings
were

"Temples, at once, and Landmarks."

Nearly four months before the holding of Hopkinton's first town meeting, there was convened a meeting
of the citizens to take steps to build a meeting house.
The date was January 5, 1724-5. Then and there they
voted to build a house "forty-eight feet wide and twenty
feet between joynts and that the house be stooded."
The second of May was fixed for the raising, which suffered the inevitable delays. Perhaps a chief reason was
that they could not agree where to erect the house, three
locations being strongly represented by the preferences
of as many parties. The town was not small in area,
neither were the sentiments of the separate neighborhoods in range of ideas. The choice was finally made
by lot. Is it not written,

"The lot causeth contentions to cease,
And parteth between the mighty?"

November came and went, and no raising. On the
29th of that month it was "Voted that the town appropriate ten pounds" for the raising, "that the meeting
house be raised with spike poles, that it be left with the
selectmen to appoint the time to raise the meeting
house," and a committee was appointed to order all

necessary things. It was particularly ordered that the committee on the raising should "see to it that all those that entertain those men with supper the evening after the raising of our publick meeting house that have been to said raising shall have one shilling 3 pence per head for each man allowed them by the town of Hopkinston, they giving theire names of each man to the town." The deed was done in December. The building is no more. The spot is unoccupied except by a few old tombs where the dead sleep under the pines which bend over the grassy plot a little one side from the modern rather sleepy village with its comfortable homes, its pleasing park, its upland sweep of horizon, its old cemetery, its town hall, its straggling stores and modern churches.

The rest of this chapter will deal with religion and its ecclesiastical habiliments worn, not by angels but by men, and bearing all the marks of toil and moil and melancholy strife. Do not blame the narrator for choosing to make somewhat meticulous transcription of these sometimes sorry records. Sorry, yet I confess, to me as I write them, by no means without a sardonic humor which makes the writing—whatever the reading of them may be—enthralling. Anyhow, the records of these months and years is barren of anything else except the dryest and most insignificant routine. This story is practically all there is to tell. Our pursuit is the homes and habits of these people. We have scoured space and time to find the people. We have at last gathered them into a compact community. We know what their inheritance has been. Herein is offered evidence out of which you, my reader, are to judge whether these Scots of Irish transplanting and American re-transplanting, are true or not to their past; whether or not they promise to erect a New Glasgow worthy of the name of their old University ideals. These pages can be skipped in the reading. But hold! the skipper of them will lightly pass over also the open sesame to the souls of these folk who henceforth will, to all such, become and abide an unlocked mystery.

Fare we forth, then. These folk were not all members of the church. But they did all look to it as the one institution which should shape the people's life, be the inspirer of their ideals, the chief vehicle of their social instincts and functions, the nourisher of their childhood and their stalwart faith. "It was not till the meeting house and minister were provided," said President Porter of Yale, "that the community was prepared to meet the duties and enterprises of their common life. In their quaint language a golden candlestick was set up, as was fondly hoped, never to be removed, and the Lord Christ was seen to be present by its side. . . . By the same rule after which in these days parents are compelled to send their children regularly to the school house, they were required to come with them to the meeting house on the Lord's day. On the same principle, till 1818 in Connecticut, and till some years afterward in Massachusetts, every citizen was compelled to support some religious organization by a tax on his estate. This was done in no spirit of religious tyranny, but on definite grounds of public policy. What it cost in toil and fear to be present at the meeting house in the first generations no one of us can adequately imagine. But the toil and fear and privation were cheerfully encountered from a sense of duty to God."

Following its civil organization the next business of the town was to obtain a settled minister. The choice, April 20, 1724, fell upon Samuel Barrett, Jr., who for some months had already been their regular supply. They voted him thirty-five pounds a year salary for three years, together with the furnishing of his firewood.

After that, seventy pounds yearly, relying upon the trustees of the township for help. They gave him thirty pounds "towards building his house upon his own land." In addition to this they voted to give him sixty pounds —a sum which they afterwards raised to one hundred— "towards his settlement, in day labor, oxen's work, boards, shingles, clapboards, slitwork, or other materials needful for the building of an house for him, and to pay it by the first of October next."

Mr. Barrett accepted these propositions, adding the expressed hope that "they will be disposed, as God shall encrease and enlarge them, to afford" him "a more honorable maintenance than they are capable of affording." This acceptance was dated July 16. He was ordained September 2, in John How's house, where all along the church had been assembled, and the selectmen had charge of the affair. The church was organized the same day, and comprised the pastor and fourteen laymen— no women. These are the names, taken from the Hopkinton church manual, published in 1881. The asterisks indicate the Scotch Irish names. These asterisks are my own insertion, not the manual's, and I am confident I have not so marked any not belonging in this category: Rev. Samuel Barrett, Elnathan Allen, Obediah Allen, *Benjamin Burnap, Sr., *Robert Cooke, *William Dunaghoi, *Jacob Gibbs, *Patrick Hambleton, *Robert Hambleton, Joseph Haven, *Robert Huston, *William Montgomery, Samuel Walkins, John Wood, *Samuel Wark. It is noticeable that John How, whose interest in this church was so great, is not in this list. While not every starred name was among the future Blandford founders, most of them were. They were a clean majority. But the minister was not of their race or sect; and there were others.

Their covenant, embodying all they felt to be necessary as condition of church membership, was this:

"We do now under a Soul Stumbling sense of our utter unworthiness of so great and high a privilege as God is now graciously putting into our Hands own and accept of God the Father, Son and Holy Ghost for our God in Covenant with us and do accordingly give up our Selves and seed according to the Terms of the Everlasting Covenant, to him to be his, under the most sacred and inviolable obligations, promising by the help and strength of his Grace without which we can do nothing that we will walk as becometh Saints according to the Rules of God's Holy Word; Submitting our Selves and Seed to the Covenant of the Lord Jesus Christ as King of his Church and to the watch and discipline of this Church managing our Selves toward God and man, all in Civil and Sacred authority as becometh such as are under the teaching of God's holy Word and Spirit: alike declaring it to be our Resolution that in all things wherein we may fall Short of Duty, we will wait upon God for his pardoning mercy and Grace in and through our Dear Lord and Saviour Jesus Christ to whom be the glory for ever Amen."

Brief, strong, dignified, Christian, this covenant of the Hopkinton church is a noble monument to the faith of these early fathers. Now it was for them to do what in them lay to incarnate it in themselves and the society they were trying to build on that sublime foundation.

The first New Year's Sunday following organization, these Irish Scots united with the church: Hugh Black and his wife, Samuel Wark and his wife and James Wark.

We now return to the meeting house. It was already covered in, but was slow in coming to completion. They were still working upon it in 1729. There were galleries on three sides. "The pulpit stood in the centre of the north side, with a large window behind, and a half-circular sounding-board above it." Pew-ground, arranged around the sides of the house, was granted to all leading families who asked for it, the size being fixed by vote of the town, usually six or seven feet long and five deep. If a pew abutted upon a window, the owner thereof was expected to keep the window in repair. Early in 1728 two tiers of seats were put down, one for men, the other for women. The seats were "dignified." For example, in 1732, it was "Voted, that the fore seat shall be esteemed the highest in dignity; the second seat below and the fore seat in the front gallery equal; the third seat below the next; then the fore seat in the side gallery the next, and so on. Voted, to seat seven in each seat below, and eight in the front gallery, and fourteen in the side gallery." They were seated according to their rate in the town tax, and a penny was added for each year of age to every person from twenty-one to sixty.

Thus constituted, both meeting house and congregation, the people assemble for worship. In the middle of the last century there ministered to the sons and daughters of this first flock of God's sheep in that new settlement a minister who was also a careful historian. To him is due our privilege to join that early congregation, and be seated in the strangers' benches.* "Walk into that old meeting house, if you please upon the day of 'seating,' and just look around you. The walls are naked, and the pulpit with its *sine qua non*, the sounding board, is rising high above you; the deacons' seats are immediately below. Here is the famous pew which Colonel

---

* The following long quotation is the reproduction of an article by Rev. Elias Nason, in the New England Historical and Genealogical Record, XX, 122ff.

John Jones (our friend, the Justice of the Peace—
S. G. W.) was permitted to build, 'seven and a half
feet long and five and a half feet wide;' here is the pew
which was made for 'persons hard of hearing to sit in;'
here is the 'ministerial pew' upon the north side of the
west door, and the remaining space is occupied by
wooden benches, those upon the right for men, and
those upon the left for women. There is as yet no choir,
no instrument of music, and no bell.

"But the time for public worship is approaching, and
the Bixbys, Burnhams, Woodwells, Smiths and Joneses
from the East; the Caryls, Bowkers, Haydens from the
South, the Woods, the Freelands, Gibbses and Claflins
from the West are drawing near; the men on horseback,
with their wives behind them; and a motley multitude
of people, old and young, in homespun garb on foot,
are gathering toward the sacred portals.

"A horn or drum announces the hour for worship;
the elders with long tax lists are standing at the door
and pointing to the seat which each may occupy; the
rich go forward and the poor sit down behind; the children and the negroes take the back seats and the galleries, and the tythingmen with slender poles, some ten
feet long, stand in the corners keeping guard. Now look
at them again. The wealthier men are quite well dressed
in powdered bag wigs, snuff-colored coats, long em-
broidered vests with wide lappels, ruffled shirts, small
clothes, silk stockings, and broad silver buckles on the
square-toed shoe; the women on the left—the hair piled
up . . . 'in curls on curls before and mounted to a formidable tower'—are robed in ample silk brocade or
gingham, or white cambric gowns, cut low and without
sleeves, and each sits just as nearly opposite her liege
lord as the arrangements of the church permit.

"Now see, from out the front door of yonder new

built house of gable roof, a young man, in a surplice, wearing a monstrous long bag wig, and having two snow white bands depending from his chin, approaches slowly with a steady step, and as he enters every whispering tongue is silent, the elders reverently seat themselves in front of the whole waiting congregation. Colonel Jones brings his sword down into its accustomed place, Scipio and Dido Dingo cease from their grimaces, and all sit *auribus erectis* for the opening of the ministrations of the sanctuary.

"The Rev. Mr. Barrett takes a pinch of snuff, invokes a divine blessing, reads a chapter from Corinthians, the Scotchmen following him closely with their well worn Bibles; he calls out the number of a Psalm from the 'Bay Psalm Book,' reads it, and immediately the good Benjamin Burnap deacons off the line:—
'The rivers on of Babylon':—
The elder Joseph Bixby—as precentor, strikes up doleful 'Windsor tune,' and here and there the shrill and untrained voices—some high, some low, some quick, some slow (for this is the dark age of church music in America), come grating in and grinding it through. The deacon reads another line:—
'There when we did sit down;'
The congregation in discordant notes respond:—
'There when we did sit down.'
The deacon reads—
'Yea, sadly then, we mourned when;'
The people sing lugubriously:
'Yea, sadly then, we mourned when;'—
The deacon continues:—
'Wee Sion thought upon;'—
The people cry—
'Wee Sion thought upon,'
prolonging the last note in cadences as charming as the

poetry itself, the genuine twang commingling with the common Scotch and Gaelic. The Psalm concluded, the congregation rise and stand through a long wearisome prayer, for Mr. Barrett's abilities were but slender here* and as the petition closes, sink into their seats and wait expectantly for the homily. The worthy pastor turns the hour glass on the green cushioned pulpit: takes out his manuscript, which is on a scanty sheet of yellow foolscap, and proceeds to read from 'firstly,' 'secondly,' up to 'ninthly,' 'tenthly,' and so on for perhaps as far as 'twentiethly,' to the great delight and edification of the people. In closing it, he adds a brief prayer, a benediction—and instantly, before the word 'amen' falls fairly from his lips, a shrill, squeaking voice is heard from the southwest corner of the house, proclaiming with a kind of sly insinuation in the tone, 'Jonathan White and Molly Black intend marriage!' and so the people wend their rough way homeward, some to think of the

'Waters on of Babylon,'

some to muse upon and profit by the sermon; but too many, alas, to inquire when and why Miss Molly Black is to be changed to Miss Mary White, and whether they themselves will be so fortunate as to receive an invitation to attend the nuptial ceremony."

Affairs were not going smoothly in Hopkinton at this time. Among the Congregational brethren of New England, church polity had not become altogether crystallized. There were simon pure Congregationalists, and there were other Congregationalists who were presbyterially inclined. A very large section of the Hopkinton church were not only presbyterially inclined, but dyed in the wool, and the color was fast. Furthermore, while

---

* Mr. Whitfield prayed, in reference to Mr. Barrett's feebleness in prayer that "the Lord would open the dumb dog's mouth."

other churches were in a more or less chaotic state, a majority vote of this church, April 9, 1731, threw it definitely into the Congregational column, with pledged adherence to the Cambridge Platform of 1649.

This voting to stand on the Cambridge Platform harked back to the time of Oliver Cromwell and to the whole movement of Independency which the Scotch Presbyterians were quite sure was of the devil. This action was an unspeakable grief and horror in the minds of the Irish Scots. They could manage to get along with a quasi Congregationalism by way of accommodation. But the pure article cut them off from the traditions of the Presbyterian fathers, and put them beyond the pale. The English descendants had got ahead of them. "The jig was up."

A couple of months after the Hopkinton church put itself by formal vote into the Congregational fold, they chose two ruling elders and two deacons. On the face of it, it seems strange that Presbyterians should take exception to such a proceeding. But Congregational ruling elders and Presbyterian ruling elders were governing saints of radically diverse strains.

The new issues were still further complicated. The neighboring church in Framingham was being torn by faction of a related if not quite identical kind, the upshot of which was the reception into the Hopkinton church of several members of the church in Framingham, the removing members, however, lacking letters of dismission. Before it was all over, one of the most famous ecclesiastical councils in the history of Congregationalism adjudicated upon this affair.

At this distance much of all this looks petty. So were many matters connected with the Stamp Act, in the years preceding the Revolution, petty. All this business might profitably be left in musty vaults of the dead past if only the past were quite dead. But it was very much alive. Our present study is one of origins, and all this temper of mind is characteristic and epochal. We resort to the manuscript records.

An entry of May, 1733, recites that "The Church being offended with Several of the members for their long absenting them Selves from ye ordnance of the Lords Supper, sent to enquire by ye Elders into the reasons of yr thus absenting." "The persons who absented were, James Montgomery and his mother Robert Cook and his wife William Henry, Walter Steward, Robert Huston and his wife, and John Hambleton, Robert Barrett and ye widdow Hambleton. The reason of their absenting being asked. They replyed as followeth James Montgomery and his Mother answered, because we had altered from what we were by coming into this way of government, and brought into so rashly or hastily and they thought they should not partake with us any more. They said likewise yt the widdow Hambletons reasons were the same. The answer of Robert Cook and his wife William Henry and Walter Steward was much to the same purpose: af'd (?) forementioned. Robert Huston and his Wifes answer was to ye same purpose: but added that their reasons were given to the ministers and they waited for an answer from them. Robert Barret said the cause was from within himself, and he hoped to Joyn with us in our communion again. John Hambleton said that they had laid ye matter before the ministers and if their advice was such as he could not comply with, he purposed to leave the Town."

So deeply had these sorrows taken root. This is the cloud like a man's hand on the horizon, portending the coming emigration. Who these "ministers" were is not stated. They may have been the "Boston Association," of whom the Rev. Mr. Swift, the Framingham minister, was seeking counsel. It was the regular, stated procedure, where a presbytery was not at hand, to appeal to a Congregational association of ministers to act as such for Presbyterians seeking unbiassed counsel.

A church meeting was convened June 26 for the purpose of pursuing these matters further. Robert Barret "gave the church satisfaction." With Barret we have little to do. Robert Cook was not so easily disposed of. He pleaded justification on the ground of their "alterations in Church Government and said he thought the Church was disorderly and that the Church should not rule over him and that he desired no dismission from ye Church, but that ye Church ought to ask a dismission from them. Robert Hustons Reasons being asked, He said our receiving the members from Framingham without a dismission. John Hambletons reasons being asked replyed yt he was not oblidged by covenant to attend the Sacrament any longer than he see himself thereto obliged and thereby edifyed and also our coming into this way of Government and our taking the members from Framingham Church. William Henry was asked to give his Reasons who replyed that he had given them in to the Ruling Elders and repeated them which were that we had broken from our first Government and if he continued in the mind he was in he should never partake with us any more. Walter Steward was asked his reasons who replyed he had given his reasons to Joseph Haven and yt he was still of ye same mind viz our coming into this way of Government, and he did not intend to partake with us any more."

These pleas in defence of independent and schismatic procedure seemed not adequate to the church, which continued trying, but in vain, to reconcile the delinquent brethren, and threatened suspension in the event of obduracy. They also voted a bi-monthly observance of the sacrament of the Lord's supper, "in complyance with our brethren from Scotland to encourage communion with us," as the record runs, and then adjourned a month to await developments; then to adjourn once more, apparently to see if the delinquents would in the meantime come to the communion table with them.

The whole matter was canvassed again September 7, with increased warmth. These "brethren from Scotland," however, were not reeds shaken by the wind. They could not understand why so many inquiries were necessary. William Henry told them that they should have no further replies from him. Walter Steward was not so laconic, but "replyed in a very angry manner that he never see people haraced about as they were," and refused to repeat what he had before said. James Montgomery put it thus succinctly: "y*t* we were one body at first, but when we altered we became two Bodys, and y*t* they did not belong to this church and were not obliged to hold communion with it." John Hambleton was equally explicit and yet more analytical. His reasons were: "1: our coming into this way of Government 2: our doing things privately as our ordaining the Elders and not giving notice. 3. our bringing in the members from Framingham either of which was sufficient to justify his absenting from communion." Some of this is very like Martin Luther's reasoning on his excommunication.

This choice and ordination of the elders seems to have given great offense to the Scotch section of the church. The secrecy of the transaction does not appear otherwhere than in this charge by James Montgomery. The church for some reason now unrevealed made no reply to that count in the charge. The ordination was in June, 1731, and the two Boston ministers, Thomas Prince and John Webb had assisted.

At the church meeting last reported resolutions were passed declaring the reasons given by the accused to be not satisfactory, and that these members should be admonished and suspended, which decision was "immediately disposed by the elders." An ultimatum was also sent to "several others" of like mind and conduct, charging them to appear and give account of themselves "on Monday ye 15th of october," else they too should suffer like penalties as their brethren. The church then adjourned to the date named. Reconvened on October 15, the church found those who had been summonsed to be not present. These were, "Hugh Hambleton and his wife Hugh Black and his wife Wm Dunugahoi Robert Black the wife of Robert Huston, the wife of Robert Cook and the wife of Walter Steward, the Widow Montgomery The Widow mary Hambleton, the Wife of James montgomery." Thus the consorts of the earlier accused were coming in and the insurrection was spreading. At last that which they had ceased to regard as a privilege should be positively withheld. The talent should be taken away. They were now requested "to absent themselves from the communion on the next Sacrament day unless they made satisfaction to the Church before that Day." Adjournment was made to December 17, when the delinquents were notified to appear at the January meeting. At that meeting four of the last named group were singled out from the rest for punishment. They were "Robert Black, the wife of Robert Huston, the wife of Robert Cook, the wife of James Montgomery." They were suspended until such time as they should give satisfaction to the church.

At this time the church took occasion to spread upon its records its grounds of justification. They say that these four persons, "professing themselves presbyterians, nevertheless joyned themselves to this church in full communion thereby rendered themselves subjects of our brotherly watch and care and entitled themselves to ye privileges enjoyed by the members of a particular Congregational Church, but have since for a considerable time absented themselves from the communion of this Church." And as the culmination of all offenses, it was added that they refused to give an account of themselves or offer a defense of their conduct.

Whatever may be the personal opinion of the writer or the readers of this story, the above surely is sufficiently clear in exhibiting this little group of people as clear-headed, precise, intelligent, and absolutely loyal to their historic traditions and inheritance. Here was the undying flame burning on their altar. When, after more than two generations, their Blandford church became itself Congregational, it was only after prolonged conditions of onerous and trying isolation from their peculiar fellowship had at last practically compelled the change.

A complete list of the Hopkinton excommunicates will be of interest, for it comprises the major part of the real nucleus of the Blandford settlement—not absolutely all of it. The dates of their joining are appended: Robert Cooke, William Dunaghoi, Robert Hambleton, Robert Huston (all 1724), Hugh Black, Mrs. Hugh Black (1725), William Henry (1727), Matthew Blair, Sarah Montgomery, Robert Black (1728), Jane Wark, Rebecca Wark (1729), James Montgomery, John Hambleton, Adam Knox (1730), Israel Gibbs, Mary Gibbs, Israel Walker (1731), Mrs. Robert Lennet (doubtless meaning Sennett) (1732). Besides these, under the inexplicable date of entry, July 5, 1772 (certainly a clerical error) are the following: Mrs. Robert Cook, Hugh Hambleton, Mrs. H. Hambleton, Walter Steward, Mrs. J. S. M'gomery, Mary Hambleton. Very few of these remained in Hopkinton. A very few of the Blandford emigrants, members of the Hopkinton church, escaped the doom of excommunication: John Wood, Samuel Wark, John Osborn, Mrs. Adam Knox. Others whose names might naturally be looked for were not members.

It may be recalled that Rev. Elias Nason, in his picture of Sunday morning worship, represented "the Woods, the Freelands, Gibbses" etc., as coming from the west part of the town. That section has for generations been known as Woodville, so named for the large number of Woods who lived there. It appears that a number of Scotch inhabited that region also. It is certain that the family of Captain John Wood was intimate with some of these Irish Scots. There was a John How—the Hopkinton church records spell it with a final "e"—among those who first took up settling lots in Blandford, or New Glasgow; and in the year 1727 Mary Howe became the wife of John Wood, eldest son of Captain John. There was, further, as we have seen, a Daniel Stone, who also took up settling lots; and he took for his wife, Mary, the second child of Captain John Wood, while, as we have already observed, Captain John's widow became the wife of Josiah Rice. Both John and Benjamin became members of the Hopkinton church.

After the Scotch Irish schism in the church at Hopkinton, a Presbyterian church was there organized. The following excerpt from the Provincial Court records will serve to show that our Presbyterian friends were still alive and active.* The date is Friday, Feb. 1, 1733. "A Petition of John How and others of the town of Hopkinton, complaining of innovations in the Church there, so that they cannot conscientiously continue in the Communion with them, and Praying that they may be

* Vol. XV.

discharged from being taxed to the support of the Ministry in Sd Town. In Council, Read and Dismissed." The Hopkinton church manual affords this illuminating note: "In 1734, they organized a Presbyterian church, built a small meeting-house about one and one-half miles west of the village, near what is known as the Ellery place. Subsequently, on the removal of many of these families to Blandford, this church organization was, by consent of Presbytery, transferred to that town." Rev. Nathaniel Howe, the preacher of that name who figures in Mrs. Stowe's "Oldtown Folks," in his "Century Sermon," gives this interesting and rather doleful historic summary:* "These offended brethren formed a society, built a meeting house, and maintained their separation for a number of years. There is no account that they ever had a minister. It is more than probable, that they met together, sung, prayed, and exhorted one another. But in process of time, their zeal abated, their society dwindled, their meeting house decayed, some died, others sold and removed, and a number of years after they had been admonished and suspended by the Church, those who remained in the town returned, made concessions to the Church, and were restored to their former standing, and admitted to communion." Had this famous worthy known what we know about the main scion of this Hopkinton Presbyterian church, he would hardly have said, "their zeal abated."

So it transpired that on November 7, 1734, evidently after the new church had started on its career, this thunderbolt was sent out by the old church: "Whereas, Several members of this Church viz: Robert Hambleton and wife, Robert Barrett and wife, Israel Gibbs and

---

* "A Century Sermon delivered in Hopkinton on the Lord's Day, December 24, 1815, by Nathaniel Howe, A.M., Pastor of the Church:" a pamphlet.

wife, Matthew Blair and wife, Samuel Wark and wife and James Wark and Rebecca Wark John Ozburn Sen*r* Adam Knox the wife of Robert Sennet and wife of John Ozburn Jun*r* have parteken of the Lord's supper with the aforenamed members of this Church who were under suspension of this Church, therefore voted that the brethren and sisters be held as offenders and accordingly be desired to make satisfaction to y*e* Church for their offence." January 3, 1735, all these just named were suspended till satisfaction should be made.

It is pertinent to remark that the mass of this Presbyterian church were tired not only of the Hopkinton church, but of Hopkinton because of the church. It was the eve of another emigration. Hungry and thirsty, their souls fainted in them, not for bread which perishes, or water which comes down from the clouds, but for the dear privilege of worshipping and serving God according to the ways of the fathers and mothers of good old Ulster, only in peace and good will. They had sought otherwheres for it in vain. They thought they had found it in Hopkinton, and were disappointed. Now they would go out and make a wilderness blossom as a rose. Be it remembered, when they went out, they went as a church already organized, to plant it in the midst of a community of their own creation where they would not be "haraced about" by other winds of doctrine, with a polity of their own inheritance, in "New Glasgow," replica of the mother of them all, their refuge and their solace.

CHAPTER X

SUFFIELD EQUIVALENT: TOILS OF THE LAW AND TOILS OF THE LAW-BREAKER

Our story is of the aspirations and struggles of a church. This church is in the world, not in heaven. It has been cribbed, cabined and confined; has been expatriated; has been a stranger and a pilgrim; has had ambition and bitter disappointment. It is now about to sally forth into the worldly business of establishing a community in which it can bear rule. So it confronts the problem of land. And land fit to occupy is hard to get. The State might give away lands, or sell them for a farthing an acre. But such lands were an untamed and cheerless wilderness. To make it fit for human dwelling, where women might sing at their spinning, and children play safely in the dooryard, and go to school without fear of beast or human foe, where there should be "no breaking in and no going forth," the land must be disciplined into orderliness and the soil made ready for the coulter and the wheel. To accomplish this men's backs became bent, women grew old and worn, and children had to wait long for their rightful inheritance of bounding and joyous play.

Contemporary with events related in the last chapter, extensive land operations were going on in the Province of Massachusetts Bay, to the west of the Connecticut river. Wild lands were surveyed and laid out into townships by speculators and proprietors who acquired these lands by purchase, inviting settlers thereto in accordance with provisions laid down by the General Court. One of these tracts was known as the Suffield Equivalent Lands. High up on the hills of western Middlesex, a

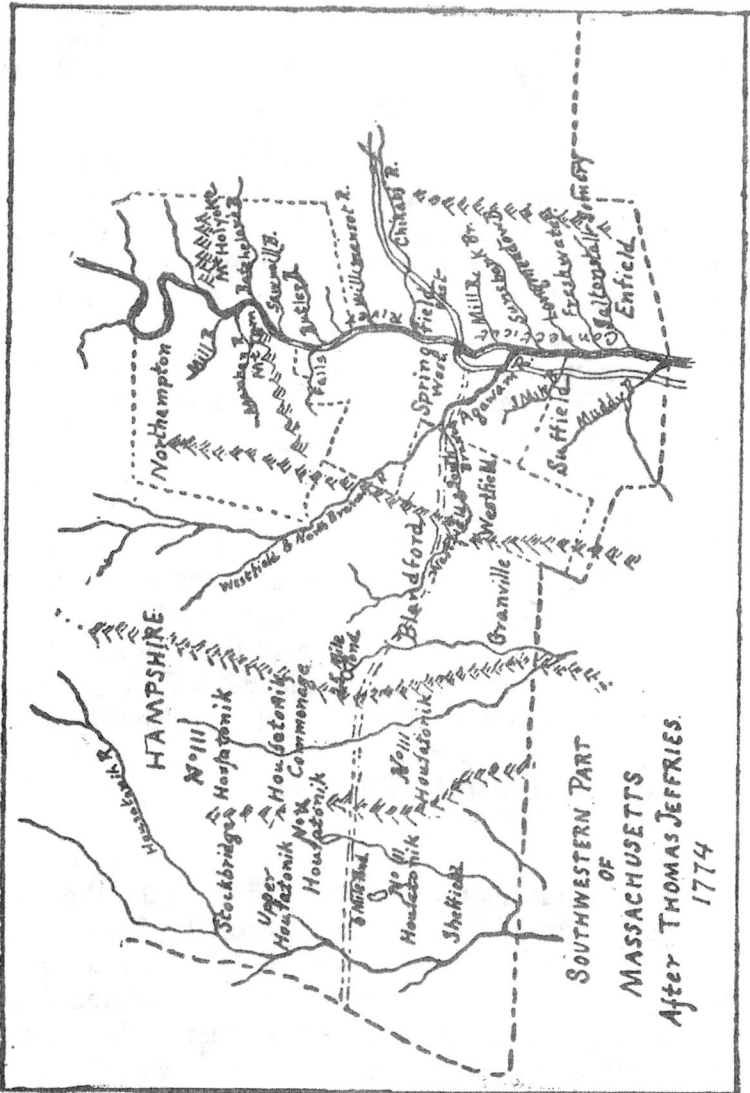

SOUTHWESTERN PART
OF
MASSACHUSETTS
After Thomas Jeffries
1774

little later set off as Hampshire, now Hampden, county, a virgin forest, this territory appealed to the imagination of the malcontents at Hopkinton, and was chosen by them to become their future place of abode.

We have first to do with the disputes of two states— for they were states in development. Colonial charters might be grants of land extending from ocean to ocean. But just the same they crowded like boys knocking one another's ribs. Connecticut was laboring over boundary disputes for nearly two hundred and fifty years. Massachusetts and Connecticut were in periodical quarrel over their common boundary nearly a century. Rufus Choate once said to the Legislature of Massachusetts concerning the boundary between that commonwealth and Rhode Island, "Why, gentlemen, the Commissioners might as well have decided that the line between the States was bounded on the north by a bramble bush, on the south by a blue jay, on the west by a hive of bees in swarming time, and on the east by five hundred foxes with fire-brands tied to their tails."

When Massachusetts had the Colony line dividing it and Connecticut surveyed, in 1642, the surveyors, Nathaniel Woodward and Solomon Saffrey, started the line from the point they thought was three miles to the south of the southernmost point on the Charles river, "and instead of extending the survey across the country, they sailed round Cape Cod and up the Connecticut to the place they supposed was in the same degree of latitude with the starting point, but which was in fact seven or eight miles to the south of it."

It would be unprofitable to review the wearying wrangles leading to the final adjustments of this boundary. Suffice it to say that Woodstock, Enfield, and Suffield, which had been settled by Massachusetts men, and had been reckoned as Massachusetts towns, were thrown into Connecticut. This boundary was ultimately settled by inter-colonial commissioners appointed in 1713. It was agreed that Massachusetts should continue to retain jurisdiction over the old border towns just named, though they fell to the south of the Colony line. But the land was to be Connecticut's. It was an arrangement bound to provoke disputes, and in time the towns passed over altogether to the Colony south of the line. Before that occurred, however, Connecticut demanded some compensation for her loss of jurisdiction over the alienated townships. So, for as much territory as Massachusetts governed south of the line, she agreed to give an equivalent in unimproved lands north of that line to her southern neighbor. Of the lands thus held in ownership by Connecticut, but governed by Massachusetts, Suffield's share was 22,172 acres. This land was sold and the money given to Yale College.

But that is not all of the story. It runs out into intricate detail which we will not follow. In short, Suffield claimed that she had not yet received all her due; that certain lands had been "taken from Suffield and laid to Windsor and Simsbury," and that these, furthermore, were the richest lands she had possessed. So the proprietors of Suffield laid the matter before the Provincial Legislature, which appointed a commission to investigate and report. The matter hung fire for several years, as is the way often with legislatures. Joseph Winchell and Joseph King represented the township, and were referred to in the legal documents as representing the "commoners and proprietors of the common and undivided lands" of Suffield.

While these matters are pending, it may be well, for the clearer understanding of the subsequent story, to take a little excursus into the meaning and implications of that last quoted phrase.

It is a technical one indicating "the original grantees or purchasers of the land of the town and their legal heirs, assigns or successors, with such as from time to time they chose to add to their number. . . . In every case they formed a *de facto* land company, as truly as did the companies which received the grants of the New England colonies."* Commonly, in New England, the proprietors of a town had been also its first settlers. This was so, for example, in the Scotch Irish town of Pelham. It was distinctly not so in Blandford. "Wherever the genuine proprietary regime existed, emigration and settlement were largely directed from a single centre, because the proprietor sought income from the land of his province; he advertised its advantages, planned its settlement, sold its lands, exacted a quitrent from its grantees, in short, developed a provincial land system. . . . In a real, though not in the fullest sense, emigration to the proprietary provinces was assisted emigration, the encouraging and directing influence of the proprietor being felt through it all." †

This element is to be found operative in the building up of New England, as in the case of Plymouth and of Salem. To a degree, it is true, it operated in Blandford, but only to a small degree. There the purpose and method were different. In Blandford the chief motive power was spontaneous. Assistance from without was incidental, or supplementary. "By far the greater part of the land in New England colonies was granted to towns, that is, to groups or communities of settlers by whom it was allotted to individuals." ‡ It was rarely leased, and rent was no appreciable part of the revenue. No distinct land office was established in any part of

---

* Herbert L. Osgood.
† Ibid.
‡ Ibid.

New England. In Blandford, however, rents, though only nominal, were exacted, as the deeds bear specific witness. It became an uncomfortable burden. Proprietorship had a hard time in New England when it came to burdening settlers with such claims. The New England air was too free.

Where proprietors of a township were also settlers in it, as in Pelham, already cited, grants of land furnished very important items in the town business. Proprietors' meetings might indeed be separate from the town meetings, as the latter would include some who were not original proprietors., Nevertheless, the proprietors' meetings were large, public, or quasi-public and local meetings. In Blandford it was never so. The proprietors were few, all were non-resident, and there is no record whatsoever now extant of any of their meetings. The final result was not so very different from that of the other sort of towns described. But in procedure it was vastly different, as later we shall have occasion to notice. Eggleston observes* "that some of the oldest towns were quite small; but in general a tract six miles square, or its equivalent, was thought of the best size for a plantation. Sixty families were considered a good number to begin a settlement. The Springfield proprietors had fixed upon forty as the suitable number."

On April 5, 1733, the General Court gave answer to the petition of Winchell and King as follows:

"A Petition of the proprietors of the common and undivided Lands in ye Town of Suffield, Shewing that upon the Settlement of the dividing Line between this province and the Colony of Connecticut a great Part of their best Land was taken from them and added to the said Colony Praying that a Grant of Seven or eight

* In Johns Hopkins University Studies, Vol. IV.

miles square of unappropriated Land be granted as an equivalent therefor.

"Read and in answer to this petition

"Voted that the Prayer of the Petition be so far granted as that the Commoners and Proprietors of the Common Lands in the Town of Suffield be and hereby are Inpowered by a Survey and Chainmen on Oath to survey & lay out at their Cost & Charge the Contents of six miles square of the unimproved Lands of this province on the West side of Connecticut River, Provided that they within the Term of seven Years from the Confirmation of the Grant Settle on the Spot Sixty Families who shall be and are hereby obliged to bring to, clear & fit for Improvement three Acres & six Acres more well stocked with English Grass, & also have a good Convenient Dwelling House on said Land of one Story high & eighteen feet square at least & that within the said Term they build a good & convenient House for the public Worship of God & settle a learned & orthodox Minister there, reserving three Lots, each Lot equal to any Settlers Lot, One for the first settled Minister, one for the Ministry & one for the School, & that they return a Plan of the Granted premises to this Court within Twelve months for Confirmation to the said Commoners & Proprietors their heirs & Assigns for ever." This tract became known for a time thereafter as the Suffield Equivalent Lands.

There were more than one hundred original proprietors of this land. One of these, Joseph King, who had bought out many, not to say most, of the others, himself presently sold his rights to Christopher Jacob Lawton, a resident of Suffield and an attorney at law. The deed recites that the said Lawton had already been at "great expense" in his measures "to obtain a grant of the general assembly of the Province," and "in viewing and surveying a tract of land whereon to lay said equivalent, and getting confirmation of the same by the general assembly." In the same instrument of sale Lawton is obligated to carry out to completion the provisions of act of the general assembly not yet fulfilled. This instrument was signed November 24, 1735.

Already, two years before this, Lawton had begun very definite measures, in addition to any thus far hinted at, for favoring the new settlement. Westfield was at this time a thriving town. To the west there lay a district, or tract, known as Houssatanick (variously spelled). Whether at this time or not, at all events not much later, Lawton, or perhaps his son* had interests both in Suffield Equivalent and Houssatanick. Naturally he would want to establish communication between the two places, a purpose running quite parallel with the desire of the Provincial Government as well, which was anxious to settle and develop into towns all this outlying region. So Lawton petitioned the Legislature for a grant of 500 acres for a tavern site situate on the road or path between the two places aforesaid, and within the equivalent tract with which we are having to do. He was granted three hundred acres and certain conditions were laid down for the tavern which he was to build and maintain. It divided the distance between two termini into two fairly even sections, and became a not unimportant or uninteresting halting-place in the pioneering days of the "Berkshires."† This was the earliest hearth-fire in the township which was to arise in this "equivalent."

An indenture of Nov. 1, 1742, between Jacob Wendell of Boston, John Stoddard of Northampton and

---

* v. Vol. M, page 25, Registry of Deeds, Springfield. The date is 1740.
† The ancient caravansary was known as "Pixley's tavern." The story of it is given in detail in "The Taverns and Turnpikes" etc.

Philip Livingston of Albany, party of the first part, and Joseph Root, John Lee and John Huston, "all of the county of Hampshire," party of the second part, certifies the sale by the first named group to the second, for the sum of 1200 pounds, of forty lots of land of one hundred acres each, "on both sides of the Housatunock river." The indenture states that the plan was made by John Huston, who is mentioned in many of the deeds of this period as a surveyor, and is associated with Roger Newbury as laying out the plan of Blandford, particularly as mapping out the home lots in the two divisions. John Huston has already come under our notice in the story of Hopkinton. He was a large landowner as well as surveyor, buying and selling land in Pontusuck, now Pittsfield, which he also surveyed, bought and sold in town No. 9, and was very early a considerable land agent in "Glasgow," was a first settler there, proprietor of a tavern, deacon in the church, and was otherwise prominent.*

Affairs connected with the land movement had developed just in the nick of time. The Scotch Irishmen of Hopkinton were not going through the world with their eyes closed. If Governor Shute's Memorial to the King had been common talk among the people there; if already, as some of the malcontents had confessed, they were on the lookout for virgin soil whereon to plant a church and a town of their own making, what the Legislature was doing for Suffield Equivalent was no secret hidden from their eyes. John Huston at least would see to that. Lawton, too, the foremost proprietor of these lands, was not asleep. It was easy for the two parties to get together, and one may conjecture, with good reason for the guess, that the men from Ulster were eager respondents to say the least. However this may have been, Lawton and a group of Hopkintonians

---

* v. Wood.

made a bargain together whereby the new settlement should be established. One would like to know—what has gone into the forgotten past—something more about the preliminaries to the agreement; what the private conversations or public addresses were like, as this large company of men and women contemplated breaking up their homes, selling their lands and betaking themselves, their children and their cattle to this wild and mountainous country, at best a darksome frontier among wild and difficult hills. Imagination must here have large room.

The agreement was drawn up and signed, July 8, 1735. It first rehearses the Act of the General Court of date December 14, 1732, in answer to the petition of the Suffield proprietors, setting forth the required terms of the settlement, then proceeds:

"And whereas the said Christopher Jacob Lawton hath since purchased of the aforesaid commoners and proprietors all their several respective rights of Josiah Sheldon and the heirs of Joshua Leavitt, deceased, of said Suffield, and hath agreed with Robert Senot, James Freeland, John Osborne, Hugh Hambleton, Hugh Black, Comeinne* Anderson, James Beard, Joseph Rice, Benjamin Woods, Samuel Karmer,† James Montgomery, Armor Hamilton, Israel Gibbs, Robert Henry, Jonathan Boyce, James Wark, Robert Black, John Osborne, John Hambleton, Jeremiah Anderson, William Province, James MacCletick, Samuel Ferguson, James Freeland Jr., John Houstin, Samuel Cook, Daniel Stone, Robert Houston, Samuel Tygar,‡ William Anderson, William Barker, Samuel Wark, Alexander Osborn, Thomas Reed, Matthew Blair, Robert Cook, John

---

* Cornelius.
† Carnahan, Cannon.
‡ Taggart.

Cockhoron, Robert Hambleton, Hugh Hambleton, Daniel Howe, Adam Knox, Joseph Freeland, John Stuart, Robert Huston, Samuel Cook, William Donaghoi, William Province, James Beard, John Cochran, Robert Hambleton. For the settlement of sixty families on said land in such manner and within such time as in the said proviso, in the aforementioned grant is contained and expressed, to whom the said Christopher Jacob Lawton hath convenanted to grant the several quantities hereafter mentioned, viz.: To fifty families 120 acres each, to two families 60 acres each, to five families 40 acres each, to one family 30 acres, rendering to him, his heirs and assigns six per cent current lawful money of New England yearly, if demanded for each 120 acres of land and so proportionably, which said settlers have given bonds and covenants to John Foye and Francis Wells, both within the province aforesaid, merchants, and the said Christopher Lawton in penalty amounting in the whole to £22,500 lawful money of New England with conditions to accomplish their several settlements and pay their aforesaid bonds. Now witnesseth these presents, that the said Christopher Jacob Lawton for and in consideration of three thousand pounds in lawful public bills of credit to him in hand paid by Francis Brinley of Roxbury, in the county of Suffolk and province aforesaid, Esq., before the sealing and delivery of these presents, the receipt whereof is hereby acknowledged," etc.

Then follows, in usual form, a deed to said Brinley of one undivided fourth part of said township. This deed is dated July 8, 1735. Lawton had already by deed, dated Jan. 17, 1735, conveyed to Francis Wells, of Cambridge, and to John Foye, of Charlestown, one undivided fourth each, of his interest in said township. And on March 30, 1737, these several proprietors executed a deed of partition among themselves; so that from that date each became the owner of certain numbered lots in different parts of the township, containing 500 acres each. That same spring the contractors also received deeds in severalty according to the contract, and a grant of ten acres was laid out in the midst of the home lots for public purposes. This manner of partition was unique among all the towns of the province.

It will be remembered that the Suffield proprietors, in whose behalf, and especially in his own, Lawton had been diligently lobbying, had asked for a grant of land "Seven or eight miles square," and that Lawton was overseeing the survey which Roger Newbury was making. That was done in the summer or fall of 1733, when Lawton went before the Legislature with a plan of the grant, as also with a diagram of the tavern site of three hundred acres. But he told the Legislature that "through Mistake" he had "left behind the Certificates of the Surveyor and Chainmen being sworn." That body appeared to think that this mistake should be rectified, and Lawton petitioned for time, which was generously granted. That was in October, 1733.

In November, 1734, Joseph Heath, of Roxbury, purchased of Lawton fifteen hundred acres of this land, "the same to lye in one Piece and in a Regular Figure or in Five Hundred Acre lots" as the buyer or his heirs might choose, to be located by lot, and the deed stipulated that this land should be "forever Free and Clear of all the Conditions of Settlement mentioned in the Court Grants and from all other Incumbrances lets or Intanglements," and to be delivered one year from date.

The next month, December 4, 1734, in the absence of the sworn statements, an Act was passed embodying a detailed outline of the equivalent grant, including the "Grant of Three Hundred Acres of Land Granted to Christopher Jacob Lawton in December 1732 laid out

by John Ashley Junr Surveyor and Chain men on Oath,"
etc. The description is given thus:

"Beginning at a Black Birch Marked with Stones
about it being the South East Corner & is near a small
brook that runs into Westfield River. & on the West
side a steep Round Mountain, from thence Running
West twenty deg north 1945 Rods to a Maple tree
marked; thence North 20 deg. East 1920 Rods to a
Beach tree mark'd with Stones about it; from thence
East 20 deg South 1945 Rods; to a Yellow pine tree
Mark'd, with Stones about it. from thence Runing
South 20 Deg. West 1920 Rods to the bounds first
mentioned." This was ordered accepted "and that the
Lands therein Delineated & described so far as the
Extent of the Contents of Six Miles Square be and
hereby are Confirmed to the Commoners and proprietors of the Common and Undivided Lands in the Town
of Suffield and their Respective Assignees forever they
observing and performing the Conditions of the Grant."

Lawton's farm also was confirmed, subject to fulfilment of conditions of the grant, "provided also that the
plat Contains no more than the quantity of Six Miles
Square & three hundred Acres of Land and does not
Interfere with any former Grant." The General Court
was moving cautiously, evidently suspecting chicanery
in the measurements, at the same time trying to avoid
unnecessary embarrassment to innocent purchasers or
holders of the land.

Two more years passed and no partition. November
15, 1736, Lawton gave to Heath another deed, promising that the desired "Sett of" should be made one
year from that date. But already this artful adventurer
was entering upon a path which no man would desire
to follow, as fully appears from an entry in the Provincial Laws, nine days following the date of the last men-

tioned document. Therein is the statement made that
Heath has asked the General Court to confirm this purchase, and the court forthwith decreed that Lawton's
deed of sale to Heath in the month of November, 1734,
"which the said Lawton had not acknowledged before
he was deprived of his Reason" should be "confirmed
& made good and valid in the Law." This was done
Dec. 6, 1736.

What drove Lawton insane is perhaps a question more
profitable for speculation than for history. What might
have driven him to the mad-house is a question somewhat easily answered. After the transactions just described, Christopher Jacob Lawton, of Leicester, in the
county of Worcester, attorney at law, takes the place
of the other Lawton, presumably his father who was
now incompetent to carry on business with the world.
The acts of the General Court concerning him may continue to treat as with the elder Lawton; but it is the
son who, in person, for his father, and finally with the
wife, Sarah, indicating the death of the father and the
son's possession of the estate finally in his own right,
conducts the business.

The "Mistake" of the elder Lawton had come back
on many a day to plague him, as mistakes and some
other things have a way of doing. For years he had been
trying to make a tract of seven miles square look to
the General Court like only six. He had not succeeded.
The General Court could wait, but how long could he
wait? The Court that had given could take away, was
loudly hinting that it would take away, and Lawton
had staked thousands of pounds on that die. Those
years could hardly have seemed to him to slide along
with swift wings lent to time by a good conscience and
a happy mind.

In that valuable treatise, "The History of Western

Massachusetts," by Josiah Gilbert Holland, there is copied a letter, written by Francis Brinley, "evidently made to an attorney," the occasion for which was a suit commenced by Hugh Hamilton, whom we have met twice before. The historian does not reveal his source of the letter, and I have not happened to run upon it anywhere else. No date is appended, but it will be seen to fit in with the narrative which we are now pursuing. This is the letter, as printed in the History aforesaid:

"It's generally well known in your parts that Mr. Christopher Jacob Lawton obtained a grant for a tract of land called now Blandford, *alias* New Glasgo, and in the time of it, in order to carry on the settlement, took in two partners for one-half, viz: Capt. Francis Welds and Mr. John Fay. Some time after, I bought of said Lawton one-half of his remaining half, (exclusive of all charges) which entitles each of us to one-quarter part. But I should have observed, before I was concerned they had agreed with 45 families to settle it, from a place called Hopkinton, and articled with them, amongst whom was one Hugh Hamilton, who could not go by reason he could not sell his interest there; so, by much importunity of him and his friends, being a man pretty well approved amongst them, I purchased his farm, (and one of his neighbors') to get them up to Glasgo, and I soon sold them to loss. However, I gave them obligations for money and lands in Glasgo. The money part I long since paid, and this man, if I remember right, was to have 300 acres, and (to oblige him, which he was to impart to no one living,) I promised him to choose out one of my lotts, when I could certainly know where my right was; and accordingly, a surveyor was appointed to survey it, and lay it out in 500-acre lotts, and before he had finished it, or even markt and bounded them, the General Court overhald the grant, (which made some disturbance) and ordered a committy, and had it new surveyed, and found Mr. Lawton had a mile or thereabouts more than was conformable to their grant. But finally they granted the overplus, as I took it, to all of us, on condition that we settled sixteen familys more. But how it happened I know not, this second grant was done in Weld's and Fay's names only. But they have always told me and Lawton that we were and should be equally entitled to it with them, and that they would give us a quit-claim, in order to make good a division we were about to make above mentioned, but they have never done it, (more than by promise) though often requested. This I told said Hamilton, and others concerned in Glasgo, three or four years agoe, and hearing he was uneasy and threatening, I wrote him I was willing to doe it, if he'd appoint when, but I thought it was a pity to let him pitch at uncertainty, and I always was and am as willing to doe it (and doe him justis) as he can be to have it, and it has been retarded on no other account on my side. But such are the circumstances often in such new settlements, that it's almost impossible — if men are so unequal in their demands, without the least injury to them. But by what I can learn, what has moved him to this resentment, or at least to give a handle to it, is as I have sold to four men a lott of 470 acres, in order to perform my quarter part of the settlers to the last grant above mentioned, in order to qualify me to my full quarter part as above hinted, with Welds and Fay, that there might not any longer remain any difficulty not being named in the second grant, and I have sold for £70 less than others, in order to perform my part therein, with a long credit. Now behold nothing will serve said Hamilton, as I am told, but 300 acres out of that lott which I can't recall."

This interesting statement throws light upon a num-

ber of little things we are glad to know about. It illum-
inates some of the ways taken to settle this grant. It
hints that the wholesale exodus about to be accomplished made land cheap in Hopkinton and hard to sell.
It reveals that some of the Irish Scots as well as some
of the proprietors had their eyes open and meant to be
forehanded. What is quite as much to the present point,
it brings out the fact that Lawton's trick was not only
discovered but was creating considerable disturbance
among all concerned—legislators, settlers, adventurers.
It indicated that while the storm was raging Lawton was
lying low, perhaps eating his heart out with remorse and
fear, and for some reason keeping Brinley in the rear,
while Wells and Foye were pushed to the front as principal agents before the public, at least before the General Court.

Brinley's statement is not the only evidence we have
of what was going on. There are also the Provincial
records. It occurred to the legislators that it might be
well to have a survey made by direct authority of their
own. That would eliminate any "mistakes" in the understanding of the affair, if not in the affair itself. This
survey was made by Joseph Wilder and John Chandler,
Jr., who reported to the Legislature, which "Ordered,
that John Hobson Chandler and William Ward Esqrs
with such as shall be joyned by the Honble Board be
a Committee to consider of this Report as far as it relates to the Survey of Suffield Equivalent Township,
and also the Petition of Messrs Francis Wells and John
Foye and that of David Ingersol;" and that this committee report what in their opinion might be proper on
the whole for the Court to do in the premises. David
Ingersoll was at this time interested in the Pixley tavern
and farm.

"In Council, Read and Concur'd, and John Stoddard

and Joseph Wilder Esq*rs* are joined in the affair."
Passed January 11, 1737-8.* Two days later the committee reported. The Record runs: † "The Committee appointed to consider the Report of a Committee of this Honorable Court so far as it related to the survey of Suffield equivalent Township; the Grant to M*r.* Christopher Jacob Lawton; and also the Petitions of Francis Wells Esq*r* & M*r.* John Foye &c—upon mature consideration thereon report viz*t.*

"That the Plat of the said Township as set forth by Cap*t* William Chandler Surveyor &c, with all the lands therein delineated and described (exclusive of three hundred Acres granted to said Lawton) be accepted; and that the full contents of six miles square thereof & no more be confirmed to the original Grantees the proprietors of Suffield their heirs and assigns respectively in full satisfaction of that Grant, they performing the conditions thereof—And upon inquiry into the petition of said Wells and Foye, it appears to the Committee, that the said Petitioners were not knowing at the time of their purchase of any wrong or overplus measure in the former survey of the said Township; and that the facts therein alledged are true and the taking away of the overplus Land will entirely destroy the settlement of their several Divisions of Land, for a great deal of which they have passed Deeds in Warranty.

"The Committee are therefore of opinion that the surplusage of the lands set forth in the plat more than the contents of the six miles square, & the three hundred acres granted to s*d.* Lawton, be granted and confirmed to the said Francis Wells and John Foye their heirs & assigns respectively for ever, on condition they settle eighteen Families more on the lands set forth in

---

* Chapter 237.
† Court Records, Vol. 17, pp. 16, 17, 18.

said Plat in as full and ample manner and in all respects, and within the time limited for settling sixty families in the original grant to Suffield proprietors; and also that the said Wells and Foye do within two years pay into the publick Treasury the sum of fifty six pounds thirteen shillings and four pence of the New tenour Bills, or one hundred and seventy pounds of the Old Tenour, into the publick Treasury to reimburse the charge of the Committee of the Court in Correcting this and other plats at or near Houssatonnoc.

"All of which is humbly submitted in the name & by order of the Committee.

January 13th. 1737-8—   John Stoddard

In Council Jany. 13. 1737-8

Read and sent down

"In the House of Representatives Jany. 13, 1737-8. Read and Ordered that the considerations of this Report be referred to the next sitting of the Court.

"Sent up for Concurrence, J. Quincy Spker

"In Council Jany. 13. 1737-8. Read and Concurred

J. Willard Secry

"14. Consented to, J. Belcher"

"In the House of Representatives Decr. 19, 1738.

"Read again, and Ordered, that this Report be & is hereby accepted; and forasmuch as it appears that the Petitioners Francis Wells Esqr. and Mr. John Foye were not knowing at the time of their purchase of Mr. Christopher Jacob Lawton, the Lands granted as an equivalent to Suffield Proprietors, of any wrong, or overplus measure in the former survey of the said Township; and that the facts suggested in the petition of the said Wells & Foye are true & the taking away the overplus Land will entirely destroy the settlement of their several divisions of Land, for a considerable quantity of which, they have passed Deeds with warranty: Voted, therefore that the surplusage of the Lands set forth in the plat more than the contents of six miles square and the three hundred acres granted to the said Lawton, be and hereby are given, granted & confirmed to the said Frqncis Wells Esqr. & Mr. John Foye their heirs and assigns respectively for ever, in answer to their Petition to which this Report is annexed, provided, he or they settle eighteen families more on the lands set forth and described in the said Plat, in as full and ample manner in all respects & within the time limited for settling Sixty families, by the original Grant to Suffield proprietors; and also that the petitioners Wells & Foye their heirs & assigns respectively do within two years pay into the publick Treasury the sum of Fifty six pounds thirteen shillings & four pence of the new tenor Bills to reimburse the charge of the Committee of the Court in correcting this plat of Suffield equivalent townships within mentioned & other plats at or near Houssatonnoc.

Sent up for concurrence
"In Council Decr. 20. 1738-9. Read & concurred
"23. Consented to

J. Belcher"

Thus was this town plat resurveyed not only, but other contiguous and neighboring town plats also, for they would all have been disturbed by Lawton's fraudulent returns. Suspicion seems also, and very naturally, to have fixed upon John Huston, but evidence does not occur, incriminating him.

The four proprietors—Lawton the son having taken the place of the father—finally executed a deed of partition. It is dated March 30, 1737, coincident with the date of all the first settlers' deeds. By this deed, Lawton, of Leicester, was granted these "farm" lots: Nos. 1, 5, 10, 15, 19, 23, 27, 31, 36, 44, 49, 32, as laid out by Roger Newbury of Windsor. Brinley was given Nos. 4, 8, 14, 18, 22, 26, 30, 34, 39, 41, 48, 11, 12. Wells was to have Nos. 3, 7, 13, 17, 21, 25, 29, 35, 37, 43, 47, 51. To Foye were assigned Nos. 2, 6, 9, 16, 20, 24, 28, 33, 38, 35, 46, 50, 42. Most of these lots contained 500 acres each; a few contained less. Lot No. 40, which is omitted in the above partition, probably by error, was afterward sold by Foye.

The date of this deed of partition is at least four years earlier than Brinley's complaint that he had not been able to secure his deed to his rights, although he had repeatedly asked for it. It is a curious fact that, while this deed bears date identical with all those original deeds conveying home lots to the first settlers, it is not recorded in the volume with them, but in a volume most of whose entrances bear dates nearly or quite a half century later. Why this so great delay? Why wait until after the Revolution to record a conveyance of lands made before the French and Indian wars? There is no one to arise to tell. It seems to have been another incident in the history of Lawton's "mistakes."

However, not the proprietors, but the settlers, of Suffield Equivalent, made the town. "Glasgow" was not begotten in a surveyor's office, nor in the strong box of a surveyor's secrets, nor in a real estate agent's office, whether honest or dishonest, not even in a wayside inn, but amidst a company of men and women who had visions of the eternal God and an unloosening grip upon the gospel of life. These men of the world who exploited the real estate markets opened a very needful avenue of approach to the homes that were to be on these heights. They were probably more polished and cul-

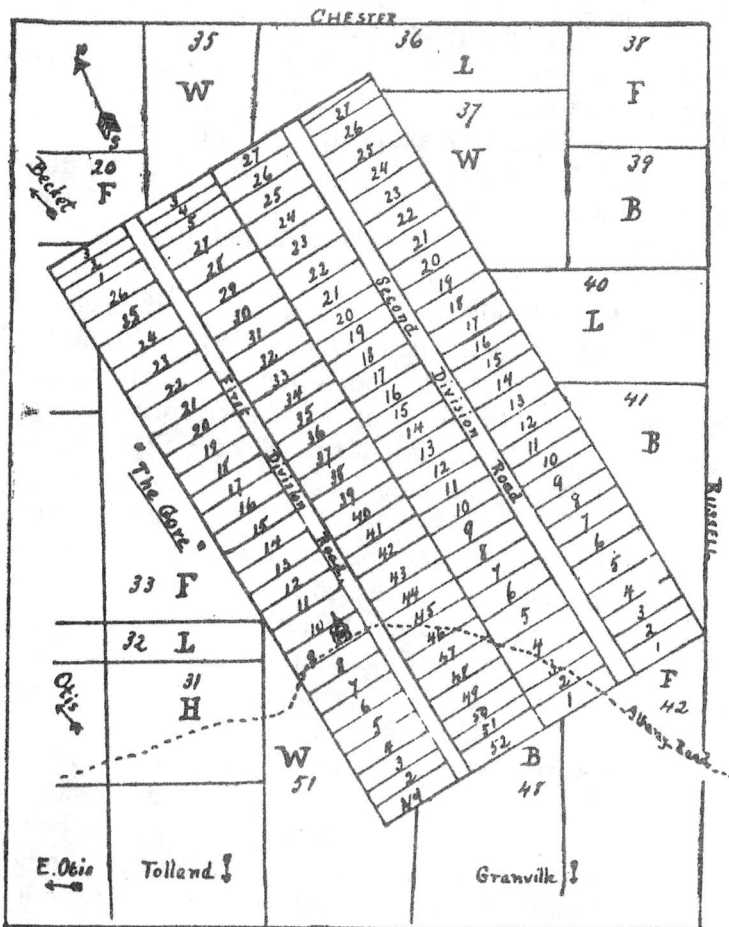

THE HOME LOTS

tured in respect of worldly ways. But the people who
had undoubted culture of soul, who had stalwart convictions which they would neither conceal nor compromise though the heavens should fall, were the material out of which to set up a miniature democracy
which should come to take its place among the self-
respecting and contributory units of a splendid Commonwealth, and be not ashamed.

We are not yet quite ready to cultivate further intimate acquaintance with the people of the new township. The town plat itself claims some fuller investiga-
tion. The "home lots," or "settling lots," as they were
variously called, were blocked out in one solid rectangle
of about four miles by two. This block of home lots was
laid out so that "The Great Road Commonly Called by
the name of the Street," to quote from one of the early
deeds,—in recent times, and still, called North street,—
ran along a high ridge forming the divide between the
Westfield Little River system to the westward, and
Black brook, Freeland brook, Gibbs brook, Potash
brook, etc., to the eastward. All these streams are ultimately tributary to the Westfield river, which in turn
feeds the Connecticut. This high ridge of land is about
fifteen hundred feet above sea level at the point chosen
for the meeting house. With the exception of the extreme southerly section, it rises here and there to sixteen hundred, and falls to fourteen hundred or thereabout. All but a very small, thin wedge of this plot lies
east and north of a diagonal drawn from the northwest
corner of the township to the southeast. Its longest sides
run north, ten degrees west, and south, ten degrees east.
The northeastern corner nearly touches the northerly
boundary of the township, while its southeast corner
runs against the easterly town bound a little to the
south of its central point.

This block of about eight square miles, approximately one sixth of the area of the township, was divided longitudinally through the center thereof, the westerly half being called the first division, the other the second division. There never was any road running along this division line, though for a time one was contemplated. But each division had a road running longitudinally through its center. In each division the lots were laid out in rectangles, with a narrow end abutting upon the street in either case. That is, while the main axis of the whole block ran northerly and southerly, the main axis of the individual lots ran easterly and westerly. The farm lots of 500 acres were laid out in squares, except as they were cut into triangles or other irregular shapes where they abutted against the plot of home lots.

For a town street intended to run straight over a length of four miles, the selection of the first division road was most wise. There is no other such extent of high and approximately level ground anywhere near the center of the township. There is an elevated plateau not as long, known as "Uhl Street" running close to the western boundary, and it became an important section, but it was too far to the west. There is another clear, high range of plateau on Beech hill, in the southerly part of town, and it has had a famous history. But that over-runs into Granville. The settlement plot was laid out easterly of the diagonal mentioned above, doubtless, to avoid the stretch of continuous meadow along the upper reaches of Westfield Little river and its tributary, Bedlam brook.

There was a saying of the fathers that there was no spot in town where a wagon could be left to stand without having to block the wheels. No road could come nearer to the truth of that witticism than the Second Division road. Its extremes of elevation are one thousand, and fourteen hundred feet or more, and the grades are broken far more abruptly and the changes are much closer together. That old road was like a titanic saw with teeth turned upward to the traveler. It was laid out one mile to the east of the Town Road, and exactly parallel therewith. It looked fine on paper, but it defied nature. It ran—and still runs in interrupted sections—in a bee line, up hill and down dale, regardless of contours, without deviation from, and defying compromise with, hill or meadow or ledge or brook, throughout its entire length. It is amazing for how long this street really did business. These canny Scotch did not easily let go of things. But the generations wore away, and long stretches of the road returned to nature. To-day it is eloquent with silent witnesses of a sturdy past: old grass- and moss-grown orchards, grizzled door-yard maples crumbling to decay; houses going or sunk into cellar holes, an abandoned school house, a mill pond securely hiding its secrets of past industry, a little cemetery grown up to thicket, with stones leaning or fallen. One runs along a surviving section of it, then suddenly turns off, perhaps without knowing that he has left the ancient thoroughfare. He dips down as into the bowels of the earth to cross a gem of ancient bridge construction and obtain a vista of brook and hill and forest and upland mowing which abides in his soul long years after his feet have trodden the ancient ways. Then he climbs up on the other side to emerge upon a height where story after story of the silent past waits in hidden places to welcome the antiquarian or sympathetic artist. "The Second Divison" still lives in local parlance, but it is an empty echo. Londonderry had a somewhat similar experience with its second division.

The numbering of the lots of the first division began at the southernmost corner, on the western, or southwestern, side, and ran on that side of the street in regular order up to and including No. 26, then crossed the street, beginning at that point with 27, and continuing to the foot of the plot at No. 52, opposite No. 1. At the northerly end of the street, above lots 26 and 27, were five other lots, two and one-half on either side. North of and contiguous to 26 was 1, then half of 2, and 3; then crossing the street and running down to 27, were the other half of 3, and 4 and 5. An explanatory note on one of the ancient plans reads: "Note each of the small Divisions contains 5 Chains or 20 Rods." These were sometimes referred to as "the first and small division." Or they were spoken of as "the forty acre division." Quite as frequently, perhaps, they went by the name of "the boys lots," by which term is apparently meant lots for young men to start life on, who were willing to cast in their interests with the older men of the company. These small farms were rather remote from the center of activity, and perhaps it stands to the credit of the young fellows who first settled them that they did not long stay there.

The system of numbering the lots of the second division was different. The numbering began, as in the first division, at the bottom of the chart, and there were 27 on either side of the street, distinguished from one another by the designation, "east," or "west," appended to the number, as No. 1 east, or No. 25 west. The size, or at least the shape, differed slightly one from another, so that the ends of the lots abutting upon the street were not exactly opposite, and on the extreme upper end on the east side was a narrow lot somewhat smaller than the 40-acre lots. This little lot, which completes the general rectangle, is neither numbered nor designated by any note, but is, by a reasonable inference, the 30-acre lot elsewhere referred to.

CHAPTER XI

HOME AT LAST—"A PLACE CALLED GLASCOW"

The would-be historian of Blandford is confronted at the very outset of his work with the lamentable paucity of records or even traditions of the earliest settlement. The proprietors' records are gone. The church records for the first half century are no more. For seven years from the time of settlement there are no town records, because there was no town. No personal letters of the time have come to light. There are the provincial records, and these have been reviewed. There are the records of the registries, of deeds and of probate. There is here and there a waif or scrap of historic material incidentally bearing on our quest. One must look upon all this as through a magnifying glass to find hidden treasures of inference, and call upon imagination to breathe into it all the breath of life.

In the early nineteenth century, the Rev. John Keep, scholar, divine and pioneer, was for a decade and a half minister in Blandford. In his later ministry he peered into the silent past of his parish and town for the earliest facts, and as a result of his study wrote a sermon, which, more than half a century later, was printed, with this on the title page: "A Discourse Delivered at Blandford, Mass., Tuesday, March 20th, 1821. Giving Some Account of the Early Settlement of The Town and The History of The Church. By Rev. John Keep, Pastor of the Congregational Church in Blandford from 1805 to 1821. Printed from a recently discovered manuscript copy by Charles W. Eddy, Ware, Mass., 1886." Some copies of this are extant. There is one in the Porter

Memorial Library in Blandford. The original manuscript also survives. There is another manuscript, a fragment, containing a small portion of the sermon, with notes, evidently made by Mr. Keep himself, and "Extracts from an Address of Patric Boies Esqr. on the Same Subject." This latter manuscript is a copy. Both these documents are of great value. The sermon carries practically all of the earliest traditions obtainable at the time it was written. There is the Historical Address of William H. Gibbs, dated Sept. 21, 1850, but it adds almost nothing concerning the earliest period, embodying the material of Mr. Keep's sermon, in somewhat modified phraseology. The sparse gleanings gathered up in this sermon, precious as they are, serve also to impress the student with the niggardly material at hand. In transcribing what this first student of Blandford history has been able to transmit to our generation, I shall in large measure—so far as the subject of this chapter is concerned, quote *verbatim*, correcting where correction may be needed, and adding some explanation or facts which later research has made it possible to add. Blandford lovers will, I am sure, appreciate the flavor of this pioneer student of "A Place Called Glascow."

Mr. Keep says: "The original records of the town were burned in Boston, and when the town clerk began his journal he was far from being very particular or lucid." Anyone who has studied these records will hardly be disposed to think that Mr. Keep has done an injustice to the primeval town records. The early historian, having briefly outlined some of the facts already passed in review, goes on to recite that after the Hopkinton company was formed, and they had "resolved upon the expedition, they sent a few young men as pioneers, to mark the course and to erect a few log huts for the temporary accommodation of the company upon their first arrival. These youths reached the centre of the town the last of April. The day of their arrival a snow storm commenced and continued three days, collecting to the depth of between three and four feet. They were ten miles from Westfield, the nearest settlement, and seven miles from the nearest house. I need not tell you what must have been their feelings in the wilderness in such circumstances. No shelter except what they could form by the boughs of trees, no fire to warm their bodies or food, except what they would make by some rock or stone. Happily for them the cold soon subsided, and in about four days the snow was so much melted as to permit them to pursue their business of felling trees and burning them, and of erecting log huts for the generous reception of their friends whom they left in Hopkinton."

Some little details of preparation had already been made, which Mr. Keep could not very easily discover, and which may detain us for a little while these "few young men" are doing their first rough pioneering. A few scanty records will help us. Imagination too must have large room, for it is needed to clothe the bare facts with flesh and blood and put a beating heart within.

It was a busy time, for they must sell their farms and homes. Copied deeds in the Registry in Worcester recite how, as early as October, 1733, Samuel Wark had sold his deed of lease for three hundred pounds; how James Montgomery, in the spring of 1735, disposed of his lease; how Robert Senat had to wait until April of the year 1736 before getting rid of his farm, also for three hundred pounds; how Samuel Ferguson followed that year with his deed of sale in June, while Walter Steward parted with his holding not until October, 1737, John Steward preceding him in a like transaction by two months. It is not necessarily to be concluded that departure waited in every instance on sale. As for Hugh Hamilton, the preceding chapter has told of some of his negotiations and difficulties. It was no light thing to dispose of scores of farms in a little new town in the course of a year or two. For the most part this is a closed chapter over which the past has drawn a heavy curtain.

Apparently the whole company waited until the return of the pioneers before signing the agreements. If these youths could return with a good report from the tender mercies of the spring snow storm in the heart of the rugged hills, the autumn frosts and the oncoming winter would hardly frighten the rest. We will return to the story of Mr. Keep: "As nearly as I can ascertain the fact, the first families moved into the town in the autumn of 1735. In the following spring the residue of the company arrived. They made their settlement upon the main street which now runs through the town.* The name of the man who first came with his family into town was Hugh Black. He settled on the place where Captain Luke Osborn lived and died. On this spot stood the first house ever inhabited in this town. Here commenced the civilization of the wilderness in the immense tract of country which overspread these mountains."

It was not, however, quite the first house, not quite the absolute beginning of civilization there. For Pixley's tavern had stood on the western border of the township for a couple of years or so. But it did have more significance than the aforesaid public house, for it was the first home of what was to become a community of homes, an incorporated unit in the Commonwealth.

The invaluable narrative of Mr. Keep goes on thus,

---

* That is, not the modern village street, but North street and its southerly extension down through the pines and on to Granville, otherwise known as "The Falls road."

following upon our last citation: "The next man who came with his family was James Baird. He erected his dwelling upon the lot where the house stands which is now occupied by William Sanderson. A distance of nearly four miles from Mr. Black, the only English family in town. To us it is a matter of surprise that the two families did not settle in the same neighborhood. But it is commonly the fact that those who have the enterprise and hardihood to penetrate with families into a wilderness manifest great fondness for independence, and choose to settle where surrounding improvements may testify *my hand has done all this.* ... At the house of Hugh Black the proprietors began to number the farms which they designed to give to the first fifty families."

There is every reason to believe that neither Hugh Black, James Baird, nor any other had the opportunity to make choice of his particular location. We have the documentary statement already cited to the fact that the farm lots were apportioned to the various proprietors by lot. William H. Gibbs definitely states, "The settlers selected their farms by lot." It was the usual way of apportioning common and undivided lands whenever the division should be made. We have, furthermore, corroborative evidence in the fact that no sooner had the settlements actually been made than the settlers began bargaining, selling, swapping lots to better suit their fancy or convenience. It is altogether creditable to Mr. Keep's imagination that he should assign to the first two widely separated homesteaders a reputable reason for all but the farthest possible separation from each other. The real explanation empties out the poetry in this instance. The statement also that James Baird was the only Englishman in town will perhaps hardly pass. There were Scotch Irish Beards, and

the name is so spelled in our records. Beard drew in
the first division lot No. 33. There were a half-dozen
sixty-acre lots north of him, besides the three "Boys'
lots" on either side. He also drew No. 24, east, in the
second division. The two men who figure in Mr. Keep's
story were, however, sufficiently far apart for their
"hands" to find plenty of room. Number 33 above designated became known as "the Baird lot;" was so called
in 1785, when Warham Parks, Esq., sold a part of it
to "Samuel Crooks Gibbs, Cordwainer." In Mr. Keep's
day it was a bustling section of the town. Several stores
and taverns were thereabout, and it was the hey-day of
the stage-coach.* Abner Pease, Warham Parks, Job
Almy, Dr. Brewster, and Gibbses and Boises galore
were all bunched together almost within a stone's throw
in the stirring days of the early nineteenth century.

We have paused a little to see two families stationed
in their mountain wilderness. While we wait for the
rest, let us look a bit upon the way they came.

The Old Connecticut Path ran from Framingham directly through Hopkinton and Grafton, then bore southerly into Dudley and Woodstock. The Hopkinton pilgrims might take this path to Grafton, and thence to
Worcester. The kingdom of heaven was far from its
coming into Worcester at that time, and here they might
meet some of their own race who were earnestly plan-
ning to cast in their lot with emigrants to other Scotch
Irish towns already spoken of in this connection in these
pages. From Worcester they might go by the Bay path
to Brookfield. As has been already noted, this was wilderness, and the path was no boulevard. Or they might
not have gone by way of Worcester at all, but instead
have kept to the Old Connecticut Path which many
years later the Boston and Albany railroad adopted,

---

* v. "Taverns and Turnpikes."

"Sackett's;" or, Washington Tavern, Westfield; Exterior, and Interior, upper Front Room

in the main, as far as to Springfield. All the main paths united at Brookfield, at the Quaboag Fort. At this time Colonel Dwight was running his tavern on Foster's hill. Our people may not improbably have spent a night there, as Brookfield was an important town, and Dwight's a standard place. The seal of the town of West Brookfield bears a likeness of the old house. Our people passed over the bridge in West Brookfield just where the present one is located. The road leaves the valley of the Quaboag here and mounts the hills into Warren and West Warren, or Western, as it was then called. Thence, Palmer, known then as The Elbows, a settlement already begun, and in a few years more to receive an influx of Scotch Irish. Beyond that, North Wilbraham, by the Chicopee River, Indian Orchard and Springfield. They would have no difficulty in finding entertainment there, and next morning would cross the Connecticut by ferries. Once across, they would push on to Westfield, finding the level meadows a grateful change from the rough hills of central Massachusetts.

Both Mr. Keep and Mr. Gibbs assert that the second company stopped at Sackett's Tavern, "at the foot of the mountain," west of the village of Westfield. It is otherwise known as the Washington Tavern. Probably they all went by that way, "the mountain road" as it was later called. This old inn is still standing, a most interesting relic. In the second story is a front room extending the whole length of the building, where a large company of emigrants might throw themselves down on their wraps and baggage and rest their weary limbs. This tavern has figured more than just this once in Blandford's checkered history. From here, the distance they had to go, says Gibbs, to reach the middle of the town, is "slightly exceeding seven miles." But the worst was yet to come. "The ascent of the mountain began on the margin of the river, and continued up a rocky ledge, which, from its rude and forbidding appearance, acquired the name of 'Devil's Stairs.'" It is no exaggeration. This stream, the Westfield Little river, flows through a mighty gorge for several miles. The mountain road soon leaves it, but for some distance hugs the almost precipitous slope of the rocky mountainside at a considerable height above the river. The view is one to inspire awe. The modern road is buttressed by extensive masonry and for such a company to attack it when in a state of nature was a task worthy of remembrance. Still more amazing is the statement of Mr. Keep which seems to imply that on this trip a cart was hauled up by a team of oxen. He says: "The team which drew the first cart that entered the town was driven by Israel Gibbs, the father of deacon Ephraim Gibbs, who still survives. ... I cannot ascertain how many families came on with this team." Gibbs's statement is this: "The team which drew the first cart that entered the town, was driven by Widow Moses Carr while the men were repairing the road. It is said that the team belonged to Israel Gibbs, who settled upon the farm now owned by John Gibbs; and his son Israel was the first male child born in this town." It would have been hardly possible to haul a cart from Hopkinton, on account of the streams. Perhaps the investment of the team was made somewhere in the Connecticut valley.

The supplementary manuscript above mentioned contains this note: "It has been said that Israel Gibbs was the first man who entered the town with team and cart. I have had a conversation a few days since with Mrs. Ann Carr formerly of this town but now residing in Westfield and ninety-five years old; who is positive in her assurance that James Baird her grandfather, was

the driver of the first team. . . . Such was the difficulty
of forcing a passage up the hills and through the unsubdued forest. It was the gloomy march of Israel in
the wilderness, but without the cheering promise of rich
and fruitful Canaan beyond it. My information is, that
provision was made by the proprietors in their reserva-
tion lots for fifty settlers. But I do not learn how soon
these lots were taken up & occupied, or whether that
number of settlers availed themselves of the grant. It
is very manifest that for years afterwards there were
not so many voters in the town. So far down as 1760
the names of 35 persons are entered upon the town records as the number of lawful voters."

This valuable note certifies pretty well the matter of
the cart. As to Mr. Keep's doubt about the population,
the long continued French and Indian wars probably
depleted the population of the town seriously. But for
the initial number of families there is documentary
evidence beyond challenge.

To return once more to our clerical guide. Mr. Keep
states that this second group of migrants accomplished
two miles that first day up from Sacket's, "and encamped for the night in the woods." It was a creditable
accomplishment. "The next day they succeeded in
reaching the top of Birch Hill* and encamped again for
the night, where beasts of prey roamed, and venomous
reptiles denned. The third day they reached the log
house on the lot where John Hamilton now lives, and
found a comfortable lodgment in the bosom of friends."
In Gibbs's time it had become David Hamilton's. I
am credibly informed that this was the Hugh Hamilton
lot on Pound hill, just south of "the causeway."

"The place which is now termed the Causeway was

---

* There is a picture of this hill from the modern turnpike, below, in
"Taverns and Turnpikes," opposite p. 248.

then a thick hemlock swamp. The whole of the next day was occupied in getting through this swamp. One of the most athletic of the men, James Baird, was so fatigued that immediately after he had left the swamp, he lay down under a hemlock tree, and there retired till morning. Some state that his family of eight persons remained with him. The others of the company urged on a few rods further to the house which had been provided for them." This swamp, or causeway as it later became, is just north of Pound hill, where North street dips down to the lower level.

"In a similar manner, all the first families urged their toilsome journey to their respective places of residence. They must have commenced their settlements under many disadvantages. This is true of every new settlement. But those who now penetrate our western and southern wilderness have it in their power to command many facilities which could not be possessed by the first settlers of this town, and one obvious reason is, that the whole country was then in its infancy." Pastor Keep—"Father Keep" as he was called in Oberlin—spoke as himself interested in pioneering, for he was about to do what he could to make Ohio appear attractive to Blandford citizens. And to him the lumbering stage coach or even the "Conestoga" was what the Rolls-Royce is to-day, or the Pullman.

Once more, our earliest historian: "The north lot taken up was the one which is now partly occupied by Israel Gibbs. The whole distance between the house there and Montreal in Canada was one trackless wilderness, without a single English family. A fort had been erected in Williamstown, another at Crown Point. But they were occupied only by a few soldiers in time of war." Mr. Keep is partly in error here. Israel Gibbs drew number 35 in the first division, just two lots to the south of James Beard, where he apparently built him a house, and lived in it. He also drew number 23 west in the second division, a little farther north, but not the extreme north. This he sold to James Worke in 1743. But he retained his other lot, and did not possess himself of the northernmost property for twenty-one years. In the year 1758 Israel gathered in "three certain Lotts of Land in the first division of the Settlers part ... Commonly known by the name of the boys Lotts all adjoining and is by Estimation one Hundred acres." They were bought "of John Crooks of Mendon." The deeds seem to indicate that he bought also a fourth small lot and the northerly half of lot 27, and there he lived. There is off there the ruin of a monstrous fireplace commonly known as the Isaac Gibbs chimney. It would require a stalwart earthquake to level it. In 1778 the place is mentioned in a deed as the "Israel Gibbs Jr. house lott," and another ten years later a similar instrument identifies it as the "Israel Gibbs home-lot."

It should not be forgotten that in this company of pioneers there were boys and girls and babies in arms. It is not idle for us to pause upon this fact for a little. These small people and their mothers had to be looked after. The adventures and hardships of the rough journeyings and the new creation of home and neighborhood were fully shared. To name them all is impossible. But a few may be snatched from hungry oblivion. We at least have record of Hopkinton births and baptisms, albeit these do not tell the whole story even of those dozen or fifteen years. There were: James Beard's Susannah, eight years; David Black,—Hugh and Elizabeth's boy, fifteen; Robert and Mary Black, both babies, children of Robert and Jenny; the Blare children, Elizabeth, Mathew and Robert, seven, five and three, children of Matthew and Mary; Rachel and Elizabeth Crooks, four and two respectively, children of Samuel. William and Elizabeth Donaghy's family was growing on this wise,—Jayn, fifteen, John, eighteen, Mary, thirteen, William, eleven, Elisabeth, eight. Israel and Mary Gibbs had John, eight; Armour and Agnes Hambleton, Patrick, three, Mary, five, and Ephraim, seven. Robert and Hepsibah Sennet had Hepsibah, a little maid of two. The little brood of Walter and Grisel Stewart comprised Margaret, thirteen, William, six, and Solomon, two. William Henry, son of Robert and Jennie, was an infant of a few months. These, though by no means all, may be taken as representative.

A few small openings were quickly made in the dense forest, and doubtless some semblance to a path was cut connecting neighbors along the four-mile stretch. The sound of the axe was heard everywhere. From the little cleared and clearing door-yards the curling smoke spiraled upward in prophetic columns. A few cows and horses grazed on the scanty grass and weeds which grew under the overarching branches and browsed upon leaves and twigs. In the immediate dooryards, under the careful and anxious watch of the elders, the little children played, and the older boys and girls, old beyond their years, assumed the airs and importance of the founders of a new, miniature republic.

This new settlement, born of travail and great tribulation, soon to be organized by legislative enactment, the people fondly called—as variously spelled—"Glascow," "Glascow Town," now and then "Glasgo Lands," or "New Glasgo." Fondly they looked back to their Scottish university city where their ministers had been educated, and where their church had been fostered. As fondly also did they look forward to the church and

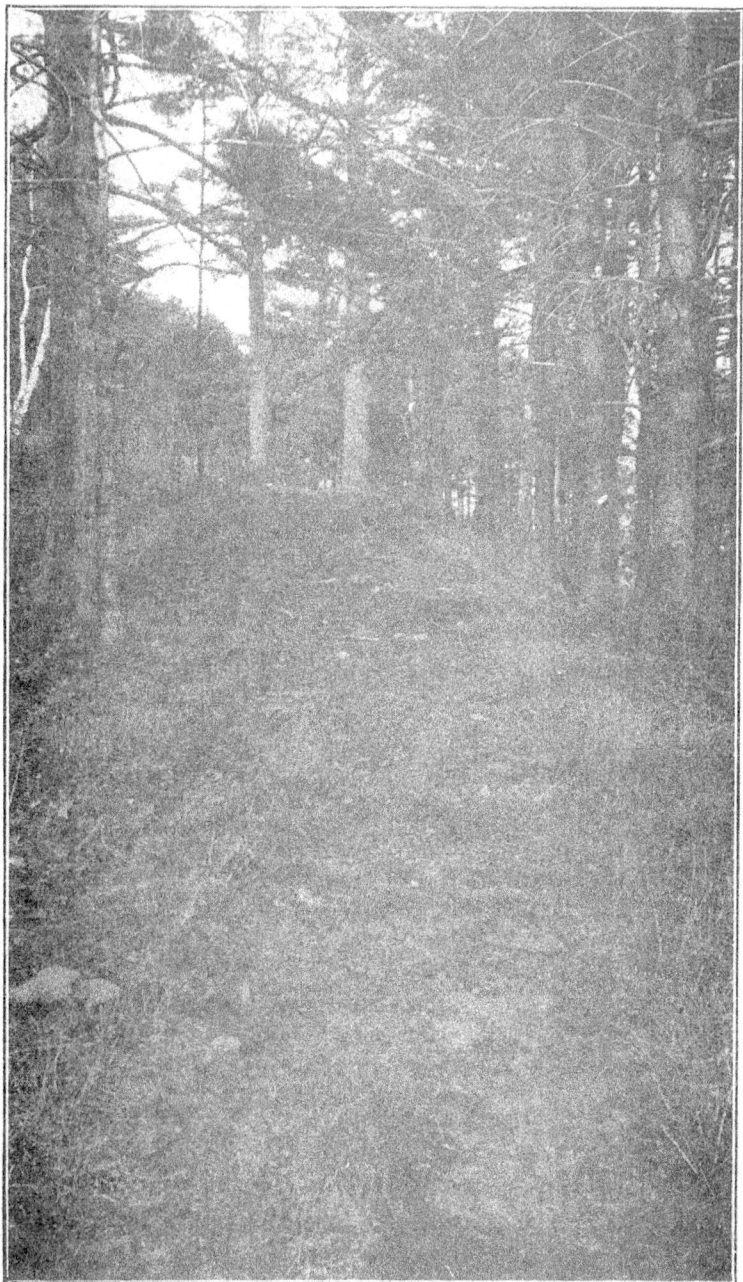

The Old Road Through the Pines: Ten-Acre Lot

the town which were to be; which, indeed, at so great a cost, had already begun to be.

Before we knock at the doors of the new homes, we must get our orientation. And to do that, we must locate the meeting-house lot. It would yet be years before any structure were raised there, and meantime we must, in the absence of records, suppose the people meeting in some one of their dwellings, as they did in Hopkinton. But the location is already fixed. As this was the high spot, ideally, sentimentally and historically, in the town's life, it is well to take account of it here and now.

In the ancient plan of the town which serves for our cartographical authority, in lot 9 of the first division, at the easterly end thereof, there is a faint square outline surmounted by a triangle, like the gable of a house. Very faintly, under a reading glass, may be discerned the legend, alongside and underneath the figure, "Meeting House." The figure rests on the dotted line, indicating that it was situate on the main highway to the eastward and westward running through the town and county.* Mr. Keep wrote, "In the original grant of the town ten acres were reserved in the centre for public uses." That is all. Mr. Gibbs wrote, "A grant was made of a ten acre lot in the center of the town, for public uses and as a general common."

There appears to have been some kind of accommodation made by way of slight change, since the deed specifies lot 8, whereas the map indicates the area as in lot 9, and probably lapping over into lot 44. Large prevision and public spirit kept it intact and immune from plunder and vandalism. Except as open spaces were required for road and school and burials, it has ever been kept as a place for worship and recreation.

---

* For detailed descriptions of this road, v. my "Taverns and Turnpikes."

For a time it was used for a parade ground. But always for the public interest. Nobody too shiftless to go to his own woodlot for his fuel was allowed to trench on this preserve.

One needs but little observation, by way of contrast, in Blandford itself, to magnify the wisdom of the fathers in setting off this sacred area. There was a time when North Blandford became a more thriving and bustling place, I have been told, than Westfield itself. This was in the tavern and stage-coach days. But North Blandford was not designed by the spirit of prophetic co-operation. Nature had provided good water privilege and spots for pleasant homes and places of business. Like Topsy, it just grew. Now, down in that snug little village, about everything is tilted up on edge. The schoolhouse is on a steep bank, apparently threatening to slide down into the street in any moment of loneliness—for how may it ever forget the past? In that village, where people have enjoyed,—and the few who are left still enjoy,—life as well as anybody in the world, there is not a school playground for the child reaching up to manhood, not a tree that the people can call their own, nothing but the open street for the boys to play ball in; and, at least a half-generation ago, nothing but curses or frowns when the inevitable ball shattered the too insistent window pane. Mowing, garden and dooryard are too valuable to give way to the universal need of that fine culture which the ten-acre lot affords those whose souls are not too pinched and mean to appreciate its generous sentiment and its invitation to a common fellowship. In the midst of much narrowness and intense sober practicality, when life's poetry too often congealed in frozen channels, it was a great thought which set apart and kept inviolate this people's Common. "In Trust"—reads the deed of allotment—"upon these Speciall Trust and Confidences nevertheless that is to Say in Trust to Permit the Proprietors of the Severall lotts of land in Glascow town aforesaid forever to hold use Occupie Possess and Enjoy the Premises as an Absolute Estate of Inheritance in fee Simple and to and for no other use Intent or Purpose what Soever Rendering therefor yearly and Every year on the Twenty Fifth day of December to the said Christopher Jacob Lawton his heirs and assigns the Rent of Sixpence lawfull money of New England if the same shall be lawfully demanded" etc. The town by solemn enactment forbade the private felling of trees upon its slopes. In 1796 it was "Voted to give Liberty to certain persons"—not to anybody, but to certain persons—"to clear off the Small Brush from among the pines to make a walk from the meeting house to the School house on the west side of the Road, the same to be done by Direction of the Select men." I fancy that then the man who should have made a common dump, whether of lumber or anything else, of this preserve, regardless of beauty and all fine sense of sentiment and public self-respect, would have been hardly dealt with, as he would have deserved.*

To gnarled and mighty pines the fathers hitched their "naggs," as they drove on horseback, the mothers be-

---

* Under the direction of the Blandford Town Improvement Committee, Dr. H. A. Gibbs, Secretary, the old burying ground has been enclosed by a substantial wall, with stone piers at each of the corners, and a wrought-iron gate hung at the front entrance, "the whole effect being one of artistic beauty, fitness and lasting solidity." "Since the wall was built the triangles in front have been graded and seeded, surrounded with shrubbery and transformed into a park upon which have been placed the General Knox marker, a Revolutionary tablet, also a tablet to the Civil War and World War veterans. Together with the old cemetery across the way it forms a most appropriate monument to the memory of our forefathers in a beautiful and picuresque setting." (Quoted from the Secretary.) This work has been done under the efficient leadership of Dr. Gibbs, with the "generous co-operation of the townspeople, city residents and descendants of old Blandford families."

hind on pillions, and little children bestowed between as best might be, and proceeded into the meeting house on a Sunday. The few remaining pines of that primeval generation, still standing in this twentieth century, scarred and broken and grim, I have been told by the late Enos W. Boise, Esq.—and he knew—have their trunks well filled with spikes and staples, as witness the luckless saw which has essayed in vain to cut into boards one or two of them blown over by a gale, or killed by lightning or by some vandal hand. Henry D. Lloyd, one-time publisher of maps, and president of the Y. M. C. A. in Mr. Beecher's Brooklyn church, Blandford-born and bred, penned some fine lines concerning these ancient monarchs of the forest.

> Five hundred years ago or more
>   These stately pines upsprung,
> Beneath the giant parent arms
>   That o'er the mountains hung.
>
> And here they grew where panther-screams
>   Outrang the wolf's wild howl,
> And Indian war-whoops echoed shrill,
>   With bruin's sullen growl.
>
> When centuries' growths had shot them up,
>   As once their fathers stood,
> Beneath decayed their ancestors—
>   They, monarchs of the wood.
>
> Then from the East some bold men came,
>   To lay the forest low;
> And many a mighty monarch groaned,—
>   They were the forest's foe.
>
> And far and wide the slaughter spread;
>   The axe, with havoc dire,
> Smote legions down: the sacrifice
>   Was finished with the fire.

But these they spared. Perchance some sage,
  By glassy spring to dine,
Had seen his own bald head, and saved
  These mountain locks of pine.

Some dame, perhaps, who heard the blast
  Come searching to her door,
Had prayed the shelter God had made
  Might waste away no more.

And here they stand, as they have stood,
  Old Blandford's beacon light,
To beckon back her children, strayed,
  To early memories bright.

Five Christian generations prayed
  Near where their verdure waves,
And four are sleeping either side;
  And still they guard their graves.

Some churchyards yield the solemn yew;
  In some the willows weep;
But Blandford's dead have these tall pines
  To direful vigils keep.

But year by year, and one by one,
  Their number dwindles fast;
Like Indian tribes they knew of yore,
  Their die of death is cast.

Long may they live! May Blandford's sons
  Ere time shall reck them down,
Plant other pines to fill their place,
  These worthies of the town.

On the bare top of this ten-acre lot, where the glaciers of the ice period scraped bare the bedrock, where
the perpetual winds blow their unresting gales from
January to January of the centuries, where, fifteen hundred feet above the tides the eye surveys the sweep of

mountain, stream and valley in three states — New Hampshire and Connecticut, with the full width of Massachusetts spread out between,—the fathers in due time planted their sanctuary. The school was to be near by, and the burying ground below. The fathers dearly loved a sightly location. Especially they loved to plant their meeting house on a height. No doubt they thought it safer, when wild Indians were about. But sentimentally they wanted it. Did they not sing, from the old rugged Bay Psalm Book, with voices as rough and rugged as the rocks that upheld them:

> Great is Jehovah, & he is
>   to be praysed greatly
> within the city of our God,
>   in his mountaine holy.
>
> 2 For situation beautifull,
>   the joy of the whole earth
>   mount Sion; the great Kings city
>   on the sides of the north.
>
> 3 God in her pallaces is knowne
>   to be a refuge high.

Osgood remarks: "On or near the common the church was built, and in not a few cases the site that was chosen for this building went far toward determining the entire layout of the town." The fathers liked a broad outlook. They wanted to see their meeting house and its spire rising toward heaven with nothing round it unless the towering pines to dispute its primacy as a physical fact. Everything conspired to make this elect spot in Glascow town one beautiful in elevation, the joy of the whole earth, on the sides of the north, the city of the great King. It was a landmark. From the eminences to the west, and in a measure, to the south also, the buildings hereabout are seen silhouetted as if on the roof of the world.

The people, amalgamated as they were by faith and strong social instincts and habits, were hardened by labor, thrift and unending conflict. They were large-boned, strong-limbed, and had "a digestive apparatus the envy of the mountain bears." * "Their women were fine specimens of their sex, about medium height, strongly built." † They were such people as would not quail before the hazards of life, and they possessed a determination and endurance which hardship might not discourage. Of the men of Coleraine, Massachusetts, contemporary with Blandford, and of the same sort, Holland in his sketch of that town says: "They were a robust set of men, six feet or more in height, with frames of corresponding size; possessing constitutions capable of great endurance, and fitted for any emergency."

* Prof. Perry.
† J. P. McLean

CHAPTER XII

As we have seen, our people were intensely religious. The conditions laid down for incorporation of the town would be far from obnoxious to their instincts and habits. It becomes impossible therefore to trace the history of the town without pursuing alongside the history of its church, or to write the history of their church without also discovering its relation to and participation in the history of the town and state.

They were given the period of seven years in which to bring their town to municipal birth. It was no sinecure: seventy-eight families of actual settlers with houses built and large lands cleared for the plow and the scythe; "a good and convenient House for the public Worship of God," and "a learned and orthodox minister." The proprietors and settlers of Glasgow occupied the full measure of time accorded to them in order to gather the resources necessary for incorporation. The task was achieved in the very nick of time.

We will continue the narrative for a little with our pastoral guide, the Rev. John Keep: "The four men who were the original proprietors of the town entered into covenant with the first settlers to set up a frame of a meeting house, and to cover the outside, and to put in glass windows. This they were to do for the people. . . . The frame of the meeting house was set up in 1740. The men who assisted in raising it were the most of them from Westfield and Suffield. The frame stood one year the sport of winds and tempests before it was covered. The boards which were used for the covering were brought from Southampton and Westfield, but the glass windows were not supplied until after the lapse of more than twelve years." How impatiently the forbears must have waited for their dear place of worship to arise, only a well informed and sympathetic imagination can at all picture. In those earliest years of opening new paths, making new homes of logs chopped down in their very door-yards, clearing the stubborn primeval forest for mowing and planting, creating a town of no mean proportions, these separated people experienced the full measure of the lot of lonely mountaineers. Young men and maids loved and married, children were born to look out upon a wild, uncouth wilderness pierced by a few narrow lines of open sky through lanes of dark forests. It was a day's journey to the nearest physician, and any minister was equally distant. Birth, sickness, death were unattended except by ministrations of kinship and neighborly help, or perchance by professional assistance only after cruel and anxious waiting.

At last all seemed to be in readiness, and a petition was duly forwarded to the provincial legislature asking for incorporation. This is the Enabling Act.*

"A Petition of the Inhabitants of the Lands called the Suffield Equivalent Lands, shewing that they have fulfilled the Conditions of their Grant, and have a number of Families settled there sufficient for a Township; and therefore Praying that they may be erected into a Township.

"Read and

"*Ordered* that the Prayer of the Peti*n* be granted and the Peti*rs* are allowed and Impowered to bring in a Bill accordingly.

(Passed April 3, 1741)"

A footnote adds, "The town was called 'Blandford'."

* Provincial Laws, Chapter 178, page 759.

Seven days later, the Act of Incorporation followed:

"Whereas it hath been represented to this Court by the Inhabitants of Suffield equivalent lands, commonly called Glasgow, in the county of Hampshire, that they labor under great difficulties by reason of their not being incorporated into a township,—

"Be it enacted by His Excellency the Governor, Council and Representatives in General Court assembled, and by the authority of the same,

"(Sect. 1.) That the lands aforesaid be and hereby are erected into a separate and distinct township by the name of Blandford; the bounds whereof are as followeth:" (whereupon follows the same description as of Suffield Equivalent Lands).

"(Sect. 2.) And that the inhabitants of the land aforesaid are hereby vested with all the powers, privileges and immunities which the inhabitants of other towns are or by law ought to be vested with. (Passed and published April 10, 1741.)"

Pastor Keep says, in his historical sermon: "The inhabitants of the city of Glasgow in Scotland sent word to the people of this town, that if they would continue its then present name, they would give the town a bell. It was the design of the people that they should bear the name of Glasgow, and they made their petition accordingly. But Shirley, who had been late appointed governor of the province, had just arrived from England in the ship Blandford. In honor of the ship he chose to have the new town, which applied for an act of incorporation, to bear its name. Hence the name of Blandford instead of Glasgow was given to the town. But this application would not have been made, it is supposed, at the time it was, had not the survey of General Newbury embraced a mile of more importance than was originally embraced in it. Hence by the unexpected gain of a mile, the people lost their expected bell."

Governor Belcher had come over in a ship bearing the name of Blandford, in the year 1730. It was a man-of-war, and the commander of the vessel, George Prothroe, was presented, by vote of the General Court, with two hundred pounds as "a Gratification for his Respectful Treatment of his Excellency the Governor." Perhaps Shirley came in the same vessel, though I have not happened to find any official confirmation of the above cited tradition. A note in one of the volumes of the Proceedings of the Massachusetts Historical Society, referring without comment to Holland's note on the incident, makes the pronouncement that the name "was undoubtedly derived from the title of Marquess of Blandford, the second of the honors belonging to the Duke of Marlborough. In 1741 the bearer of the title was Charles Spencer, third Earl of Sunderland, who was son of Anne, second daughter of the great Duke of Marlborough. His cousin William, Earl of Godolphin, son of the eldest daughter, died S. P. in 1731; and in 1733, on the death of the mother, Spencer succeeded to the dukedom also." Amen!

Let him who cares to bedeck his poor, shrivelled soul with such flummeries meekly bow down and adore. But to the sympathetic student of the men and women who were making this church and town of old Hampshire's first line of lofty hills it would seem that if a ship's name were to be taken for the name of the town then building, it might have been after the brave bark that carried the chief of them; or if for a duke or a lord, then for some old Scottish laird or other worthy who had really done something for this company, or was held in endearment by them who never toadied to any dignitary bearing—to them—vacant and meaningless though high-sounding titles.

It was a pity to have lost the bell, for these poor folk had to wait pitifully long before they could see the way to buy one. But in sooth they lost more than their promised bell. As so often is the case when someone does wrong, it is the innocent who have to take the penalty. This christening of the town, "Blandford," was a wretched and melancholy piece of flunkeyism on the part of a Governor too recently come from England to be blessed with that artistic sense of propriety—let alone any genial sympathy with the people—which the occasion demanded. These men of Glasgow Lands were not immaculate, indeed. But whatever they were, they were not snobs. It is a thousand pities that the dear old name, theirs by right of inheritance and by fond choice of a people who always knew their mind if they knew anything at all, could not have stayed; a thousand pities that when Independence crowned the history of State and Nation, to which these Scotch Irish stalwarts contributed their full share of devotion, they could not have dealt with a readier government which would have given them back the name of their choice. Over and over again, in the official lists of Massachusetts Soldiers and Sailors of the Revolution, is the residence of some soldier entered as "Glasgow." So tenderly and persistently, for more than a generation, did they cling to the endearing name. We will, for them, lay down our emblems of devotion at no Baal's shrine. Glasgow was the university town of their ordained sons. Concerning this city they could fondly say, "This one and that one was born in her." Not alone from martial rosters, but from the sacred transfers of homesteads and farms, transfers which, significantly, are called "deeds," the name of "Glasgow" echoes and re-echoes down through the years, a reminiscence wafted back like spicy breezes from the pine groves of these hilltops, infallible witness that it was the familiar spoken name in the talk of the fireside.

"The name that dwells on every tongue
No minstrel needs."

Following the Enabling Act, after one week again the voice of the Provincial Government spoke*: "*Ordered that Robert Huston one of the Principal Inhabitants of the new Township called Blandford in the County of Hampshire be and is hereby Impowered and directed as soon as may be to notifye and warn the Inhabitants of the said Township to assemble and convene in some convenient publick place in said Town to make choice of a Town Clerk and other Town Officers to stand untill the Anniversary Meeting in March next. (Passed April 17, 1741)." I have found no record of this meeting.

The first regular election of record is of date, March 21, 1742-3. Not alone on account of the persons chosen to various town duties, but also as indicating something of local interests, the full list is herewith transcribed: Moderator, David Boies; town clerk, James Hassard; selectmen, David Boies, Robert Cook, 2nd, James Hassard, John Stewart, John Young†; treasurer, John Hamilton; constable for the south end, William Pro-

---

* Vol. 2, Chap. 195.

† The Youngs having early established themselves in this town, and early rising into prominence there, it will not be out of place to insert here, from William Lincoln's History of Worcester, a double inscription on one common gravestone standing in the old burial place in Worcester:

Here lies interred the remains of John Young, who was born in the isle of Bert, near Londonderry in the kingdom of Ireland He departed this life, June 30, 1730, aged 107 years.	Here lies interred the remains of David Young, who was born in the parish of Tahbeyn, county of Donegal and kingdom of Ireland. He departed this life, December 26, aged 94 years.

The aged son and the more aged father
Beneath (these) stones, Their mould'ring bones
Here rest together.

vence; for the north end, Walter Stewart; assessors, James Hassard, John Young, David Boies; Surveyors of highways (very important in those early days): (1) "for the two west streets in the south end," James McClintock; (2) "from the Meeting house Eastward in the Main road, William Knox," (3) "in the north end," Robert Young and William Donaghy. Tithing man, Adam Knox; "hoge Constabol for the North end," Samuel Carnahan; "for the South End," John Wells; "fence vewers this yeare," Mathew Blair and Robert Henry. —"from the Meeting house Eastward in the Main road" can hardly be any other than the little artery of travel east and west across the province. It was becoming more and more of a province-wide thoroughfare, as new towns to the westward of Blandford were rapidly developing. Already it is called "the Main road." In this town election three men are chosen office-bearers whose names were not in the Lawton contract nor in the original list of settlers.

Five town meetings were held in 1742. Their moderators were, in order, Robert Cook, David Boys, William Knox and John Huston (twice). Sixty pounds were appropriated for repairing roads, and the wages were to be six shillings per day, "old tenor." At this same meeting it was ordered that "the Inhabitenes" should meet at the burying place on Sept. 16, at eight o'clock in the forenoon, "to Clear the Buring place." A fine of six shillings was imposed upon every absentee.

We now once more place ourselves, in part, under the guidance of Mr. Keep for a condensed story of the stormy experiences of the town in providing themselves with the regular ordinances of the gospel:

"Till a little previous to Mr. Badger's ordination, all the most important theological concerns of the people were conducted in town meetings. There is no church

TWO GATES HUNG FROM CROTCHED TREE STUBS:
BARNYARD GATE; POUND GATE

record of any certain date until 1781, more than forty years after the town was settled. Between this and 1787, when Mr. Badger received his call, only a few things were noted: nor is there any account even of his ordination or dismission, and only a very few things are mentioned which occurred while he was a minister. My dependence, therefore, has been placed upon very important town records, and upon verbal testimony of persons now living, who have been conversant in some of the transactions I shall mention.

"This church was organized in Hopkinton, by the aid of Rev. Mr. Prince of Boston, in the presbyterian form. When the settlers had determined upon a remove to this town it was judiciously resolved that all who were professors of religion should be formed into a private church. I regret that I cannot state the number of the members at its organization. It must, however, have been small. Most of the members had emigrated from Scotland, and were Irish Independents and Scotch Presbyterians.* In doctrine they harmonized. And as the Irish Independents had no form of government to which they were especially attached, they all readily united in the presbyterian form. John Huston, John Steward and David Boies were the first deacons or elders. The presbyterian mode of government was continued, though maintained very imperfectly for the most part, till the year 1801. In the month of September of this year, the church finding it inconvenient to practice according to the presbyterian form of government, adopted a new and separate form of government. This constitution is strictly congregational, and is given at length in a fair hand, on the records of the church. It was transcribed

---

* I wish I knew Mr. Keep's authority for his statement about "Irish Independents." If there were indeed any at all, they must have been an excessively minute proportion of the whole.

by Mr. Gordon Johnson, who was then preaching in town. Rev. Timothy M. Cooley was moderator of the church when this change took place. John Caldwell was the first person who preached in town, of whom I can find any account. He preached in town in the year 1741. Some time in the course of that year he was invited to accept of the pastoral care of the church and people. While Mr. Caldwell was making his preparation for an answer, Rev. John Harvey was employed as a preacher. He was requested to go to Worcester to meet the presbytery, and to urge for an answer to the call they had given Mr. Caldwell.

"Some of you need to be informed that in the presbyterian form of government, when a parish wish the person who is preaching to them to settle, they must lay their invitation before the presbytery, and this body is to decide whether the candidate shall answer in the affirmative or negative."

Embarrassed as the people were by extreme poverty, they appealed to "the Gentlemen," their proprietors, "to see what help they will give the town to mentain the gospil without going to Cort." The town's committee to look after these matters were David Boies, Israel Gibbs and James Hassard, and they were directed to retain the services of an attorney, "Squair Jugason." They further appealed to James Wark, who had returned to Hopkinton, to draw up their "Artickels," presumably the articles of this petition. As though this were not trouble enough, some shadow rested upon the character of their candidate, and the presbytery were taking time for deliberate judgment. The day for ordination was finally set for the second Tuesday in November.

But before that day arrived much happened. Matthew Province was gone as a second delegate, on a thirteen days' errand to the presbytery, at an expense of ten shillings a day for his time. While he tarried the fire burned, and a solemn protest, spread upon the town records, was made against the whole movement by this strong array of citizens: "David Boies, John Young, John Steward, Armor Hamelton, John Boys, William Steward, Thomas Clintock, James Gomery, James Clintock, John Wells, William Boys, James Steward, William Donasey, James Freeland, Joseph Freeland." One town meeting followed another. A proposal to refer the difficulties to the decision of the neighboring ministers was rejected. The attempt was made to gain the consent of Caldwell to relinquish the privileges of first minister in the event anything should be made out against his character, but in vain.

Winter passed, and spring and summer. In the interim John Harvey appears to have acted as pulpit supply more or less. In September, 1743, "the autumn after the trial," again quoting Mr. Keep, the presbytery was asked to "send on a preacher for any time, less or more, and anybody except Mr. John Caldwell. We may conclude, therefore, that his character and principles were deficient, and that the attachment of his friends had abated. . . . The same year Mr. Dunlap was employed a short time as a preacher. He was followed by Mr. Morrison. In their disappointment respecting Mr. Caldwell, and finding no general union, either in Mr. Morrison or Mr. Dunlap, at a meeting in October they presented a petition to the presbytery for permission to send to Ireland for a minister. They still cherished a tender remembrance of the country they had left, and imagined that if a preacher who had been bred in their habits, could be obtained, they should be united and happy. Their request was granted."

We will pause a bit to get more acquainted with the

Rev. John Harvey. He had been born in Ireland, probably of Scotch parentage, and was a university graduate. After teaching school in Londonderry, New Hampshire, he went to The Elbows, now Palmer. The Hampshire Association gave him a quasi-recommendation, containing the signature of Jonathan Edwards, to the effect that nothing was known against the man. By 1738 he had already confessed drunkenness, answering a charge by the grand jury, and he was repeatedly charged by his people with "other gross immoralities." Dissension over him (continues Mr. Keep) went by appeal to the General Court, which pronounced him innocent. Then he went to Peterboro for a time, and later came to Blandford, where, the historian of Palmer says, he bought a farm. The same historian says that Harvey spent the remainder of his days in Blandford.

The messenger who was sent abroad to find a pastor "returned with a man whose name was McNeil. But the reception of Mr. McNeil did not correspond with his expectations. He had been here but a short time before evil reports respecting him were circulated, and countenanced by the people. The good man's spirits were broken down and he left the town in disgust.

"The next year the committee to supply the pulpit obtained the return of Mr. Harvey, and by appointment of the town, he was to preach at the fort on some day of the week, besides the usual services of the Sabbath. Mr. Harvey was at no time considered as a candidate for settlement, and frequent consultations were held by the committee to devise the best method for surmounting the obstacles which now seemed to meet them at every step they took toward the settlement of a minister. The town directed their committee to employ no preacher on a longer trial than six weeks. This vote evinces a very disturbed state of the public feelings at that time.

"In this year some questions arose concerning the doctrines of the gospel, and the town voted to adhere to the doctrines of the Church of Scotland, as contained in the Confession of Faith, the longer and shorter catechism.

"Mr. Munson was their next candidate. The Rev. William McClenathan followed Mr. Munson. He was a man of respectable talents, and thought to possess unusual gifts as a preacher, but somewhat unhappy in his temper. In July 1744 the people were happily united in giving him a call to settle, with the offer of ninety-three dollars salary and ninety-three dollars settlement. The first minister was also entitled to one sixty-acre lot, to become his own on the day of his ordination. James Hazzard was sent to Boston to present the call to the presbytery. In September he was installed, and in December the town transported his goods from Boston. The next year every man in town over twenty-one years was required to work one day for the minister in getting his wood and assist in repairing his house."

The remainder of this story will fall into another chapter.

If it was found toilsome in the wild forest of these rock-ribbed hills to build homes, it was even more difficult to found a church. In all this period "Massachusetts was kept in a miserable state of indigence and discomfort." * This general condition would be intensified where racking toil was unremitting, bare existence obtained only by intense battling against nature, and nerves strained almost to the breaking. Moreover, the century-long inheritances of this people were chapters of bitter, sometimes bloody, strife. Princes, lords and

---

* Palfrey.

prelates had persisted in goading these liberty-loving souls to desperation. On this western soil they were thrust into thorny hedges of prejudice which involved both race and creed. Once and again exiles for conscience' sake, huddled together as sheep torn by wolves fondly believed to be shepherds, destitute, afflicted, tormented, they still wrought on, and in the midst of all, in spite of all, in hope of a better day, in pledge of allegiance to the one institution through whose faith and ministry they firmly believed the better day must come, they erected their temple, set up their altar, and diligently sought for a true minister who should be herald of the gospel of peace. Believing, blundering, praying, battling, holding on, like the scarred and storm-swept pines of their sacred enclosure, they gathered there, they stood, they called:

"VOX CLAMANTIS IN DESERTO!"

CHAPTER XIII
THE STORY OF THE HOME LOTS

NOTE: This chapter will over-run the chronological limitations of most of the chapters in this book. It seems better so, in order to preserve unity of treatment. This unity, however, will be necessarily broken by reason of the fact that "The Taverns and Turnpikes of Blandford, 1733 to 1833" has already in part covered the subject matter with a good deal of detail. I must per force refer my readers to the book just named, as the limitations of this present writing will not allow so considerable repetition. References will be given below,—to chapters, in Roman letters; to pages, in Arabic numerals, and all included in brackets. The initials "TT" stand for the book just named.

Our procedure in this chapter will be, to begin with Hugh Black's first division lot, No. 1, and proceed northward along the first division street, at the same time taking into account the second division lots as these were coupled with their respective holders in turn. We will glean what little we may, as we go along, of the pioneers and their doings—and it will be but little for the most part—lingering in each lot long enough to jot down some of the historic landmarks of the same for a generation or two following.

From the ten-acre lot southward the road bears away a little to the westward from the midrib of the first division, in order to keep on the general level of the landscape, which is broken down along that midrib by the deepening depression through which the upper waters of the Falls brook run. It may also be well to observe that, on the easterly side of this first division, and also overlooking this same valley, there is another road, approximately parallel to the one just mentioned, traversing the westerly ends of the first division lots from 45 to 52 inclusive. Settlers on both sides of the first division to the southward of the ten-acre lot thus had the opportunity to choose on which side of the road, in either case, they would build.

We will pause to note some significant terms of the title deeds to the lands in the New Glasgow, or Blandford. These included "the Trees Woods Waters Mines Quarries Rights Priviliges Profits Emoluments Heridataments and Appurtenances there unto belonging and the Reversion and Reversions Remainder and Remainders thereof," etc. Most of the home-lot deeds bore date of March 30, 1737. Very few varied a day or two, or a few days, from this.

Lots 1, and 15 East. We have already located Hugh Black on the first lot. It remained in the family twenty-five years. April 23, 1762, "David Black, Gentleman," otherwise then known as "Lieutenant," sold the same to William Carnachan, then living "in ye Green Woods on Sheffield Road," "with House and building standing thereon." This gentleman sold it the same year to Robert Montgomery, who in turn sold it to "Captain Luke Osborn" in 1776. Then the lot began to be broken up into sections, but the Osborns continued there down to my own ministry in Blandford, 1901-1911. The buildings were near the old soapstone quarry. Black also drew lot 15 east in the second division. That lot passed on to David, then Glass Cochran bought it in 1745. This would be handy for Cochran, as near his own people, by the mill pond above. Black, like most of the company, was a "husbandman."

Lots 52, and 6 East. Opposing 1 is lot 52, assigned to Robert Cook, who was a blacksmith. It is hardly believable that he would not soon have set up a smithy's forge, for aside from the necessary shoeing of horses and oxen, there would be immediate call for such universal home-made implements as barn tools, nails, hinges, door-latches, etc., cranes, andirons, pot-hooks and trammels and numberless like things.

Cook's other lot was 6 east, second division. On this there was a small mill privilege, as Gibbs brook with its tributaries runs through the ravine at the eastern end of this and neighboring lots. The early nineteenth century saw a good deal of business transacted hereabout. A good deal of drinking also was done, as a consequence of which local innholders got their unyielding grip on the estates, foreclosing one property after another. These men reached out long arms towards every thirsty throat. In this lot there was "a little brook that takes its rise near the barn." The business was done lower down. John Hastings came upon the scene in the early nineteenth century, and by and by the Rev. Horace L., [228] whose genius and faith helped Blandford to a finer reputation and tradition.

Robert Cooke (so spelled in the inventory) lived until 1749. The heirs agreed to the settlement of his estate on this wise. Two brothers had, between them, the 300 acres in farm lot 19. Apparently one, Robert Hazard, was brother in law, the other being Cornelius [282]. The son, Samuel, had the homestead including the lot, so there was a house on the first division lot, for the other lot went to Mary, a daughter, who had married Joseph Pettingal. Jane, another daughter, wife of James Hazzard, [133, 244] had the second division lot, and 10 acres on the side of farm lot 19. Here is insight into the home circle living in and swarming from this Robert Cooke home in lot 52 in these early days.

On this lot, in 1750, John McKinstree, of Suffield, Ct., settled [224ff.]. Seven years later came James and Samuel Loughhead (Lloyd), from Hartford [195, 204]. Two classic Blandford names thus enter, of the second generation of settlers. A deed mentions that there were "buildings and fences," a fence being another mark of advance in comfort and self respect. Later, Robert

Henry came, [26n, 85f., 104] who by and by sold to "Elisha Parks Esq.," from Westfield [24n., 138]—another new name which did not soon disappear. There was a "house and barn" there then—1771—and Robert Henry was living there, the homestead being bounded "West on the Town street." It would seem to indicate that the lot had been extended westward into the Osborne lot, as the town street was there, and the Osborne place was on the other side of the street. On the family lot, 6 east, before the Hastingses came, appeared James Campbell. The Campbells, always interested in mills, became long resident, though not on this lot. They will command attention later.

Lots 2, and 7 West. Back on our town street, lot 2 was held by Thomas Reed, elder of the church. He also had 7 west in the other division. In 1761, James Montgomery [177, 180ff.] had the first division lot, "with buildings and improvements," indicating that progressive operations had gone on from the beginning. Montgomery lived there, and William [48] after him. By the beginning of the next century, Jacob [271] and James Blair took possession of the west part, where the house was, while a blacksmith by the name of King established himself east of the road, to be followed by Amos M. Collins, of Hartford [173, 246].

By 1744, Reed parted from his second division lot, 7 west, to William Blair. Through this lot ran the road to Matthew Blair's [103ff., 128, 142, 163, 271] saw mill, on Gibbs brook. This road left the town street between lots 45 and 46, practically the present Russell road. Wherever there was water power in the early years, there look for Blairs [105, 129, 166, 170, 184, 231, 271]. Following William, in this lot—7 west—were, in order, Robert, Jr., Jacob and James, until the first quarter of the nineteenth century had passed into history. "Jacob Blair's homestead" is definitely located as in the northwest corner of the lot, on or near the late Deacon Hinsdale homestead. The northernmost boundary of the Reed first division lot, number 2, was on "the road to the mill," down in Smoky hollow, on Peebles brook.

Lots 51, and 27 East. Number 51, opposite 2, was the investment of Benjamin Wood, and along with it went 27 east. The two lots were about as far apart as they could possibly be—considerably farther than the homesteads of Hugh Black and James Beard, whose separation so impressed the Rev. John Keep. The second division lot was promptly disposed of. It was taken up by William Boies [v. TT index] in 1752, and held by him for many years. Benjamin Wood's first division lot he sold in 1738. It would naturally be inferred that he put up the log house and proceeded with the clearings as required, then abandoned his interest. He sold it to James Hazard. Following that, this lot shared similar transitions of ownership as the lot to the south (52), and by the same men, until 1777.

Lots 3, and 7 East. James MacCletick, or MacClintock, drew the two lots, 3 and 7 east. On the first named he built his house and lived in it, passing both his lots on to his son, Thomas. Something after the middle of the century, the first division lot passed into the hands of the Campbells, mill men, and the second came into the possession of Captain John Ferguson, [143] who held on to it until his death. This lot corresponds nearly or very nearly with the modern Haley farms on the road to Russell.

Lots 50, and 26 East. Lot 50, opposite 3, first division, and 26 east in the other division, were taken up by Samuel Crooks. Not quite as far apart, but nearly, as Benjamin Wood's two lots. But unlike the latter, the

Crooks family held on to both their separated possessions until well toward the end of the century. The sale
by "Samuel Crook" to "William Crooks" [221] —they
recked not of spelling—in 1767 does not read as though
this family were letting go of their holding: "a Homelot
(viz., 50, first div.) with a Mansion House Barn Malt
House Standing thereon," about 103 acres for 200
pounds, evidently some considerable new land having
been gathered in. The year previous he had sold his
other lot to John. Samuel died in 1776, at eighty-seven.
The Crookses married extensively into other local families. Their early history is thoroughly interwoven with
the early history of the town.

Lots 4, and 17 East. Lot No. 4 fell to Samuel Taggart,
along with No. 17 east, second division. This latter is
just south of Cochran, or Second Division, pond, on the
opposite side of the road. On which of the two lots he
had his home I am unable to say. Perhaps both were
occupied. Nathaniel [293ff.] took possession of both
lots in 1753; but the next year Samuel and Nathaniel
sold the first division lot to William Proven [177] and
the Provens sold to Dr. King [176, 181] in 1781. Following Dr. King came Thomas Herrick, well on in the
nineteenth century. The Taggarts probably moved to
their second division lot, close to mill and six corners.
In 1765 the Rev. James Morton [v. TT index] bought
the place on his dismission from his ministry, and the
Taggarts sought another location. Nathaniel was a
blacksmith, then an innholder.

Lots 49, and 21 West. To William Knox, weaver, [v.
TT Index] went possession of lots 49 and 21 west.
Blandford has had members of this historic and re-
sourceful family through all the days of its history.
Much might be written of them. On this lot 49 William
built at once, and in due time established himself in

business there. One of the deeds mentions his "dwelling house and shop." The west end of the lot underwent some changes in ownership in the early years, but the family interest in some part of the lot persisted through the decades. It passed to (Deacon) John, then to William, then John, then Elijah. [For all the Knoxes, v. TT Index]. The east end of the lot was on or very near to the western thoroughfare, and I infer that the family homestead was there. It was also close to other properties yet to be indicated under the caption "2 W." In recent years this has been in the ownership of the late E. W. Bennett, and later of S. W. Peebles.

William Knox's other lot was 21 west. His son, William, took possession in 1742. This son, and William Provin made some exchanges of property in or near the Knox lots in both divisions, as their various estates adjoined one another. The Knox interest in this second division property passed along through William, Jr., James and David until close to the end of the century, and I know not how much farther. In 1749 William Knox was "Ensign," also "Gentleman," one a military honor, the other civil; if unofficial, yet socially significant. The Knoxes found Blandford climate and society congenial. Like so many other families of Blandford history, these pages will have to carry some seeming negligence concerning them. As to property holdings, this numerous family had, at or near the "noarth end," foothold at one time or another, of 19, 20, 21, 22, 24, and 25, in second division west, also 21 east; and, near by, in the first division, of a part or the whole of 23, 24, 25, 29 and 30, besides those down on the Albany road already indicated.

Lots 8, and 45, both of first division. The old burying ground was located in lots 8 and 45, at the adjoining ends. We have already progressed to lots 5 and 48, some of which is in the very heart of "the new village" [VI.]. Even in the earliest days, before town incorporation, the infant thoroughfare running diagonally athwart the settling lots up to the meeting house lot, then down the hill between lots 8 and 9, and on to the westward, must have been visioned by the far-sighted as containing large possibilities for future business.

Lots 5, and 17 West. The first to settle in lot 5 was Cornelius Anderson. By 1761 he was living in Windsor, Connecticut, and sold the lot to William Provin. Somebody, at some time or other, set out an orchard here— where tavern business began in right good earnest. Over and over again, in the passing of deeds, this "little orchard" figures. When James Nimock, in 1785, bought here of James Provin, the "small orchard" [172, 226ff.] was excepted. It was "a little orchard . . . called the South orchard." It was "between the road and the brook," and contained "14 apple trees" in 1772, when it fell into the possession of "Benjamin Conners, Mill Wright, of Murrayfield." The Ashmuns, and Watermans, and Dr. King, and John Watson, and Benjamin Scott, and Moses A. Bunnell, and Russell Atwater, and Reuben Frary, all [TT *passim*] had their hands at one time or another on this desirable lot, in late years known as the Herrick place.

Anderson's second division lot was 17 west, a desirable location for the time. The second division pond was just north of the north end of this lot. Anderson sold it in 1765 to Samuel and Paul Steward. Then, in 1777, Paul sold his share to Joseph Frary, "including house, barn, orchard, fences, Meadows, pastures, Ploughing fields, woods, trees, brush, underbrush, nothing excepted but the nursery Apple trees." Frary calls it "my late home farm." We might pursue the interesting history of this lot, were it not that we are after germinal matters, prophecies, forces in their incipiency, all of which make a society. And we are getting much. At least, I know that the thoughtful are. We have so little contemporary record to guide us, about our only resource is to jump ahead a little, then creep back. This lot, 17 east, fell into possession of the Rev. James Morton, along with lot 16 adjoining, in 1765. That reverend gentleman had a sharp lookout for "orchards"!

Lots 48, and 5 East. We can soon dismiss Daniel How, who took up lot 48 of the first division and 5 east of the second division. He sold his first division lot the very year he got his original deed, and that lot passed into the thick of the story of town life. Rev. William McClenachan got in there in 1744. Rev. Joseph Badger—a very different and most noted "divine" and Ohio pioneer, lived there near the end of the century. Timothy Hatch had his hat shop there, when the road became known as "the Albany road," etc., etc. The other lot, 5 east, Anderson also sold, though not quite so early. Here were the mill and mill yard of John Hastings. The Bodurthas got in there, and—of course, in those days, the tavern men got a strangle hold. All this may have been a real estate venture on the part of How. Or it may have been a real interest to further the settlement, but short of wanting to abide long—a kind of adventuring.

Lots 6, and 20 West. James Provin—variously spelled —Province et al. [181] settled lot 6 in the first division. It stayed in the family a full half-century. Here is where they had their home. Their second division lot was 20 west, a couple of lots north of the pond lot over there. By 1742 it was sold to William Knox, Jr. More of this anon. The Provins appear to have done their part.

Lots 47, and 12 West. James Hambleton had lot 27, but left it soon, we trust for the golden streets. William Forbes, of Worcester, October 31, 1738, sold to John Huston, "sixty acres in first division in Glasgow No. 47

laid out to James Hamilton Late of Worcester deceased, and by sd Hamilton bought of Christopher Jacob Lawton." It went for forty pounds. This lot falls right in the center of the modern village and shares its history [V, VI, etc.]. James's other lot was 12 west. That also soon passed out of the hands of the Hambletons. Rev. James Morton had it awhile. At that time it was known as "the Forbush lot."

Lots 7, and 13 East. Armour Hambleton next, at No. 7 [178]. We are now just a little to one side of the busiest part of modern Blandford, but in the very thick of Blandford of the Indian wars. Both Armour and his widow, Agnes, ran a tavern here. His second division lot was No. 13 east. It continued among the Hamiltons for a generation or so, then passed to the Cochrans, and I know not to whom else. I can tell nothing of interest of this lot, except that it holds together still. Nobody lives there.

Lots 46, and 22 West. Lot 46 in the first division was taken up by Adam Knox [69, 71], who also drew lot 22 west, in the second division. John Knox, who had a lot next but one above the last named, bought 22 west of Adam in 1755. Then it passed to John Beard and became known as "John Beard's Homelot." So we may know there was a residence there, though of how early a date is not revealed. Adam's first division lot was in the very heart of the modern village.

Lots 45, and 25 West. The last remark is true also of lot 45, just north of Adam Knox. It went to William Anderson, of whom we know too little. It was very soon in other hands; sooner than his lot, 25 west, in the other division, where perhaps he lived. This lot went to Matthew Blair, the younger, in 1783, by sale from a considerable group of Anderson heirs.

Lots 8, and 13 West. No. 8 went to the minister, the

first to occupy it being Rev. William McClenachan, in 1745 [11]. Rev. James Morton succeeded to it in 1748. These were lively times in all respects [I, II, III, IV, V, VI]. McClenachan dabbled in the Pixley tavern property even before his settlement as minister, and held on to it for some years. Much is to be written of Rev. James Morton, whose career is woven into the warp and woof of early Blandford. After him this lot, so centrally located, right on the main street and the "Road to Tunak," just opposite the burying ground, passed into the hands of the tavern and business men of the town: Ashmun, Bradley, Sage, Atwater, Watson, Scott, etc., and became familiarly known as "The Pickle Lot."

We are about to enter, in our pioneering dooryard calls, upon a whole string of lots, on both sides of the street, and even beyond, prophetic of tavern and turnpike activities, [all very fully told in TT]. The first building ever erected in the township was a tavern; the first minister dabbled in the business; taverners became pillars of the church; town meetings adjourned to the tavern; the tavern built up the town—and almost ruined it too. And at last, with opened eyes, the church cast it out.

The other ministerial lot was No. 13 west. Gibbs brook cuts through this lot something like three-quarters of a mile below the pond. The lot became Rev. Mr. Morton's "home farm."

Lots 9, and 21 East. In entering the next lot, 9, along the street, we begin to climb meeting-house hill, where even yet is left a clump of the ancient towering pines. This lot was drawn by William Henry, who sold it the very next year to John Wells. But Robert Henry had it in 1757, selling it eleven years later to John Watson, who established a tannery there. This has been one of the most historic places, and John Watson was one of the most noted men, in Blandford history. It is too long a story to detain us now. The other lot of William Henry was 21 east, second division, in the old "Number nine" school district, on the upper reaches of Black brook. He kept this lot five years, and then sold it to Samuel Cochran. From him it passed to his widow, then living in Boston, and to James, perhaps a son, certainly administrator, whose business was that of "Wharfinger." In 1766, it was bought by "William Knox, Gentleman," "paying the yearly rental." This lot adjoined, end to end, William's original lot.

Lots 45 and 44, first division, and 25 West. The two first division lots, 45 and 44, together comprise the upper section of the modern village street and the lower end of North street. Opposite the west end of 44 stands the meeting house, while the old burying ground cuts off the western end of 45. The corner tavern of long and checkered history, some of the stores, and an important group of men who did much to make the town, all found or made this a focus of religious, social and business life. William Anderson stayed on his lot, 45, first division, only until the year of town incorporation. He appears to have settled on his second division lot, in 25 west. William Knox bought this in 1746, and it became a part of the great block of Knox possessions in this part of town.

Lots 44, and 11 East. Lot 44 in division one was Robert Huston's. He built his house there and lived in it nearly twenty years, at the end of which period Elisha Parks took it over. Then Hewitt Root bought it, when it was mentioned in the deed that there was a "Mansion House & Barn" there. Root was an innholder too. Then came the Peases, Dewey, Justus Ashmun, etc. Huston's other lot, 11 east, seems to have afforded him little interest. He parted with it in 1746, to Jonathan

Dwight, a Boston innholder. Then it passed to Nathaniel Dwight, "Gentleman," in 1750, and two years later still, to William Babcock, of Milton, another innholder. Some of these land sales are flitting illustrations of the contacts which our hilltop forbears had with the world abroad.

Lots 43, and 18 West. The same coterie of men that handled affairs in lot 44, also in due time moved into lot 43, which was John Huston's. Robert Huston bought it first, in 1742, and held it until 1756. Then entered the rest of the procession. The names of Noble, Tuttle and Shurtleff are to be added to the train of the others in this lot. The end which abuts on the street has long since been the display ground of the Union Agricultural Society. John Huston's second division lot was 18 west, containing at its easterly end the second division pond. He sold that lot to Andrew Graham in 1741, then Duncan Graham had it, and in 1745 it was bought by William Mitchel, [159, 284, 293] who for a long time ran the mill, the lot being known as the "William Mitchel homelot." Mitchel and Steward were near neighbors.

It begins to appear that changes were rapid, in the early years. They generally are. It was no new thing, and it has not become outworn. Tastes differed then, and differ now; talents vary both in kind and degree. We are now too far from the beginnings of things in the "place called Glasgow" to say who were incompetent, who were shifty, who mercurial. We can without prejudice note here and there some who were substantial town builders. That is what we want to know, and we shall meet these again, in the future story of church and town. The women, though not speaking much in these pages, had much to do with it all.

The Hustons were forward men in the early history

of the settlement [II], then the town knew them no more.

Lots 10, and 19 East. Lot 10 in the first division fell to Robert Black. It too was a lot with a large tavern history [99f., 104]. On this same lot Capt. Abner Pease had his tavern. Here is where Almon Smith lived in recent times. The old building, the rear section, was undergoing changes in the early nineteenth century. The chimney bricks bore the date of 1774. The beams in this house were of oak, 12 x 8, and 13 x 8, inches square respectively. Cross-beams were dovetailed in, to prevent spreading. The rafters rested upon an additional set of great beams laid down on top of the frame. The iron furnishings, such as hinges and latches were the manifest work of local blacksmithing.

Black's other lot was 19 east, second division. It was sold to John Crooks in 1742, and remained in the Crooks family until near the end of the century.

Robert Black naturally felt that his first division holding was superior to his other lot, 19 east, albeit the latter was located close to the little community forming about second division pond. The road "to murrifield" which was projected in 1755, and thirty years later became a county road, perhaps he did not then vision. But he sat close to a greater thoroughfare. He sold 19 east to John Crooks in 1742, and this purchaser settled down there, the property remaining with the family to the end of the century.

Lots 11, and 3 West. We come to lot 11 in the first division [V, 103ff.]. The old road to "the gore," discontinued generations ago, ran between this lot and the one next north. Down there in the meadow, on Freeland brook, just how early I cannot say, was a saw mill run by the Blairs. This lot 11 was first owned by Matthew. No more important or trusted functionary of church or town ever breathed Blandford air. The Blairs were both numerous and influential; none, from first to last, more so than Matthew.

His second division lot was number 3 west. Potash brook, taking its rise just below the village, running through the meadow of the modern Hinsdale farm, provided another mill privilege for Matthew. The Blairs were born mill men. Matthew was also a surveyor, and pursued that business more or less locally. His first division lot remained in Blair hands until the Revolution, when Samuel Sloper [29, 36ff., 70, 104ff., 221, 227, 244, 272, 298, 304]—Captain Sloper—soldier, merchant and landlord, a most picturesque and amiable personality, took possession. In the northeast corner of this lot, or possibly the southeast corner of lot 12 just north, is the fine old colonial mansion now used as a country club house, formerly the country home of the late Mrs. John Addison Porter, built by Dr. Silas Wright in 1822. This was known as the parsonage before Mrs. Porter's occupancy of it.

Matthew Blair's second division lot, 3 west, being not far from the village, and one corner of it on the great western thoroughfare which later became known as the Albany road, was early cut up into various separated or inter-related holdings. A long list of names might be given in this connection but for very weariness to the reader [VI]. The Blairs kept some kind of hold upon it, while along came also the Walkers, Crookses, Frenches, with Phelps, Button and Hatch; McKinstry, too. At last, down in the corner, on the south side of the Albany road, John and William Knox obtained foothold.

Lots 42, and 5 West. No. 42, first division, was Robert Henry's and he held on to it [VI, 171]. It remained in the family for more than a generation. It is now occupied by the fine summer home of the William H. Dexter heirs.

Robert Henry's second division lot was number 5 west, a holding which remained in the family possession for more than a generation. In 1763 Robert devised it by will to his son Samuel. As late as 1780 it was known as "the Samuel Henry Home lot." The Henrys appear not to have been very numerous in Blandford, but they made an esteemed contribution to Blandford life.

Lots 12 and 41, first division; 1 East. We have reached, on the town street, the fine upland lot, now the (late) James P. Nye place, where also is the modern fire-district's reservoir, originally lot 12, drawn by John Stuart; and opposite, No. 41, the modern Candee-Cooley place, the front end of which was in 1796 taken for the parade ground [VI, 117, 171]. These homesteads along here afford a sweeping panorama of the splendid Connecticut river valley and the hills beyond. No wonder these sightly uplands along the street are becoming increasingly the choice locations of summer residents. Here, in number 12, John Stuart erected his dwelling. In 1747 he willed the house to his wife, Sarah, and the rest of the "Home place" to his son, James. Then it began to suffer division by one sale after another. William Donaghy had it. In 1757 Matthew Blair bought forty acres of it, and that passed on to his son, Matthew. James Ferguson, blacksmith, had twenty acres along the north side, and William Carnahan followed him in this holding. John Upson came in and lived there in 1796, and the lot became known as the Upson farm. Dr. Charles H. Little lived there in the early nineteenth century. Presently the tavern men got their mighty leverage under it, and the gloomy history of foreclosures or embarrassments was enacted there as in so many other homesteads.

John Stuart's second division lot was number 1 east. The great western thoroughfare cuts diagonally athwart it. This lot John passed over to his son-in-law, Robert Black, in 1741, by will. Elihu Sperry came into possession of part of this lot, also Giles Dayton, these transactions happening in the nineteenth century. Curtis Knox had a clothing shop down there. Gurdon Rowley came in. The usual mortgages to the dealers in ardent spirits passed in review through those bibulous generations. Finally, be it noted, here is the little territory where local Methodism was born, and from which it swept like the winds of heaven [32n., 160, 205ff., 231].

Lots 41, and 26 West. Lot 41 commands a more extended notice than has been given it in the preceding paragraph. It was Alexander Osburn's, then William Doneghy's, and by 1760 was in possession of Matthew Blair, Jr., and curiously denominated in the deed of sale as "Lot 12 East." The last named owner was there as late as 1788 and perhaps later [104]. Yet in 1795 it was still spoken of as "the donecoy lot so called." May we infer from this little reminiscence that it was William Doneghy who first developed it? In 1792, when Benjamin Chapman [117] took possession, the deed relates that there was on the lot "a small house now occupied by David Knox and a barn." Quite an occupancy! Then followed kaleidoscopic changes. The parade ground was put in trust of "William Knox 3rd, Reuben Boies, Asa Blair, Samuel Knox & Reuben Blair yeomen." It was ten rods deep and occupied the entire west end. Solomon Ferguson had the lot in 1795. The next year it had passed to John Upson, except the parade ground, the property then having "a small House thereon standing." In the following century it was carried along in succession by Amasa Shurtliff, Thomas Sheldon and Alvah Ferguson, and had in the mean time acquired a mortgage to the State of Connecticut.

The second division lot drawn by Alexander Osburn [240] was 26 west, overlooking Murrayfield, and in the heart of what became the Knox district. The lot remained with the family or connections by marriage, until near the end of the century. This neighborhood later contained several families of Nye. There is out this way what appears to be one of the oldest houses in town, and very primitive, known as the Welcome Nye house. It may possibly be in farm lot 37, adjoining the lot under discussion. This little old home is very small, of a single story. In the front end there is a central garret window, and on either side of it is another, but they are not mates, so to speak, and there is one large window, down stairs, out of line with anything. The thoughtful would guess that these little windows were afterthoughts, to lighten wee bedrooms of the children as they came along. The quizzical might be tempted to say the windows look as though they were thrown on. Worthy of mention also is the old Logan Crosby place [160, 282]. This house must be very ancient, and is of more ample proportions than the last mentioned. I have never seen the interior of either of these.

There are two Knox places worthy of mention in the northerly section of the second division; the old homes thereon, however, being only a reminiscence, as one was torn down twenty-five or thirty years ago, the other being the melancholy scene of a destructive fire somewhat more recent. The first named is the John Knox [28n., 69, 159, 277] place. I never saw the old house, but am the possessor by gift of some of the fireplace irons in it. After it was demolished, the well in the yard was enclosed within a high wall made of boards from the ancient building. Standing close up to it, I could barely reach up to the upper edge of the fifth board.

The other house was that of the late James Knox, possibly a relic of the old Beard place. It was a fascinating, single-story house, with broad gable roof, covering a rather generous area, admitting a little window just above the larger gable window under the peak. During the last years of its occupancy, Mr. Knox removed the old chimney, replacing it with a modern one. The space so released contributed a whole new room to the old house.

I suppose the reason why there seem to have been more upstanding houses of primitive, or near-primitive erection, in the northerly section of the home-lot quadrangle, than in other localities, is that population receded from these parts, leaving less occasion for new building to disturb the old.

Lots 13, and 19 West. I cannot transcribe a great deal about lot 13, first division, or its first owner, Jeremiah Anderson. The Andersons all appear to have been transient operators or residents in Blandford. He did not retain this lot long. The Stuarts, or Stewards (variant in spelling), came in for a time, then the Carnahans, or Cannons, and it became known as "The Cannon Farm."

Jeremiah Anderson's second division lot was 19 west. James Beard and his son were there in Revolutionary days, then the lot was taken over by William Knox, thus becoming a unit in the Knox family holdings in this region. It would look as though the Andersons either were disappointed in their Glasgow estates, or that they entered upon them with the intent to "turn them over."

Lots 40, and 23 East. Joseph Freeland settled in lot

40, first division. If his neighbor, Jeremiah Anderson, just across the way, was in haste to sell and get away, this man was content to abide. The inventory of his estate, 1767, mentions this as his "Home-lot 60 acres with Buildings and Improvements." It must have been these dwellers in the heart of the old village who gave their name to the little brook which rises on the easterly slope of this and the lot next north, and which furnishes the present village with an abundance of pure water. It is a relief to find no trace of tavern tragedy or history connected with this home lot. Joseph Freeland's other lot was 23 east. It, too, descended to his heirs. In the latter quarter of the nineteenth century, Nelson Nye was there.

Lots 14, and 4 West. Back again to the street. Hugh Hambleton had lot 14. So far as I am aware, this has remained with the descendants of the family down to modern times; and this family estate has also had no tavern history that I know about. It too must have enjoyed great peace. The companion lot to this one was 4 west, and this was sold in 1741 to Matthew Provin, who lived in the opposite lot in this division. Then it passed on to Provin heirs, "Widow Rachel Provin" being there in the eighties. In the early eighteenth century Perry Button [230] established himself there, with his shop, and the merry dance of business, mortgages and restlessness set up. How quiet it all now is!

Lots 39, and 8 West. Opposite Hamilton's and Pound hill was number 39, the lot of John Osborn [V, 137]. It passed through these rapid metamorphoses of ownership: Adam Knox, 1740; David Boies, 1749; James Freeland, 1754; Samuel Boies, 1779. Presumably John Osborn put up his log house and did the necessary clearing. The lot became known as "Deacon Samuel Boies' home farm" [TT *passim*]. Then David Boies had it.

We shall know this important personage better farther on in our story.

Osborn's second division lot was 8 west. This is just below the Deacon Hinsdale place on the Russell road. The lot passed into the hands of John Knox in 1750. He was an innholder. Then in 1764 it was Lt. William Knox's ('third'). After that it had a checkered history.

Lots 16, 17, 38, 37,—all first division. Our path now takes a decided dip down to the swamp which so exhaused the pioneers on the second day of their arrival, and which had become a "causeway" in the time of Pastor Keep. It takes the drainage of the easterly hill, which slopes down toward the road, affording some opportunity for building on high land somewhat back from the street. It is impossible for me to determine accurately the boundary lines of these lots. But lots 38 and 37, on the east side of the street, fall within the description just given. The opposite lots, 16 and 17, were more level meadow land [V, 142].

Lots 15, and 16 West. Our next call is at lot 15, which John Osborne, Jr., drew, and did not like, perhaps because it was too low. Anyhow, he and James Montgomery [177, 180ff.] swapped lots in 1738, Osborne taking Montgomery's second division 1 west, down on the "tunak" road, and Montgomery taking 15, first division, which transaction gave Montgomery two adjacent lots on the street, for he drew number 16.

Young Osborne's second division lot was 16 west. This was one of the busy sections of this secondary street, which as early as in 1740 was sometimes called "the town and common Road," just a little below the pond. Its owner parted with it in 1749, to Nathaniel Taggart, the blacksmith, who in turn sold all west of the brook—a little more than half—to William Mitchel, who for many years ran the mill [159, 284, 293]. Rev.

Mr. Morton settled in the eastern end of this lot and the one to the south. The first division lot of the Junior John Osborne got back into the Osborne family, in the person of Alexander, in 1764, and passed to the heirs of the latter.

Lots 38, and 3 East. The opposite lot, 38, was David Boies's—whose covenant with God has already been noted. It remained the family homestead for very many years. He was no reed shaken by the wind. David Boies was a "Taylor," and would doubtless find employment at his trade round about among the people of the infant town. His second division property was number 3 east. Captain John Ferguson bought the western section of this lot in 1779. The rest of it contained a mill privilege. There was a sawmill there which had a checkered history, involving some of the tavern men. Gurdon Rowley, apostle of Methodism, took a chunk out of the center of that and the lot to the south, also in the early nineteenth century.

Lots 16, and 1 West. At No. 16, on the main street, we find James Montgomery, as noticed just above. When he sold this, in 1764, to Alexander Osborn (along with lot 15 just south), it was mentioned in the deed that there were "a dwelling house and barn and other implements," but as this applied to both lots, we are left in uncertainty just where Montgomery settled. It is pretty certain that he built on one of the two, and lived there. Mr. Keep thought James Montgomery drew "two lots" here. He drew one and bought the other. We have already noticed his early disposal of his second division lot (1 west).

Lots 37, and 36, first division, and 16 East. These were the lots of David McConoughey, substantial citizen and public officer, as was his son, David, after him. William Donaghy "first settled and Improved" lot

37. We are on high ground once more when we reach lot 36, an elevation of sixteen hundred feet or more extending northward for a mile [V]. Dunakey (the name variously spelled) sold his second division lot, 16 east, to John Scott, in 1738 [221]. The Hamiltons had it later.

Lots 17, and 14 West. We come to the John Boys lot, opposite the McConougheys' long-time home, No. 17. He had also 14 west, second division. He settled down on the lot on the street, and lived out his life there. His son Samuel succeeded him, and when he sold to Rev. Joseph Badger in 1787, he writes it down in the deed that it is the "Homelot whereon my late honored Father John Bois lived." Both father and son were substantial and prominent men in church and town. On the tombstone of Samuel in the old burial ground it still may be read that Samuel was "a ruling Elder of Christ Church in Blandford more than 40 years." The lot became divided by sale. Dr. Brewster was here late in the century. Not many years later, Dr. Nathan Blair came in, who was not by any means another Matthew. Drinking and tavern business with the inevitable disturbances, mortgages and foreclosures would unfold their tales of human frailty enacted on or from this lot, if its records were closely inquired into. There is little to be said of number 14 west, the second division lot which went with the holder of 17, first. Rev. James Morton operated there after his retirement.

Lots 36, and 9 West. The northwest corner of lot 36 [V, 136] on the street, is sufficiently elevated to allow comfortable building. It was Samuel Cannon's, or Carnahan's, and was known as his home lot as late as 1780. Its later history need not be repeated here. It involved much. I pause simply to observe that when Joseph Eells came here to do a store business and sell liquor, he little appreciated that his son Cushing would make the family name great among the thousands of Judah for his association with Whitman in saving Oregon and building Whitman College. The corner is still known by elderly people as Eells hill. The Eells home was in another neighborhood. Samuel Cannon's other lot was 9 west, on Freeland brook road. It was kept in the family for quite a number of years. The Blairs became interested in it early in the next century.

Lots 18, and 15 West. We move on up the street to number 18, the home lot of Samuel Ferguson. He was an old man, and did not many years survive the rigors of pioneer life in Glasgow town. Before the community had become incorporated he had passed on.

Samuel Ferguson's second division lot was 15 west. We are already acquainted with the region, through which ran Gibbs brook, and where in later years Taggart and Rev. Morton operated. It shared the various changes of ownership and fortune of that mercurial neighborhood, and many names might in this connection be passed in review. The very first sale was to one Stephen Coots, and was made by "Samuel Forgeson Jr.," perhaps to clear off the debt to Lawton.

We will return for just a moment to the homestead lot which we have left on the street. It is the Deacon Amasa Stewart place of recent memory, and has borne the sobriquet of "Broad Acres." The house does not fall within our early era, but we may pause a moment by it. It was erected about 1785, as so many others in the village were,—a fine specimen of the old country farm house. In this home there is a wide door whose lower panel is of one huge board. What monarchs of the forest those were which were laid low by the axe of the builders!

Lots 35, and 23 West. Israel Gibbs [135ff., 141, 271],

pillar of the church and a true father of the town, settled down on lot 35, which a good fortune assigned to him. There he built, and there he lived, and his son after him. Then, in 1780, Warham Parks [36f., 82, 135, 137ff., 224, 282] bought it, and in five years more it was taken over by Samuel Boies, second, who set up in the tavern business. This is the house which, according to the story, when three new structures were going up in that neighborhood, racing for the landlord's business, won first honors [V]. In the stage-coach era just opening it was a principal stopping place.

Israel Gibbs's other lot was at 23 west. One wonders how it ever escaped the Knoxes' hands. It went to James Worke in 1743, who still kept up some kind of interest in real estate development here. Then William, Walter and Paul Steward had it successively. Finally one half of it was added to the Baird home lot just to the south.

Lots 19, and 25 East. To James Freeland was assigned lot 19 [V, 136] on the main street, and 25 east in the other division—rather remote from the busy life of the settlement. He sold both lots in 1739 to William Brown "Living on Land Called the Gore Lying Between Worcester and Oxford in the County of Worcester." That was on February 11 of that winter. We observe, again, how rapidly population was shifting.

This property passed to Elisha Parks in 1769, then to Warham Parks; next, to Samuel Boies, Innholder, 1787, and to his heirs in 1812. Luther Laflin [139, 174, 255] came into possession of the east end in 1830. In one corner of this lot, next the street, the Episcopal church [143, 145, 175] was built. The parsonage of that society—I hardly think it was called rectory then—stood in the lot next north, while diagonally opposite was Job Almy's store. It was the liberal nucleus, and Almy [136, 143, 145, 190f.] was one of their pillars. Probably it was here that the Scioto company of Northwest Territory development, and its passionate revolt from Calvinism found its nursing fathers and nursing mothers. But we have wandered far. In more modern days this has been known as the Chapin place.

Lots 34, and 11 West. We will cross the street to lot 34, and call for James Wark, for he drew this lot and No. 11 west, second division. But we shall not find him. However much or little he did in person to improve his lots, or either of them, may be a question. The Warks did not settle in the new town. I conjecture that it was not from inability, but taste. James was a man of parts, and once and again the town of Blandford turned to him for literary, or legal, or scribal, assistance, even when he was in Hopkinton. This lot 34 early passed to Israel Gibbs, already living on the lot immediately adjoining to the south, and in 1754 it was in the possession of Israel's son, John, and became known as the "John Gibbs Homelot." If I mistake not, it has never been alienated from the family, unless in small sections. James Babcock, [142] blacksmith, had his shop in the southwest corner late in the century. A county road "to Babcock's corner" from the eastward was laid out in 1796, on the line, at least in part, of a town road of date 1750 "between sd Gibbses Loots," that is, Israel's, which puts it between lots 35 and 34 [X, 271, 281ff.] There was a store also in the northwest corner of lot 34 —only we have wandered a century from our starting out. An imaginative backward look, when contemporary facts are wanting, may be a help. From the fruit judge the seed.

We are now nearly to the top of the wind-swept "Dug hill" of this old street, where shade trees long ago planted by the side of the thoroughfare show only gnarled and stunted branches on the windward side. Where the rising land to the east up here shuts out any broad view, to the westward the great rolling hills of the Berkshires display their graceful curves.

James Wark did not part with his second division lot—11 west—until 1768, and then to John Carnahan. Wark thereupon wrote his name as "Gentleman" in the deed. Just how much and what this man did in and for Blandford lies in the deep shadows, as does so much of the early history. He may possibly have developed several holdings. This lot, 11 west, by the way, was known as the "Wigwam lot," form some rare and forgotten Indian tradition.

Lots 20, and 2 East. Samuel Cook came to lot 20, on the street. For reasons not revealed he cared not to stay, and sold out to David Campbell in 1739. Why David Campbell should want this place is as much of a mystery as why Samuel Cook did not. For the Campbells were mill men. How long David Campbell was here I am unable to say. That enterprising man of business, Warham Parks, had it in 1787, when it was known as Parks's Bagg lot. The Bagg well [138] was in it, at the northeast corner. Quite probably the fathers had found that at the beginning, for they were shrewd observers, and water has not everywhere been easy to find on Blandford hill, and pure water still less so. This well privilege figured in deeds of real estate hereabout. The history of this homestead and farmstead is notable in several respects. Dr. Brewster was living here in 1788, before he moved farther down the street. The same is true of Babcock and his blacksmith shop. The lot became divided into east and west parts. The Episcopal parsonage stood on this lot—in its little day. Somewhere up here—I have never been able exactly to locate it, whether in the east part of this lot or of

one to the north, was a "Whetstone Quarry," a separate property, which in 1810 belonged to Benjamin
Scott and Robert Cannon. Mention of it occurs
again and again in the deeds. It may have been worked
out, or superseded by a better product, and it certainly
seems to have been forgotten. But the fathers found it
and opened it up. Running through this section of
Blandford, continuing in a thin line southward, and in
a broader band northward through Chester, is a band
of Chester amphibolite, "a dark, flabby hornblende-
schist, in places changed to serpentine, and emery." *
A little of this last may have been found. Or, some little
spot may have been discovered containing granular
quartz fine enough for whetstones. The Scottish fathers
were keen for all such things. The other lot, 2 east, lies
down at the foot of Tarrot hill near the Russell line,
and did not prove very attractive to the first comers.
This lot was bandied about from settler to buyer for
a score of years, nobody seeming to care much for it.

Lots 33, and 24 East. Opposite Samuel Cook was
James Beard. It became known as "the Baird lot"; was
so called in 1785, when Warham Parks, who had become possessed of it, sold a part of it to "Samuel Crooks
Gibbs, Cordwainer." This was a bustling section of the
town in the early nineteenth century. Several stores and
taverns were thereabouts [TT, V and VI]. Abner Pease,
Warham Parks, Job Almy, Dr. Brewster, Gibbses and
Boises galore were all bunched together almost within
a stone's throw in those stirring days.

Baird's second division lot was 24 east. I cannot give
the story of this lot except to say that John Beard appears to have been living there in 1787, and that it has
been known in recent times as the Welcome Nye place
—at least, the east end of the lot.

---
* Geologic Atlas of the U. S., Holyoke Folio.

Lots 21, and 10 West. Daniel Stone obtained ownership of lot 21 in the first division, and 10 west in the second division. It was his second division lot to which he gave the preference. Apparently he settled there. In 1751 it passed to Josiah Stone, not improbably a son. The latter was a "house carpenter" in Hopkinton, and it is particularly mentioned in the deed that the three-pence yearly rental was still being paid. That same year he sold the lot to Samuel Carnahan, who was living on the lot next south. Nathan Cannon had it as late as 1806, all of which means that Samuel and his family from the first established a family tradition down there on Gibbs and Freeland brooks. Stone sold his first division lot to David Boies in 1738. Then, in 1742, it passed to William Boies and became known as the "Deacon William Boies home farm." It remained with the Boises [TT *passim*] until near the end of the eighteenth century, and perhaps later. Justin Wilson bought at the eastern end, then at the western end also. It still bears the name of the Justin Wilson place. In the middle of this lot, which fifteen years ago—whatever may be true to-day—was in summer a luxuriant and splendid field of white daisies, once a fine mowing, stood a boarded enclosure around a well. Near there was the Boies home, and the licensed store of Deacon William Boies. This daisied area, broad and open, is fringed at the farther edge by a vigorous forest growth, over which can be observed from the street a majestic line of Berkshire hills towering skyward.

Lots 32, and 22 West. Opposite this lot of Deacon Boies is number 32, drawn by Walter Stewart. There a homestead was reared from the first. In 1769, when it passed to Solomon Stewart, it was written in the deed that it was the Stewart "Homelot with a Mansion House and Barns on the same." Not until 1812 was it alienated from its three-quarters of a century of Stewart associations. Then Job Almy came in. This stirring man of business and liberal churchman brought a very different atmosphere. In fact, by the time he had taken possession there and (as we have seen) in the lot immediately to the south of it, old things had passed away, all things had become new. Four acres in the southwest corner were set off at this time, and on it a blacksmith shop was erected and operated. Quite likely a house was also built. One blacksmith succeeded another. In those days the place of the village smithy was a busy one, not alone for horse-shoeing and general blacksmithing, but for talk, a veritable hatchery of politics and the ways of the world. In 1828, Justin Wilson bought the eastern half of this lot, which was just to the north of the "Road leading to Northampton," and there were "buildings" there too. In this lot still stands what is familiarly called "the old red house," a picturesque relic.

The second division lot of Walter Stewart was 22 west, pretty well to the north. He held on to it until 1769, perhaps for an outlying farm lot. In the year just noted, he sold it to Samuel Ferguson. This was Samuel the younger. It is not improbably a case of swarming, since Samuel the senior, on lot 18, first division, scattered the property by will to his several chidren. At any rate, Samuel passed on this second division property to Solomon Ferguson in 1784.

Lots 22, and 20 East. It may be remembered there were two Warks, James and Samuel. James we have already taken into account. Samuel drew lot 22 in the first division and 20 east in the second. It looks as thought he had died early. At any rate, the two lots soon fell into the possession of "Elizabeth Wark, Spinster," of Upton, and she sold them to John Crooks in

1739, who also turned them over in a year or two. Duncan Graham bought the lot on the town street in November, 1740, and it is recited in the deed that there was on it a "Mansion House and Fence." Now that means a frame house and a yard that the owner cared enough about to keep out the wandering pigs and other animals, and perhaps to keep in the children. But who built it? That is any one's guess. Whoever did it, there was enterprise worthy to be jotted down, meaning a good many things which the reader can work out in his fancy as well as the writer of this tale. Duncan Graham kept the place only a couple of years, and sold it to John Wilson in 1742, who passed it on to his heirs, who were holding it at least as late as 1787.

John Crooks established his home in the lot adjoining on the south side the second division lot of Wark's, so this purchase from Miss Wark seemed like a convenient addition to his farm. But he parted with it 1742, when it fell into the hands of the Henrys—William, then his heirs—who stayed on until late in the century, perhaps longer. The Murrayfield road ran between the two lots just commented on.

Lots 31, and 8 East. Francis Bryant comes next, in lot 31 on the town street, opposite Samuel Wark's lot, and 8 east in the second division. Bryant is another of the inexplainables. He sold both his lots to John Huston in 1738, the meaning of which is that he would not wait for a purchaser who was wanting to settle, but resorted to a real estate dealer to relieve him of the burden. Then "John and William Ferguson, both of Pelham, Taylors," bought both lots. Confining ourselves now to the first division property, Samuel Willson had it by 1745, then James Freeland, James Beard, Jr., Solomon Stewart (east end), then the Boieses, William, Jr., having the whole of it by 1788. So dizzy a career lends small chance for locating anything, and I have nothing else to tell about it worth recording.

The other lot embraced Gibbs brook, and drew the Blairs [TT *passim*] to it as a loadstone the needle—Matthew, Robert, Isaac, Jacob, beginning 1749 and continuing for years. If only it had been Abraham instead of Robert, it would seem worthy of a place in holy writ. A sawmill privilege figured in the processes, sometimes half, sometimes the whole. James Blair, Elam Blair, Israel Cannon, Sharon Bradley, all, and more beside, had their little day here. In the midst of it, John Ferguson, the redoubtable captain, who lived on the lot just south of it, had his hand on it too, before the Revolution. Francis Bryant did not know what he had lost.

Lots 23, and 27 West. Our next calling place, lot 23, first division, has a very different story engraved upon its rock. Robert Senot (Sennet, Sinnet, etc., etc.) drew it, settled down on it, and spent his life there. When he willed it to his son in 1763, he mentioned it as the "Homelot on which I now Dwell." This clan were originally Anglo-Normans, and settled in Ireland in the twelfth century. Their seat was in County Wexford. They were Roman Catholics, and fared ill at the hands of Cromwell. The Blandford families of this name appear to have become assimilated with the Presbyterian Scots. Time and tide and inter-marriage finally opened the way for Captain Samuel Knox to enter the lot. One of the most interesting old houses in town stands on this home lot, built, according to tradition, about 1785, by Captain Knox.

Robert's second division lot was 27 west, the northernmost lot in the quadrangle. It passed by will to John in 1763, with the statement in the deed that there were "Houses and buildings" there.

Lots 30, and 9 East. Branching off to the west-northwest from the town street, opposite lot 30, cutting off a little corner of 23, is a road, set off very early, which became dotted with taverns and is rich in tavern and turnpike story [TT, *passim*]. The "old town road or street" continues on its north-northwesterly course, a little crooked here and there to accommodate itself to the contours. Up here was "the noarth end" of the settlement. We pause for a little at lot 30, where William Barker settled. Then Robert, another William, and forthwith John. And then the Barkers vanish from the town, about the middle of the century. They seem to have gone to Upton. Robert Wilson followed, from the eastern end of the province, then Andrew. Names only, all of them. "Phebe Knox, Widow," was there in 1820.

We pass to lot 9 east in the second division, Barker's other possession. It was sold in 1756 to Robert Blair, who was followed by Isaac and Jacob, as in the lot immediately to the south. Some of the Cannons, Isaac, followed by his son Nathan, then, still later, Israel, had the west end late in the century; and finally Sharon Bradley shall close our rather vain pursuit.

Lots 24, and 10 East. Hugh Maxwell arrests our brief attention next, on lot 24 in the first division. He sold it in 1738 to Alexander Osburn, who in turn parted from it to Robert Young in 1739, "as laid out by Robert Huston"—so runs the deed. Maxwell gave his residence as Bedford when he sold out. So we speed the parting and greet the coming guest. Then the Youngs came in. They sold out to William Fisher in 1749. Ten years after that, Fisher sold to William Brown in 1759. Fisher was a weaver. Brown came to stay, and was succeeded by his son of the same Christian name. Thence the lot bore the title of "The Brown Farm, or Homestead." A little old house, on this lot as I suppose, on the northerly side of the stage road running slantwise through these lots, was familiarly known as "the Brown sisters." It gives—or gave—every appearance of great age, yet can hardly represent the early period we are trying to picture. It is a little single-story house: plain front door between two windows. Many times have I visited it with fascinated interest, its fire-places and cupboards all tumbling to ruin, silently eloquent of a sealed past. Zadok was apparently the last of the Browns here, and he sold to Solomon Noble, Jr., in 1810, Noble selling it the same year to Samuel Hinkley, Esq., and Hinkley to Eli Knox in 1818.

The other Maxwell lot was lot 10 east. That, too, was sold in 1738 to Alexander Osburn. Then William Donaghy bought it, who sold to Samuel Carnahan in 1749. From that time on, to at least near the end of the century, it remained in the Carnahan family [TT, *passim*]: Samuel, William, John, Ezekiel, Nathan and other heirs. For a time this family were in possession of 9 west, on the opposite side of the street. How ever it escaped the Blairs is an interesting speculation.

Lots 29, and 14 East. Josiah Rice, "House Wright," was located at lot 29, first division, and 14 east, second division. I have no definite indication of any kind as to which of these lots he selected for a homestead. And I am unable to say whether he ever really lived at all in Blandford, or Glasgow. He died in the summer of 1745. His death is not recorded in Hopkinton, nor is there any existing stone marking his grave in Blandford, if indeed he were buried there. He bequeathed to one son-in-law a piece of land "lying near the Mansion House of Capt. John Wood, late of Hopkinton." To his "well beloved wife, Elizabeth," he left "all the remainder of his estate, Real or Personal, wherever it may be found." Elizabeth, it may be repeated, had been the widow of Capt. John Wood, who had spread such a feast in Hopkinton before a traveling minister, and who had talked over with his guest Governor Shute's memorial to the king. Before Josiah Rice's death, however, he had gone back to Hopkinton, for in March, 1744-5, the two, husband and wife, together sold both these Rice lots to John Wood, Mrs. Rice's oldest son,— "as laid out,"—so runs the deed, "by John Huston," "Together with the Messurages Tenements & hereditaments." This would look as though Rice had built more than one house on his lands, and not impossibly on both his lots. His trade would invite him to do this, and might have occupied not a little of his time building for others in the infant community.

John Wood kept hold of both lots until 1757, then sold. John Wilson bought the first division lot, and he continued there at least until 1787. It passed to Samuel Knox in 1793, and Samuel sold to William the eastern half in the same year. That was close to the growing estates of the Knox clan in that part of town. Rice's second division lot was bought by John Freeland, who kept it five years, when it was bought by Glass Cochran, who was already occupying the lot just to the north.

Lots 25, and 24 West. The first division's twenty-fifth lot was taken by John Knox—classic old Scotch name—and it passed on to Adam Knox in 1753, with possibly William coming in between the two. The ever alert Warham Parks took it up in 1779, when it had "thereon standing" "a Mansion House and Barn," expressly stated as "lying about two Miles and one half North from the Meeting House." How long it had been built is not told. If I mistake not, this is the site of the old Taggart tavern, with the cellar stairs of solid quartered oak, [pictured in TT, opp. p. 304] the modern H. H. Cross place.

The second division companion lot was 24 west—Knox territory almost by divine right. Nevertheless, it was sold to David Scott in 1762, and John Scott had it in 1783.

Lots 28, and 18 East. John Cochran had lot 28, in the first division, and 18 east in the second. The lot first named passed to John's brother, Glass, in 1744. The other one went to "the widow Cochran, and in the latter part of the century Cornelius had it. On this second division lot is, or was, a score of years ago, a picturesque old wreck of a home, just opposite the mill pond, known then as "the Cochran house." It must now be in the cellar, an old, old house, carrying down with it the traditions of the Cochran generations. On the other lot is the old Warfield house, so called, with its well sweep. Or, possibly, this home may be located in the southwesterly corner of the lot to the north, lot 27. It is hard to tell. This lot, 28, had an uneasy history. In 1762 it was in the hands of Solomon Stewart. In his day the ever watchful Warham Parks got a grip on it. For a time Samuel Knox crept in at the southeast corner, close up to the Knox possessions in the second division.

Lots 26, and 12 East. We come to the last two sixty-acre lots in the first division, numbers 26 and 27. The first named fell to the hand of James Freeland, Jr., together with 12 east, second division. He appears to have settled on his first division lot, for he kept hold of that until 1754, when it passed to Samuel Wilson, whereas his other lot he disposed of in 1739 to Robert Huston. In that same year he bought of John Huston the first forty-acre lot, adjoining his homestead lot on the north, which William Huston had already sold to John Huston. And when Samuel Wilson bought lot 26, as above stated, he also bought this forty-acre lot, so that the two passed along together. These two lots descended to the Wilson heirs.

The second division lot, 12 east, got into the hands of non-resident innholders for a series of years, probably by way of mortgages, whence any record of it on my part disappears into oblivion. The second division road between lots 10 and 19 became impassable and was closed to traffic—except, as related on another page, to an inquiring and adventurous minister—years ago. It never should have been laid out.

Lots 27, and 6 West. Our last remaining lot of the full-size first division home lots, is number 27. Its owner was John Hamilton, and the companion lot was 6 west. Whether he built here I am unable to say. In 1765 he sold to John Gibbs; and in the same year Israel Gibbs, who had already consolidated into his holdings a considerable section of "the boys' lots," bought the northerly part of this one, and it continued in the possession of the family and descendants a long time. A deed of 1778 speaks of it as the "Israel Gibbs Jr. house lot," and one of ten years later carries a similar designation with the "Jr." dropped out.

The other lot, 6 west, whose easterly end abuts on the second division road, begins to descend as into the bowels of the earth, about where the modern road to Russell also descends through the Haley farms. Between 1773 and 1782, in two separate sales, Hamilton sold the eastern end of this lot to John Ferguson, who, in 1792, willed it to his widow, Doratha, or Dolly; and apparently John, the son, had it ultimately. Lieut. William Knox, 2nd., had the west end in 1782. This western end of the lot abuts on the lower village property, in which the Knoxes took so large a part a half century after the town settlement, and later. On the whole this is a rather impersonal story, but the angel with the ink-

horn by his side did not always write his story with in-
delible liquid and a pen of steel.

The Boys' lots, 1, 2, 3, 4, 5. All that now remains of
the westerly half of our settlement block is that section,
well known in the old days as "the first and small Divisions," or in shorter and more intimate terminology,
"the boys' lots." I have already treated of these in considerable measure, incidentally, by the way. "The boys"
were William Huston, John Donaghy, Glass Cochran,
William Stewart and John Crooks—five young men distributed over as many forty-acre lots. They comprised
a not altogether pleasing block of real estate for a group
of young bloods. In the first place, it was at the jump-
ing-off place. If the fathers had been wiser, they would
have blocked out these lots in the midst of the settlement. For one thing, the girls were too far off, and hard-
surfaced roads and swift cars were not yet. Besides,
what young man of spirit would choose to be far from
the anvil, the husking bee and the store? By the time
we reach the northernmost sixty-acre lots, we are already leaving the great central plateau along the back-
bone of which the street runs, and by the time we reach
the *ultima thule* of the small lots, we have descended
nearly two hundred feet. It is indeed an imposing frontage of landscape seen as one begins the descent, for
there are rolling billows of hill country of marvelous
grace beyond the intervale. But young men are apt to
seek out other beauty than that of distant hills, and
young women are not less eager, too, to mix in the life
of the throng. We have already seen William Huston
quit his location before the beginning of the decade
which should see the settlement receive its charter. John
Doneghy, on lot 2, put his holding into the hands of the
land agent, John Huston, that same year,—1739. I am
unable to state just how long the other young men

stayed by. The Crooks brothers, William and John, bought the divided lot 3 (east and west), along with 4 and 5, thus relieving Glass Cochran. And themselves sold to Israel Gibbs in 1758. By that time all this Crooks holding appears to have got into the hands of John Crooks, and when the sale was made to Israel Gibbs, John Crooks had gone back to Mendon.

However, we are not hereby necessarily to conclude that these youths had done nothing with their holdings. The very fact that they did not revert to the proprietors is witness to the contrary. Very likely they built their log cabins and cleared their lands according to contract with the proprietors, then sold out and "did better" for themselves.

Lot 2 West. We have nearly completed our survey of the original home lots. But a few fragments remain. In the second division, lot 2 west was assigned to William Carr, and he had no other. This is down on the old turnpike road, successor to the primeval path, or trail, that ran past Pixley's—"the road from Boston to Albany." I am unable to say what Carr did on or with this lot. By 1767 it was called by the family owning it "the Matthew Provin Homelot," and it passed on to Matthew's heirs. Very late in the century the Knoxes —another clan who thought much of one another's company and loved to neighbor together—came in. They all settled down on this Albany road: John, John, 3rd., William, William, 2nd., Elijah, Ranar, Curtis. I may not have them in the right order, and probably have omitted some. John Knox was the pioneer, by purchase, down this way, and he and his heirs held number 1 west for generations. Down a little private way to the south stood the old house, another cruel victim of the hungry flames in the first decade of this century, a roomy, hospitable home of the ancient type, "a mansion house" indeed, of the rural, homey sort.

Lot 4 East, Second Division. Matthew Proven had but one lot, that one being 4 east, second division. It passed on to his heirs in 1773. We should not go far astray in picturing his log cabin chimney sending up smoke on the second division road at the foot of Tarrot hill. In the early nineteenth century, Caleb and Elihu Sperry sold their liberties to the innholders of the town, who took their inevitable course.

The 30-acre lot. Robert Hambleton drew one lot of thirty acres, not further described in the deed. But as there was but one such lot, it is easy to locate him, just to the north of 27 east, as indicated in our plan of the town. He wrote himself down as "yoeman." The deed which turned over to him the title to this lot states that it "is now in possession of the said Robert Hambleton with all the Buildings therein erected." From which one may draw the inference that "the said Robert" was at least forehanded.

The above survey completes the enumeration of the settling lots and the first settlers thereon, being exactly sixty in number, if we include the first minister, not yet on the ground, but located by anticipation. Sixty, remember; not fifty; nor forty. Various documents quoted—not official, but nevertheless influential, usually cite one of the smaller numbers. We have the sixty names of heads of families,—barring the possibility of less than a half dozen bachelors with expectations or hopes of marriage. There must have been at least count three hundred people ranged along the two divisions, busy men and women, subduing a wilderness, creating homes, building a town.

No one can be wise enough to say just how this first settlement found its homes distributed. My guess would be, about two to one in favor of the main street, or first division road.

Two of the parties of the second part fell out,—William Province and James Freeland, Jr. In the list of actual first settlers, these names appear which were not in Lawton's contract: Matthew Proven, John Doneghy, William Stewart, William Carr, Hugh Maxwell, John Crooks, Glass Cochran, William Huston, Francis Bryant, James Hambleton.

These are all matters of record. The Rev. Mr. Keep, in his historical sermon, essayed to publish a partial list of first settlers. He says: "I have it in my power to give you the names of the twenty-five who obtained the farms on the west side of the town street. He then proceeds to give them, according to the information he had. He did not consult the deeds, all recorded in the Springfield Registry. He obtained his results by inquiry of his contemporaries, who remembered some, and forgot some, and disarranged some. Both men and women, and the homes they built, and lived and died in, were so easily forgotten! Only the momentum of succeeding generations rooted to some little spot of earth can impress so much as a family name on our kaleidoscopic humanity.

The trouble between Hugh Hamilton and Francis Brinley over a purchase of a part of a farm lot in Glasgow, will be recalled; also, that on account of Lawton's fraudulent dealing with the Legislature, that body required that eighteen additional settlers' families should be obtained for the new township. The home lots having been all taken up by the original sixty families, there remained nothing to do but to locate these eighteen families out on the farm lots, unless possibly through the pioneers already on the ground being willing to sell off from their settlement lots portions for newcomers to build on. Either or both of these methods may have been followed. There is no definite record of any of this, so far as I know.

CHAPTER XIV

THE STORY OF THE FARM LOTS: OR, FROM PROPRIETOR TO FREEHOLDER

Note. This chapter, like the preceding one, will contain much detail uninteresting to the general reader, but of intimate interest to the Blandford descendant. But there is a unique importance also inhering in the fact that there is herein put on record a process of land settlement unlike that observed in any other town in the Commonwealth of Massachusetts. Furthermore, herein are contained some incidents which may catch the eye of the seeker after general knowledge of pioneer conditions. It includes some essential elements of the scouting story.

This township, of seven miles square, was laid out, as nearly as could be, conveniently, into farm lots of 500 acres each. Upon this general scheme, and interrupting its continuous procedure, was superimposed the block of settling lots of sixty acres each. And this block was laid down somewhat diagonally. Hence many irregularities in shape and size where the farm lots abutted upon the settling lots. There were 51 farm lots. The numbering of them began at the northwest corner of the township, and ran down along the western town line, there being nine in that tier. Doubling back, the second tier, beginning with 10, ran up. The third, doubling in like manner, ran downward, the fourth turning again and running up. Here the disturbance began, but the procession was continued after the same fashion so far as conditions would permit. Easterly to westerly, except where interrupted by the home-lot rectangle, there were seven lots. Thus, those which were in regular form were seven-ninths of a mile by one mile in dimension. Mathematically this would yield 497 acres and seven-ninths of an acre to the lot. Pixley's farm, nominally of 300 acres, but actually 362 acres as surveyed,

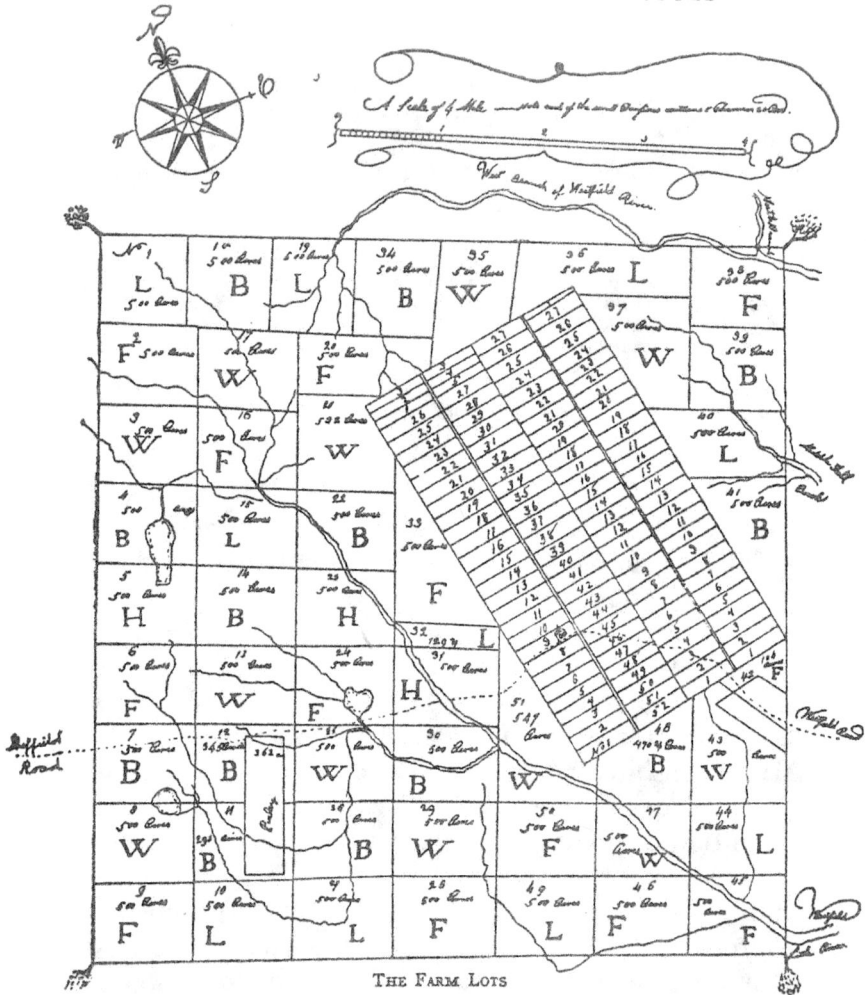

THE FARM LOTS

"THIS PLAN DESCRIBES the township of BLANDFORD. In the County of Hampshire, Lying upon Sheffield Road. It also describes the several Lots Belonging to the chief Proprietors (as is Represented by the first Letter of their Name) and the Number And also the subdivision of the Settlers part. And ten Acres for the Church laid out between the Lots No. 9 West and No. 44 East in the First Division of Said Settlers Lots. And also the Streams in sd Township Surveyed partly by Mr Roger Newbury of Windsor in Connecticut Surveyr and partly by John Huston Surveyr. It was Surveyed in the Year 1742 . . . as will Appear by the Original as this is taken from a true copy Drawn by David King—and now recopied at Westfield April 19th 1767 by BARNET HARKIN."

came out of lots 11 and 12. There were left in lot 11, 293 acres; and in lot 12, 345. Lot 21 contained 532 acres; lot 32, 129 and three-quarters acres; lot 42, 104 acres, and lot 51, 547 acres.

Supposedly, the drawing was by lot. In fact it was by turn, or approximately so. And notwithstanding Lawton had been deprived, by act of the General Court, of any share in the overplus of lots, his heir managed to get the full allotment just the same. Wells and Foye possessed the statutory right to make the partition. A little study of the plan will indicate conjectural reasons for irregularities in the drawing, the result of which should be an approximate equality of acreages in possession of the four. In the plan, No. 7 is assigned to Brinley, and No. 8 to Wells. This seems to be a mistake, for the deed of partition, and Matthew Blair's plan as well, give No. 7 to Wells and No. 8 to Brinley. The lion's share, in point of acreage, seems to have gone to Brinley, while Foye fell behind. In actual sales, Foye or his executor was grantor of parcels of land in No. 8.

The proprietors had entered upon this business and municipal venture in an unfortunate time for real estate sales. When Gov. Barnard made his first address to the General Court of the Province, in 1760, the House replied, referring to current topics of discussion, that "this colony ... for more than a century past has been wading in blood, and laden with the expenses of expelling the common enemy." * The Proprietors had no easy task in Blandford. Much of the land which they held for sale passed to their heirs, and to the heirs of their heirs. Another century dawned before proprietary ownership ceased to be.

There were several early sales out in the farm lots, by the proprietors to first settlers and a few others,

* Palfrey, Vol. IV., p. 296.

while as yet the settlement waited for town incorporation. I do not claim to know about all of these. But I am able to make record of certain of them, and herewith spread them on these pages as luridly illustrative of primitive conditions. For here is exhibited the real scouting instinct.

The land was yet, for the most part, unsubdued forest, packs of wolves driving through, not to mention other beasts, dangerous on occasion, and there was always the suspicion of Indians. No roads, only the most primitive paths or trails, and travel not yet considerable. The township was seven miles square. Well, four men made purchases near together in lots 26, 27 and 29; between, that is, Pixley's tavern and Beech hill. Samuel Ferguson bought 200 acres, James Henry 100, Robert Wilson, Jr., 100, and James Caldwell of Boston, 200. A fifth man, Henry Caswell of Boston, bought 249 acres on "the West line of Glasgow," but whether inside the line, or outside, I am not sure. Quite a little business in real estate was going on at this time in "Belfast," southwest of Glasgow, apparently in the neighborhood of the ponds in Otis, or Louden, or "Number 3." One of the Crookses bought an original settling lot in the last named.

Fix it in mind, these men took pains to locate together. It was a lonely wilderness. Two are better than one, and a threefold cord is not quickly broken. There were other groups. James Montgomery bought 200 acres in lot 1, in the extreme northwest corner of the township. William Dunakee bought an equal area in the same lot. They could go and come together. Walter Cook and Walter Stewart bought, respectively, 300 and 200 acres in lot 19—the whole lot, that is. There was but one lot separating these two purchases from the two mentioned just before. William Knox and John

Stuart bought, the one, 300 acres, and the other the remaining 200 of lot 10. That was close to the first group named, and close to Pixley's; and the Housatunnock road, or path, traversed all that territory. James McClintock took up 240 acres in lot 44, away down in the river land, and Robert Sinat secured 150 in that same lot—two more companions, and incidentally near "Youngs 200." Finally, Robert Henry invested in 100 acres in the northeast end of the town, lot 36, immediately abutting on the north end of the second division settlement. What could they do with all this outside land, when their own home farms gave them more than they could possibly develop in years? Perhaps it was speculation. Certainly it was adventure. Possibly some of them built on them as soon as their own homes were comfortably closed in, hoping to sell. Every locality chosen by these men above named came to be pierced by important thoroughfares. Life sprang up and surged on there. These men were far-visioned. It offers to us insight into their souls. And that is what we care about. Incidentally, four of these men were not first settlers: Robert Wilson, James Henry, Henry Caswell and James Caldwell.

In his History of Western Massachusetts, Dr. Holland has told a thrilling incident connected with a Becket ("No. 4") early settler, which also touches upon our present story of Blandford's lonely acres. The location is the southeastern part of Becket, contiguous to Blandford. Our historian relates that "on Walker brook is the site of the first mill built by the settlers of 1740. Here was where the original settlement was made, and, for a time, Jonathan Walker and his wife were the only inhabitants. During the first winter of their residence here Mr. Walker cut his foot badly, and on that account needed assistance. Their nearest neighbors were in

Blandford, several miles distant, with an unbroken wilderness between. Mrs. Walker did not think it safe to leave the wounded man alone, while she could go for aid, so, with necessity, she became the co-mother of invention, and taking the bloody bandages from her husband's wounds, she fastened them around the horse's neck, and started him in the direction of Blandford. There at length the dumb but eloquent animal arrived with his blood-written message, and obtained the desired assistance for his owner." This path of the horse was in part at least over the continental road of a later day.

In the early years of the Revolution, the General Court, for the purposes of war revenue, passed an act in which was the provision that "where no Person appears to discharge the taxes on non Resident Proprietors unimproved lands to the Collector he shall after notice given as in said Act" proceed to sell the same, or so much of it as might be needful to discharge the obligation, the sale to be at public auction. Scores of such sales of the proprietors' lands in Blandford are on record, and many thousands of acres of such land were taken up by the inhabitants, such sales being always made at some tavern, as might be most convenient.*

The three farm lots marked "H" in the plan, were assigned to Col. Heath, a distinguished citizen of the Province. The first of these lots, No. 5, in the extreme westerly side of the township, beyond Walnut hill, contains the upper section of Long pond, that superb beauty spot so loved by the late Edward Uhl, and wrangled over as between succeeding owners and the public—whether, that is, it should be a one-man lake, or an all-men's lake. The sovereign law of the State has

---

* See, e.g., Vol. 16, p. 151, Registry of Deeds, Springfield, Mass.: sale by James Sinnet, Collector, to Asa Blair.

recently declared for the latter. Of old, William and Joel Boies invested there. Later in the eighteenth century Rev. Joseph Badger, later of Ohio fame, executed his sardonic *coup d'etat*, and settled down, six miles away from his flock of sheep, until his sheep should better appreciate their shepherd. Heath's next lot, 23, was largely taken up by Squire Reuben Boies. That ancient worthy well chose for his residence not only a much traveled road from the north and west over Beech hill and down into Connecticut, but also a sightly homestead commanding an unforgettable expanse of meadow and hill and the glory of the seasonal procession of cloud and color. Heath's third assignment, or purchase, cornered southeasterly on No. 23, and is numbered 31. It passed wholly or in great part to one "Susannah Loring, non compos," whose guardian, Nathaniel Appleton, sold lands to others, notably to Archibald Black. Poor Archibald had as big a thirst as his big double farm, drinking it all up (or down), little by little, at Captain Pease's tavern. Mortgage after mortgage was followed at intervals by appropriate foreclosures, until the places which had known him knew him no more for ever. This farm, in No. 31, was on the old Gore road running past Blair's mill, a road long ago discontinued, and the mill, on Bedlam brook, now a forest-covered ruin.

Lawton also sold to Wells and Foye numbers 27, 40 and 49. Then Foye bought out Wells's share in them. They had for outlander neighbors in No. 1 William Dunakee and James Montgomery. This was out toward Becket and Chester. Israel Gibbs bought the whole of No. 15, between Little River and Long Pond, and parcelled it out by will to his children. Robert Cook bought a farm in No. 19, on the west branch of the Westfield River, as early as 1737. Part of the lot waited for the collector's sales, when it passed into the possession of the Stewarts and the Fergusons, and is known by their names to this day. There you may see cellar holes and turf-grown ridges, the last vestiges of old-time homes, where still stand rows of majestic maples bordering an ancient road into whose leafy luxuriance north-end residents looked out of their windows. All this, or nearly all, has long since been hidden from the eyes of the common traveler. Gnarled apple trees, more than centenarians, cluster together in reminiscent silence in the midst of old upland mowings, peaceful, silent, inviting to reverie.

Hovering close upon the edge of this one-time community, between it and the deep river valley, is a tract, wild and forbidding, a place of ancient legends and ghoulish imaginings. The mountains, sixteen to seventeen hundred feet in elevation, dip down to meet the river twelve or thirteen hundred feet below, and are seamed and separated by deep gorges through which flow babbling brooks. In the primeval forest then uncut the whole region was dark and vaporous. The late Samuel Bartholomew—"Squire Bartholomew" he was sometimes called, with a fitting flavor of the olden time about that title of honor—used to tell this story about this region. A lonely resident was at work, in the depths of these gulfs between the towering hills. At noon he sat down by the brook to eat his solitary dinner, leaving his jack-knife carelessly upon a log. Going back to find it after a time, to his astonishment he discerned a man occupying the place himself had left vacant sometime before. The stranger had the lost knife, and held it in his outstretched hand toward the owner of it, silently pointing at the same time with his long index finger down the brook. The knife was taken by the owner, who without comment obeyed the silent signal, and departed down the ravine. No word was spoken, as though wild nature here in the gloom and solitude could brook no sound other than that of "the murmuring pines and the hemlocks," and the fretting of the brooks impatient to reach the open and cheerier glades of the river valley.

No. 32 was sold by Lawton in 1749 to Estes Hatch. The peculiar deed of conveyance has been mentioned in an earlier chapter. Lot 36, down on the Westfield river at Murrayfield, was early sold to Robert Henry and Samuel Ferguson, as also already noted. The remainder of the lot waited many years, to be released at last by collector's sale. At nearly the opposite end of town, down on the Westfield Little river, between it and Birch hill, with Birch meadow brook running through it, lay No. 44. Here, as noted above, Robert Sinnet and James and Robert Sinnet took estates in 1737. Here also James Wallace settled in the latter part of the century, a man of large capacity and some business enterprise.

The story of Wells's proprietorship is soon told. He secured John Hill, Esq., and William Story, Gentleman, both of Boston, in 1754, to help him lift his financial burdens, assuming them again for himself two years later. Before that, he appears already to have taken into partnership a namesake,—Francis Wells, Sugar Baker. The original proprietor of this name was a distiller. After their connection with Hill and Story was severed, they appealed to David Vanhorn (or Vanhorne), of New York, to whom eleven tracts were mortgaged, namely, all that were originally set off to Wells. Meantime, Wells and Foye together had purchased of Lawton lots 27, 40 and 49; but apparently unable to carry them, Wells had sold his share in them all to Foye in the same year that he looked to Hill and Story to help carry his other burdens. He struggled along for ten years more, when (Aug. 31, 1764) Vanhorn foreclosed the mortgage, and Wells was out of it altogether.

In this transaction two notables appear. One is that exceedingly versatile and altogether interesting clerical character, the Rev. James Morton, whose ministry— but by no means his residence—in Blandford was now drawing near to its close. The other is Col. John Worthington, an able and popular lawyer whom the people of the town had the good sense more than once to retain as counsel, and who did much to elevate the bar in old Hampshire county into a position of liberality and influence. In one of the deeds recorded at the registry in Springfield* the statement is made, that James Morton and Moses Bliss, of Springfield, Gentleman, on April 27, 1762, "Saw John Worthington, Esq., of said Springfield, as attorney to and in Behalf of David Vanhorn of New York, Merchant, Enter into & upon one certain Tract of Land in the Township of Blandford," namely, lot No. 51, and took possession of the same in behalf of Vanhorn, and "of all the Several lots of land" mentioned in the indenture of mortgage.

In the nearly or quite thirty years in which Wells held proprietary right over these farms, or tracts, he appears to have sold but little. In lot 29, just north of Beech hill, he sold 200 acres to James Caldwell and 100 to James Henry. The Moors and Lloyds came into possession of most of the rest before or during the Revolutionary period. He also sold 100 acres in 1748 to David Campbell in lot 51, contiguous to the southwest corner of the settlers' rectangle, where this investor had a mill.

The names of Vanhorn and his executors,—"John Jay, Esq. and Ann Vanhorn of New York," "John Jay Esq. and Ann Edgar," or "John Jay Esq., William Edgar and Ann Vanhorn, executors"—appear in the

---

* Vol. 5, p. 447.

deeds of sale as late as the early nineteenth century. Valuable and desirable property much of it became, notably lot 13 and Foye's 24, out in the Blair pond and Pixley farm district. This became the favorite stamping-ground of the Watsons and Blairs, both clans predestined to developing water privilege in some way or other, though the Blairs for the most part operated elsewhere. Through this region ran the famous provincial highway to Great Barrington and Albany.

No. 3 was not sold until 1806, when Aaron Beard, Rufus Boies and Elijah Gibbs bought the whole of it, 515 acres as surveyed by Timothy Blair. Forthwith the last named of the triumvirate bought out his other two partners. Curiously, this far westerly lot is the only one of the 51 original farm lots which has continued to this day to be known and popularly called by its original number. "Number three" is a familiar phrase locally. Everybody knows where it is—everybody in Blandford, and it continues to be,* wholly or largely in Gibbs holding.

No. 7 lies just westward of the northerly end of Pixley's and abuts on the township of Otis, the ancient Louden. It waited for buyers until after the Revolution. Then Capt. Nathaniel Wood, Gentleman, of Louden, took up 75 acres on the county road and the Louden line. A road in the neighborhood was named for him. Nine years later he sold to John Knox, Jr., who also bought 75 acres more of the Vanhorn heirs. The rest of the lot was bought by Ebenezer Bartlett.

Ephraim Hamilton, Nathaniel Taggart and the Bairds took up lot 17, through which runs the Greenwoods road. It lies on the upper sources of Westfield Little river, known in early times by the euphonious name of North meadow brook. Through the southerly part of

* I.e., 1911.

this lot ran the newer stage line to Albany. Here also is "the crater," which is not a crater, but a drumlin. This must have been the path by which Walker's faithful horse took his solitary and critical way to Blandford in the early days.

On the extreme northernmost tier of the home lots lies No. 36, overlooking Westfield river. It is so wild and forbidding as never to have encouraged extensive settlement, though on its northernmost slope the country is inviting enough. Here the Vanhorn heirs were making sales late in the eighteenth century to John Osborn, Ezra Baird and perhaps some others. Now and then a section passed to new ownership by public sale in lapse of tax payments. But on the whole the tract was wild, gloomy and forbidding in the extreme. A dozen years or so following the Revolution—so a persistent tradition relates—John Baird, living in the northerly part of the second division, was wandering around in this lonely wild where he discovered a mass of lead and silver ore near the northern boundary of the township. The tradition has it that he cast some of this ore into balls and sent a pound of it to the town representative at the General Court, who had it assayed, with the result that it yielded nine ounces of lead and two of silver to the pound. An attractive financial offer was made to Baird for the property, and he was to show the prospective purchasers the location of the metallic vein. This he attempted to do one bright day, but a river fog arose and enveloped the party in almost impenetrable gloom, and they had to make their way toilsomely home without the coveted knowledge. The experience so terrorized Baird, "who was superstitious," that neither promise of wealth nor the pleading of friends could ever induce him to repeat the search. "Hundreds," says Mr. Gibbs in his Historical Address, "have searched for that mine, but they have never discovered it." It may be added that in somewhat recent times borings have been made in the ledges of that general region, where the quartzite rock has yielded gold, but not in sufficient quantity to attract the gold-seeker.

Lot 37, abutting upon the northeast corner of the settlers' block of homesteads, is the next in order of the Vanhorn property. It constitutes a part of that inviting "east part," once so thriving and populous, now so deserted and forlorn. The old Murrayfield road of 1766 traverses it, and a parallel road laid down in 1770.

Black's brook, which furnished the water power for the busy east part, takes its rise in this lot. In this section Vanhorn sold wide-stretching farms to James Nutt, in 1771. The year previous he had already negotiated similarly with John and Robert Cochran and William Mitchel, while his successors sold to Jonas Henry in 1796, Justus Ashmun meanwhile having come in for a big slice of 170 acres through collectors' sales. The Crookses were secondary investors hereabout. There is a farm, or section of one, on this area, still known as the Mitchel lot. The above are all classic names in the town's early history.

There is a piece of land marked out in the early plan of the town in lots 42 and 43, through the center of which ran the old highway by which the settlers came. In our plan it is designated as "Young's 200." The first named lot was Foye's, the second Wells's. But the transfer of the aforesaid 200 acres was made by Francis Brinley and Francis Wells, for five shillings "and for Divers other Considerations," while a deed one week later by Lawton for 200 pounds conveyed the same transaction. There is something a little mysterious about the sundry transfers and the marking out of the plot. The division line between the two farm lots appears to run nearly or quite through the middle of Young's purchase, the date of which was 1742. According to Professor Perry, the Young's were "Celtic Irish." It was this family of Youngs, of whom four generations came over together, and it was they who brought the potato to Worcester. Professor Perry tells of the tradition, which he says was lively in his boyhood, of the presentation of a potato to each of the several English families by these ardent Celtic advocates of that vegetable. But the seed was in every instance scornfully thrown away. Some Andover families treated similar gifts more hospitably, but cooked the balls instead of the tubers, and pronounced them unfit for food. In this lot 43, the Vanhorns sold other land to John Noble, David Hamilton and Rufus Blair in partnership, and to James Campbell in 1792-3. In 1778 John Sinnet took a small lot there through a collector's sale.

The Westfield Little river cuts lot 47 in two diagonally. Here John Thompson bought 100 acres of Vanhorn in the year 1776. The Thompsons and the Morrisons, who later came into this neighborhood, became members of the Scioto company, being among the earliest local emigrants to Ohio.

We pass next to the proprietorship of Francis Brinley, whose connection with the new township seems not to have been very fortunate, either early or late, though he did not, like Wells, succumb. His sale of the land in 11 and 12, where Pixley's was located, has been already related. His first lot in order was No. 4, which contains the major part of Long pond. It was largely disposed of by forced sales, John Gibbs buying 188 acres in the piece. The Gibbses came in for primordial rights to the western sections of the town, and some of them are there yet (1911). Rev. Joseph Badger's brief sojourn in No. 5 lapped over into this lot also.

Lot 14 contains Walnut hill, the highest elevation in town, 1760 feet. It did not prove to be a popular location, and its first sales were altogether, or very nearly all, under the hammer in Revolutionary or later times. Warham Parks took 170 acres, John Gibbs 217, Jonathan Shepard 26, David McConoughy 43. No. 18, in the northwest part of town, shared a similar fate—it would seem unreasonably, for broad acres and fair fields are there. Its distance from the village probably was against it. In 1780 Solomon Brown bought at collector's sale 200 acres, while Justus Ashmun, Nathan Cannon and Archibald Black possessed themselves similarly of considerable fractions. This section became later known as "New State," and contains some of the finest acreage in the town.

Lot 22 is traversed by the road to North Blandford—the old turnpike. David Boies bought of Brinley 200 acres on the eastern side, which is the best part of it, in 1743. This is still known as Boies meadow (but under the modern spelling, Boise). In the 90's Apthorp sold to David McConoughy 79 acres, and to the Rev. Joseph Badger, 60. The reverend gentleman just named, Dr. Joseph Wadsworth Brewster and Dr. Nathan Blair —three professional men—all obtained large holdings in this lot, yet none of them ever lived there. Time and distance in those days of slow traveling meant so little!

Lot 25, lying to the south of Blair pond, for some unknown reason became known distinctively as Vanhorn land. It entered the market late. Adam Blair bought a large section of it of the Vanhorn heirs in 1804. This region has been by "title clear" Blair property for generations. And, of course, it had water privileges. Here, in these latter days, was the hospitable home of Hiram Blair, as genial a gentleman as could be found in the community, with his family, following in the footsteps of the preceding generations. His little ancient sawmill, out in the woods among the birds and forest ferns and flowers, did its leisurely work with a perpendicular saw. Here he would attach the log on the carriage, set the saw agoing, leisurely, up and down, up and down, then fare forth with his guest to explore some interesting relic or feature of the old farmstead, and stroll back again without hastening his step, to see how far the old faithful saw had cut its way into the log. It was idyllic. Those days are gone forever.

No. 30 cornered at the northeast on No. 26. The Pond brook runs through it, to "join the brimming river," entering Little river near the northeastern corner of the lot. Here Brinley sold to Thomas Moor, in 1742, 200 acres along the north side. In 1793 Apthorp sold to James Moor 102 acres on the west side. Some of the land went by collectors' sales. Cellar holes or traces of old homes abound over this lot, without any visible evidence of a neighboring road. No highway so much as crosses any part of it to-day, nor has there for many years.

No. 34 lies on the northern slope and partakes of the general character of the others of its neighborhood, already described. Data are not at hand to outline much of its earlier history. Apparently it waited for buyers until the period of the Revolution. John Gibbs in partnership with John Durlam bought the northerly part by collector's sale.

Lot 39, one lot removed from the northeast corner farm lot, overlooks the valley of Westfield river, and embraces a part of that once thrifty east part already spoken of. Black's brook begins to be a considerable stream before leaving the confines of the lot. Near the close of the eighteenth century Warham Parks appears

THE LITTLE ANCIENT SAW MILL

to have become possessed of about the whole of this tract. Lawton's lot 40 is next to the southward, then 41, a triangular piece abutting upon one-half of the easterly tiers of the second division lots, and contains a valuable mill privilege. James Campbell, John Hastings and Isaac Blair were operators.

Lot 48, just south of the first division lots, irregular in shape, was sold in 1742 to Robert Wilson. He bought the whole of it, and it became known forthwith as the Wilson farm. Two thoroughfares running southerly toward Granville and already mentioned in connection with the first settlements, opened it to considerable activity. Its slopes of southern exposure invited and received somewhat extensive occupation. Here were Nobles and Blairs and Knoxes and Fergusons and Morrisons and Johnsons and Atkinses and Gunns, not to mention others whose names are less familiar. Some even of these have been long forgotten by most.

John Foye needed no guardian. He handled his estates with vigor, without doubt making a good thing out of his proprietorship, and the heirs to his property continued the tradition. Foye died shortly after the Revolution, and David Munroe of Northborough, a leather dresser,—so called in the deeds,—was by act of the General Court made administrator, July 1, 1785. Other members of the Foye family are named in connection with the transfers. Sarah Foye, widow, is also mentioned as administratrix.

Taking up Foye's lots in order, No. 2 on the upper reaches of Little river, in the northwest part of town, has not yielded to inquiry any very rich results. In the early nineteenth century the Bairds invested in the southeast corner. Elijah Gibbs was in evidence in the lot, thus extending his other considerable holdings farther northward. Across this lot ran the road to Becket, where the Walker family settled.

No. 6, just north of Jackson hill and west of Louden, went in large part to Nathaniel Wood and Ebenezer Bartlett already mentioned in connection with lot 7. In the southeast corner of this lot was Capt. Wood's first investment in town, in 1779. Alexander Blair bought of David Munroe, in 1784, 140 acres in the northeast part of the lot. John Blake, or Black, was still earlier to the south of him.

No. 9 is the southwest corner farm lot of the township, and appears to have been disposed of largely by forced sales of collectors to Justus Ashmun, who in turn passed it along to other buyers. This part of town lies high, and much more level than most of Blandford's area. Its early settlement was seriously handicapped by its distance from the village and the rough country between. Lawton's ungodly trick in laying out a township seven miles square when ordered by the legislature to make it six, has been an unending burden and vexation "to this day." For years there was a persistent agitation on the part of dwellers hereabout to be "set off to Louden," but the town would have none of it. The modern village of East Otis is close by lots 8 and 9.

To No. 8, just north of No. 9, we go. Warham Parks appears to have been the first purchaser here. Himself was pretty nearly ubiquitous. He possessed himself of 80 acres in this lot in 1783. Samuel Pelton bought 47 acres in 1798. Both these purchases were made on the western side. Jonathan Shepard, another versatile man and one of considerable note, secured the northeast corner of the lot in 1779. Hugh Hamilton became a considerable landholder hereabout, selling 140 acres in 1803 to Benjamin Scott, a gentleman of business who had already located on this lot. His first investment was secured of David Munroe, on the Hartford and Albany road, where he established a tavern.* Lying within this lot and in No. 7, is "Great swamp," otherwise denominated "Red Ash swamp," or "Black Spruce swamp." In our plan this swamp appears to be a pond, nearly the size of Blair pond. It is traversed by a road running across the southerly part of it. In driving across it one wonders why the swamp does not settle down and engulf the traveler. I have been told by the late Enos W. Boise, who was meticulously familiar with the early traditions of the town, that a large section of this great swamp had never been deeded from the original proprietor.

The next lot in order belonging to this proprietor is No. 16, and was early known as "North Meadow farm." It was good property. It became Louisa Foye's, who sold the whole of it in 1777 to Robert Blair, Jr., who mortgaged it back immediately to the grantor. North Meadow brook runs through it, furnishing considerable water power. On this brook was a beaver dam, and later a manufacturer's dam, the pond thus created becoming well known as North Meadow pond. A quarter of a mile or more down on the same brook, was another beaver dam, in the lower meadow, in lot 15, through which the same brook runs. This is Little river in its upper reaches. The work of the beavers was interrupted by the early settlers, four miles away, taking possession for the purpose of making hay. North Meadow thus received its name. In the latter part of the century manufacturing began to develop here, and North Blandford thus became a busy and thriving village. Now it is melting away again. Business long ago left it in possession of rich and varied memories. The little church there heroi-

---

* This is described in "The Taverns and Turnpikes of Blandford, 1733—1833," along with other notations concerning this interesting individual.

cally struggles on, the villages and outlying neighbors "sit closer" and make the lingering and dwindling community life worth while, as the city of Springfield closes out their mills and homes one by one for the thirsty throats and insistent interests of the widening urban life of the valley metropolis.

The twentieth farm lot is a quadrangle, except for a clip taken out of its southeast corner by the northwest corner of the settlement quadrangle. Its longer sides extend easterly and westerly. Its southwest corner is in close proximity to the historic community just mentioned in the last paragraph. When John Gibbs, in 1770, bought of Lawton in lot 21, he also purchased large areas in No. 20, the whole parcel of land covering 221 acres. William Brown had preceded him by eleven years, by the investment of 90 acres in the western end. Adam Knox was Gibbs's contemporary at the opposite end, on a farm of 61¾ acres. Ten years later this farm passed into the ownership of the Rev. Aaron Crosby, who sold it in 1785 to William Brown, Jr. Then and thereafter it became known as the Brown farm. It passed successively to Andrew Wilson, Zadok Brown, Solomon Noble, Samuel Hinckley and Eli Knox. The last named purchase was in 1818. At that time the Knoxes were largely in evidence in that part of town, notably Samuel Knox, who built several houses there which are still standing. This lot was one obtained by John Foye by purchase after the original division. This and the adjoining lots northerly and westerly constituted the North end, so called in the town's early history. It is a fine, splendid stretch of country, comparatively level or rolling like a prairie. This is the locality of which William H. Gibbs proudly wrote:* "Perhaps it will not be boasting for us to state that for six miles

---

* Historical Address, p. 47.

on this road there are better farms than on any other road for the same distance upon the mountains." In 1759 Samuel Taggart bought 125 acres of Foye in this lot 21, in the northwest corner. Nathaniel Taggart at the same time secured 125 acres adjoining on the east. John Sennett bought 110 acres on the eastern end in 1768, abutting on the home lots. David Munroe sold to Samuel Knox another strip in 1791. This lot figured extensively in the tavern history of the town, and is told in the book once and again referred to in such connections. The neighborhood is still called the Taggart district, and the school there, the Taggart school.

No. 24 was known as the Pond lot, or Twenty-mile, or Blair, pond. Samuel Patterson and James Moor were perhaps the earliest investors there, in 1759. David Black came in in 1770, and John Black in 1780. The Watsons and Blairs were there too, and will be noticed in the following chapter.

Another of the later purchases of Foye was lot 27, on the Granville line. Its southerly section embraced a part of the locally famed Beech hill. There Robert Wilson took up 200 acres as early as 1740, and Robert Wilson, Jr., secured 100 acres at the same time. Later buyers were Timothy Hatch and Abner Pease, but not for home-making of their own. The easterly part of the lot went by collectors' sales.

No. 28 is east of 27, and adjoining. We have entered upon the soil which Beech hill's sacred aristocracy came to claim with a peculiar pride, where Devil's half-acre on the one hand, and Methodism's primeval possession of soil to the westward of the Connecticut, on the other, made sacred by Bishop Asbury and many a heroic circuit rider, set up their rival claims.* As early as in 1759 Robert Loughhead came in, buying 60 acres, and the

---

* Again I must refer the reader to my "Taverns and Turnpikes," etc.

next year 60 more. Contemporaneously Francis Moor bought 100 acres, the property later passing by marriage and inheritance to the Loughheads, who built a large and substantial residence, used also as a tavern, close to the Granville line, and within easy reach of Beech hill Methodist meeting house aforesaid, where the old theology and the new were to engage in the mighty wrestle for mastery. This farm lot and the next easterly—No. 49, which Foye also bought of Lawton and Wells, saw no forced sales under the hammer. A little study of the deeds gives one a mighty respect for the staunch community which there sprang up in the closing quarter of the eighteenth century. The story belongs to a later chapter, but may halt us for a moment here and now. In this lot 28 the names of other homesteaders before the dawning of the nineteenth century are Montgomery, Diver and Bancroft. Abner Pease was here in 1770. The name of Provin appears early both in 28 and 49 (next east). The latter lot became the residence of Jedediah Smith, a most important functionary in the history of the town. Sarah Foye sold to the Rev. Jedediah Smith, of Granville, 100 acres in this lot in 1772, from whom it passed to his son and namesake. Dr. Holland* gives us a bit of biography which, though ahead of our chronology, may as well come in here: "Rev. Jedediah Smith, a graduate of Yale in 1750, was ordained pastor of this (Granville) church in 1756. He was an impressive preacher, and in a revival of religion under his ministrations in 1757, as many as thirty persons were added to the church. His views subsequently became 'Stoddardean,' and excited the decided opposition of many members of the church. He had a stormy time for years, but was not dismissed until April 16, 1776. Mr. Smith was hostile to the Revo-

---

* II, 66.

lutionary cause, and sailed with his numerous family, one son excepted, for Louisiana. In going up the Mississippi, he was attacked with a fever, and in a delirium leaped overboard. He was rescued, but soon died, Sept. 2, 1776, at the age of 50 years. He was buried on the banks of the river at a point which was subsequently swept away, 'so that no man knoweth his sepulchre unto this day.' His descendants were among the most respectable people of the Southwest." The remaining son probably differed from the political sentiments of his father. The Smith house in Blandford has remained in possession of the family into this twentieth century. David and Jonathan Hall were other principal settlers in this Beech hill lot. Not without some show of reason, albeit not at all understood by a certain (grossly ignorant) hotel clerk in the city of Boston, a modern descendant of some of these classic grandsires and grandames of old Beech hill, sojourning a bit at one of the great hotels of the Hub, registered his name and address, with the concluding addendum, "Beech Hill"!

Immediately to the northward of the last named lot is No. 50. It obtained not the celebrity of its Beech hill neighbors, though the deeds bear evidence of a good deal of business done there. The Smiths reached over into this lot, and so did David Campbell, from his mill lot in No. 51 to the northward. Pudding hill is located in the southeast corner of the lot. A very ancient story-and-a-half house stands on the top of this hill. It has its own long history. This old house was an infant compared with some, long since gone to utter wreck, in this southern upland of Blandford. At least one sojourner for a decade used to roam about and stumble over these ruinous heaps, fondly longing to know their hidden secrets of the generations gone.

"The harp that once through Tara's halls
    The soul of music shed,
Now hangs as mute on Tara's walls,
    As if that soul were fled."

Indeed, the soul has fled, for the very walls have tumbled down to decay and mold.

No. 33 was, and still is, "the Gore," doubtless so named because the settlement lots necessitated its form of a right-angled triangle with the long hypotheneuse abutting on the westerly side of the first division. It was also known in early times by the beautiful name of "Intervale lot," for it is an intervale where the swamp grass grows heavy and the summer evening fogs brood upon it. Robert Blair bought the whole farm in 1753. From him it passed to various other Blairs and to some Boises. Stories of it are elsewhere given in this volume.

Foye's share in the northeast part of town fell in No. 38, the northeast corner farm lot, now almost wholly in the town of Huntington—and the village of Huntington. Here again he was most fortunate. Robert Lindley, or Lindsay, was down there "on the river bank" in 1768, with a holding of 100 acres, and four years later he and Paul Stewart together bought nearly all the remainder of the lot, of Sarah Foye.*

As respects that part of town distinctively known as "the east part," Foye was long-sighted enough, or lucky enough, to buy of Lawton and Wells No. 40—the best there was in that section. Important thoroughfares were laid through it, and Black's brook, flowing through a mighty gorge, furnished power for the mills and shops. Sarah Foye sold to David Provin 60 acres there in 1773. The year before that, Amos Fenn and Philemon Doo-

---

* The story of this lot is given in my book so often referred to in preceding pages.

little took up 144 acres. The Parks and Knox families soon succeeded to large domains.

No. 42, a small and irregular lot, was taken up in 1759, except the earlier holding of Young.

No. 45 occupies the southeast corner of the township, Little river cutting it diagonally into almost equal parts. This is the opening into the river gulch which the Federal geologist of the region pronounces the wildest section of country in Western Massachusetts. Following the Revolution it passed to the Boises, Knoxes and Nobles.

No. 46 adjoins the last named lot to the westward, which in turn abuts upon other possessions of this enterprising proprietor, Foye, and his heirs. This man seems to have had a predilection for this part of town. Through David Munroe, Justus Ashmun and Jedediah Smith he came into large possessions hereabout. Foye and his successors gave little for collectors to dispose of, but 370 acres in 46 went at one stroke of the auctioneer's hammer to Capt. Samuel Sloper in 1781. A beautiful stream, bearing for some unaccountable reason the name of Borden brook, runs easterly through this lot. Of old it was Peebles brook, appropriately so called from the dwellers in the immediate vicinity. It is a confluent of Little river, and furnished its full share of power for sundry mills.

Very much of this vast outlying territory of 51 farm lots was mortgaged to the sundry proprietors of whom the property was bought. The people were saving, and generally the mortgage was paid. The relation between "gentlemen proprietors" and the residents was delicate and always trying, the more so that the proprietors were non-residents. New England laws, institutions and traditions did not favor fiefs. A good honest mortgage was one thing. Proprietorship was quite another. It was the design of the Province that the lands should pass as rapidly as possible into the hands of resident owners. The only celebration of Christmas on record in the town of Blandford in these passing generations is the yearly payment of rent to these "gentlemen proprietors," namely, "the Rent of . . . . . lawfull money of New England if the same shall be lawfully demanded." This charge was a survival of the old English quit-rent, "an elusory rent due by one who has paid a substantial price for his holding, such nominal return being an acknowledgment of the king's or lord's rights." * On precisely what conditions this yearly rent was demanded or paid in Massachusetts there seems to be little or nothing now to explain. That it continued to be paid for a long time there is testimony abundant. The payments varied in amounts with the acreage held. For example, Robert Henry in 1763 made transfer of a home lot to his "beloved son Samuel," with the proviso that the said Samuel should pay "always the yearly Rent if any there be legally reserved thereon, if the same be legally demanded by my former Proprietor of the Said lands or his Heirs." Again, October 11, 1766, Margaret Cochran and James Cochran, administrators of the estate of the late Samual Cochran, sold to William Knox lot 21 on the east side of the second division, stipulating in the deed that the grantee should pay "the yearly Rent thereof of three pence if Demanded." In towns where there was common land for wood or pasture, quit-rent appears to have had special application to this. But in Blandford all the land was held by somebody in severalty. James Truslow Adams† observes that "New England had been settled by emigrants to whom (such) possession of land in fee simple had been

---

* Standard Encyclopedia.
† P. 419.

the main attraction. . . . it was in this free and abundant land that were sown the seeds of democracy and revolution."

The proprietors' lands were generally called in English phraseology, "the Gentlemen's lands," and were technically known as wild lands that is, unimproved, whether for clearing or for cutting. Taxes were an oppressive and vexatious burden, however necessary. It is not strange that the inhabitants regarded the proprietors as "gentlemen" of ease. In 1745-46, the town appealed to the General Court that "a tax may be laid on all the unimproved lands of the Non Resident Proprietors" in view of the fact that the town had "built a Meeting House & settled a Minister, that many of the Proprietors that are benefitted in their Interests thereby live in other places and cannot be taxed for the charges of the said Town, without the order of this Court." The request was granted, the tax to be levied not in perpetuity, however, but for the three succeeding years, at the rate of "one peny per Acre in the Bills of the last Emission in each of said years." These charges were to be collected in the same manner as the ordinary town taxes, the proprietors meantime being allowed by the Court the right of appeal.

When this provision ran out, the town "voted that Matthew Blair shall go to Springfield to get mr witherenton (*i. e.*, Worthington) to draw a petition to send to Cort to get a tax laid on the wild Lands" again. The proprietors on their part responded in generous spirit, as the Province Laws of the following year bear witness:* "A Memorial of Francis Wells Esqr & John Foye, shewing that (as principal of the Town of Blandford) they were notified of the Petition of the Inhabitants of said Place, Praying to have Liberty to tax the

* Vol. XIV, Chap. 156.

unimproved lands, for the Support of the Ministry & other Charge, And signifying their free Consent to ye levying of the said Tax." The tax was reimposed for a further period of five years. This tax, of course, applied equally according to law to such of the inhabitants as had become possessed of wild lands, but by vote of the town these were forthwith let off, as the legislative act was permissive, not mandatory like the earlier one. A bargain was furthermore made with Wells and Foye whereby these gentlemen should be exempted on condition of their paying into the town treasury during the term of years contemplated in the act the sum of forty pounds, old tenor, yearly. This would save the bother of careful assessment and avert the danger of quarrel and litigation.

Matthew Blair, that faithful and efficient servant of the people, was collector for this purpose. Already in August, 1748, he had been instructed that when he should go to Boston with the province tax, he should also take up their "writings from the Gentlemen," meaning, perhaps the written agreements. In 1750 this trusty man was still at work in Boston "to manag the affair with ye Gentlemen proprietors . . . on behalf of ye town." Before the whole business was completed this town worthy was through with all things earthly. In the year 1761 Robert Henry and Henry Seward* were appointed a town committee to "take up" the original articles of agreement between the gentlemen and the first settlers." But the business hung fire, and the year following it was put into the hands of the redoubtable James Morton, minister, who was then directed to "Reeve the obligations" which had become so obnoxious to the people, that is to say, the whole business of quit-rents. It all reminds one of the larger

---

* Meaning, doubtless, Henry Steward.

negotiations and quarrels going on between the whole people and the crown during these eventful and portentious years, as looking toward an era of political independence.

Meantime the town was petitioning the Legislature to compel the proprietors to assist in highway repairs, and, perhaps failing in that, in 1764 they begged the Legislature itself "to make and maintain Roads through ye Gentlemens Lands." A bargain was finally made with Mr. Foye in 1766, that gentleman being then the chief remaining proprietor—at least it was sought to be made—whereby he should pay the town five pounds yearly in lieu of the grant confidently expected from the "Honorable Court" in answer to the town's recent petition. The "wild lands" were fast diminishing, and presently there ensued the easement whereby great tracts passed by public sales into the hands of resident buyers. Finally, in 1782, the town itself resolved to become a purchaser of all such lands as failed to secure a bidder at public sale. The unbending spirit of insistence in the despatch of this whole business, and the unrelenting energy with which the town pursued it to the end is indicated by a minute in the records of May 20, 1779, when that long-time collector, John Scott, appeared to be in difficulty: "Voted to see if the Town will sink the forty Pound in John Scotts List—Laid on the Unimproved Lands of the Town—Being part of three Hundred pound Granted to Support the Gospel— Passed in the Nagative."

Thus endeth the lesson, except the personal predicament of poor Scott. By little and little, proprietorship, alien and unrepresentative, became a thing of the past. The people owned and occupied the soil of the everlasting hills, unfretted by landlord or lord. And in the midst of it all the people had been fighting other battles, not without blood.

CHAPTER XV

The Early Homes of the Blandford Scouts

Of the log houses first inhabited not a rack remains. If you are known to be initiated, and share a friendly intimacy with some old farmer of the hills, he may gently lead you across the road from the ancient frame dwelling—the "mansion house" which thrift at last made possible—and show you an oval depression, small, smoothed and well grassed. Over it the log house stood. The place whereon thou then standest is holy ground; —more so than the site of the still near by. Or another good friend plunges with you into the deep and silent woods and points you out at last a less shapely depression than the other. You would never have guessed it.

I have stumbled on two deeds making mention of the old log house. One was written March 26, 1784, and by it William Stewart, yeoman, conveyed to Charles Culver, also yeoman, a fifty-acre lot received from his father, in farm lot number 38. This territory is in or very near the present village of Huntington, and the house doubtless was down on the river road in old Murrayfield. The sale conveyed, with the land, "a log dwelling house, and is the same," the instrument continues, "I now live in."

The "mansion house" came into being very early, before the town received its incorporation. This phrase, "mansion house," echoes and re-echoes adown the years. I have tried in vain absolutely to fix upon one which I can affirm quite without hesitation to be now standing. As to the distinguishing marks of it, I have my own opinion which I will express for what it may be worth. It must have been somewhat more spacious, provided more of comfort, and to the eye presented more of dignity, than the log house. It must also have been a frame dwelling. It may have been little else than a big box with a roof over it; but there would be larger room in the loft, and probably more ground area. Some, more fortunate or successful than others, would build better, and there would soon come to be a variety of comfort and style comparable to what we see everywhere and always. So the lowliest and the highest would live on the same street, and be neighbors. "The rich and the poor meet together; the Lord is the maker of them all." There was no Fifth Avenue then.

Whatever the material or style of the house, conditions were primitive in the extreme. The tradition is well authenticated of the old William Randall Nye homestead in the northeast part of town, that the family horse used to be hitched up to draw great back-logs, not to the kitchen door, but into the room itself, where they were deposited in the capacious hearth.

It may appear like a solecism to refer in this connection to an early nineteenth-century kitchen fireplace. It certainly was not in a log house, neither was it in one as primitive as the very first "mansion houses." But it was a lineal descendant of the primitive hearth, and if modification needs be made in the picture to make it contemporary with our present story, it will have to be in the direction of greater, not less, rudeness. It is the story of the Butler house on or near Beech hill, and was related by the Rev. Daniel Butler, D.D., who came with his parents from Hartford in his early childhood: "A huge chimney occupied the centre. The kitchen fireplace could not have been less that eight or nine feet between the jambs.* In the winter we drew in upon the hand sled a log often not less than two feet in diameter, and the rest of the fire corresponded with this. The fire occupied only a portion of this fireplace and the oven was in the part unused, the oven door standing in line with the back of the chimney. The space in front of the oven and at the end of the fire afforded a standing place for us children from whence through the wide chimney we could look up and see the stars, and hear the roar of the winds. Our home, like most of the homes of that day, freely admitted the air through the seams round the doors and windows, so that while the great fire roasted us in front we were cold behind. Green wood was burned from an impression that it gave out more heat than dry, and a huge fire was always necessary to keep it from going out altogether. In cold weather we have burnt a half cord daily in the kitchen, which was the only room with a fire when we were alone."

There are many of these old chimneys left standing in the midst of half-filled cellars, silent reminders of a life of hardship and resourcefulness, pathos and promise, idealism and toil, patriotism and piety. A big clump of immortal lilacs, or of roses, flourishes in the area where once was the front yard, or some scrawny and broken trees linger in decrepitude, perhaps a pair of tall Lombardy poplars stand, ghostly sentinels over fallen altars, or a tansy bed blossoms to remind one of the ministry of bitter herbs in the passover of the fathers.

Whatever the style of house, the first fact to hold in mind is that the structure was built around a chimney, which was not an adjunct, and was something other than a mere necessity. For into it went the finest sentiments of centuries of home building. Such a chimney

---

* I have myself measured more than one such fireplace in Blandford, and the above estimate is not an inch beyond the actual facts.

Two Ancient Homes

was the one standing in the center of John Baird's house, afterward passing into the ownership of James Knox,—gentleman of kindly spirit and culture of soul —in lot 22 west in the second division. Until its destruction by fire, it was one of the oldest houses then standing in town. In the room into which the front door opened, on the side toward the outer wall, stood two great upright joists, supporting the beams of the roof. Probably the same was true of other of the lower rooms. Those posts had been hewn, each of them, out of a separate tree trunk, and stood with the larger ends up, in order to afford ample support for the roof. Enough two-by-fours could have been carved out of them to stud the side of a house. This place is reached by taking the old Northampton turnpike, later known as the Huntington road, which intersects the northerly home lots in the old second division, on the west side.

One of the earliest types of house in Blandford was that still familiar to observers of ancient rural architecture all over New England. The ground plan is square, or nearly so. The gable has a much wider spread than the modern gable, whose frontage is sufficently occupied by one central window in the center. Not so the old house. This type of house is truly a story-and-a-half high, for through the center is space enough for one or two rooms with upright walls, directly under the ridge-pole, there being one full-size window in each end. Above and on either side of these rooms are little garrets, lighted by little windows,* each of them usually square, and of six panes in two tiers. Rarely these little windows are rectangular. The appearance gives the impression of rather stilted and mathematical exactness.

---

* It may be taken for granted that the earliest homes in Blandford had no glass windows. These were confined to the settled towns. The wilderness settlements for a long time used heavy wooden shutters, oiled paper serving under favorable weather conditions to let in light.

But this is sometimes contradicted—not to say relieved—by an airy nonchalance which throws an extra window in anywhere, of any shape or size, to suit convenience. The family grew, but the house itself not having the power to grow or reproduce itself had to be dealt with by force. One of the side garrets might be made off into a bed room. There slept the children, under the roof, where the pouring rains or the howling of the ceaseless winds on Blandford hills made monotonous music, the lullabies of Mother Nature.

Another and very familiar type of ancient homes is that of the unequally sloping roof. No better description of it can be given than that by Jane de Forest Shelton, in her book, "The Salt-Box House": "Built after the fashion that ruled largely in Connecticut for half of the last (i. e., the eighteenth) century, it was more convenient and commodious than graceful or picturesque. Colloquially, it was called a 'salt-box house,' its lines repeating those of the wooden salt-box that hung in the kitchen chimney. The ridgepole was set far to the front, from which a short roof pitched to the top of the second story, but the back roof sloped long and curveless to the outer line of the ceiling of the ground floor, reaching out a wing beyond that to cover the L that cuddled close to the main house." There were three examples of this type in Blandford in my day there. One was at the old north end, and was built by Captain Samuel Knox just after the Revolution. It was a ruin. Another was on Beech hill, occupied by Mr. Harris. The third was very small, and must have been very ancient. It stood on the North Blandford road, just west of the ten-acre lot and south of the "new cemetery." It was torn down some years ago. It was a favorite object to lovers of the ancient, inviting the brush of the visiting artist.

The town is dotted over with cellar holes or other traces of ancient dwellings close to which no modern road ever ran. To this day there stand the two fine rows of maple trees shading and beautifying the approach to the Shurtleff place on the Sheffield road a little below the old Elijah Knox house. This entrance entices one to find out what there is, or was, at the farther end. Nothing rewards the search but a hole in the midst of trees and brush, with other neighboring relics near by. Another such approach, not so fully arched by trees, but quiet, retired and dreamily inviting the pilgrim to inquiry and reverie, is the Oatley or Sperry place, on the turnpike to North Blandford, at the gore. Years ago there was a wrecked and tumbling fragment of an ell to a once more imposing dwelling. The curving and spreading branches of an ancient elm bent over it, lending reminiscent and artistic interest to the landscape of open meadow and pasture. Here were the Blairs, while up on the hill to the north, a full third of a mile from the highway — ancient or modern — nestles the lovely old home of the late Mr. E. E. Herrick, one of the oldest houses, as I suppose, in the gore, a story-and-a-half house, snug, reposeful, hospitable, modestly resting under magnificent maples, its windows looking out over a rolling country of hill and intervale. In pausing at these solitary old homes I run serious risk of exciting the jealousy of many a worthy and ancient Blandford family that might put in a claim for mention here on the ground of more primitive origins. I might have drawn a few pictures of the northernmost section of the town, where are majestic ranges of fine old shade trees eloquent of a forlorn but courageous attempt at village building, and apple orchards, moss-grown, grizzled, and—at last,—sober.

Sundry descriptive phrases in deeds of sale are picturesque and fragrant reminiscences of years spent as a tale that is told. "Home lot" is the most frequent:

Self-denials, pains and struggles transformed the wilderness and solitary place into a home where mother cradled the baby, and from which with lamentations an early father or mother was borne to an unadorned grave,—the epic of the pioneer. These "homelot" designations should not be allowed to die
"Unwept, unhonored and unsung."
There were the "Israel Gibbs homelot," "the Brown Farm, or Homestead," "the Cannon Farm," "the West Sloper Lot" and numberless others. All are eloquent of "our altars and our fires." As years were multiplied and little family incidents, farm interests and neighborhood associations were interwoven with the web of community life, one needed but to mention certain familiar incantations to produce instant telephotographs of history in the making; of history wrought into patriots' fibres, into the emigrants' passionate remembrance of home, into the eloquence of a statesman, into letters which were treasured more than bank accounts or jewels: the "Harper Lot," the "Bagg Lot" and the "Bagg well" in it; "Luther Laflin's Bear Lot," holding the reminiscence of some long remembered incident; "the Pickle Lot" and "the Little Orchard."

Dry-as-dust deeds furnish material for poet, musician, painter. One has built a new house, but "the old house" may never be forgotten. There are two parts of a certain home lot, one history, the other prophecy: parts "both improven and unimproven." There are "the mowing lot and the hill pasture," the "intervale lot," "the brook," "the branch." Abroad are "the gore farm" and "the black spruce swamp." In the midst of the small openings, widening ever through the toil of the settler, the smoke of three-score or more of log dwellings had begun to rise in curling and prophetic columns.

These early years were frightfully disturbed, and life

for long stretches of time was filled with terrors and racking uncertainties. One stands in reverence and in reverie before the slumberous ruins, or shadows of ruins all but gone back to dust. One has wished the time might be prolonged when these ancient homes with ridgepole sharply curving to the center, kitchen floor already down in the cellar, windows no more and doors wrenched and sagging on their hinges, shall become— as most have already become — a shapeless heap of broken and twisted lumber lying in and about the cellar, wrapping round the huge hulk of a once hospitable chimney. You essay to enter by the unbarred and open door. But Time has already told you Nay, and you pause reverently on the threshold before the yawning grave into which the floor has already gone. You behold the stairs, hugging the chimney of stone, to the second story, then turning and ascending again to the garret. And you seem to hear the clatter of young and nimble feet which have so many, many times, run up and down there. You go over to yonder silent yard, filled with dark gray slabs and ancient mounds bearing no other monument than an unhewn stone, and speaking no language other than that of its own gentle curve concentric with the arching skies which look down on them through all the days and all the nights.

The initiated, turning from these shady and perhaps brush-grown abodes of the first generations, to the highways of the living, will find now and then a survival of the ancient dwellings still held up for longer service by association with another generation of rural architecture. An ell or lean-to is discerned, once the entire home, or the main part of the home, of some of the ancients. The unpracticed eye will pass it over. But the trained and sympathetic observer finds it, and greets it like an octogenarian taking refuge with the grandchildren.

The folk were all tillers of the soil: minister, doctor —when such worthies were on the ground—tradesmen of every name, tavern-keeper, squire. All alike bore the smell of the field and were horny-handed. "Husbandman" was the common title of the householder or youth become of age. When he rose to the dignity of yeoman, he still was not above work. The "gentleman" and "squire" probably did less muscular toil, but they too were busy men. Poverty they knew about and could understand. But pauperism, laziness, shiftlessness were a kind of mystery, or provocation to wrath. If any man would not work, neither should he eat, unless in sorrow. Every stranger was watched as soon as he came to town, and jealously shadowed until his record became established. Whether man or woman, if suspicion of laziness or dependence rested upon any, that person was thereupon transported, or bonded in some way, or harried out of the place.

So it happened that every now and then such persons were "legally warned to Departe from this town." If so be—and it was a rare occurrence—the obnoxious person could not be got rid of, if question or obstacle of any kind blocked the way, the difficulty was strenuously and persistently attacked. What the antecedents of one James Welch may have been I do not know. But from the time, namely, in the year 1758, when this individual was appointed by vote of the town to be boarded one week by every householder, and then over again in the same round, and when at last they voted to petition the General Court for relief from this intolerable incubus, Welch continued to be the subject of anxiety, vexation and expense. The poor man was hopelessly crippled, and he was wholly dependent. All expedients were tried. The case became mixed up with the Rev. Mr. Morton, whose troubles seemed endless.

It found its way into the courts. Pity was lost in weariness and impatience. He who runs may read that for a man who would not, or even could not, work, the town had no welcome and little compassion, and the poor man himself had little peace. The town must be one of thrifty homes, whether or not they were generous.

The tavern was the place for intercommunication and advertising:

1746: "John tramen notified the Select men of Blandford that he the sd tramen put in to a hous in Blandford the Wedow watkins and her Children within 20 days after he had done it."

"Upon the thirteenth day of august 1774 Robart Henry took into his house a young woman & she calls hur name Rebeckah Knox and Ses She was Born in Ireland   august the 24   1774   he gave her in to the Select men."

These people, as we have seen, brought with them what they could, but it was not overmuch. One ox cart would not carry a great lot over such a road as "the devil's stairs." Some of the families had not so much as a horse, or an ox. It was nearly a generation after the settlement of Glasgow was made that one John Smith went from Northampton to our neighboring town of Murrayfield, all the way on foot, carrying on his back a five-pail iron kettle.* A settle, or a table, or a bed could hardly be carried on the back of man or ox, in addition to other necessary articles of more modest dimensions. Furniture had to be made, and they were obliged to begin before the era of local sawmills. The home was "ever so humble." "Gibbsey" things were better than none, better than borrowing.

We are not left altogether to conjecture. There is documentary evidence. The death of Samuel Ferguson

---

* History of Murrayfield.

occurred in 1741. He signed his will August 7, "in the year of our Lord god 1739," "being very sick and weak." In it he mentioned his home lot "and purches land." He had children, Samuel, Isabel, James, Joan, otherwise called "Ane" all minors under fourteen years of age. He also had a daughter married to William Mitchel. At his death he was in debt to Lawton for his estate, twenty pounds, and "to Reats 2 pounds." This is the inventory:

"viz. a house 10: 10: 0   a Cow 12: 0: 0
a Cow 8: 0: 0   a Chain 20/   31 - 0 - 0
Axes 2£ 2s 0   old Tools 14s plough & horse
  tackling 2£ 2s   a harrow 30s   a pot &
  trammil 50s   8 - 18 - 0
a Barr 20s fork   scythe & Sundry Iron tools
  3 - 7 - 0 Fryingpan 10s   a pannel 20s   5 - 17 - 0
a Rasor & hoan 12s Cloaths 3 - 0 - 0 Wooden
  Vesel 2 - 0 - 0 Corn 5 - 0 Wheel & Rook 30s 10 - 02 - 0

— o —

Of ye Goods Belonging to Moses Mitchel
  Brooght unto sd Fergusons Estate By his
  Widow Now Eleanor Ferguson viz a Bell
  & tools 35s Beds & Beding 10 - 0 - 0 Pots
  & tongs 20s a gun 2 - 10 - 0 a Wheel &
  chairs 20s Bellows 3s a Third of Which
  Belonging to Sd Ferguson is   5 - 16 - 0
The real estate is a house a true record of the Prizal
  Lot of 60 acres out land made by us
        her   his
Elener E Ferguson Admx Hugh Hamilton
        Mark   mark
                              Israel Gibbs
                              David Campbell"

In the will it was provided that, in view of family

prospects, it "beg uncertain" whether the expected child "be a son or a daughter I do make this provision viz:" if a son, and when arrived of age, Samuel shall give him one third of his land; or if a daughter, then 30 pounds "in curant money of this provance" etc. Israel Gibbs and Robert Young were to be the executors of the will. For some reason the judge appointed the widow administratrix. She was to have the use and improvement of the home lot, which after her decease was to pass to their children.

These instruments are worthy of some searching thought. Run over the articles named, and in imagination place them, one by one, where they belong in barn and house. Take a mental photograph of the interiors. How pitifully, how appallingly meagre they are! All this the combined possession of two families now become united because of a death. Let it be noted, furthermore, that this family was getting on, and continued to get on. The manhood capital was beyond the assigned function of the court to make appraisal of. Doubtless this slender equipment was in essential respects true of many another pioneer family in Glasgow Lands in those early days.

I do not know how better I can close this chapter on Blandford's earliest homes than to transfer to these pages a word picture written by a one-time school-girl there twenty-five years ago. Her home was away out in the northernmost border of the second division, in what was then called Beulah Land. The production was one of a series of school essays contributed to "The Blandford Monthly" by request of its editor. This literary gem was handed in by the teacher of the Center Grammar School, and is here reproduced just as it was written, without any thought of its ever being spread before the public eye, and without addition, subtraction or correction of any kind, first or last:

A LITTLE COUNTRY HOME

A long road leads to it. A delightful one too. Green woods on either side. Mossy carpets under low, green laurel bushes. But at the end there is a small home cottage. Very modest and unassuming. It is in a large field which has woods on all sides. In the early morning, when the sun first appears, the deep dark shadows from the woods on one side fall across the green field. And at evening the scene is so enchanting that one can almost wish the beautiful, red sun might stay in that spot so that the deep shadows of that side might remain in contrast with the tinted grass blades that are in the fading sun light.

About this time the farmers come, bringing the cows. Only a short time now until the scene is entirely changed and a twinkling light appears at the window and the only sound is the singing of the whip-poor-will.

INA M. CARTLAND.

Jan. 24, 1902.

TABLE AND BENCH

CHAPTER XVI

The Early Habits of The Blandford Scouts

Not two centuries have passed since Blandford began to be, if we compute time by the calendar. In reality, two or three new worlds have dawned and passed and dawned again in this interval. It all is equivalent to the procession of millenniums. To visualize the habits of these scouting squads of eighteenth-century builders of home and commonwealth one's sympathetic imagination must make some strong leaps. They camped down in the forest primeval amidst rough and rugged hills nearly a dozen miles removed from store or mill or social contacts. With only here and there a bit of an open meadow miles apart, with trees big enough to furnish masts for the king's navy growing in their very dooryards and crowding their charted streets, possessed of only the barest furnishings and meager implements of toil which had been carried by hand or piled on the backs of horses, they were there to begin social existence from the bottom up. What could they do in one brief summer, before winter snows should fall? for they fall soon and deep on Blandford hills. Well, they were resourceful. Poverty had long disciplined and hardened them. They knew the fundamental industries. Mass production had not come, was not within remotest vision of producer or seer. The individual was self-reliant. The home circle practiced a score or two of trades. Then there were the "hawkers and walkers," the peddlers who passed not by but did pass through every settlement in that part of the planet.

There were some specialized trades, and these were

well represented in this infant community. Blacksmiths, tanners, house carpenters, weavers were all there from the very first. Much raw material was in the soil, lying upon it, or growing out of it. Brick-making was done right there and then, as detailed on another page of this chapter. That would account for the forge of the smithy. The tanners would contribute their skill to the setting up of the bellows. Coal pits were early constructed in the midst of that forest primeval. Thence the smith got his specialized fuel. All were workers in wood, and cordwainers would complete the circle. Iron casting was probably done to an extent. I am the fortunate possessor of a diminutive anvil (not, however, of Blandford artisanship) which bears strong evidence of home production. The stem of it is driven securely into one end of a section of a tree trunk, which is shaped and strongly hooped. I can easily carry the whole contraption with one hand. I have no evidence that iron ore was ever dug out of Blandford earth, or was smelted there. This metal must, I suspect, have been brought in, and precious it must have been. Woods were a drug. They were of great variety, from the tall pines reserved for the king's navy to the alder or creeper.*

They had brought with them their precious implements for spinning, spooling, weaving; but how long must they wait and how hard must they work to furnish themselves with wool and flax? Hardihood, courage, ingenuity, the patient wearing out of the swift summer and slow winter by unremitting labor, the ingenuity of creators, the unflagging determination of men and women bred in the disciplines of hardness and deter-

---

* One who is curious to learn the almost infinite variety of woods and wood workings which entered into the labor and life of the early colonial homestead will do well to turn the pages of "Candle Days," by Marion Nicholl Rawson—The Century Company. There is also an extensive setting out of the smithy. And all is abundantly illustrated.

mination and buoyed by the spirit of prophecy and the consciousness of mastery,—all this and faith in God which their Ulster past had won, were their mental and spiritual assets. And they were sufficient.

Try to picture in imagination the resourceful labors of these advance scouts of civilization on their upturned slopes and narrow plateaus. Every tool was kept bright and sharp. Every boy old enough to handle a knife whittled out some useful implement by the blazing hearth after the evening meal. Every man was busy until sheer weariness drove him to bed. Every mother and daughter plied busily the instruments of female toil. By and by the spinning wheel, the reel, the sewing and knitting needles, and later still, and only here and there the loom, added their cheery clatter and hum to the other noises of the busy hive. Raising and preparing flax was a long, long process. Wool was available much sooner.

The combined Ferguson and Mitchel inventory reproduced in the last chapter lists a "wheel and rook." "Rook" is an Ulsterism for "rock." Burns sings:

> "Oh leeze me on my spinning-wheel,
> Oh leeze me on my rock an' reel."

The rock was a distaff, and the phrase, "Oh leeze me," is Scottish equivalent of, "I love." The poet goes on:

> "Wi' sma' to sell, and less to buy,
> Aboon distress, below envy,
> Oh wha wad leave this humble state,
> For a' the pride of a' the great?
> Amid their flaring, idle toys,
> Amid their cumbrous, dinsome joys,
> Can they the peace and pleasure feel
> Of Betsy at her spinning wheel?"

Another inventory soon to be spread on these pages lists sheep, woolen yarn, linen yarn, wheels, reel, but no loom. At first the weaving may likely have been done in the weaver's shops, of which there were a few. These acquisitions were gradual, as the first grind of hard drudgery wore off a little.

In the year 1762, nearly a full generation after the date of purchase, William Brown deeds to Solomon Brown, both "yeomen" now, the first division lot, under strict and explicit conditions. The instrument of sale will serve to show how affairs were moving on these hills, and will afford some true picture of the approved standard of living in the second generation of Blandford's existence. William sold to Solomon, presumably his eldest son, the whole of lot 19, sixty acres, "With all the buildings & Housing Standing on the Same," for the sum of four hundred pounds, Solomon to "Make Such Provision for the Said William Brown & his wife Martha Brown . . . as shall be good and Comfortable for their Subsistence both in times of health & Sickness viz. one Room in the House & So much of the Cellar as he or she shall have a Need of, also to keep two Cows & one horse Somers & Winters, also thirty Bushels of Grain, also one hundred & Eighty pounds of Beef, & also one third of the Cyder & apples the Said Land produces and Such Necessary Sauces as ye Land produces all of which if the Said Grantee faithfully perform towards ye Grantor & his wife then this Present Deed & Sufficiancy of fire wood also Drawn to the Door, To Remain in full force & Virtue otherwise to be Null & Void & of None Effect."

his

Dec. 10, 1762. Signed, "William   X   Brown & Seal"

mark

If he was illiterate, he was not unthrifty nor uncalculating, albeit he came "within an ace" of forgetting the wood.

Among my copied inventories, transcribed in whole

or in part at the Northampton probate registry nearly a score of years ago, is a brief extract from the inventory of John Knox's estate, of date 1741. The items are these:

1.	Second Division 60 acres	£16– 5
2.	One Coat	2–10
3.	one fine Shirt	15
4.	one fine Shirt	5
5.	Two neck bands	1–3
6.	one Pair of Stockens	6–3
7.	one pair of Breaches	5

Adding a little sympathetic imagination to the above brief catalogue, one may easily paint a mental picture of a self-respecting head of a family in Blandford when dressed up in his Sunday best.

One more inventory will suffice for our present purpose. This is of Armour Hamilton, and is dated 1748. It included these items, illustrative of stock raising and farm tillage:

	£	s.		£	s.
a black cow	20		Fine Cloth	23	
a fore (farrow?)			Coarse Cloth	26	
Cow	18		Wool	3–	8
a black Heifer	8		Woolen yarn	4	
a year Heifer	14		Linen yarn	2–	9
a black Calf	5–10		Hay	40	
a little Calf	1–10		Beef	10	
a brown Calf	5–10		Hied (Hide?)	2–	5
Sheep	9–15		Pease	1–10	
Hogs	32		Turnips	2–	2
a horse	40		Wheat	3–10	

The tools and implements are:

	£ s.		£ s.
Horse Traces	1–20	Harrow Teeth	1–10
a Spade	1	Wheels	1–10
Stillyards	1– 5	Areel	5
Axes	1	Scythes	1– 2
Hoes	15	Hay-forks	8
a Chain	1–15	Churn	5
a Hamer & axe	1	Square	16
a Coulter & Share	1–10		

This is a pretty good inventory for the time and place. Notable is the item of Wheat. Armour Hamilton had been an innkeeper, and intended to provide good fare, of grain and meat. His widow, Agnes, carried on his business after his death.*

David Boies, first selectman in the town and ruling elder in the church, dying about 1770, tything man true and tried in the fifties and sixties—years of the French and Indian wars—left to be divided among his heirs, along with other sundries eight chairs and a table, thirteen old barrels, a weaver's loom, two great wheels, one foot-wheel and "real," one box iron and heater. Page after page of the records in the probate registry in Northampton reveals that the earthly wealth of the days consisted almost solely of the unwilling soil and what come out of it by hard labor. It is recorded how Elder Matthew Blair, selectman for several terms and repeatedly moderator of town meetings, had one gun worth ten shillings—every man had use for a gun—one great coat worth twenty-four shillings, one "Brown Strait Body Coat," twenty-four shillings one penny; one

---

* Armour Hamilton's inventory, in full, as well as some account of his tavern, and that of his widow, is given in my "Taverns and Turnpikes," pp. 177ff.

black coat and vest, twenty shillings; woolen breeches, three shillings, one hat, two shoes, two shirts.

Of women's attire I have too little information. Mary Provin's is listed after the Revolution. Probably it differed little from what might have been before it. She had a "Black Gown," a brown gown, a skirt, a petticoat, a blue apron. Money, in any of these inventories, is not so much as mentioned, except in two or three instances, and then a few shillings only. There are saddles and pillions, farm tools and tools for general work. Little pewter is mentioned. James Caldwell, 1751, is said to have had three pewter platters, six plates and three basins; an old Camblet coat and Jacket with no sleeves, worth six shillings, and a pair of old leather breeches, worth three. Rarely we find such luxuries as a pair of silk-thread stockings, a fine shirt and neck-bands. In the early inventories, books are for the most part wanting. The Bible is about all; usually one, rarely two, sometimes a very few other books worth a few shillings or a pound or two; always bottles, seldom a looking glass.

In the northerly part of the town of Granville there was a fine brick building,* made of clay from the farm. In this house was discovered a document recording a province tax levy of King George II. This levy provided that payment might be made in kind, at stipulated rates, twenty articles being named as acceptable. Among the twenty are these: Hemp, Indian corn, winter rye, winter wheat, barley, barrel pork, barrel beef, beeswax, tried tallow, peas, sheep's wool, tanned sole leather, all of which might be and many of which certainly were available by Blandford farmers for the purpose named. The other articles listed were mostly of iron or products of

---

* My impression is that it has been razed by the City of Springfield in the interests of their water supply—a progressive policy which has been pursued for the last fifteen to twenty years.

the sea. Doubtless local barter was carried on in this way.

Look at some of those utensils and furnishings. They worked with them not only; many of them they made. The dung fork, the hay fork, the drag teeth—I know not how many common tools of the barn and the farm —were hammered out at the village blacksmith's forge. I have some of these primitive tools in my possession. From the John Knox farm I have the precious gift of the old dung and hay forks. The former has three teeth —one broken—of straight and stout construction. It would do duty as Neptune's trident. The hay fork is curved and much slenderer, but very small. The handles were cut in the woods, were carefully selected, hewn with the axe, then taken into the kitchen, where they were whittled into shape and smoothness of a winter evening.

The tradition lingers. I myself have seen the handle of a Blandford blacksmith's hammer cut and shaped by his younger brother, the elder carefully directing the younger how to do in order to insure the hammer its proper rebound from the anvil. The crane, the slice, the door hinges and latches, even the nails were home-made. Many an ancient house or ruin contains them still. "The farmer bought rods, and in many hours, when debarred from outdoor labor, often at the kitchen fireside, he hammered them into nails,—as important in his vocation as the claw-tips of his own fingers were to the work of his own hands. . . . . The mill took the bar iron, rolled it into ribbon, and slit into these rods." * When these nails were sold, they were sold by the hundred.

I have seen an ancient Blandford hammer thus used for making horse-shoe nails. The handle was worn nearly through by the pressure of thumb and fingers.

---

* Economic and Social History of New England, by William B. Weeden.

The owner remembered its replacing a predecessor similarly worn. How many other predecessors there may have been who can tell?

J. G. Holland's monumental work on the History of Western Massachusetts is a repertory of knowledge as to the farming methods of the early population. As to the plough, he says: It was "composed almost entirely of wood, and of clumsy construction — of itself almost heavy enough for a single team, and admirably adapted to load itself with earth, until its influence upon the soil was but little more than would result from the drawing a log across it, unless it was frequently relieved of its load by the wooden shovel which the ploughman always had at hand for the purpose." Then he proceeds in detail to describe the successive improvements made in this wonderful instrument of civilization.

It was long before any considerable grass crop could be cut on the new clearings. In the Gibbs historical address it is related that "when the early settlers broke down the beaver dams at North Meadow, most of their hay was obtained there, for the grass sprang up and grew luxuriantly."

"The method of harvesting this hay, (says Mr. Gibbs) was curious. Tradition informs us that the laborers — especially Israel Gibbs — used a straight stick, which answered a threefold purpose, viz.: as snath, rake, and fork; and it was so bungling that it was then, and even now (1850) anything that is coarse, is called 'Gibbsey'. A cow was taken to the meadow, fastened to a tree, and fed with the hay while they labored there. The milk afforded them a healthful and nutritious beverage. From the circumstance of their harvesting hay at this place, they gave it the name of 'North Meadow'; a name it has borne ever since."

Some of these "Gibbsey" implements survive. All

praise to a man who had the spirit to invent, and to construct, and to push ahead when beginnings had to be made with almost nothing. Let it not be forgotten that this Israel Gibbs brought the first cart into town. Possibly, with all this ridicule, a bit of jealousy may have been mingled.

Blandford never had any "commons" strictly so called, such as Salem and other old towns had. There must have been pastures considered common by general consent, certain groups of landholders banding together to fence their lands in common. Such enclosures included cultivable lands, and might surround other smaller enclosures held exclusively for individual use. At the very first there would seem to have been one general pasture, but if there were, none arises to say where. There is sufficient evidence to show that for a time the herding of cattle was a town affair. March 21, 1743, the town "Voted granted to Hugh Black and James Gumery for the youse of their Bulls this yer £3–10–0." The year preceding each farmer whose cow had a calf was obligated to "pay to the owner of the bull: 2: shillens." Action was taken yearly in town meeting to regulate these interests. The times when the males of the herd or flock should be kept in pastures were regulated by the town. The sheep, "the Naggs," "the Hogs" were some years allowed to run at large, and sometimes not, according to the whim of the voters, or the previous activity of the animals. "Hogg Rives" and fence viewers were chosen. After a time the condition laid upon the running of the swine at large was that they should be "lawfully youked & Ringed." Once—in 1768—the term "Commons" is used, when the liberty of those lands was accorded to the swine. The whole subject is provokingly obscure. The apparent chaos attending the subject is

due in great part to the peculiar conditions of proprietorship in the town of Blandford.

All this concerning brute beasts. But what of human
lives? Let us hope that the entry in Rev. Mr. Ballantine's diary, pastor at Westfield, cites the exception, not
the rule, among these hills. It was in September, 1767:
"Awakened this morning by the ringing of the bell to
collect men to go in quest of a lad in Blandford, who
was lost. He was absent three nights, but was found
alive. His father and mother had forsaken him, but the
Lord had mercy. . . . A man in Murrayfield knew the
child was lost, and thought he heard a child cry, but he
had a hired team and could not afford to let it lie still
while he searched."

Chimneys were built of stone up to the first floor.
All the oldest houses surviving even in ruin have or had
brick chimneys at the least above the ridgepole. The
bricks were home-made. Bricks even to top off a chimney
could hardly be brought into primitive Blandford on
horse-back or in a cart. Clay was abundant, even if not
of the first quality. One may range about among old
cellar holes and find bricks containing pebbles half or
three-quarters of an inch in diameter, and as close together as raisins in grandmother's plum pudding. They
were rough and coarse and rude, cut out of the clay soil
of the farm and laid down in the door-yard ready for the
kiln. One such precious relic has been preserved having
plainly stamped upon its face the footprints of two feet
of the family porker as he nosed about the yard. He
made "his mark."

As for mortar, that too was of home manufacture.
One's admiration of the ingenuity of the fathers in-
creases with every old document or ruin brought to light.
Here they were, in a country of hard schists — horn-
blende, flaggy mica, Hoosac and Savoy — and as barren

of limestone ledges as of salt water. Yet they went to work making lime and mortar. In a northwest and southeast swath across the town is a scattering of limestone boulders, emptied down by the glaciers of the ice period and left there, weathered and dull, to look like all other common stones except to the eagle eyes of men whose wits had been sharpened by necessity and adventure. How long these limestone boulders lay there untouched I know not. Presumably not so very long. Anyway, the bricks of those house chimneys, and what few brick houses there were, were laid in mortar in the days before stage coaches and wagons — and it takes wheels to carry much lime very far. Along that swath of limestone fugitives were kilns where the men who beat the French and Indians and drove out the British burned their lime, that they might sit in comfort by their hearthstones with their families in peace and gladness. One is still to be seen by the interested seeker, near the brook which makes fertile the intervale where the Rev. Josph Badger had his farm, and on the banks of which many a shop and mill now silent dipped the buckets of its busy wheels in the descending stream. It lies behind a sugar house in a sleepy little hollow in the woods. Near by is the tree-covered mill-race of a long abandoned sawmill, silent and smoothed by the fallen leaves of years, while the brook, like waters forgotten of the foot, goes slipping down to Little river, unvexed except by an occasional fisher. In that secluded dell is a mound made of stones generously padded with sod and overgrown by flowers and shrubs. It looks as though it might be some old cromlech of a forgotten time. It is the ruin of a primeval lime kiln, an industrial monument standing, like many another stone-heap of the past,—in old Canaan or Babylonia,—"unto this day," and certain to stand, unless molested by irreverent hands, for ages to

The Old Lime Kiln

come. A few rods away, scattered thickly about, are limestone boulders, brought by the kindly ministry of Nature, or Providence, for the behoof of these wanderers whose successors depend so completely upon the commerce of the world.

The windows and doors were home-made, doors sometimes containing a panel cut out of a single board from the wood lot. Doubtless tables were so made, also the baby's cradle and the coffins in which the dead were carried to the grave. Wooden utensils turned out by the lathe were a later product.

In short, about everything had to be created. Hard work and ingenuity, all imaginable kinds of work the situation invited, demanded. Farmer, or husbandman, or if you will, yeoman, had to get down at it. There was the subduing of the earth—this forest-grown and stony earth—in such wise as that the daughters and sons of Blandford grew up on the consciousness that mastership over nature, not slavery to it, was their calling and election. Put a Yankee on Juan Fernandez, said Lowell, "and he would make a spelling-book first and a slat-pan afterwards." I incline to think—the spelling-book having already come, in Blandford,—the slat-pan was the first care. But the spelling-book was not forgotten. When it was, they made their own spelling. Slowly and painfully, yet steadily, they forged out a community which took an honorable part in the commonwealth.

There was resource; there was mother wit; there was increasing comfort; meager at first, but growing. And self-respect there was, which led them to tackle toil, endure hardship and grapple with the lusts of the flesh.

We have not yet for the most part strayed very far afield. But the great Outside was all about them. This was much, even when confined to the forty-nine square miles of the township itself. In this great forest the wild beast had his lair. Traditions have come down concerning early surveyors getting home just in the nick of time after a hot chase by wolves. The days of the French and Indian wars were close at hand in the very beginning of the town's life. For years the whole countryside lived in watchfulness and recurring panic. A gun and plenty of dry powder and lead were as necessary as the scythe and the plough. The inventories bristle with arms: "1 gun"; "firelock and ammunition"; "1 gun and sword," —in Matthew Blair's, 1753.

Probably much the larger outlay on road-building at first was made upon the two main parallel streets which were the dividing lines between the tiers of lots in the two divisions, and the road from the valley towns westward—to Pixley's and beyond. The first and second division roads were connected by one from the second division pond to the main street, corresponding to the Northampton road of later years, and entering the main street between lots 35 and 36; that is, just south of the Samuel Boies tavern of a later generation. That was in 1742, when also a short section of the present road to Chester was extended past and beyond the Knox-Stewart house and the Brown sisters'—to use landmarks which did not then exist. Another, of uncertain identification, which looks much like that over Sunset Rock, ran southerly for about a mile toward Granville. The rest, so far as there were any, were nothing better than bridle paths leading out into "the Gentlemen's lands." As to this, one tradition is sufficiently eloquent, to the effect that two men on their way to Great Barrington, past Pixley's, sank down in exhaustion and died. Probably "the town and common road" was little if any better than an ox path. Everywhere outside the settlement the silence and dense shade of the forest brooded over all. In the early deeds no settlements are mentioned except this one and

Westfield. There were none anywhere about, though townships were laid out, and some few scattering beginnings were being made. Some local determinations which seem now to have passed out of mind come back to us out of musty records like voices of the past. One was the "Tract of Six Hundred acres" lying "Between Glascow and Westfield at a Pond called Twelve Mile Pond Ten Mile Pond," which must be that later known as Hazzard's pond, now Russell pond, on the shore of which a half-century later the Rev. Joseph Badger organized a Congregational church. There was another tract in " ye South west Corner of Glascow," 780 acres in extent, belonging to Lawton, as did the one last mentioned, and, like the other, containing a pond later known as the Great Lake, or Big Pond, now the upper Otis pond. Apparently this same tract — for the ambiguous phraseology of the deed leaves one in doubt — was Belfast (already mentioned), "in which Lyes a Pond and thro the same Runs a River." To the northward, indefinitely, there was unbroken forest.

I think it is Sydney George Fisher who has remarked that in those old days everybody rode a horse or walked, that New Englanders lived in the saddle, taught their horses to pace in order to favor long-distance travelling, sixty miles in a day being not over-tiring to a good pacer. And he observes, further, that no very great love of riding developed. Probably conditions were too stern, and necessity left little room for the element of pleasure.

Of early education, Rev. John Keep in his historical sermon says: "Very limited were the means of Education which the children of the first settlers enjoyed. Parents taught their children what they could, without any expectation of sending them to school. The first school was taught by James Carter, a sea captain, in the house of Robert Black, because it had in it two rooms.

For several years the schools were taught in dwelling houses. Two months in the year were all that could be allowed. No school was taught by a woman till about 1770."

There are some ameliorations and compensations to take account of. The first struggle with nature was biting and cruel. The daily round and common task as already outlined was itself a discipline which amounted to a good deal of education of children of the generation which then was. The men of Blandford were not an unlettered and ignorant crew, if we compare them with the general condition of New England society. Their spelling was original, but notoriously so was the spelling of pretty nearly everybody. The signatures were those of men more used to the scythe and the axe than to the pen — scrawling, uneven, angular and labored. There were exceptions, and David Boies was a shining one. Comparatively few were the men among them that could not read and write. There were more women, for the education of girls in all early New England was not esteemed important. But there were strong mothers and worthy daughters.

The earliest records of the town are absolutely silent about schooling. For some unexplained reason there is no extant evidence that the proprietors complied with the statutory requirement that a lot of sixty acres should be set aside for the benefit of schooling: nothing but a portion of the ten-acre public area.

In his "Three Episodes of Massachusetts History," C. F. Adams says: "The town clerks were not then, any more than they are now, chosen for conspicuous illiteracy, and the records prior to 1800 are conclusive as evidence of the instruction in writing given in the public schools of the period; nor is there any reason to suppose the instruction in other respects was better, or the results attained more creditable. In point of fact the children were neither taught much, nor were they taught well; for through life the mass of them, while they could do little more in the way of writing than rudely scrawl their names, could never read with real ease or rapidity, and could keep accounts only of the simplest kind." But that was about all the average child or man was expected to do. "The New England schools of the eighteenth century," continues this same writer, "doubtless reflected the usages of the homes." It would appear that Blandford school history, after all, might not, considering all conditions, and especially all manhood products in its history, be more barbarous than the like history of other towns. The life of the day sharpened wit, cultivated resourcefulness, invited invention, and afforded unceasing and ever-changing direction to self-reliance and to association. The eye and hand, brain and heart were trained. Life was hard; toils were unceasing; pleasures were few. Standardization was unknown, and there must often have been an exhilaration in work not now appreciated by the unionized worker. Wit and brawn were given free movement.

One needs to read the gravestones in the old burying ground under the pines to learn the tale of sickness and early deaths. It is pitiful indeed to muse upon the oft-told tale of infant mortality and of youths stricken down in the day of their promise. Families were large and sorrows multiplied. The drinking habits of the people all over the country brought on a frightful train of diseases: "kidney or bladder troubles," and "running sores which could not be closed."* Small-pox was periodical. In 1759 the town was agitated over the question of building a hospital, but nothing was done about it. Inoculation had not yet won the confidence of the people. In

* C. F. Adams, "Three Episodes" etc.

1761 the town by vote declined to allow it, and the scourge went unchecked.

How through all these years the gaunt ghost of poverty haunted this frontier settlement of Western Massachusetts may be sufficiently illustrated. The town clerk made this entry under date of May 13, 1742: "The inhabitines of Sd town being warned ass the Law Directs Did meet att the Publick Meeting houes of Sd town David Boys Moderator:

"Voted) thatt there be an excuse sent to Cort by
) Westfield Debility for our Nott sending
) man to Cort."

"Westfield Debility" was not some despatch express. The meaning seems to be that the neighboring town in the valley, where their grist was ground, would, through their representative, present the "Debility" of Blandford as a suitable reason for excusing this town from present representation.

The matter receives further illustration from records of county taxes paid by the town. The first one charged was (English notation of pounds, shillings, pence) in 1752, 1-2-0. Bedford (Granville) had that year, 1-15-7; Westfield, 9-18-13. Blandford's tax was paid by John Cochran, constable. Figures for other years are: 1753, 1-10-8, by John Hamilton; 1754, 2-1-1, James Moor; 1755, 1-17, smallest tax in the county; 1756, 0-14-8; 1757, 0-14-4-2 (farthings), paid by John Cannon; 1758, 1-4-8, John Scott; 1760, 1-18-9-2; 1761, 2-3-7-1, John Wilson. Granville paid, that year, 3-9-1-2. 1762, 3-3-4-1, Samuel Wilson; 1763, 4-4-6-1, John Boies; 1764, 6-2-11, William Mitchel; 1765, 7-3-4-3, Robert Blair; 1766, 4-14-8, Robert Henry; 1767, 5-11-0-2, John Gibbs; 1768, 3-18-1-1; 1769, 11-2-0-3, Paul Stewart; 1770, 10-3-11-2, Nathaniel Taggart; 1771,

7-14-10, William Carnahan; 1772, 5-11-0-2; 1773, 8-8, David McConoughy; 1774, 20-14-11, Silas Noble.

In 1763, a census ordered by the mother country and "negligently executed" * by the province owing to suspicion of its purpose, credited Massachusetts with a population of 245,000 white persons and 5,000 colored. Blandford was reported as having 316, and all of Hampshire county (including the present Hampden county also), 17,516. Boston had then 15,520, Springfield, 2,755. By 1776, Blandford had reached 772, when the fathers of men to become famous were coming forward.

I cannot account for the tradition that the first physician in Blandford was Dr. Ashley, in 1745. There is documentary authority for the following named, gleaned from deeds, or more generally from inventories of estates. The dates given are those of the documents: Dr. Smith, 1759; Dr. John White, 1760, 1770; Dr. Mather, 1770; Dr. Josiah Harvey, 1774; Dr. Benjamin Cross, 1774; Dr. Robert King, 1774.

Roads and industries go hand in hand. Imagine the colossal labor required to pull stumps and remove boulders through miles and miles of forest and swamp. The cart road was an evolution. It would never be cleared except as necessity created the demand, and the demand became imperative. Down in Westfield, in the summer of 1762, the Rev. Mr. Ballantine set out for Suffield in his sulky. "Having got about 3 miles," he says in his diary, "there being a cart in the way, my horse started, ran back, threw me from the sulky, and ran over me, but through God's goodness, not much hurt." This was in a valley thoroughfare, on the way to Hartford.

Down to the year 1749, little or nothing was done by the town in road-making outside the rectangle of set-

---

* Barry, II, 272.

tlers' home lots. Aside from "the road to Tunak," the first long outreach was the road "to North Meddow Brook" and thence to the town line. This became later in the century the northerly stage route, past the Bruce and Baird taverns. Like the town street, it was established four rods wide; that is, on paper. It was an ideal. Land damages were allowed where it seemed just. Not infrequently the building of a fence was esteemed sufficient satisfaction.

In describing the primeval difficulties of the first settlers, Mr. Keep says, in his historical sermon so often quoted: "For the first years, and from what I can find, for about ten years the inhabitants were obliged to go ten miles to a grist-mill for their grinding. This would occupy a day for a man who owned a horse, but many had not this accommodation. When the families first came on there was little hay cut. A cow and a very few sheep, a man forehanded could keep through the winter. Hence many were obliged to keep their horses in the winter season at Westfield. For such it would be necessary, in order to get their grain ground, first to go after their horse, then take their corn to Westfield to mill, and return with the meal, and then go back again with the horse and come home on foot. This would make a man sixty miles travel to get home to his family with one grist of meal. This was a common occurrence in the first settlement of this town." Mr. Gibbs adds that home mortars were used by some to prepare coarse meal. Mr. Keep further says that "Indian corn was the chief support of the inhabitants when the land was new." I wonder why this early historian did not mention potatoes.

The story about getting grist in Westfield a whole decade would be almost unbelievable were it not for the fact that Mr. Keep was close to the evidence. Old

Old Mill-Wheel and Watering Trough

people were there who knew, and he diligently inquired. The compiler of a "History of the Connecticut Valley,"* is responsible for the statement that a grist mill was probably erected in Blandford before 1745 by Captain Kelso. No authority is given for the statement, and no details are offered. Kelso is an unknown name in Blandford early history. Mr. Keep states that the first grist mill he could learn anything about was erected in 1755. But it is possible from documentary evidence to push that date back a good deal.

October 1, 1748, as by deed of record in the Springfield registry, Francis Wells, the proprietor, sold to "David Campble of Blandford" "all the Grist mill as it now Stands on Lott No fifty one w. *th* Dam and appurtenances belonging to said Mill, and also one Hundred acres of Land of Said Lott." This land was to abut upon the settlers' homestead lots, and to lie in a square. The sale carried with it the "benefit of y.*e* Streams." How long this grist mill had been there who can say? But there it was, indisputably, doing business, and Campbell thought it, with the farm, a good bargain at two-hundred pounds. Is it possible that this is the mill vaguely indicated in the treaties above named, and that transcribers misread "Kelso" for "Wells"? Campbell seems to have preferred to live alongside neighbors, in No. 3 of the first division settling lots, where "James McClintock built a House." By 1760 he had developed the milling business until he had "Corn-mill Sawmill & Bolting Mill," and sold a half-interest to his son James, who sold it back to his father three years later.

David Campbell died in 1769 at the age of 58. The inventory of his estate indicates that he owned "Two Bibles and some other Books" valued at thirteen shillings, and that he died possessed of "½ a pew in the

* Published by Louis H. Everts, Philadelphia.

meeting House" appraised at one pound ten. "His Dwelling House & Farm" were valued at one-hundred pounds, and he is credited besides with "two old Mills & two Saws" worth fifty pounds. His life had been a simple one, if busy, for the inventory indicates nothing of large resources or even comfort beyond the usual modicum enjoyed under the severe conditions of the time and place. His old miller's hat was either worthless, or it served for seven days in the week, for the catalogue itemizes "one Hat and his wearing apparel," all appraised at one pound ten—the same as his pew. Farming and milling had been interspersed as occasion and the seasons demanded. That it was not always easy to collect bills is illustrated by his having to take by execution process in 1752 a piece of land on the "Highway or Town Street," in first division lot Number 3, at the top of the hill above his mill. The unfortunate creditor was Thomas McClentock, son of James, and he had built a house there which became the residence of James Campbell.

Of course there must have been a "road to the mill." It was not an easy matter to build or maintain, for the mill hollow is deep down between the hills, and the plunge is precipitate, the road having had to be changed once and again on this account. The first way was displaced in 1750 by another which was made to run along the northerly side of lot two in the first division, and it was "voted" in town meeting "that the man that Clears ye mill Road (which was a rod wide only) shall have their pay alowed them in thair next Highway Rates." The importance of this road is indicated by the unusual allowance of forty shillings per acre damages to Thomas Reed for the land taken. In 1764 David Campbell gave the town, "forever" a "Rood two Roads wide," the transaction being duly recorded in the town clerk's

book. That road, or something approximating it, passing
the present-day house of Samuel Richardson, is still
open, or was a few years ago, being a section of a rural
delivery mail route, but for ever claiming the distinction
of reverting to the condition of a mountain torrent's
stony bed. A "new road," so called, laid out only after
another century had dawned, diverging to the southward at the foot of Tannery hill, was hardly constructed
and well sampled before "Reuben Boies & 18 others"
addressed the court of general sessions in a petition to
have it discontinued. They maintained that the old
was better, especially that it was "dryer." Thus with
lagging footsteps and slow do reforms come in.

Campbell's mill besides being important in itself was
located on a main highway between Beech hill and
Granville on the one hand and the village on the other.
The mill buildings were on an island in the river. How
long the inhabitants were satisfied to ford the stream
the records fail to tell. In 1772 the town granted ten
pounds "in addition to a grant of twenty Days' work
Granted by the town March the 12 1770 to any Person
or Persons that shall Buld and mentain a good Sufficient
Bridge (for the tearm of ten years) over the Little River
near David Campbells Mill." This was the second
David, who also became a substantial citizen. He was
for a time collector for "the wild land rates," knocking
down under the hammer every now and then a piece of
real estate wrested from the always irksome tenure of
the original proprietors. This David Campbell was not
a son of the first David, but evidently a kinsman, and
the administrator of the elder David's estate. In 1777
he sold the whole property to Jonathan Frary, coming
from Middletown, Connecticut. This is a little beyond
our present period of review, but to complete the chapter it may be added that in the deed of conveyance the

statement is made that "on the sd Land is one dwelling house & one Mill House two Barns one Grist Mill & Saw Mill." The property became known after this as Frary's mills, and it grew in importance with the growth of the town. Down there in that mill hollow stood, a decade and a half ago, an old, old house bearing all the hall-marks of the ancient architecture of these colonial days. Among the developments of water power would inevitably be the sawmills. From the nature of the material handled, these would naturally be more numerous than the grist mills. The earliest one of which I happen to have record is mentioned in a deed of sale, of date, July 3, 1745, by John Walker of Londonderry, carpenter, to John French, of the same town. The location is lot 3 on the west of the second division, sixty acres, "Together with a Sawmill on the aforesd. Lot." This was on Potash brook, near the Rowley place of a later generation.

More important, apparently, was a saw mill enterprise undertaken by Matthew Blair. It was located on the "Branch," in the second division, in lot 8, east. This is at the foot of the hill below what is popularly called "the second division school house," which latter is where for a few rods the modern Russell road coincides with the ancient second division road. "The road to the mill," as it was called, takes a precipitate plunge to the north down into the bowels of the earth to the level of the brook's bank, crosses the same and ascends the opposite bank of the stream. Spanning the brook is a gem of an old bridge, and the whole bit of landscape down there is one of the beauty spots of the township. In 1760 the town voted to build a road to it "Eastward from the metting House." The mill, of course, was within the boundaries of the settling lots, and was for many years known as "Blair's mill." Matthew Blair, May 25, 1753, conveyed to Robert Blair of Blandford, Carpenter, the whole lot on which the mill was situated, and one-third of the mill. The conveyance imparts the information that the mill was "lately Erected," and bears date of May 25, 1753.

Another saw mill, outside of the home-lot rectangle, like David Campbell's, was on the "gore road" so called, to be sharply distinguished from the modern gore road. This road was laid out by the town in March, 1768. It left the town street between the lots of Matthew Blair and William Carnahan, at about the location of the late J. P. Nye's homestead, and ran westerly then southwesterly, crossing the present North Blandford road, over hill and stream and meadow, through the gore to what the modern maps call Bedlam brook, and to Robert Blair's saw mill. Trout fishermen familiar with Blandford streams know the place, a little way below the house of the late Mr. Millard. The mill-dam embankment is still there, and in the midst is an old elm, gone or going to decay, with trunk something like two feet in diameter. At the beginning this road was called Gore Lane. By 1770 the selectmen, by order, opened another road, starting near Robert Blair's saw mill, crossed "madle (middle) Branch," and ran southwesterly to David Campbell's mill. This last road has remained. The old Gore Lane was long years ago abandoned. How early Robert Blair's mill was operated I do not know. But the story of these roads reveals a rather early extension of local activities to the southwest.

It would seem almost beyond doubt that other early saw mills sprang up on Gibbs brook, which was known also as Gulf brook. Guess-work is not necessary, however, in connection with the mill privilege at the northeast corner of lot 8 east in the second division, at the foot of the hill on the modern Russell road, at the fork of the roads where the late Lyman N. and Mrs. Nye lived and carried on — as hearty and hospitable souls as ever lived. It is a beautiful spot, a gem of a mill pond with the gorge below it. One who has climbed the hill above the mill and looked down over it all cannot soon forget the picturesqueness of the scene. Here James Campbell located in his day. The town meeting of March, 1771, allowed a road past it provided the abutters would give the land. It is thus described: "Beginning at the Second Division street & running East on the line between John Ferguson & James Campbell half on Each Lott to the steep hill above the Brook then Running across James Campbells Lott on the Bank of the Brook to the Bridge then Running east betwen sd Campbells Lott and Robert Kings Lott to the end of the said Lotts." This is substantially as the road to Russell still runs. Nine years earlier than this a mill was operating there, owned by "Robert Blair of Westfield," selling to John Ferguson on this wise: part of lot 8, second division, east, "containin a road 21 rods & 2/3 running quite through said Teer of Lotts"; a lot of twenty-five acres bounded easterly on land of a proprietor, together with one-half of a "Certain Sawmill" adjoining, "called by the name of Blairs Mill Standing on Middle or fall Brook." The description is specific and unmistakable, and is not to be confused with the mill down in the meadow of "Madle Fall" in the Gore. The arrow points still backward to an indefinite beginning.

Thus they did. Running mills and shops became a "habit"— Blairs or no Blairs. The running brooks invited it. The necessities demanded it. The proclivities of an industrious folk led them to revel in it. As the decades slipped along, mills larger or smaller sprang up all over the territory, and manufacture branched out into diversified and multiplied production. But this is the story of a later period, when little mills could be operated only when water was flush, and so became known as "buttermilk mills."

Potash brook was sprinkled all along with them to the boundary of Russell. Following along its banks one summer day, for several miles, noting every broken dam or stray relic of an unremembered water power, I saw lying in the grass and shrubbery a diminutive mill-stone, perhaps two and one-half feet in diameter—so small and light that, alone, I raised it and rolled it from its bed, wishing I might carry and lift it into my buggy and take it home. Its story I know not, for it kept its own secret, and there was none else to reveal it.

Potash brook received its name from the manufacture of that product so necessary in the making of soap. The everlasting burnings connected with clearing the forests furnished the raw material for lye, and potash would afford one of the bases necessary to home soap-making, and an article of barter for the peddler. Potash works were established at the first turn of the road which now runs from the center of the village to Russell, at the head waters of the little stream. The capital and mechanical outlay for making potash were almost negligible; the product was used also in bleaching and quite a variety of manufacturing operations. Before the end of the century potash works in Massachusetts were numbered by the hundred.

Robert Huston, one of the original settlers, was a tanner. There seems to be no extant record of his working at his trade in Blandford. It however is past reasonable belief that he did not. It is and was, an elemental industry. Blandford folk would of course take their cows' and sheep's hides to him to tan, for shoes, harnesses and straps. Huston lived just east of the meeting house. On the lot just opposite, in the year 1768, a young man, John Watson by name, apparently a tanner, attracted from abroad by the growing enterprise of the place and the opportunity to ply his trade, bought and settled down. Near to his house, and on a little brook flowing from a living spring a few rods above the place, Watson established his tannery. The slope is still known by the familiar name of Tannery hill, and traces of tan bark were discoverable on the place well into the present century.

In those early days tanneries consisted generally of oblong boxes or hogsheads sunk in the earth near small streams, and without covering or outlet below, thus serving as vats or leaches. A few similar boxes were placed above ground for lime vats and pools. There was an open shed for a beam house, and in a circular trough fifteen feet in diameter, hemlock bark was crushed by alternate wooden and stone wheels turned by two horses —usually old or blind (poor things!)—a half-cord of ground bark being thus turned out in a day. The industry was sufficiently important, as early as the middle of the century, to warrant the province receiving "good tanned sole leather" in payment of the province tax. John Watson speedily prospered and became one of the wealthy and influential men of the town.

Of course, cider mills were everywhere, as the tavern business ever more and more flourished. Distilling also was done. Liquor flowed freely, and, as already noted in Chapters XIII and XIV, real estate business was made feverish by mortgages, foreclosures and all the legal paraphernalia of court proceedings. Even ecclesiastical councils had liquor served to the delegates and ministerial members, appropriations therefor being duly entered in the town records.* The days of social reform had not yet come.

Certain registries had to be made in the town clerk's book:

"Blandford Septembr ye 21: 1746

"upon ye fourth day of sd month Isaac Goodeal swapt or Chainsed a hors with John Boies of sd town and Delivered him at his own proper Esteat befor or in presence of Israel Gibbs and Samuel Carnochan being witnesses the hors which sd Goodeal Delivered to sd Boies is a white hors with some gray hairs upon his Leges and Reeps with a Brand Lightly Branded with ye Letter C upon ye near Buttock and by Estimation six year old

Israel Gibbs
      his
Samuel Carnochan
      mark"

"October the 29 1749

"then taken up by James Caldwel of Blandford a red lined steer Coming in two years old with white on the face & belly with a peace cut out the off Ear."

All sorts of notices were nailed up in the taverns: town meeting warrants, notices of sales, administrators' notices, legal notices of every imaginable kind, lost and strayed notices. "Vandues" were held there. They were the common meeting places, the club houses of provincial days.

There was always a large interchange of life between the Scotch Irish towns in New England, and even farther away. A century later, in the days of the Ohio migrations, men walked back and forth between the east and west — between Blandford and the "New Con-

---

* These matters are treated at length in "The Taverns and Turnpikes" etc.

necticut"; did it repeatedly, some of them habitually.
It would appear to have been almost as common as
riding. In these earlier times it was not an every-day
occurrence, as note the long intervals, already observed,
between signing and registering deeds of sale of land.
But it was done, over and over. Young men rode or
walked abroad to woo their brides. Look over the columns of banns and marriages in the Appendix, and see.

Whenever Matthew Blair, or some other neighbor,
went abroad on business, he did errands for his friends
—beyond a doubt. Letters were so carried every
whither; they were even entrusted to the itinerant peddlers. Post riders there were, at intervals, but the expense was great, over two pounds to carry a letter from
Boston to Portland. Recall the story of the gathering of
the Blandford Scouts from every whither to Hopkinton.
Considering the paucity of news-print in those days, this
interchange of news was little less than a miracle.
"Every one who went upon the road bore messages." *

* Richardson Wright.

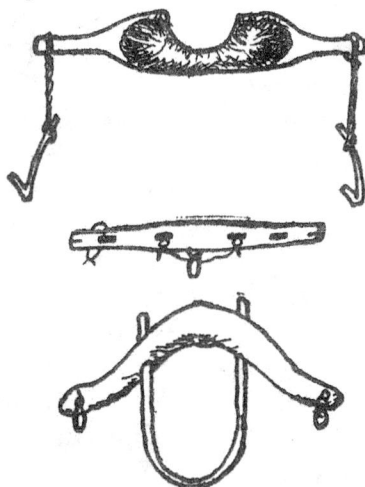

TOOLS OF DEACON ISRAEL GIBBS; FORMERLY IN POSSESSION OF MR. ENOS
W. BOISE, A LINEAL DESCENDANT

TWO MILL SITES
(1) CAMPBELL'S GRIST MILL, 1748, SMOKY HOLLOW
FRARY'S MILLS, GRIST AND SAW, 1777
(2) ROBERT BLAIR'S SAW MILL:
RUSSELL ROAD, SECOND DIVISION

NOTE

List of Pew-holders, May 28, 1760.
The starred names were also listed, Jan. 11, 1760,
as legal voters.

Baird, John
*Beard, James
*Black, Robert
*Blair, Matthew
Blair, Matthew, Jr.
*Boies, David
*Boies, John
*Boies, Samuel
*Boies, William
*Brown, William

*Campbell, David
*Carnahan, Samuel
*Carnahan, William
*Cochran, Glass
Cochran, Widow Margaret
*Crooks, Samuel
*McConoughey, David

Ferguson, Samuel
*Freeland, Joseph

*Gibbs, Israel

*Hamilton, John

Hancheet, Thomas
*Henry, Robert

Knox, Adam
*Knox, John
*Knox, Ens. William
*Knox, Lt. William
McKintry

*Mitchel, William
*Montgomery, James

Pease, Nathanael
Provin, Matthew
*Provin, William

*Scott, John
*Sinnit, Robert
Stewart, Pearl
  (Paul, probably. S. G. W.)
*Stewart, Walter

*Taggart, James

Willson, Samuel
*Wilson, John

Legal Voters not Pew-holders

Black, Lt. David
Cochran, John
Dalremple, John
Doneghy, William

McConoughey, John
Root, Henert,
  (Henry? S. G. W.)

CHAPTER XVII

KING GEORGE'S WAR:

BLANDFORD ON THE SCOUTING LINE

NOTE: This and the following chapter had their nucleus in a series of articles contributed by the author to the Magazine of History in 1909-1910, and copyrighted by the editor and publisher, William Abbatt. These articles are used here by permission. Much has been added and the arrangement has been altered.

The little municipality of Blandford may almost be said to have begun its existence as a foundling laid at the door of an army barracks.

It was in the maelstrom. Jealousies of the Gaul and the Briton, wild passions and war-cries of aboriginal Americans, old-world ambitions of empire, new-world importations of age-long history writ with sword and fire and blood were here. They had leaped over the mountains, run along the rivers, spread over the prairies, and already had their bloody nurseries and training grounds from Acadia to Florida, and from the Atlantic to the Father of Waters. The rivalries of fighting religions, the hatreds of sects, the suspicions and fears and the unresting propaganda of their militant confessors and missionaries were all here, dragons' teeth and militant men, whether with the sword of the flesh or of the spirit, or both, and were boring into the soil like the roots of the mast pines in their forests.

When France and England came to grips again over there, the whole world was their battle field, and New Englanders adopted their full share. Maine had been penetrated by the missionaries of Rome. French trading posts and French priests had drawn far-flung lines of communication to the northward and the westward.

They easily affiliated with the Indians, and had most of them as allies. If these posts and garrisons were a hollow shell, it at least was hard to crack. When war was proclaimed from the two capitals separated by the English Channel, nearly all the Indians of the eastern half of the country at once became the implacable foes of the English and of their provincials. No matter how friendly they had become, the change was immediate and the enmity was ruthless. In varying density they were scattered everywhere. For the most part they struck the trail for Canada where they might join the French as confederates, and from the spot where each brave started he went across country forthwith as the unpitying enemy of the English, and lost no opportunity to make it known.

None entered into this strife with more spirit than did the Scotch Presbyterian from Ulster. His whole blood was stirred for the safety of his home and for the defence of his faith. The campaigns to the northward were joined by these scattered fighters with a zeal which burned deep. All New England, in fact, regarded these as holy wars, since they were fought between a Protestant and a Roman Catholic power. Days of fasting and prayer were provided and ranked by both legislature and populace along with supplies of war, and the war was commonly called the Protestant cause.

The peace of thirty years between England and France was terminated early in 1744. It had been prognosticated for some considerable time, and quiet preparations had been made by the provincial authorities to meet the issue when it should come. Even before Boston was apprised of the declaration of war, a New England garrison, on the Island of Canso, had been captured. So early as Nov. 11, 1743, the provincial legislature passed an act looking to the protection of its inhabitants and the garrisoning of its western county.* It provided, "in order that the Inland Frontiers in this province be put into a better posture of defence," that the following appropriations should be "laid out in some of the settlements in the County of Hampshire, vixt: to Fall Town, Colerain, Blandford, Stockbridge, Sheffield and Upper Housatunnock, one hundred pounds each; and to New Hampton, sixty pounds, thirteen shillings, and four pence." It was specifically provided, further, that the sums named should be laid out, "in the most prudent manner, in erecting in each of the before-named settlements, for their securing during the War, a Garrison or Garrisons of Stockades or of Square Timber, round some dwelling house or houses, or otherwise, as will be most for the security and Defence of the whole Inhabitants of each place."

"PROVIDED, nevertheless, that if the apprehensions of War be over before the money be laid out, what Remains shall be returned into the Treasury, there to ly for the further order of this Court."

On the last day of this same month Governor Shirley issued instructions to the committee as follows (in part): "The particular places in said Settlements for Erecting these Works must be such as will best accommodate the Whole Body of the Inhabitants in those Settlements; and so far as that end may be attained, I direct you to erect these Works in such a situation as may Cover any other of His Majesty's Subjects Settled in the exposed parts of the Frontiers within the District, and of such Forces as in case of War may be sent out for the annoyance of the Enemy in any of their Settlements" etc.

There were urgent reasons for looking after Blandford. It was a new settlement and still struggling with

* Register, 13, p. 21.

poverty; about it were other towns or settlements still weaker, and the Albany road which cut athwart its southerly portion was the avenue by which most of the military supplies and men of these wars just about to begin were to pass from the eastward to the Hudson and the northerly forts. These forts were particularly needed to guard against hostile raids of Indians whose guerilla instincts everywhere precluded their being kept within the bounds observed by civilized nations in warfare. They were an ever dreaded foe whose pitiless massacres had for generations already filled New England homes with terror.

Concerning the local defences, Mr. Keep's manuscript has this note: "Early in the settlement three forts were erected for the safety of the people: one upon the lot now occupied by Captain Elijah Knox, the other where Mr. Tuttle now lives, and the other the lot occupied by Samuel Boies." The Elijah Knox place was in lot 49 in the first division, about threee-quarters of a mile below the center schoolhouse, on the road to Westfield—"the Albany road." The Tuttle lot was number 43, just north of the meeting house, where the agricultural fair ground now is. The Samuel Boies place was at number 17, on the west side of the old town street, just south of its junction with the modern gore road. A square mound is still very faintly discernible in the meadow where the fort was said to be. The three forts were located approximately a mile apart, two of them guarding the town street with its homes and public buildings, and the southernmost one overlooking the great highway. The middle one practically did duty for both roads. All this is more than a tradition.* By 1748

---

* Dr. Holland knew of only one fort in Blandford, and that a small one. But he was not informed on that point. Just when each of these three forts were erected is not told. Perhaps Dr. Holland's small one was the original.

the three forts are definitely referred to in the town records of that year.

The building of the forts was entrusted to Colonel John Stoddard who was at the head of the militia west of the Connecticut river. Work of construction began at Fort Shirley, in Heath. Specifications were given for its building, which was to serve as a model for the rest. The fort was sixty feet square, and was made of pine timbers squared and smoothed to fourteen by six inches in diameter, interlocked and pinned together at the corners, and the courses doweled together at suitable intervals with red-oak pins. The height was twelve feet. Two mounts, twelve feet square and seven feet high were erected on two opposite corners of the main structure for fighting purposes. The ground story was made solid. Houses, or barracks, eleven feet wide, with shingled roofs, sloping up to the top of the walls of the fort, in old "salt-box" style, faced the center of the fort. The whole cost of Fort Shirley was about fifty pounds sterling. There were four stone chimneys standing against the wall, each chimney apparently accommodating two houses, one on either side of the partition. If these abutted upon two sides of the fort, the open space in front would be forty-eight feet square.

Fort Pelham appears to have been only a stockade. Just what the Blandford forts were, or what officers and forces manned them, has gone from record and tradition alike, barring the scantiest notice now and then.

The Indians were great travelers, great path-makers and resourceful guides, and the routes followed by the opposing forces of these wars were in large measure what the American aborigines had already worn.

To be thoroughly understood as it affected Blandford and New England generally, the war paths must be mentally mapped in their grand outlines.

The north and south avenues are thus clearly indicated by Professor Perry*: "The upper Hudson and
Lake George were a warpath for the English and Mo-
hawks to Lake Champlain and Canada, and the Riche-
lieu and upper St. Lawrence were routes for French
and Indians to Lake George and Oswego. It is these
immemorial routes and battle-grounds of the Indians,
and later of their civilized confederates on the one side
and on the other, that connect the valleys of the Hoosac and the Deerfield and the line of forts flanking the
two with the vast events and issues of the last two
French wars."

Lake Champlain was an easy channel southward. The
Indians would leave their canoes at Crown Point and
travel on foot to Hoosac, between Williamstown and
North Adams, where their progress would be challenged
at Fort Massachusetts, located in a meadow between
the mountains. It is a natural Thermopylae. Or they
would go farther east and down the Connecticut. There
was a fort on this river at Charlestown, then known as
Number Four, within the new province of New Hampshire. There were other forts along down the stream,
notably Dummer, on the river a little south of Brattle-
boro, in Vernon. Massachusetts manned and took care
of these. In the next war, the Seven Years, so called,
there was another fort, Rice's, in Charlemont. Approximately at least these forts, ranged from Pelham to
Fort Massachusetts, were along the Mohawk trail.

No Indians were locally in evidence in the first year
or two of the war. Nevertheless, garrison duty was not
neglected. The day before Christmas, 1745, Gov.
Shirley wrote to Col. Stoddard to the effect that Capt.
Ephraim Williams was asking for more soldiers at
Stockbridge, and the proprietors of Blandford were

---

* Origins, 75.

urging similarly in behalf of that town. Williams was also begging for a band of scouting Indians. No definite orders accompanied the letter, but the Colonel was advised to give the matter his attention. This was in accordance with the general instructions sent out by the governor, Nov. 30, 1743, to the committee who were to look after the building of the forts. On the fourth of March following, another letter was addressed by his Excellency to Stoddard, on learning "respecting the Tracks which have been discovered near Number Four." In a postscript to this letter the governor wrote: "I have sent you, by Colo Dwight, £187.10s as advanc'd Wages for Miller's, Huston's & Pomroy's Comps, and £50 as Bounty money for Pomroy's Company." This Huston was Capt. John of Blandford.

The town records for these years are lost. The muster rolls and official returns from this war were all sent over to England for inspection, as a basis for the payment of the soldiers and were never returned. A very fragmentary list has been compiled from sundry sources and published in the Massachusetts Historical and Genealogical Register.* Therein occurs the name of John Huston, just now mentioned, tavern landlord, surveyor, land agent, man of the world, and withal elder in the Blandford church. He is first mentioned in connection with his agent, Sergeant Enoch Davis. Huston duly received his commission as captain, and thereafter became locally addressed by that title, incidentally corroborating his identification as our old friend of tavern and turnpike history of this enterprising town. His was company the eighth, Fourth Mass. regiment, Samuel Willard, Esq., colonel, the date of the com-

---

* Vols. 24, 25.

mission being Feb. 15, 1744.* Would that we had the
roster of his company!

In the autumn of 1744 the General Court "Ordered,
that twelve men out of each of the five snow-shoe companies in the western parts, amounting to sixty in all,
be detached and sent out under a captain commissioned
for that purpose, to scout and range the woods, for the
four months next coming, their march to be from Con-
toocook on the Merrimac River to the westward as far
as the Captain General shall think best." These, as
developed throughout the course of hostilities, were the
famous "Ranging Forces," or "Rangers." Professor
Perry thus describes their make-up in the later years
of the struggle: † "The Ranging Corps required men
of great strength, inured to fatigue and danger. They
must start with thirty days' provisions on their backs,
and in addition carry their muskets and equipments,
with the requisite ammunition. At night their camp was
upon the bare ground, with no cover unless it were brush
huts. In winter the march was upon snow-shoes, to the
use of which they were sometimes trained before the
campaign began. . . . If a man became sick, or was
wounded, he was either sent back or carried on by his
companions. There was little room for medicine or sur-
gery, and consequently little chance for recovery. In
forest stratagem these forest rangers of the last French
war showed themselves little, if any, inferior to the Indians, and in sustained fighting on equal terms, generally superior. They knew nothing of general military
tactics, and if they had known, it would have been a
constant impediment to them in the woods. . . . Provided they were brave and hardy and good marksmen,
—and these were their general characteristics,—nothing

* Op. cit., Vol. 25, p. 251.
† Origins in Williamstown, p. 274.

more was supposed needful to qualify them for this partisan service." The most famous of these rangers was Major Robert Rogers, a Scotch Irishman. Trained dogs were their companions, and a bounty of thirty pounds on every Indian scalp—so pitiless had these wars with Indians become—was an incentive to sharpen every wit and intensify every day's march.

When the war was declared, early in 1744, the General Court responded with spirit to the proposals of Governor Shirley. Five hundred men were promptly impressed, and powder was distributed at original cost to all the towns in Massachusetts. In January of the following year the governor made the astounding proposal to the legislature that a sudden and secret campaign be set on foot to surprise and take Louisburg, which was by far the strongest fort north of the Gulf of Mexico. He recommended a force of four thousand men for the purpose, a proposal which was promptly declined, but on maturer deliberation was considered and adopted. One reads this item in the histories with a kind of shock of surprise which continues to haunt one spite of all we know of the slowness of communication in those olden days. When the news was carried to the towns of New England, none sprang to enlistment with more agility and eagerness than the men from Ulster who were now scattering all over the edges of New England as it then was. They "hated popery as they feared the devil," to quote a phrase of Professor Perry, and incidentally "they were becoming numerous and continued poor."

The forces were to be raised on this wise: from Massachusetts, 3,250 men; from Connecticut, 500; from Rhode Island and New Hampshire, 300 each. The troops were to go by transport under the popular leader, William Pepperell. The campaign was inaugurated by a day of fasting and prayer called by the General Court, and the surprising and glorious victory was followed by a day of thanksgiving. In leading them on to the conflict Pepperell had given to his forces this motto: *"Nil desperandum, Christo duce."* * It was said to have been given to him by Whitefield, the famous preacher.

In this campaign the town of Blandford was represented, of course. But it is impossible to say by how many. Doubtless she bore her full share. A few certain echoes have returned to us in the documents already cited and reproduced by the Historical and Genealogical Record. Jonathan Boyce was one who volunteered "under the command of Daniel Bacon to attack the Island battery." This may have been John—sometimes called Jonathan—Boies of Blandford. Feb. 7, 1745, Samuel Black was commissioned Second Lieutenant "in the 3rd Massachusetts, whereof the Hon. Jere Moulton, Esq., (was) is Colonel." John Huston and James Wilson are listed as "under command of Col. John Storer." There is this item of date Sept. 16, 1745: "Sergeant Enoch Davis made agent of the following persons to receive their plunder. Joseph Huston" et al. This same sergeant was also constituted agent for like purpose to John Huston. On October 2, of that year, the following correspondence occurred:

"To

His Excellency W*M* Shirley, Esq*r*

This is to inform your Exelency That my Regiment is not Settle*d*: so as to be in any Capassity of doing their duty. as they ought to do—and it is by Reason of y*e* Companys being Very much Broke; and in order for the Settlement of the Companys In my Regiment. and for the Peace and Quietness of the Soldiers: I

---

* Nothing is to be despaired of with Christ as our leader.

shall take it as a Grate Favour Done to me: if your Exelency would See Cause To Commissionate Those Gentleman Hereafter Nam*d*:

James Huston,
James Fry John Fry Nath*ll* Pettengill To be the officers over the men that belong*d*: To Lev*t* Collo: Chandlers Company & Cap*t*—James Stevenss Camp*a*." etc.
Signed by "Sam*ll* Willard."

On the very same day, pursuant to the tenor of this letter, the four men above named addressed this letter to His Excellency:

"Louisbourg 2*d*: Octo*b*. 1745

"We the subscribers the Officers to the four Companys within mention'd humbly proposed to Your Excellency by Col*o* Samuel Willard for the settlem*t*. thereof; untill the Spring Ensueing, or the first of May next desire the favour of your Excellency that we with our respective Companys may be joyned to the Regiment of Brigadier Generall Waldo; and that your Excellency orders or Commissions may Issue accordingly."

The leading signature to this letter is that of John Huston. Presumably the document was in his handwriting, and reveals a remarkable literary accuracy for the time it was written, far beyond that of his superior officer, Colonel Willard.* Huston was recommissioned, along with James Noble, Major, and John Moore, Lieutenant.

Other reminiscences have strayed along our way, and may as well be bunched in here. The redoubtable Captain John Huston was acting as agent for his regiment, along with other agents of other regiments, "which met May 20th, 1746, at Capt. Peter Prescott's." These

---

* S. S. Green's "Three Military Diaries," p. 5f.

agents were detailed for the purpose of receiving bounties or spoils of war. Capt. Huston being a surveyor in a large way, and prominently connected with the layout of numerous towns in Western Massachusetts, was a man of considerable business experience and an entirely suitable person for such diplomatic affairs when "to the victors belonged the spoils." Capt. Estes Hatch was over the 10th company in the same regiment, his commission dating from Feb. 4, 1744. Whether he was resident in Blandford at precisely that time may be in doubt. He is the same Hatch who, Sept. 21, 1749, took the deed of a farm in Blandford, paying for the acquisition "two Mares & a Colt & a gold Watch." Oliver Watson is listed as a private in the 5th company, Eighth Mass. regiment, Col. John Choate. The Watsons, however, did not come to this town until later. The name also of Hugh Hamilton is returned on several lists of the provincial war records in the year 1747 and '48.

These scattered and fragmentary notes are enough to establish the belief that Blandford men liberally swelled the ranks of the expeditionary forces which saw the walls of Louisburg fall.

The fortress of Louisburg capitulated to the Provincials in the early summer of 1745. It was a notable triumph, and the people were tense with the desire to push on to the conquest of all Canada, a thing which was least of all wanted by the English government, whose military leader, the Duke of Bedford, did not by any means care to have the colonies become over-much conscious of their might. It was ordered that this particular campaign in its main movement should be transferred from land to water.

It is one thing to capture, another to keep. It cost the provincial soldiery 150 men to bring the fortress to subjection. But shortly after, while they lay encamped round about it, they lost by sickness ten times that number. The ensuing campaign also was inglorious, as things born of jealousy are apt to be. England wanted 3,500 more troops from Massachusetts to co-operate with the fleet against Quebec, and these were immediately raised.

This was known as the Crown Point expedition. The other colonies were to furnish three thousand additional men to operate as a rear guard against Montreal. This they did. The spirit of Massachusetts is attested by her promptness in all this action and by the resolutions of her legislative assembly, which avouched in their record that the additional grant was willingly made "notwithstanding the great difficulties and charges to which this province is exposed by reason of the numerous attacks made on all parts of the Frontiers, which burthens are made much heavier by coming immediately upon the loss of so great a number of men as were killed and died in the late expedition against Cape Breton." * The Governor requested the legislature to appoint another day of fasting and prayer in view of this military expedition.

Three days after this legislation, two hundred and seven men were called for in order to reinforce the garrisons "in the Western Frontiers," meaning Western Massachusetts. This requisition included a company of fifty men "to range the Woods with Fifty large Dogs, to be provided and fed at the charge of the Government." † The strain of constant watchfulness out on these frontiers was heavy, the garrisons were generally inadequate to meet an emergency, and these brave men had little of the excitement of a regular campaign to spur them on. It was dogged, wearing, dangerous, and

---

* Province Laws, Vol. XIII, Chap. 3.
† Ibid., Chap. 5.

required prolonged readiness to respond any day, any minute, to a sudden alarm with a tragic ending.

To return to the Crown Point expedition. The men were to march to Boston, whence they would be conveyed in transports to the Hudson.* The movement was delayed until autumn, when the state of feeling was such that again the legislature was moved to ask the Governor to appoint a public fast. It was just then that France was sending out an immense armada to reduce New England. It spread terror throughout all these borders, and the formidable menace was averted not by the prowess of man, but by the Providence of God. The ships were wrecked by a mighty storm at sea, and New England was saved from the "destruction which wasteth at noonday."

The wretched military misfortunes which attended the armies in the field will not now detain us, except to add that they necessitated still further enlistments for reinforcement, particularly in the heart of Nova Scotia. A body of troops was embarked at Boston for this destination in the winter of 1746, not without impressment riots, however, in that city.

To the terror inspired by the French fleet was added the melancholy surprise at Fort Massachusetts in the summer of 1746, and the fall of that stronghold, followed by the sickening Indian massacre of the inhabitants of Deerfield, then the principal settlement in those parts. Earlier in the summer isolated small raids and killings by Indians had occurred, in Falltown (Bernardston), Northfield, Colerain, Greenfield and in New Hampshire. Williams was absent on August 20, when the attack was made on Fort Massachusetts, and there were but few men at the fort, and a few women and children, half of them sick, and none of them well. The

* Ibid., Chap. 124.

ammunition was nearly gone, and Vadreuil, with his French regulars and Indians, outnumbered the little fighting force within the fort something like forty to one. It was as gallant a fight as ever was made. Sergeant John Hawks's little force kept the enemy at bay for twenty-eight hours, and the capitulation was made on terms of the defeated. All Western Massachusetts was thrown into much confusion by these events, and the Scotchmen of the Ulster migration all about enlisted in the war in large numbers. At Fort Massachusetts, which was razed after Hawks's fight, a John Cochran, identical with the name of a Blandford settler, had been a member of the garrison.

The part taken by Blandford in all these campaigns can be indicated only by fragments of intelligence picked up here and there. The historical sermon of the Rev. John Keep contains this enlightening paragraph concerning certain local events falling within the period now under review,—the only coherent relation extant of the town's part in the early campaigns of this war:

"The Rev. William McClenathan* followed Mr. Munson (as pastor). He was a man of respectable talents, and thought to possess unusual gifts as a preacher, but somewhat unhappy in his temper. In July, 1744, the people were happily united in giving him a call to settle, with the offer of ninety-three dollars salary and ninety-three dollars settlement. The first minister was also entitled to one sixty-acre lot, to become his own on the day of his ordination. James Hazzard was sent to Boston to present the call to the Presbytery. In September he was installed, and in December the town transported his goods from Boston. The next year every man in

---

* The spelling should be—McClenachan.

town over twenty-one years was required to work and assist in repairing his house."*

"Mr. McClenathan was twice sent abroad on the business of the town. Once he was chosen representative of the town, and they voted him thirty dollars additional to his salary. The next year the town, by a general vote, required that Mr. McClenathan be dismissed. The cause of this sudden change was as follows:

"A war existed between the French and the English, and the seat of it was the vicinity of Nova Scotia. While Mr. McClenathan was in Boston as the representative of the town, his feelings became enlisted in this war, and he obtained both captain's and chaplain's commission. On his return he succeeded in engaging the feelings of several young men in Westfield, and in Blandford. As he was the minister, and made promises to defend and protect young men, their parents permitted several to enlist under him.

"When he reached Boston, with his company, he was not permitted to hold both offices, and sold his men to another officer. Four of the young men died. This by the people was deemed traitorous, and they refused to receive him again as their minister. But he held as his own the ministry lot. He was arraigned before the presbytery, tried and dismissed. All who testified in this case were required to be put on oath. Afterwards he relinquished his right in the ministry lot. He removed to the South, became an Episcopal preacher and soon after died." It would seem as though, in the game of war, death should be discounted as a probable event. It may be inferred, therefore, that the fault laid at the

---

* As matter of fact, they gave him the two lots, that for the minister, and that for "the ministry." The deed, recorded in Springfield, was given by Robert Huston, Davoid Boies and John Osborne, by whom the property was held in trust, and was "Signed Sealed & Delivered in the Presence of James McClintock" by James Hazzard.

minister's door was his "selling" the young men to another officer, thereby lightly esteeming a solemn pledge of personal oversight. The names of the unfortunate dead were long since forgotten. The survivors also are, with an exception or two, a nameless company. There is no roster, and the number of them as well as their names is unknown. A faint echo or two comes back to us from the silent years, a forlorn fragment of a message as if caught by a wireless station and given to a world hungry to learn the rest, which imagination alone may fill out. It occurred to the Rev. William McClenachan and to one or more of the youthful volunteers who followed his uncertain leading that prudence might dictate that they should set their house in order before going. The cleric's disposal was on this wise:*

"Whereas God in his Providence is Calling me forth to the Present War, and as I am persuaded of the uncertainty of my being in this World and having (I trust) a Disposition to do Justice & Maintain a Good Conscience, I therefore do hereby signify my Inclination & Oblige my Self if I Die in the Expedition to Resign my Claim & Title to the land I Received in the Town of Blandford as first Settled Minister of the Same and Said Land & House to be for the next Presbyterian minister Presbyterially Settled in Said Blandford The Inhabitants of Said Town Paying to my heirs or assigns what the building & Improvement Cost me on said Lott or Land: In Testimony whereof I have hereunto Set my hand this 16*th* of Sept*r* 1746.

"W*m* McClenachan & Seal." The date of this deed indicates that this enlistment was for one of the Crown Point expeditions.

One of the young men who went with his rather irresponsible minister was, almost certainly, William

---

* Springfield Registry.

Knox, Jr., who made a somewhat similar assignment of his property to Robert Young, of Wallingford, Connecticut, who for the sum of two hundred pounds was to receive all the estate, real and personal, of young Knox. The farm thus assigned consisted of second division lots, west, numbered 20 and 21. The instrument reads: "Whereas the said William Knox Junr Is Inlisted a Soldier in his Majesties Service against the French and Indian enemy in North America, and is now going forth on the Said Service, and if in Case it shall so happen that the said Wm Knox Junr. Shall Proceed therein & afterwards Return Home again The Said Deed shall be null & void." This young soldier did come home again and received his estate, as by deed signed in June, 1749.

In 1774, previous, that is, to the ministry of Mr. McClenachan, while all was as yet quiet, but apprehension of danger was grave, Rev. Mr. Harvey, as temporary supply of the pulpit, "by appointment of the town," preached "at the fort on some day of the week, besides the usual services of the Sabbath." * Probably this was at the fort near the meeting house. Without assigning any definite date to the period covering the intelligence, Mr. Keep remarks that "Often were the people driven to their forts by false alarms, and when Indians were seen they were either friendly or harmlessly pursuing their game." This sounds more like conditions early in the war than late in the forties and in the fifties.

During the year 1747 the enemy were active along the Connecticut river in the southern part of New Hampshire, and there was a notable fight at Charlestown. The next year occurred Hobbs's gallant fight lower down the river, and there was another battle at

---

* Mr. Keep's sermon.

Fort Massachusetts, which had been rebuilt and regarrisoned after its destruction by Vaudreuil. All these bloody events of course revived panic conditions in Blandford. To all these western forts the people of the province looked for protection with vigilant and anxious attention. It was a wild and fearsome tract of country to guard, vast in its solitudes and unlimited in its possibilities of terrors, where imagination heaped up uncounted perils beyond those well known and sufficiently definite and numerous. The use of those literal dogs of war seems to smack of barbarism. But war is barbaric, never more so than in this twentieth century. How else could the long and gloomy stretches of country between the far-separated blockhouses be so sentineled as to protect at all the villages and scattered homes of this far "western frontier"? It sounds strange to our modern ears to read of Massachusetts offering a bounty for Indian scalps. Yet such was the universal fear inspired by the horrid tortures of the Indians that mercy for them almost departed. Our expedient is poisonous gas, and that for non-combatants. The bounty extended to scalps of females.*

In the summer of 1747—it was June 23—an engagement at Fort Saratoga had been fought with disastrous results to the colonial forces, and following this reverse, Clinton, Governor of New York, ordered the fort abandoned and burned. The cannon were taken back to Albany. It had been the only barrier against the enemy between Fort Massachusetts and the country to the northwest. This cruel exposure sent a shiver of fear throughout Massachusetts.

During these years of peril the old men were apt to seek refuge where the last days of life could be breathed out in greater degree of safety and quiet than on Bland-

---

* Province Laws, Vol. XIII, Chap. 306, 1745-6.

ford's ragged edge of wilderness. John Stewart, black-smith, went to Suffield, Connecticut, to die, and made his will there, July 27, 1747. On August 14 following, his children and heirs met for the settlement of his estate "at ye hous where David Boies dwells," probably where the old man had died. David Boies, of course, was also a Blandford refugee. Besides these two, deprived of their peace and domicile by wars and rumors of wars, we know not how many others had sought asylum abroad, but enough to provoke agitation in town meeting concerning their exemption from taxation or abatement thereof. Certain documents indicate that the exodus had been considerable. Precocious and discerning infants of Blandford that year chose to open their eyes to the light of day also in this same valley town so closely associated with the birth of the town itself, for the town clerk's book contains these entries for that year: Samuel, son of John and Anna Boies, born in Suffield, May 26, 1747; and, Ebenezer, son of Robert and Jean Henry, born in Suffield, June 7, 1747. The records refer to it as having transpired in the spring. The debacle at Fort Saratoga occurred a week before July arrived, only two or three weeks after apple blossom time in Blandford, where winter is inclined to linger in the lap of spring. There was diversity of opinion on the subject of tax abatement, but the final judgment was that the fleeing inhabitants must bear the burdens of the town along with those who stayed by.

The peace of Aix-la-Chapelle was signed October 7, 1748. It really was only a truce, for nothing was settled. The Indians continued more or less active—how should they understand European politics? But in general there was quiet in the western part of the province, there was a breathing space for a few years, and frontier settlements had opportunity to take new hold and extend their peace-time interests. The provincial garrisons were reduced, but as there was little confidence in the perpetuity of the peace, small forces were kept at Forts Dummer, Massachusetts, Deerfield, Northfield, Pontoosuck and Stockbridge. Forts Shirley and Pelham were abandoned. There was little use for them anyway. Especial attention was given to Fort Massachusetts as supremely strategic. Meantime great numbers of religious exiles were entering the province from the old country and the desolated settlements of Acadie,—the "French Neutrals" whose sorrowful story Longfellow's "Evangeline" has made immortal. New townships to the westward were laid out and occupied. German pioneers were taking possession of the Mohawk valley. Ulster was still emptying out her population to swell the settlements of Pennsylvania. An Ohio company was organized under Lord Halifax. It was movements such as these, and the empire which was bound to be, that fired the ambition of the Old-World powers to seize possession of the New.

William H. Gibbs, in his "Historical address," * based on a statement in the sermon of Mr. Keep, says that in the spring of 1749 "the Indians began to make encroachments upon the white settlers of the town, and all the families but four fled to the neighboring towns, some to Westfield, others to Windsor, Suffield, Simsbury, and Wethersfield, Connecticut. A portion of them returned the following winter, the remainder the next spring." It is beyond belief. Perhaps the lecturer confused the events of this year with those of 1747. In 1749 there were town meetings in Blandford on March 6, May 17, June 12, August 18 and Sept. 29. In the spring of that year the town clerk made this entry:

---

* P. 8. Judge Copeland, in his History of Hampshire County, follows this authority.

"John Beard heath provided a bul according to the vot of the town and desired me to list him." In August of this same year was this minute: "voted that those that Came to this town last winter and spring shall be freed of one half of their rates for the last year." That is, the church tax. It looks like a return instead of a flight. Furthermore, in that same month the Rev. James Morton was ordained.

On March 10, 1748, in addition to a vote previously passed establishing garrisons along the northerly line of forts, the provincial government voted to ask of Connecticut 60 men for Deerfield, 60 for Northfield, and "the other 80 to be posted in the most exposed places of New Hampton Blanford No 1 & 2 Stockbridge & Colrain & Sheffield."

More than a year passed, and the men for Northfield, New Hampton and Blandford had not yet been raised. The General Court, June 15, 1749, asked the governor "to cause such deficiency to be supplyed by an Enlistment or an Impress of Sixty two men in their Room." *

It remains to be remembered that the town had been limping along through depletion and terrors, with a portion of its normal population probably still non-resident. It is not impossible that the tradition just commented on told the exact truth in all but the date. When, Dec. 1, 1747, the provincial legislature of Massachusetts Bay resolved † that it was necessary to send out 4,000 more men to take the Crown Point fort, it was with the grim determination of desperate men who recorded their deliberate decision that the requisition upon the people must be made "notwithstanding the full Persuasion of the Commissionrs that these Burdens must be beyond-

---

* Vol. XIV.
† Provincial Laws, Chap. 158, Vol. XIV, Appendix IX.

the Ability of said Governm*ts* if continued, they being constantly harassed by Invasions or Incursions on their Borders by the French & their Indians for nearly five Hundred Miles . . . & many of their Settlements already broken up & destroyed, & divers others in the most imminent Danger, the Case being such, that if these Governm*ts* do not lay these heavy Burdens on themselves (under which if they are not relieved, they must sink) they must much sooner be destroyed by their inhumane Enemies above s*d*" etc.

CHAPTER XVIII

THE SEVEN YEARS WAR

"Watchman, What of the Night?"

If wild Indians could not understand the meaning of the Treaty of Aix-la-Chapelle, which stopped the war in the midst and handed back to France the fortress of Louisburg once more, which satisfied only the politics of Europe, neither could they be expected to observe it. And since it left absolutely nothing of current western conditions decided, no more could the colonists put confidence in it. It furnished a sort of hazardous breathing space. Some trade was carried on with the Indians. But there were Indian attacks too. It was a time when there was desperate need of the colonies coming to a common understanding and some large unity of procedure. An attempt at this was made, headed by the astute Franklin, at the convention at Albany, but it miserably failed. Much statecraft yet remained to be learned, and military schemes meantime suffered woefully from want of strong centralization. But of valor there was no lack.

Some extracts from a letter under date of Dec. 16, 1754, from Colonel Israel Williams, to Major Ephraim Williams, who was then in Boston, may serve to throw some light on the situation at this time:

"I am sorry ye publick affairs are so many of 'em retarded, and am very much dissatisfied with ye conduct of his Majest's wise Council in some particulars. I hope you are satisfied as to the necessity & prudence of your remaining at Boston, and that you do good ef others dont. . . . The great schemes on foot we are not inform'd. I wish well to my country, & hope others will be directed right, and a foundation laid for our tranquility & well being. . . . What is in ye womb of Providence, or what ye event of ye present projections may be I desire humbly to refer to ye wise Governour of ye world, who can save His people and advance ye Redeemer's Kingdom in ways unthought of by us. May Zion's peace be prolong'd and establish'd. There will be occasion for a considerable number of magasons* if Mr. Wheelwright will give order, our leathr will do for that purpose. There are but a few left that are good, they are now wanted for ye scouts. If you can find at ye leathr-dressers a good fine oil dress'd skin that is clean & white I desire you to get me one large eno for a p'r. breeches. . . . The men ordered to Stockbridge Sheffield Brewers Kings Glasgow † &c are not needed, and ye main of them at present are a needless expense to ye Gov't. I hope unless they are needed for some service ye Gov't will give orders for their discharge, which may be of advantage hereafter. Those in line for scouts, and some at Pontoosuck are necessary, & at present ye Cont. soldiers are at ye last place. I fear ye great schemes afoot will prevent due care of ye frontiers, and also prevent ye building of Forts, & before we put our schemes into execution the French will theirs, surprize us in ye spring, & very much distress us." There was much of truth in this prophecy. The suggested dismantling of the forts named in the letter was doubtless with the thought of comparative security on account of the strong line of defences to the westward and northward of these posts. It will be noticed that no such thought was entertained concerning Fort Massa-

---

* I.e., moccasins.
† The fond name persisted.

chusetts. There are strong reasons also for believing that Blandford was allowed to keep her garrison.

On the frontiers generally during the year, 1755, there was diligent preparation for war. On January 4 the legislature had ordered* in connection with other measures "relating to the putting the several Forts and Garrisons throughout this Province into a proper Posture of Defence. . . . That there should be two good Cohorns † with a sufficient number of Shot & Shells to every Fort & Block House in the Government: That a sufficient number of Wheels of Cast Iron be procured for the Cannon at the several Garrisons of the Province," etc. In June there was an Indian massacre at Charlemont, when three captives were taken, first to Crown Point, then to Canada. The picketing and ranging had begun again along the lines of forts in Western Massachusetts, just south of the present Vermont and New Hampshire lines, and along up the Connecticut river to the north. In October, the legislature voted "to give Orders to the Chief Officers of the Towns of the Eastern and Western Frontiers to Oblige the Soldiers under their respective Commands to go compleatly Arm'd to their several places of publick Worship on the Lord's Days in this time of Danger." ‡ If fear inspired the inhabitants, at least the proceeding of armed garrisons to divine worship must have supplied an element of quickening interest and martial enthusiasm to the boys of the town as they congregated at the meeting house for the weary hours of the weekly service, at once the victims and the terrors of the tithingman. And many a blushing maid of Blandford town surely cast sly or winsome glances at these foreign youths bristling with arms, themselves not beyond dan-

---

* Provincial Laws, Chap. 228.

† A cohorn, or coehorn, was a small brass or iron mortar used for throwing grenades.

‡ Provincial Laws, Chap. 152.

ger of wounds from eyes which "looked love to eyes that loved again."

Serious Indian hostilities occurred in succession along the Connecticut in New Hampshire, and the settlers in those parts appealed to Massachusetts for help, and received it, New Hampshire doing nothing for them. The scouts, or rangers, did most valiant service. Holland says:* "The history of the watchful nights, the daring feats, the tedious marches, and the almost unexampled toils of these men, may not be written, but the imagination may conceive something of the almost ferocious hardihood which characterized and sustained them."

Meantime, three formidable military expeditions were fitted out for the more distant campaigns: Braddock's,† from Virginia, against Fort DuQuesne at the forks of the Ohio; Shirley's, against the French posts on the Niagara river; and Sir William Johnson's, from Albany, against Crown Point; campaigns to be attended by disaster and bitter disappointments. In preparation for all these movements, Massachusetts promptly raised two regiments for Crown Point, and gathered in no small part from local frontier garrisons or from those who had served in them, hence principally from the old county of Hampshire. One of these was the regiment commanded by the immortal Colonel Ephraim Williams, founder of Williams College, who met his death in the battle of Lake George. The other went out under

---

* Vol. I, p. 189.

† In her "Home Life in Colonial Days," Mrs. Earle, citing Benjamin Franklin, gives a list of articles making up one pack-horse load in the commissary department of Braddock's army: Six pounds loaf sugar, six pounds muscovado sugar, one pound green tea, one pound bohea tea, six pounds ground coffee, six pounds chocolate, one-half chest white biscuit, half-pound pepper, one quart white vinegar, two dozen bottles old Madeira wine, two gallons Jamaica spirits, one bottle flour mustard, two well-cured hams, one-half dozen cured tongues, six pounds rice, six pounds raisins, one Gloucester cheese, one keg containing 20 pounds of best butter.

Colonel John Worthington, of Springfield.* Colonel Worthington was a young man when he joined the army, and died long years after at the advanced age of eighty. Blandford men learned to lean on him for counsel in peace as well as in war. He and Israel Williams,— "river gods,"—with Ephraim Williams also, cousin of Israel, were the three most influential men in secular affairs in that part of Massachusetts which is comprised within the watershed drained by the Connecticut.

As valorous fighters these troops won immortal glory. The campaign, however, came to nothing. The army never reached Crown Point, and prospects everywhere were dark at the end of the year, when Massachusetts attempted to muster 3,500 additional soldiers, with a few from New Hampshire. Only a little before the battle in which Colonel Ephraim Williams met his death, he wrote a pathetic letter to his superior, Colonel Israel Williams, lamenting the fact that they had but 3,000 effective men, whereas they needed 10,000 or 12,000. "Had Braddock, Shirley and we struck at the same time," he wrote, "it might have answered to have proceeded with our number. But y't is over, and if we should be beat, our country is lost. Therefore suffer me once for all to beg of you to exert you self for your country—it's upon the brink of ruin. It's who shall remember—what King William said, when the case of the Dutch was prity much the same with our's—I pray God unite your Councils, and show the world you are true patriots of your Country, and give to us to behave as becomes Englishmen." †

In September the Court made provision for munitions of war, including a mortar, a lighter, and "a sufficient Quantity of Suitable Shells and Shott for the Use of

* v. Appendix.
† Origins, p. 338.

the Province, and that they immediately forward the same to Albany, for ye Use of ye Army on the Expedition to Crown Point.

These campaigns as planned proved highly popular among the people, and enlistments were made with zeal and rapidity. Old Hampshire county nearly filled one regiment, made up largely from the frontier garrisons, or soldiers who had served at the frontier forts. Ephraim Williams was commissioned colonel of this regiment. The Rev. Stephen Williams of Longmeadow was made chaplain. Military activities in every quarter were speeded up, and the militia officers were charged to see strictly to it that the people go armed to public worship.

But these activities were not the only ones to be accounted for. The French were equally busy along with their hosts of Indian allies. The provincial armies were slow. They had not even yet thoroughly learned the lesson of the Indians' craft and suffered almost fatally because of it. Col. Ephraim Williams, brave beyond a shadow of doubt, had forebodings of coming ill. August 16, he wrote to his cousin, Col. Israel Williams, condoling with him for the death of a brother: "Pray God to sanctify it to all of us, & fit us for our own turns which will soon arrive—how soon God only knows. I beg your prayers for us all, & me in perticular. We are a wicked profane army, more especially New York troops & Road Island, nothing to be heard among a great part of them but the language of hell. I assure you, Sr, if ever the place is taken, it will not be for our sakes, but for those good people left behind." On the other hand, the New England men, particularly from Connecticut and Massachusetts, received enconiums from their officers. General Johnson, at the head of the Crown Point expedition, wrote of the good effect of the

prayers, and others wrote in similar vein. "Not a chicken
has been stolen," wrote one.

As matter of fact, not a single one of the three expeditions in this campaign ever reached its objective.
Braddock was ambushed and his force cut to pieces.
Williams was caught and his entire regiment in the famous "bloody morning scout," and his force extricated
at heavy cost, September 8.

All this had happened before any formal declaration
of war between the two great fighting nations. That
came in May, 1756. Great Britain reduplicated her efforts looking to the capture of the French cordon of
posts on this side of the ocean. Indian maraudings and
massacres on the frontiers of New England recurred, in
New Hampshire, in Greenfield, in Northfield, and in the
vicinity of Fort Massachusetts. The prayed-for successes failed to come that year, and 1757 was no better.
The next year the aspect changed, Pitt having come into
power in the English government. Louisburg fell and
other French strongholds, then Quebec. All Canada
came into English possession by 1760, and in 1763
France ceded Louisiana to Spain. It was during the dark
year of 1757 that Pownal, then governor, ordered all
the cavalry of the province and a large body of militia
to Springfield, under the command of Sir William Pepperell, lieutenant governor.

We are now prepared to enter upon certain intimate
incidents of this period within, or closely related to, the
town of Blandford.

A curious and interesting story is told by William H.
Gibbs in his Historical Address* on this wise: "In 1755
a special favor granted by the Court is noticed upon
their records, and acknowledged in the following terms:

"'By virtue of a petition put into the Great and Gen-

---
* P. 18.

eral Court of Boston by the Rev. Mr. Morton in behalf of this town, the Honorable Court was pleased to grant one *swivel* gun as an alarm gun, with one quarter barrel of powder and one bag of bullets for the same, and also one hundred flints for the use of the town, which we have received and paid charges on the same from Boston to this town, which is two pounds and sixteen shilling old tenor, to Captain Houston.'" There is no such action recorded in the provincial laws under this date, nor is there any surviving entry of the sort in the existing town records. The tradition as related by Mr. Gibbs is too circumstantial to be disregarded, and the lecturer would not have passed it on had he not considered the source of it historic. Probably this authority in our town history has put the date one year too late, and that the incident coincides with that of the sending of the "cohorns" as related on a previous page.

In connection with his relation of the planting of the three forts, Mr. Keep passed on to his hearers a vivid description of their use. He assigns no date to it, though it might appear that he thought it to have been the same year as the great exodus from the town. Whatever the date, this is his story:

"For more than a year all the families were collected every night into these forts as a safe lodging place. How great the inconvenience and discouragement of such a mode of life! And after the people presumed to lodge in their own dwellings the cases were frequent, in which, upon an alarm, they would in the dead of night hurry with their families to the fort. When they were in the field for work, they would take with them their arms, set one as a sentinel while the others labored; nor did they deem it safe to meet on the Sabbath for religious worship except they took with them their arms." This condition seems to coincide with the period of general alarm already described in this chapter.

"The way* by which Colonel Williams was ordered to take his companies to Albany, and did take them, was a rude road laid out as such by the Colony of Massachusetts in 1735, from Westfield through Blandford and Otis and Sandisfield and Monteray and Barrington to the New York line in North Egremont. This came very shortly to be commonly called the 'Albany road.'† Like all the other oldest roads in New England of any considerable stretch, this was undoubtedly an Indian trail from immemorial time.

"In connection with the laying out of this road, and during the same year, a committee of the General Court reported, that they were 'of opinion that there be four new townships between Westfield and Sheffield, and that they be contiguous to one another, and either joined to Sheffield or to the township lately granted to the proprietors of Suffield,'‡ These townships were first numbered, and afterwards named in order, Tyringham, New Marlborough, Sandisfield, Becket. The new road led to the settlement of these townships, and especially of the more important townships on the Housatonic,—Stockbridge and Barrington, in one or the other of which occurred Talcot's fight in King Philip's War. For some years the new road was passable only on horseback; but in the winter of 1738-39, ten of the principal dwellers on the Housatonic, two of them, John Sargeant and Timothy Woodbridge, missionaries to the Stockbridge Indians,—'did undertake and with great fatigue and

---

* I am again indebted to Professor Perry's most instructive and interesting "Origins in Williamstown," p. 303ff, for this long excerpt. Further detailed information about this ancient highway may be found in preceding pages and in "The Taverns and Turnpikes of Blandford, 1733-1833," Chap. IV.

† Now known as the General Knox highway.

‡ The present Blandford.

difficulty upon our own cost and charge make a good and feasable sleigh-road from New Glasgow, being according to estimation thirty five miles, by which means a much more safe and convenient way of transportation is now oppened from said Sheffield and the several settlements upon the Housatonic river to Westfield and the neighboring towns, and whereas, before it was very difficult for anybody, and for strangers almost impossible, in a snow of any considerable depth, without a track, which often happens in the winter season, to find the way, now by our having marked a sufficient number of trees on each hand, an entire stranger cannot easily miss it, and the people living in those parts are now able, and in the winter past did pass and repass to and from Westfield, with more than twenty sleighs, well laden, through a wilderness which before that was almost impassable on horseback, which by reason of the badness and length of the way, it was almost if not utterly impossible, for his Majesties' subjects living in these parts of the Province, to supply themselves with foreign commodities, the never so necessary in life from any town within this section.'

"It is almost certain, when Williams's ten companies, one after another, averaging perhaps forty men each, made their way over it as best they could in obedience to the marching orders received, that no organized military companies had ever before straggled and struggled over this Albany road; but four years later, and earlier in the season, Major-General Amherst took a large army of British regulars and American militia over this road to the Hudson, and from the Hudson to Ticonderoga and Crown Point; and in less than twenty years after Amherst's final overthrow of French America, Major-General Burgoyne, with a part of his captured army, traversed the same in the reverse direction; while many a regiment of New England soldiers, in the war of 1812, passed and repassed that way in both directions."

There were hospitals in Sheffield, Tyringham and Westfield, where sick soldiers were cared for, seventeen of whom died in the one at Sheffield in less than a year, 1756-'57. The Province line was run from Westfield west in 1717 through a trackless wilderness, the roadmakers returning home from Sheffield—now Great Barrington—by this old Albany trail. In 1754 it was made a county road, receiving the name of the "Great Road from Boston to Albany."* It should be understood that the westward continuation of this road in these years was "over the mountain," as the pioneers had already come in 1735.

The year 1756 proved no better than the year before it. The next year was a practical repetition of the ill success of the other two. How affairs were going in Massachusetts, including the town of Blandford, is somewhat lighted up by a letter of Colonel Israel Williams, written to the Governor at Boston (1756).†

"Sir, This acquaints you that at Capt. Bridgman's Farm about Eight miles above Northfield a week since 3 women 11 children were captivated by the Indians— 1 man killed, and one Endeavoring to make his escape supposed to be drown'd in Con't River. The buildings burnt—and Tuesday last one man killed or (?) captivated at ye Ashuelots. The enemy are discovered dayly, and within these few days—in almost every part of our Frontiers, 150 are said to come down with design to murther and destroy our people. We have full evidence of their being very numerous. This Morning by Express from Capt. Wyman of Fort Massachusetts

---

* I have culled the above information from an article in the "Berkshire Gleaner" of fifteen or twenty years ago.

† Origins, p. 284.

John Hamelton

John McQuilby

Alexander Osborne

John Knox

Samll Boies

Adam Knox

James Baird

John Gibbs

Let William Knox

John Baird

John Croops

James Taggart

John Scott

John Boies

Robert Henry

Samuel Henry

SOME ORIGINAL SIGNATURES OF 1764

I am informed that the scouts from that garrison this week discovered the tracks of 30 or 40 Indians steering towards pontoosook, besides divers other small partys— their course southward—Two men present in order to inform ye people at pontoosook saw five, fir'd upon 'em & probably killed one.

"The people in the new places above keep close— business is at an end, and they will be impoverished and ruin'd. And if our enemys continue to press upon us at this rate, we must quit our husbandry and other business and take to our arms. I can't think the people at Southampton Blandford No. 1—New Marlborough &c, &c, and the other places between Westfield and Sheffield will be safe and secure any longer. I sent 8 men yesterday to Wings garrison at No. 4—and expect 8 men more from below, which I design for Southampton. It is not in my power to grant relief to any other at present. Several places before mentioned are a cover to your people, and unless protected, they tell me they must and will leave their habitations. Notwithstanding the gloomy prospect our people support with the hopes of being soon delivered from ye cruelty and inhumanity of our inveterate as well as savage foes.

"To have our people women & children butcher'd and captivated by such miscreants is very provoking, but not wholly to be prevented. The murdhers & deaths of so many innocents, & the Cruel oppressions we now groan under, Cry aloud to Heaven for vengeance. If our iniquities don't prevent may we not hope to have an Almighty arm engaged for our help. Pray God turn to flight the armies of the aliens, & crown all our enterprizes with success.

"I have directed ye bearer to wait yr. answer.

"I am w*h* sincere respects to y*r* Hon*ble* Council of war, Sir,   Your Most Ob*t* Hum*e*, Serv't,
I. W. (Israel Williams)."

Robert Blair, brother of Matthew—so we are told by William H. Gibbs*—"purchased that tract of land called 'The Gore.' Here he built a log house for the accommodation of his family, and began to clear the land. The whole region about was one unbroken forest, and the footpath which led to the nearest fort, a distance of two miles, was through the same undisturbed wild of nature. He remained a few years, when his fear of Indians and the distance from the fort induced him to return to Worcester. The journey was performed upon horseback, carrying his wife and three children and household furniture with him. They staid five years in Worcester, and then returned to Blandford. Mr. Blair was chosen deacon of the Presbyterian church, and served many years in that capacity. He died in 1802."

This little echo of tradition speaks with eloquent voice of hardships and sorrows and the colossal labor of making a town and commonwealth. There is a deed of date, December 12, 1753, given by John Foye, the proprietor, to Robert Blair, Jr., of Worcester, "Taylor," for 160 pounds, conveying to the latter "a Certain Farm or lot of Land Number thirty three Commonly known by the Name of the Gore Farm Containing Five Hundred acres be the same more or less." It was Robert's son, Robert Junior, who made the purchase, the date of which is established by the deed just quoted. How long he remained in his new and lonely dwelling is not said. But the traditional return would approximately coincide with the establishment of peace.

The capture of the English posts at Lake George in the summer of 1757, ending with the capitulation of Fort William Henry to Montcalm, and the fearful massacre by the Indians which accompanied that event, threw the colonies into a state of resentment and terror.

* P. 56.

As a matter of fact, the French general did not follow up his advantage. But it was expected that he would, and Pownal, then Governor of Massachusetts, ordered all the cavalry of the Province, with a large body of militia, to Springfield, under the Lieutenant General of the Province, Sir William Pepperell. This latter was a new officer, elevated for the occasion. Orders had previously been given for the establishment of a magazine of provisions and military stores at the same point. A train of artillery was ordered to be provided, and a regiment of artillery raised. Sir William was instructed, in the event of the advance of the enemy, to have the wheels struck off all the wagons West of the Connecticut, to drive in cattle and horses, and make a stand upon the east side. The similar order given eighty years before, for the inhabitants of the west side to repair to the east, will show how comparatively painful had been the progress of settlement during this long and disturbed period. The garrisons at Fort Massachusetts and West Hoosac were strengthened, and preparations made in every quarter for defence, against a foe which never came."* There were no "wagons" in Blandford until long after this, but by this time there might have been a goodly number of carts.

A fatality of this campaign is brought to light by an inscription in the old burying ground. It reads thus:

> In Memory of Miss Eleanor
> Ker who died March 27, A D
> 1778 aged 27 years. Daughter
> of Mrs Katharine relict of Mr
> William KER who was slain
> by the Indians at Fort George
> in a morning scout August
> 4, 1757.   Aged 46.

* Holland, Vol. I, p. 194.

band,
There fell the parent by the savage
hand;g
Here was I snatched by deaths unerrin
hath done
Now gentle reader see what death
sertain doom.
And humbly wait your own your

William Ker was not a citizen of Blandford, however, at the time of his death. The family came to town a little later, as the following document, on file among the deeds in the Springfield registry, bears witness. While only incidentally illustrative of the immediate story of the war, it is nevertheless somewhat illuminating:

"Pursuant to a Warrant under the hands of the Select men of the Town of Blandford bearing date of the 24th of December 1759 Daniel Murphey Eleanor Murphey his wife Edmund Murphey who came from Sambreey* The widow Susanna Phelps Samuel Phelps Susanna Phelps junr. who came from the nine partners The widow Katherine Kar William Kar James Kar Eleanor Kar Katherine Kar Junoir Who came from Westfield George Mc. Muray who came from Kenderhook and Mary Phelps who came from the nine partners and Frederick Murphey who came from Sambreey on the Last day of the same December were warned forthwith to depart and leave said Town of Blandford by Glass Cochran Constable of said Blandford as pr Warrant on file appears. Feb. 12, 1760."

The William Kar herein named was probably son of William Ker of the tombstone inscription. The immigration seems considerable for a time of so much unrest. The town authorities, unmoved by the late William

---

* Perhaps meaning Simsbury, Ct.

Ker's valor, but greatly disturbed by the coming into town of so many widows and helpless children, took full legal measures to become exempt from liability should any of these prove unable to support themselves or their children.

The military reverses above related made urgent the calling out of new troops, of which Blandford town had no mean share. One company, raised and officered in Blandford, went out under Lieut. David Black.

Echoes come back to us of tavern business, always considerable in old Blandford in time of peace, stimulated and even glutted in seasons of war. April 6, 1756, the General Court* made the following allowances "out of the public treasury:" . . . "To Robert Henry two Shillings and six pense; to David Boise, Seven Shillings; To Robert Black Seven Shillings; To James Moore Thirteen Shillings & six pense; To James Carter Fifteen Shillings . . . being in full Discharge of their respective Accounts of Entertainment afforded to Soldiers on their Return from the Army in the late Crown Point Expedition herewith exhibited." The license of some of these as taverners is on record. Robert Henry dwelt just below the meeting house, on the highway to Albany; Robert Black kept tavern almost under the eaves of the sanctuary; James Moore was on the road to Albany, a little before one reaches Blair pond; David Boise was on the town street, not far beyond Robert Black; James Carter is unknown; Samuel Crooks had his home on South street, or the old road to Granville.

July 7, 1756, it was "*Ordered,* That there be allowed and paid out of the Public Treasury to William Hurston † the sum of Nineteen Pounds seventeen shillings & four pense And to John Knox the sum of Five Pounds

---

* Province Laws, Chap. 404.
† Huston.

six shillings, in discharge of their acco*ts* of Entertainment to Sold*rs* on their return from the Forts near Lake George." Huston's tavern was just below the meeting house, on the Albany road, and Knox's was a mile or two farther down the road toward Westfield. Legislative action was taken in the fall of that year providing for the sustenance and care of the sick of the army. Taverners along the road were by one of these legislative acts required to board returning sick soldiers at the rate of six pence per meal. March 8, 1748, the provincial government had voted to pay, on the account of "Billeting Ye Canada Soldiers. Blandford, 122 weeks, 2 days," at 7/6, 45. 17. 2. Westfield had on her account, 224 weeks, 6 days, at 6/3. Stockbridge had 711 weeks, 2 days, at 7/6.

The ministry and personality of the Rev. James Morton may be treated of at length in a later story. Suffice it here to say that Mr. Morton was a man of lively temperament and liberal theology, which became a chronic provocation to his conservative flock. He lived "in a house by the side of the road," and he did not propose to be asleep when opportunity awaited him to serve his commonwealth and race. Willy-nilly he found himself in the midst of martial bustle and both as minister and patriot he was bound to do his bit. His people felt that he should keep strictly within the bounds of a narrow ecclesiasticism, and became deeply aggrieved by his nervous activities outside the pale. To them it seemed needful that he should stand rebuked by presbyterial authority, and in accordance with a recognized custom of the Presbyterians, when presbytery was too distant to appeal to, the nearest association of Congregational ministers should be asked to serve in such capacity. This was done in Blandford over and over again.

Such a council was convened there on Feb. 15, 1757—
in the midst of winter,—and in Blandford! Some of
Mr. Morton's flock made charge against their minister
"in his acting unbecoming the Carecter of a ministre
of Christ in his taking it upon him to entertain Grate
Numbers of Soldiers as they pass up and Down on
Sabbaths and at other times for the Sake of Gain theby
Rendering himself odeous not only by making his hous
like a tavern wethout any Nececety but also in taking
Pains to send and Envite Pople of all sorts to Come
to his house whare they are Entertained for money but
more Espately in Denying that he Entertains any but
out of pure Neccity which is absolutely falls."

The findings of the council are eloquent in their reference to the "hurry and confusion of business," to the
presence of "so much to lead the minds of the People
from Religion," and so on. The definite answer to the
charges against Mr. Morton is of sufficient interest to
quote in its entirety. The paper is written with exces-
sive carelessness. I quote it *verbatim et literatim:*

"As to this Article—we cant find Mr. Morton in
any measure guilty as Charged.—Tho we own that it
appears—that Mr Mortons house was much like a
tavern and its Evident that Multitudes frequented his
house for Entertainment Both on Sabbath days and
week Days—And we also Confess that its unbecoming
the Character of a Minister of Christ and is sufficient to
render a Man odeous that does it without Necessity
oblige him—But how evident is it that it was a Necessity for Mr. Morton to entertain pple—for the occasion
was very extraordinary when they were pass along in
hundreds; Soldiers that were going to Jopard their lives
in the high places of field for the Defence of their Country—and it was impossible for the Tavern to accommodate and he only upon the Road that could afford

relief to passing Soldiers etc.—Must he Because a Minister lay aside his humanity and Common Civility? Must he no bowels of Mercy to his Necessitous fellow Creatures? but treat them as brutes; Nay worse tn Brutes, for our blessed Lord Says, if he see a Sheep fallen into the pit, will he not lay hold upon it and pull it out? and this on the Sabbath Day? and shall a Minister treat his fellow Creatures worse God forbid—and if Soldiers traveled or Marched on Sabbath Days: reason good that they should be taken Care on those as well as other times—and it dont appear that he invited any, unless once, and that Supported by a Single Evidence which appeared to be a party Concerned: But on the Contrary many Evidence that Mr Morton was loath and actually refused to Entertain—But as he did Entertain, and that out of Necessity should he do it upon the free least, without any Consideration—It seems Surely if he Did, Deny the faith and worse than an Infidel: for not taking Care of and providing for his own, and Especial for his own household. Now how can Mr Morton be Charged with falsehood, for saying that he did out of Necessity, when the thing is so Evident that Necessity lay upon him—that he must thro if not only Christianity but humanity to refuse such a time as this was."

Similar labors were thrust upon the Rev. Samuel Hopkins, of Great Barrington, who later became famous as one of the exponents of the New England theology. And the same was true of Jonathan Edwards, at Stockbridge. As for Dr. Hopkins, his parish seems to have been the scene of military movements for twenty years. One record in Hopkins's diary is, "Near twenty soldiers lodged at my house last night."

Coincident with our stories of the march and the relief of the colonial troops are some incidents gleaned from the pages of "Three Military Diaries," published by the late Dr. Samuel A. Green. That one of the three which is of particular interest right here is by David Holden, of Groton, and is entitled, "Of What was Transacted In the Expedition For the Total Reduction of Canada in the year 1760." The company that marched, according to this story, included 74 officers and men, with "a Team" to carry the baggage and provisions. They began the march Sunday, May 4, 1760, and passed through Westford, Leicester and Brookfield, spending the first night in the place last named. Thence they marched to "Palmore," spending the night at Landlord Shaw's. Another day's march brought them to "Landlord Persons on Springfield Plain." Springfield itself was next reached, where "Four of Cap*t* Hutchings's men was put in prison for abuseing the people by the way."

"May 8. Past muster this morning before Lieu*t* Campbell, Drew Seven Days Provision Took a Team to Carry our Baggage in and Marched about (10) miles to Lanlord Cap*t* Claps in Westfield where we tarried all Night.

"Here we left Jonas Butterfield (of Dunstable) Lame at the widow Ingolsols under the care of D*r*. Clapum.

"9. We marched 4 miles & a half to the foot of the mount of Glasgow, where our Team Left us & we was obliged to Carry our Packs on our Backs to Shuffield, So we marched Seven miles to Landlord Pees's in Glasgow where we tarried all Night.

"here we left Freeborn Raimond & Thomas Hildreth (both of Westford) Sick.

"10. Marched Through the Green-Woods to N*o* one to M*r*. Jackson which was about 20 miles & tarried all Night."

So the journal continues, illustrating in a single detailed narrative, not alone the experiences of men on the march, but certain locations and personalities of particular interest to us just now. "Landlord Pees" was Nathaniel Pease, predecessor of Levi Pease, later of national fame.

Nothing of the glamour of actual warfare by soldiers on the field is reflected back to us from the long, silent years, as to Blandford's part therein, except the dry official lists contained in an appendix, and a faint tradition or remnant of a document which hints of heroisms and sorrows, victories and pains, and the terrific sacrifice. After the affair at Fort William Henry, there was little military activity in Western Massachusetts, except the passing and repassing of troops along the great highways.

Wrung from the reluctant hand of forgetfulness which has concealed so many more local incidents of the war than have come to light, is this tradition contained in a private letter from Mr. John I. Hastings, of Stillwater, Oklahoma: "Ephraim (Hamilton) had, I believe, two brothers, Patric and Armour, both killed by Indians. As I heard it from my grandfather, Armor Hamilton, son of Ephraim, Patric was killed at Fort George in the French and Indian wars. He was at the fort in company with one James Larrabee; and Hamilton was killed, while Larrabee got inside the fort and was not hurt." This looks like an incident in the fight in which Ker, as above related, was killed.

There is an eloquent waif from the last will and testament of Robert Wilson, of date, July 2, 1764: "Being advanced into years, but of perfect Mind & Memory and Health of Body," providing for his wife, Elizabeth, and on this wise for his son, Andrew, who, he says, "If now alive is in captivity provided he ever returns Home again or is known to be living elsewhere and sends for it or value," is to have the sixty-acre lot. If that was lot 31, of the first division,* the son came back to claim his own, for in 1788 that lot was known as "Andrew Wilson's land."

There were not only patriots, but also deserters—as always. These latter needed, for the sake of the morale of the army and the honor of the cause, to be searched out and brought to justice. Again the Blandford minister comes to the foreground, and again to the scandal of his jealous people. Mr. Morton engaged himself in this business with his trusty tithingman, William Proven — fit occupation for a man of so stern a calling. "William Province says"—so recites a document now yellow with age—"that Mr. Morton and he traveled togʳ in pursuit of Deserters," the reverend gentleman asserting in reply that he had given William Proven "2 Dolars" as the latter's share. From all of which it would appear that the business was not abundantly profitable, or that to some forward judges it seemed more profitable to the cleric than to his deputy.

The rear of an army is not the most inspiring place from which to take a view of it. Yet one may not know all about a war without knowing something of what is going on behind the scenes. The pain of a war, and the demoralization resulting, are to be traced back to petty and incidental issues which in mass are not petty nor incidental. In June, 1755, Colonel Worthington had written a letter from Springfield, embodying these complaints of the way some things were going:

"Lieut Taylor informs the officers here that the present design respecting the soldiers is that they march to Westfield on their tour to Albany & be muster'd & receive the residue of bounty, wages, &c there at West-

---

* The description as given in the deed is a little obscure at this distance of time.

field. This S'*r* gives them uneasiness, very considerable,
& if orders peremptory are given for it I am very sorry,
& I may S'*r* say it to you tho not to them that tho
I am all submission to the wisdom of our Fathers (if
their Wisdom is in it) yet that this must needs be mis-
judged. The soldiers ought in all reason to have been
muster'd ten days ago, & to have known certainly who
would be accepted & who not, that such as were accepted might have had their money to have furnished
themselves w*h* necessary cloathing &c for their march,
& to have provided to have left their families (such as
have them) provided for at home, for many such there
are who depended on their money to do those things,
& will be reduced to great difficulties without they receive it in season, & where they can dispose of it to these
purposes. This sh'*d* have been done also that such as are
so unhappy as not to be admitted to risque their lives
for us, may be saved as much trouble as might be, &
be denied the favour on the cheapest terms," etc.* The
letter goes on to complain that the soldiers should be
mustered as near home as possible, and all unnecessary
trouble avoided.

Once more the Rev. James Morton comes upon the
scene. He was charged by some of his people with "in-
equity" in negotiating the wages of James Moor, a
soldier who was probably a member of this very regiment, at or near this very time. According to an ancient
document, said Moor made deposition that "y*e* Col. was
displeased, Cooly's Name put in y*e* list," with the result
that Moor feared he would not get his wages. The
"Col. spoke disparaging, moor refused to do duty, not
expecting wages." One Cannon, who was going to Boston, agreed to look after the matter. The reverend
gentleman must have cordially regretted having med-
dled with the matter at all, for Moor was dissatisfied

* "Origins in Williamstown," pp. 331-332.

with the returns, and the minister was accused of sharp practice. Sickness, desertions, mutinous conduct, mismanagement and numberless ills aside from glorious deaths constitute a war, and entered into this one.

The above story, so fragmentary, so unsatisfactory, and so often inglorious, is after all a rather characteristic and fairly adequate one as such history goes. The impression left by these disjointed details clinging about the skirts of a continental struggle and a fateful crisis in the history of a people is after all a true one. It all needs the addendum of musterings in and musterings out, along with accounts of mileages, wages, and shadowy reminiscences of marches and campaigns, which an appendix supplies.

The town of Blandford felt profoundly the terrific drain upon its homes and man power through the repeated requisitions and drafts of troops. By 1758 the little municipality was so depleted and depressed that an agitation arose over the question whether to petition the Legislature for exemption from further enlistments. It is fine evidence of the spirit of the people that "it passed in the Negative." But four days later—March 28—another meeting reversed the vote of the preceding one, and "chos Ensign William Knox to go to Col Worthington to make Applycation to Him to be Esced in sending men into the War." They did well to choose their own colonel, and to present their application through so trusted a leader whether in peace or war. Mr. Keep informs us that "In 1768 the court gave the town five pounds for the benefit of schools, and several times excused them from sending their equal proportions of men into the service."

Out of the hodge-podge of provincial military records, the names of at least fifty to sixty Blandford men have been identified as having taken part in the wars of this period. But the condition of the lists indicates many unknown in addition. The population of Blandford in the opening of the war was as already noted probably something above three hundred. There was a man out, first and last, from nearly every home. It would look as though, at one time and another, nearly every able-bodied man was in the war for home and country. When at last they asked to be excused, it was because they felt the last reasonable extremity had come.

It is of interest to learn that, of the proprietors of the town, Francis Brinley and John Foye were officers in the wars, the former having been a colonel. Heath obtained a like title, probably in similar service.

Closing his chapter on the last French war, Dr. Holland* eloquently and truly says that during the struggles of more than a hundred years then concluding, "Children had been born, had grown to manhood, and descended to old age, knowing little or nothing of peace and tranquility. Hundreds had been killed, and large numbers carried into captivity. Men, women and children had been butchered by scores. There is hardly a square acre, certainly not a square mile, in the Connecticut valley, that has not been tracked by the flying feet of fear, resounded with the groan of the dying, drunk with the blood of the dead, or served as the scene of toils made doubly toilsome by the apprehension of danger that never slept. It was among such scenes and such trials that the settlements of Western Massachusetts were planted."

Out of isolated fragments picked up from every whither and gathered as best one may into a somewhat disconnected whole, one glimpses the story of these terrible wars and their tragic meaning for an infant frontier town in Western Massachusetts. A sympathetic and fertile imagination alone may suffice to add what

---

* Vol. I, Chap. XII.

The Old Lloyd (Loughhead) Homestead

may be necessary to a real vision of the period as Blandford folk passed through its weary and terrifying years. Men appear and disappear in ghostly fashion, not a few never to come on the scene again. Women and children are everywhere hiding in the general obscurity. There they all are, the named, the unnamed; the young, the old; the living, the dying. Such was the cost of building a state, of erecting a town, of creating home life and making it secure and abiding. Looking back over the generations, such have been the taxes levied to the last drop of blood.

There were large rewards, too. In Green's Larger History of England Edmund Burke is cited as making the assertion that during this period there were not in Connecticut and Massachusetts Bay two men who could afford at a distance from their estates to spend one thousand pounds a year. The settlers were men, adds the historian, "whose will was braced and invigorated by their personal independence and comfort, the tradition of their past, and the personal temper which was created by the greater loneliness and self-dependence of their lives." "With the triumphs of Wolfe," writes this same historian, "began the history of the United States." Then also began the larger growth of the town of Blandford into self-reliance, prosperity, substantial comfort, greatening numbers and widening influence, until before a half century more was added to her history she had begun to lay a guiding hand upon the rising empire of the great West, and to bring forth sons and daughters of vision and resource greatly worthy of the Commonwealth which had asked of the migrant Scots of Ulster in the year 1718 to go out and stand as a wall of defence on her frontier. And they went, nor did they need to be ashamed as they met the enemy in the gate.

BLANDFORD SOLDIERS IN THE SEVEN YEARS WAR

The following lists were carefully copied from the various muster rolls among the State archives in Boston a score of years ago. In the original documents, as well as in the card index, there is in multitudes of instances no designation of the soldier's residence. The embarrassment is further complicated by the fact that any certain name may represent many individuals. Very careful restrictions were attached to the use of this card index, and still more to the consultation of the documents. The conditions of research were at first most discouraging. As my search, however, was of a somewhat comprehensive nature, extraordinary courtesy was extended to me, and I was allowed access to the original documents, themselves. I am informed that such privilege was long ago withheld. Familiarity with old-time Blandford names opened to me what would otherwise have been a maze of mysteries. The groupings helped me not a little. A large number of the documents are undated, and in such instances conjecture must come to the rescue of ignorance.

1. From Vol. 94, p. 2, undated, but the date, 1755, has been written in pencil upon the document:—

A list of Men Voluntarily Inlisted into his Majestys Service for reinforcing the Army destin*d* for Crown Point, out of ye Southern Regim*t* in the County of Hampshire

Capt Elisha Noble	Samuel Stoddard	James Beard
John Sinnet	Robert Blair	William Crooks
		Samuel Loughead

2. A List of Persons in the South Regiment in the County of Hampshire under Com*d* of Col. John Worthington that have been employ'd in his Majesty's Service within Two Years past Accord*g* to ye Returns of the Several Captains Viz

Cap*t* William Hustons Compa*a*

John Donhester	Robert Blair	John Sennet
Sam*l* Belknap	John Beard	John Gibbs
Geo Cannaghee	Sam*l* Loyd	W*m* Crooks
Armour Hamilton	W*m* Steward	W*m* Barfield
James McCullock		

(Note: The diligent reader of the preceding chapters will easily identify some of the above names in a little different dress: Donhester = Donaghy, or Doneghy; Cannaghee is not so plain—perhaps Carnachan, or McConnoughy, or Kennedy; McCulloch = McClintoch, or McClenachan; Barfield possibly = Warfield.)

3. Vol. 94, p. 423.

An Ac*ctt* of the (some undecipherable words here. S. G. W.) Subsistence money p*d* Cap*t* John Mosleys men for the Crown Point Exped—1756.

		Miles	
Viz Capt John Moseley	West*fd*	95	0-9-6
Sam*l* Lah head	Glascow	95	0-9-6
John Forguson	Do	95	0-9-6
James Sennett	Do	95	0-9-6
W*m* McCallett	Glascow	"	0-9-6

4. Vol. 94, p. 24. (Excerpts, S. G. W.):

Matthew Blair appears on "A Muster Roll," date not given, but sworn to, Boston, March 2, 1756, "of a company . . . under the command of Capt. John Worthington, Centinel. Entered service Nov. 7; served until Nov. 18" (year not given. Endorsed Co. Westward from June 20 to Nov. 22, 1755).

In connection with the "Subsistence money" paid the soldiers as in the above account, it is of interest to note the allowance (v. Provincial Laws, 1755-56, Feb. 26, Chap. 316) given to the soldiers "after the arrival at the Place of general Rendezvous":

To each Man, Fourteen Ounces of Bread	Per Diem
Ditto of Pork	ditto
One Jill of Rum	ditto
Half a Pint of Peas or Beans	ditto
Half a Pound of Sugar	per Week
Two Ounces of Ginger	ditto
One Pound of Flour	ditto
One Pint of Indian-Meal	ditto
Four Ounces of Butter	ditto
One Pint of Molasses	ditto

5. Vol. 95, p. 552.

A Muster Roll of Lieut. David Black's Company of Blandford that went from the South Regiment of the County of Hampshire Under S*d* Blacks Com*d* and For the Relief of the Garrison &c of Fort W*m* Henry in the Alarm Aug*t*: 1757.

Men's Names	Quality	No. Miles they went from Home	No. of Days of Service	At what per Day	Total Wages
David Black	Lieut.	130	18 1/3	3/9	3- 8- 9
John Willsons	Ser.	do	do	2/10	2-11-11
Robert Blair	do	do	do	do	2-11-11
David McConothee	Corpor*l*	do	do	2/9	2-10- 5
Sam*ll* Bois	private	do	do	do	2- 8-10
David Bois	do	do	do	do	2- 8-10
John Knox	do	do	13	do	1-14- 8
John McKinstry	do	do	do	do	1-14- 8
James Moor	do	do	do	do	1-14- 8

Men's Names	Quality	No. Miles they went from Home	No. of Days of Service	At what per Day	Total Wages
James Lohead	private	130	18 1/3	2/9	2- 8-10
William Carnahan	do	do	do	do	2- 8-10
John Beard	do	do	do	do	2- 8-10
James Ferguson	do	do	do	do	2- 8-10
John Ferguson	do	do	do	do	2- 8-10
John Sinnet	do	do	do	do	2- 8-10
James Willson	do	do	do	do	2- 8-10
John Gibbs	do	do	do	do	2- 8-10
Mathew Blair	do	do	do	do	2- 8-10
Jacob Blair	do	do	do	do	2- 8-10
William Steward	do	do	do	do	2- 8-10
Solomon Brown	do	do	do	do	2- 8-10

50-10- 8

Ex S. Y.

(Note: There is a column inserted between "Quality" and "No. of Miles," etc., headed: "Masters &c.," under which no entries are made. There is another column, "Received of ye Tavernor," under which is written, "Nothing" for the whole list and still another, "Remains Due to Each Man," wherein is written for all the list, "The Whole Wages," a pathetically eloquent entry. Under all is the signature:

"A True Roll
OK David Black."

The back of the document contains the following:—

N B. The Day of Reparation is aded to the other Days of Service & Carried out in the Sum Total

Hampshire Ss Decr 30—1758 Than Lieut David Black appeard Before me And Made Solemn Oath That the within is a Trew Roll According to the best of his Knowledge.

before Me David Mosley Justice Paies
Muster Roll of Liut
David Blacks
Company in ye Alarm
Augst 1757
Exd S. Y. £50-10-8

Committed Jny 27:1759
Repsd A(2 undecipherable letters S.G.W.) Comtee
Wh. Advised Jany 30. 1759

(Note: Later in the year David Black was at the head of a company of 46 men, serving under Col. Worthington.)

6. Vol. 97, p. 17.

A Return of the Bayonett men

Belonging to Blandford under Command of Lieut David Black in a Regiment Whereof John Worthington Esqr is Coll.

Agreeable to an act of the Great and General Court of the Province of the Massachusetts Bay Entitled an Act for Regulating thee Malitia we Proceeded to Draft one half of the Effective men Belonging to S*d* Company to the Number of Twenty three and have fix*d* their Guns with Bayonetts according to the directions Given in S*d*, Act.

Names of the Men

Joseph Freeland	James Sinnet	Isaac Blair
Glass Cochran	William Brown Jr	Jno Gibbs
William Carnahan	Jno Boies	Ephraim Gibbs
Jno Hamilton	Jno Carnahan	Samuel Boies
Jno Baird	William Lohead	David McConoughey
Sam*l* Ferguson	Jno Sinnet	Israel Gibbs
James Ferguson	Mathew Blair Ju*r*	Solomon Stewart
Jno Crooks	John Ferguson	

the Number of Men is twenty three,—

Each Man and Bayonet the amounts at 7/pence

is £8-1-0

David Black
Hampshire Ss December 30—1758
Then Lieut David Black the
subscriber to the following amount
appeared and Made oath to the
truth of the Same — Before
me David Moseley Justice

Paies.

(Note:—The muster roll of Lieut. Black's entire company is not extant, as I have been informed from the Secretary of State's office. I am further informed that the bayonet men, consisting in this instance of half the entire number, were the able-bodied men in the company, ready for action, whatever the emergency may have been.)

7. Vol. 97, p. 236.

(An undated return, the receipt of which is dated April, 1759:)

Return of the inlisted or impressed for his Majesty's Service within the Province of Massachusetts Bay in the Regiment whereof   is Colonel, to be put under the immediate Command of his Excellency Jeffry Amherst, Esq. . . . for the Invasion of Canada

	Inlisted	Impressed	Names of the Fathers of Sons under age and Masters of Servants
James Beard	April 2	Blandford	
Jacob Blair	6	"	
John Sinnet	6	"	Robert Sinnett
John Gilmore	do	"	
David Scott	do	"	John Scott
John Campbell	do	"	
Thomas Happer	do	No. 4	
Solomon Brown	April 11	Blandford	

8. Vol. 96, p. 444.

In this return Matthew Blair, private, is listed as having entered his Majesty's service April 14 — year not given —, the return being endorsed 1758, Capt. Jonathan Ball, in Col. William William's regiment, for the reduction of Canada. The return bears date of Jan. 27, 1759.

9. Vol. 98, p. 229.

This is an undated document containing a number of Blandford names. It is a muster roll of the company "Under Command of William Shepard." The document was endorsed, 1760. It contains these items:—

John Ferguson, Sergeant, Blandford, at 2:3:1 per month. Began service, June 25. Served til Dec. 1, 22 weeks, 6 days. Miles traveled at 8d per diem, 60. Received, 2.8. Whole of Wages due, 12.0.10. Received of the Paymaster, 72; of the Sutlers, 1.1.; for baking bread, 2.1; of the Captain, 6s. Bal. due, 9-3-9.

Francis Moore, Private, Blandford, began service Feb. 28; served till Dec. 1, 22 weeks, 3 days; traveled 60 miles at 8d per diem; received 2.8; 10.4.7 wages due; received of Paymaster, 18; of the Sutlers, 1.1; for baking bread, 2.1; of the Captain, 6s. Bal. due, 7-17-6.

John Clarke began service June 28; served till Dec. 1, 22 weeks, 3 days; traveled 60 miles at 8d. per diem; received 2.8; Whole of Wages due, 10.4.7, received of the Paymaster, 18; of the Sutlers, 1.1; for baking bread, 2.1; of the Captain, 6. Bal. due, 7;17.6.

William Moore began service June 23 and served till Nov. 8, 19 weeks, 6 days; traveled 60 miles at 8d. per diem, rceived 2.8; whole of wages due, 9.1.5; received of the Paymaster, 12; of the Sutlers, 1.1; for baking bread, 2.5; Bal. due, 7.6.4.

William Karr began service June 30, and served till Dec. 1, 22 weeks, 1 day; traveled 60 miles at 8d. per diem; received 2.8; whole of wages due, 10.2; received of the Paymaster, 18; of the Sutlers, 2.11; for baking bread, 2.1; of the Captain, 9. Bal. due, 6.1.11.

John Miller began service June 30 and served till Sept. 28, 13 weeks, received of the Sutlers, 1.10; for baking bread, 2.1; of the Captain, 9. Bal. due, 6.1.11.

Isaac Blair began service June 30, and served till Dec. 1, 22 weeks, 3 days; traveled 50 miles at 8d. per diem; received 2; whole of wages due, 10.12.11; received of the Paymaster, 12; of the Sutlers, 1.7; for baking bread, 2.1. Bal. due, 3.11.

Note:—There are some mathematical inconsistencies in this document, but the whole stands as an eloquent story of camp life in the Crown Point campaigns.

APPENDIX II

TABLES OF BIRTHS AND BAPTISMS

Note:—This book is not at all primarily one of family genealogies. Nevertheless, a laborious attempt has been made to furnish such raw material as has been available from which Blandford descendants may glean the facts contained in original sources, or as close to the original as possible. No data are herein given beyond the year 1775. Even this date extends by a few years beyond the time of the events narrated in the closing chapter of this book. The vital statistics of towns other than Blandford extend but little, if any, beyond the period of Blandford's settlement.

There is a somewhat indefinite borderline difficult to define. Family roots run back and intertwine in a most puzzling way. First settlers and early settlers of Blandford bear names which were borne by many residents of provincial towns years before the migrations of 1718 and following years. It has been impossible to ferret out these inter-relations. In entering to a very slight degree upon this borderland in some of the tables, some names have doubtless crept in which do not belong there, while some which do belong there may be found to have been omitted. The author is not a genealogist, either by talent or choice.

There were family remnants in Worcester, Hopkinton and not a few other places, following the time of Blandford's settlement bearing surnames identical with those who planted our own hill town, and these names became established. It has been impossible to follow after these.

It is regretted that no genealogical pick-ups could be gathered from Suffield, Connecticut, since that town became a convenient refuge for Blandford families in the French and Indian war periods. Diligent and unrewarding search has been made for these at the Boston Public Library and at the library of the New England Historic Genealogical Society. The author was assured at the latter resort for such material that the vital statistics of Suffield had never been published.

The town of Brookfield was an early border town of great significance. Gibbses were there; Hamiltons were there in numbers; Reeds were there, and Rices, Walkers and Woods, not to mention others. Some of the Christian names furthermore suggest close kinship with families who settled in Blandford. Here is rich ground for genealogical rooting about. In addition to the published histories of the towns, and to the books of vital statistics, the registries of deeds yield rich material for those who have opportunity and patience for such research.

Some few embarrassments attend all these studies. One needs a microscope, an imagination, an almost supernatural keenness and a phenomenal gift of accuracy and research to extract the truth, the whole truth and nothing but the truth from some of the town clerks' and other records. Axes and scythes and guns were better handled than pens by some of these worthies. Dates in contemporary documents do not always agree. Dates of baptisms and of births are not always distinguished. Records are made sometimes by "old style" and sometimes by "new style." The difference in the contrasted records sometimes appears as a whole year.

These records following are put forth after prodigious painstaking and repeated checking up by reader and listener, and finally committed to the printed page with fear and trembling.

HOPKINTON BIRTHS

Beard, Susannah, d. James, 1727 (church record between Oct. 22 and Nov. 21, baptism).

Black, David, s. Hugh and Elizabeth, Nov. 8, 1720.
    Mary, d. Robert and Jeney, May 3, 1735.
    Robert, s. Robert and Jenny, Feb. 4, 1733-4.

Blare, Elizabeth, d. Mathew and Mary, Aug. 28, 1728.
    Mathew, s. Mathew and Mary, Nov. 14, 1733.
    Robert, s. Mathew, bap. Oct. 4-12, 1730.

Cook, Andrew, s. Thomas and Sarah, 1729.
    Andrew, s. Thomas and Sarah, 1736.
    Elizabeth, d. Thomas and Sarah, 1734.
    John, s. Thomas and Sarah, 1727.
    Joseph, s. Thomas and Sarah, 1738.
    Sarah, d. Thomas and Sarah, 1732.

Crook, Ann, d. John and Sarah, Jan. 22, 1749-50.
    Eliz., d. Samll., bap. Apr. 29, 1733.
    Jane, d. John and Mary, May 31, 1740 (bap. Jennet).
    Mary, d. John and Mary, June 15, 1742.
    Rachael, d. Samll. bap. Oct. 19, 1731.
    Jane, d. William, bap. Dec. 14, 1732.

Donaghy, Elisabeth, d. William and Elisabeth, Mar. 1, 1727-8.
    Jayn, d. William and Elisabeth, Mar. 14, 1720-1.
    John, s. William and Elisabeth, Feb. 1, 1717-18.
    William, s. William and Elisabeth, Mar. 20, 1724-5.
    Mary, d. William and Elisabeth, Apr. 3, 1722-3.

Fargison, James, s. Samuel and Elener, June 28, 1733.
Forgason, Ann, d. Samuel and Elener, July 20, 1735.

Gibbs, Esther, d. Jno., bap. Oct. 31, 1731.
    Jacob, s. Jno., bap. Apr. 28, 1728.
    Jacob, s. Jacob and Martha, Jan. 4, 1731.
    Joseph, s. Jacob and Martha, Nov. 7, 1727.
    Lydia, d. Jno., bap. Mar. 15, 1730.
    Martha, d. Jacob and Martha, Nov. 2, 1725.
    Phinehas, s. Jacob and Martha, June 23, 1732.
    Rebeka, d. Israel, bap. July 22, 1732.

Gibs, Jacob, s. Jno., May 19, 1734.
    James, s. Jno., bap. June 12, 1726.
    John, s. Israell and Mary, Apr. 8, 1730.

Hambleton, Ann, d. Patrick and Ann, Sept. 3, 1726.
John, s. Patrick and Ann, June 13, 1724.
Mary, d. Patrick and Ann, Sept. 29, 1721.
Paterick, s. Almer and Agness, Dec. 31, 1732.
Sarah, d. Patrick and Ann, Sept. 29, 1729.
Hamblton, Ephraim, s. Almor and Agnis, July 13, 1728.
Mary, d. Almor and Agnis, Apr. 22, 1730.
Henry, William s. Robert and Jane, May 9, 1735.
How, Abigail, d. Peter and Thankfull, Aug. 18, 1731.
Jotham, s. Peter and Thankfull, July 23, 1733.
Peter, s. Peter and Thankfull, Aug. 20, 1724.
Phinihas, s. Peter and Thankfull, Oct. 22, 1735.
Thankful, d. Peter and Thankfull, Oct. 17, 1726.

Maxwel, Elizabeth, bap. Jan. 26, 1728.
Montgomery, Mary, d. James, bap. Mar. 11, 1733.
More, Ann, d. Archibald, bap. Sept. 22, 1728.
Mountgomery, Sarah, d. John, bap. Sept. 22, 1728.

Osburne, John, s. John, bap. July 18, 1736.

Senate, Hepsibah, d. Robert and Hepsibah, Mar. 25, 1733.
Sennet, Elisabeth, d. Robert and Mehepsibath, Aug. 22, 1730.
Robert, s. Robert and Mehepsibath, Aug. 1, 1728.
Steward, Solomon, s. Walter and Greasel, Apr. 15, 1733.
Stewart, Margret, d. Walter and Grisel, Mar. 23, 1722-3.
William, s. Walter and Grisel, Apr. 18, 1729.
Stone, Daniel, s. Daniel and Mary, Dec. 6, 1732.
Josiah, s. Daniel and Mary, July 29, 1730.
Martha, d. Daniel and Mary, Nov. 12, 1726.

Walker, Abigail, d. Israel and Abigail, June 30, 1741.
Benjamin, s. Jason and Hannah, May 24, 1743.
Ebenezer, s. Israel and Hannah, Oct. 17, 1731.
Hannah, d. Israel and Hannah, Dec. 16, 1734.
Hannah, d. Jason and Hannah, July 8, 1741.
Israel, s. Israel, bap. Apr. 22, 1739.
Jason, s. Jason and Hannah, Jan. 23, 1733-4.
Israel, s. Israel and Abigil, June 30, 1743.
Joseph, s. Jason and Hannah, Feb. 9, 1738-9.
Josiah, s. Henry and Mary, Feb. 17, 1726-7.
Lois, d. Israel and Abigail, May 20, 1736.
Lois, d. Israel, bap. May 20, 1739.
Mary, d. Henry and Mary, May 14, 1729.
Phebe, d. Josiah and Mary, Sept. 19, 1730.
Solomon, s. Elizabeth, bap. June 3, 1739.
Thomas, s. Jason and Hannah, Aug. 12, 1735.

Wark, Elizabeth, d. James and Elizabeth, Dec. 8, 1736.
 Hannah (twin), d. James and Elizabeth, Mar. 9, 1739.
 James, s. James and Elizabeth, Nov. 22, 1731.
 James, s. James and Elizabeth, Aug. 14, 1743.
 Rebeccah, d. James and Elizabeth, Aug. 23, 1741.
 Rebeckah, d. James and Elizabeth, Aug. 27, 1734.
Wark (twin), Sarah, d. James and Elizabeth, Mar. 9, 1739.
Wilson, Elizabeth, d. James and Deliverance, Oct. 16, 1726.
Wood, Benjamin (twin), s. Thomas and Mary, Apr. 30, 1751.
 Elisabeth, d. Thomas and Mary, Dec. 11, 1748.
 Elizabeth, d. Thomas and Mary, Nov. 15, 1744.
 John, s. John, bap. Nov. 2, 1729.
 John, s. John, bap. May 2, 1731.
 John, s. Benjamin and Martha, Apr. 22, 1739.
 John, s. Benjamin and Mary, Jan. 12, 1742-3.
 John (twin), s. Thomas and Mary, Apr. 30, 1751.
 Mary, d. John and Mary, Jan. 31, 1727.
 Mary, d. Thomas, bap. Dec. 18, 1748.
 Saml., s. Thos. and Mary, Dec. 21, 1746.
 Sarah, d. Thomas, bap. Oct. 7, 1753.
 Thomas, s. Thomas and Mary, Apr. 2, 1743.

(ADDITIONAL, FROM RECORDS OF REV. ELIAS NASON)

Gibbs, John, s. Jacob and Martha, Sept. 11, 1735.
Gibbs, Mary, d. Israel and Mary, Feb. 15, 1728.

Hambleton, Mary, d. Almor and Agnes, Apr. 22, 1730.
How, John, s. Benjamin and Hannah, Sept. 20, 1731.
How, John, s. Isaac and Hannah, Aug. 18, 1731.
How, Lois, d. Peter and Thankful, Mar. 7, 1729.

Knox, Elizabeth, d. William and Elizabeth, May 15, 1730.

Osborn, Ann, d. John and Jane, June 24, 1727.
Osborn, Elizabeth, d. John and Mary, June 6, 1733.
Osborn, Mary, d. John and Mary, July 23, 1734.

Senate, Hepsibeh, d. Robert and Hepsibeh, Mar. 25, 1733.
Stewart, Margaret, d. Walter and Grizel, Apr. 4, 1725.
Stewart, Paul, s. Walter and Grizel, Mar. 2, 1723.

Wark, Samuel, s. James and Elizabeth, Nov. 22, 1731.
Wilson, James, s. James and Deliverance, July 8, 1730.
Wilson, Lydia, d. Josiah and Hannah, Mar. 3, 1737.

(ADDITIONAL, FROM MANUSCRIPT RECORDS OF "BIRTHS AND BAPTISMS")

Hassard, Moses, s. James and Lydia, Bap. March, 1730.
Montgomery, Mary, d. James, Bap. March 11, 1733.

Sennett, Robert, s. Robert and Mahepsibah, . . . (sometime in 1725).
Sennit, Robert, s. Robert, Bap. Aug. 11, 1728.
Stone, Elizabeth, d. Daniel, Bap. Aug. 2, 1730.
Tobias, Negro, a servant of James Hassard, Bap. Mar., 1730.
Wark, Rebecca, d. James, Bap. Sept. 1, 1734.

BLANDFORD BIRTHS

Baird, Ezekiel, s. James Jr. and Martha, Nov. 12, 1762.
Baird, Grace, d. James Jr. and Martha, Oct. 13, 1765.
Baird, James ye 3rd, s. James Jr. and Martha, May 16, 1761.
Baird, Martha, d. James Jr. and Martha, Feb. 8, 1768.
Baird, Mary, d. James Jr. and Martha, Feb. 1, 1770.
Barnes,
Bement, Anne, d. Judah and marcy, Apr. 27, 1775.
Bement, Letty, d. Judah and marcy, July 9, 1771.
Bement, Lucy, d. Judah and marcy, July 1, 1768.
Bement, Triphena, d. Judah and marcy, Apr. 13, 1773.
Bement, marcy, d. Judah and marcy, Oct. 22, 1765.
Black, Ann, d. Robert and Margarett, Feb. 1, 1744/5.
Black, David, s. Robert and Margarett, July 27, 1746.
Black, Elizabeth, d. Robert and Margarett, June 28, 1750.
Black, George 2nd (no parentage given), Aug. 10, 1774.
Black, Isabell, d. Robert and Joan, Sept. 4, 1740.
Black, John, s. Robert and margret, Oct. 14, 1748.
Black, margrat, d. Robert and margret, Dec. 7, 1761.
Black, Submat, d. Robert and margret, Feb. 28, 1753.
Black, thankful, d. Robert and margret, July 5, 1756.
Blair, Elizabeth, d. Jacob and martha, Mar. 21, 1768.
Blair, Enoch, s. Isaac and Bathsheba, Nov. 15, 1771.
Blair, Hannah, d. Robert Jr. and Hannah, Sunday, Nov. 21, 1773.
Blair, Jacob (twin), s. Jacob and martha, Jan. 6, 1774.
Blair, James, s. Jacob and martha, Jan. 4, 1772.
Blair, John, s. Jacob and martha, Sept. 18, 1765.
Blair, Martha (twin), d. Jacob and martha, Jan. 6, 1774.
Blair, Nathan, s. Jacob and martha, Aug. 20, 1776.
Blair, Reuben, s. Jacob and martha, Feb. 12, 1763.
Blair, Robert, s. Robert Jr. and Hannah, Friday, Mar. 20, 1772.
Boies, Abigail, d. William and Mary, Jan. 20, 1764.
Boies, Anna, d. William and Mary Hambleton, Dec. 1, 1746.
Boies, Anne, d. William and Marey, Nov. 3, 1748.
Boies, Anne, d. John and Anna, June 24, 1754.
Boies, Dan, s. David and Rachel, Jan. 12, 1756.
Boies, David, s. David and Rachel, Jan. 22, 1758.
Boies, David, s. William and Mary, Jan. 15, 1750.
Boies, David, s. Samuel and Elizabeth, Jan. 7, 1764.
Boies, Doley, d. Samuel and Elizabeth, Sept. (?—"soour") 18, 1758.
Boies, Elias, s. William and Mary, Aug. 21, 1768.

Boies, Eunice, d. John and Anna, Aug. 3, 1760.
Boies, Gardner, s. David and Dolley, May 2, 1775.
Boies, Jenny, d. Samuel and Elizabeth, Sept. 19, 1774.
Boies, Joel, s. William and Mary, June 7, 1753.
Boies, John, s. John and Anna (Crooks), Nov. 22, 1744.
Boies, margret, d. Samuel and Elisbath, Feb. 29, 1761.
Boies, martha, d. John and Anna, Apr. 22, 1756.
Boies, Miriam, d. John and Anna, Mar. 17, 1749.
Boies, Molley, d. William and Mary, Sept. 22, 1760.
Boies, Rachel, d. John and anne, Feb. 3, 1758.
Boies, Rubin, s. Samuel and Elizebath, Dec. 13, 1752.
Boies, Samuel, s. John and Anna, May 26, 1747. in Suffield.
Boies, Samuel, s. Samuel and Elizabeth, Aug. 4, 1756.
Boies, Sarah, d. William and Mary, Jan. 5, 1756.
Boies, William, s. David and Dolley, July 24, 1773.
Boies, William, s. William and Mary, Oct. 21, 1758.
Bois, James, s. John Jr. and Sarah, June 28, 1774.
Bois, Patty, d. John Jr. and Sarah, Jan. 2, 1772.
Bois, Rachel, d. John Jr. and Sarah, Oct. 19, 1769.
Brown, David, s. Solomon and Jenne, Nov. 4, 1769.
Brown, Elenor, d. William and Martha, Mar. 23, 1770.
Brown, Jean, d. William and Martha, Dec. 20, 1764.
Brown, John, s. Solomon and Jenne, Sept. 8, 1767.
Brown, Martha, d. William and Martha, May 25, 1762.
Brown, Samuel, s. Solomon and Jenne, Aug. 11, 1765.
Brown, Sath, s. Solomon and Jenne, Jan. 21, 1771.
Brown, Silas, s. Solomon and Jenne, Nov. 2, 1761.
Brown, Solomon, s. Solomon and Jenne, Sept. 3, 1765.
Brown, William, s. Solomon and Jenne, Mar. 3, 1760.

Campbell, Cyntha, d. James and Janne, June 23, 1772.
Campbell, David, s. James and Janne, July 11, 1767.
Campbell, Elanor, d. James and Janne, May 18, 1765.
Campbell, hette, d. William and Mary, June 21, 1760.
Campbell, Isaac, s. John and Rebakah, Jan. 6, 1765.
Campbell, Israel, s. John and Rebakah, Mar. 2, 1772.
Campbell, Janne, d. James and Janne, Nov. 30, 1774.
Campbell, John, s. James and Janne, May 11, 1761.
Campbell, Rachal, d. James and Janne, Sept. 9, 1769.
Campble, James, s. James and Janne, Apr. 16, 1763.
Car, Anne, d. William and Cathrine, Mar. 13, 1741.
Carnahan, David, s. William and Mary, Aug. 22, 1766.
Carnahan, Elisha, s. Lt. Samuel and moly, Dec. 28, 1770.
Carnahan, Elizabeth, d. William and Mary, Dec. 20, 1772.
Carnahan, hette, d. William and Mary, June 21, 1760.
Carnahan, Isaac, s. John and Rebekah, Jan. 6, 1765.
Carnahan, Israel, s. John and Rebekah, Mar. 2, 1772.
Carnahan, John, s. John and Rebekah, May 22, 1758.

Carnahan, merram, (Miriam?), d. William and Mary, Sept. 5, 1764.
Carnahan, martin, s. William and Mary, Nov. 21, 1770.
Carnahan, molley, d. William and Mary, Nov. 6, 1768.
Carnahan, Nathan, s. John and Rebekah, Dec. 3, 1759.
Carnahan, Rebekah, d. John and Rebekah, Apr. 12, 1770.
Carnahan, Sally, d. Lt. Samuel and moly, Feb. 10, 1774.
Carnahan, Samuel, s. John and Rebekah, Jan. 27, 1763.
Carnahan, Sarah, d. William and Mary, June 2, 1762.
Carnahan, Stephen, s. John and Rebekah, June 8, 1761.
Carnahan, William thompson, s. William and Mary his Wife (pen marks drawn through last three words), Sept. 1, 1758.
Carnahan, Zekiel, s. John and Rebekah, May 6, 1767.
Clark, Battey, d. James and Sarah, June 29, 1760.
Clark, Caldwell, s. Daniel and Anne, Jan. 21, 1770.
Clark, Holley, child of James and Ruth, Aug. 11, 1773.
Clark, Simon, s. child of James and Ruth, June 13, 1771.
Cochrain, Abner, s. Glass and Sarah, June 6, 1758.
Cochrain, Amos, s. Glass and Sarah, Jan. 1, 1763.
Cochrain, mary, d. Glass and Sarah, May 11, 1761.
Cochran, Cornelas, s. Glass and Sarah, Sept. 4, 1754.
Cochran, John, s. Glass and Sarah, May 30, 1749.
Cochran, Robart, s. Glass and Sarah, Apr. 9, 1748.
Cochran, Susanna, d. Glass and Sarah, Feb. 4, 1752.

fenn, Lois, d. Amos and Eunice, Jan. 11, 1772.
Ferguson, Ealenor, d. John and Dolley, Nov. 3, 1760.
Ferguson, Hannah, d. John and Dolley, Feb. 24, 1768.
Ferguson, Isabel, d. John and Dolley, Oct. 31, 1770.
Ferguson, John, s. Samuel and Margret, July 12, 1756.
Ferguson, mary, d. John and Dolley, Nov. 18, 1761.
Ferguson, Rachel, d. Samuel and Margret, Sept. 13, 1758.
Ferguson, Rhoda, d. Samuel and Margret, Aug. 3, 1753.
Ferguson, Ruth, d. Samuel and Margret, Oct. 8, 1763.
Ferguson, Sarah, d. John and Dolley, Jan. 1, 1766.
Ferguson, Solomon, s. Samuel and Margret, Dec. 9, 1754.
Ferguson, William, s. Samuel and Margret, Feb. 2, 1762.
Freeland, Anna, d. Joseph and Elizabeth, Aug. 15, 1745.
Freeland, Elizabeth, d. Joseph and Elizabeth, Apr. 15, 1748.
Freeland, John, s. Joseph and Elizabeth, May 26, 1749.
Freeland, Marey, d. Joseph and Elizabeth, Jan. 10, 1744.
Freeland, Rechal, d. Joseph and Elizabeth, Dec. 18, 1750.

Gibbs, Elam, s. John and Rachel, Oct. 12, 1774.
Gibbs, Abnor, s. Ephraim and Nanse, Jan. 4, 1773.
Gibbs, Israel, s. John and Rachel, Dec. 22, 1760.
Gibbs, John, s. John and Rachel, Oct. 13, 1768.
Gibbs, mary, d. John and Rachel, Aug. 12, 1765.
Gibbs, Samuel Crooks, s. John and Rachel, Apr. 10, 1763.
Gibbs, Sarah, d. Ephraim and Nancy, Apr. 7, 1775.

Hamelton, Agness, d. John and Sarah, Oct. 20, 1748.

Hamelton, Armour, s. Armour and Agnes, March 11, 1736, in Hopcentown.

Hamelton, David, s. John and Sarah, July 1, 1742.

Hamelton, Doley, d. John and Sarah, Aug. 15, 1740.

Hamelton, Ephram, s. Armour and Agnes, Jan. 17, 1741/2.

Hamelton, Isabla, d. John and Sarah, May 29, 1746.

Hamilton, Armor, s. Ephraim and Margrit, Apr. 2, 1775.

Hamilton, Hugh, s. David and Mary, Oct. 31, 1770.

Hamilton, Isabel, d. David and Mary, Nov. 11, 1768.

Hamilton, John, s. John and Sarah, July 31, 1755.

Hamilton, martha, d. Ephraim and margrit, Mar. 25, 1771.

Hamilton, Molly, d. Ephraim and margrit, Apr. 23, 1769.

Hamilton, Sarah, d. John and Sarah, Sept. 12, 1752.

Hassard, Jason, s. James and Joahn, Aug. 18, 1739.

Hassard, Jon, s. James and Joahn, July 9, 1741.

Hassard, Robart, s. James and Joahn, Sept. 9, 1737.

Henry, Ebenezer, s. Robert and Jean, June 7, 1747, in Suffield.

Henry, Elesebeth, d. Robert and Jean, Mar. 4, 1744/5.

Henry, James, s. William and mary, Dec. 29, 1773.

Henry, Jemes, s. Robert and Jean, Apr. 23, 1751.

Henry, John, s. William and mary, Apr. 27, 1775.

Henry, Jonathan, s. Robert and Jean, June 18, 1749.

Henry, Louisy, d. William and mary, Sept. 10, 1770.

Henry, Mary, d. Robert and Jean, Oct. 6, 1742.

Henry, Samuel, s. Robert and Jean, Aug. 3, 1740.

Henry, Wells, s. Robert and Jean, Aug. 6, 1753.

Knox, David, s. Adam and Elenor, May 12, 1758.

Knox, Edward, s. Lt. William and Jenne, Dec. 25, 1773.

Knox, Elenor, d. Adam and Mary, Apr. 14, 1764.

Knox, Elenor, d. John and Rachel, May 21, 1759.

Knox, Elenor, d. William and Isable, Sept. 15, 1752.

Knox, Elezebath, d. Adam and Elenor, Mar. 17, 1754.

Knox, Elijah, s. John and Rachel, Aug. 23, 1761.

Knox, Elisabath, d. William and Isable, Oct. 10, 1756.

Knox, Elisabeth, d. John and Rachel (freeland), Nov. 19, 1747.

Knox, Hanah, d. John and Rachel, May 28, 1757.

Knox, James, s. John and Rachel, Aug. 14, 1755.

Knox, Jan, d. Adam and Mary, Sept. 16, 1762.

Knox, Jean, d. John and Rachel (freeland), Jan. 23, 1744.

Knox, Jenne, d. William 3rd and gene, Oct. 17, 1770.

Knox, John, s. John and Rachel (freeland), Dec. 10, 1745.

Knox, John, s. William and Isable, Jan. 13, 1759.

Knox, John, s. Lt. William and Jenne, Oct. 17, 1775.

Knox, Margerett, d. Adam and Sarah, Aug. 12 (1744?).

Knox, Mary, d. Adam and Mary, Jan. 20, 1766.

Knox, Mary, d. John and Rachel, Feb. 19, 1751.
Knox, Mary, d. William and Isable, Apr. 11, 1763.
Knox, molley Boies, d. William and Mary Bois, Sept. 22, 1760.
Knox, Nancey, d. William 3rd and Jenne, Dec. 27, 1768.
Knox, Nathan, s. William and Isable, Feb. 13, 1761.
Knox, Olever, s. Adam and Elenor, June 23, 1752.
Knox, Rachel, d. John and Rachel (freeland), Sept. 6, 1749.
Knox, Rachel, d. William 3rd and Jenne, Apr. 10, 1767.
Knox, Samuel, s. William and Isable, July 29, 1754.
Knox, Sarah, d. John and Rachel, Oct. 17, 1753.
Knox, William, s. Adam and Mary, May 6 (8?), 1768.
Knox, William, s. John and Rachel (freeland), July 11, 1742.
Knox, William, s. William and Isable, Sept. 15, 1750.

Lawhead, Andrew, s. James and Sarah, Mar. 2, 1775.
Lawhead, David, s. James and Sarah, July 21, 1771.
Lawhead, James, s. James and Sarah, Mar. 8, 1773.
Lawhead, Rachel (Loughhead), d. William and Isabella, Aug. 26, 1764.
Lawhead, William (Loughhead), s. William and Isabella, Jan. 29, 1767.
Loughhead, Achsah, d. William and Isabella, Apr. 9, 1769.
Loughhead, Elisabath, d. William and Esibal, June 14, 1760.
Loughhead Isaac, s. William and Isabella, Nov. 5, 1773.
Loughhead, James, s. William and Esribal, Mar. 21, 1762.
Loughhead, Mary, d. William and Isabella (Lawhead), Aug. 15, 1775.
Loughhed, Abigail, d. Robart and Daborah, Jan. 13, 1769.
Loughhed, Betse, d. Robart and Daborah, Oct. 15, 1771.
Loughhed, Darkis, child of Robart and Daborah, Aug. 26, 1775.
Loughhed, David, s. Robart and Daborah, July 11, 1767.
Loughhed, Isabella, d. William and Isabella (Lawhead), Aug. 7, 1771.
Loughhed, John, s. Robart and Daborah, May 10, 1765.
Loughhed, mary, d. Robart and Daborah, Dec. 7, 1766.
Loughhed, Robart, s. Robart and Daborah, Nov. 16, 1773.
Loughhed, thomas, s. Robart and Daborah, Aug. 21, 1763.
Loyd, James, s. William and Isabella (Lawhead), Mar. 21, 1763.

McConoughey, Anne, d. David Jnr and Anna, Mar. 14, 1772.
McConoughey, David, s. David Jnr and Anna, Aug. 6, 1767.
McConoughey, George, s. David Jnr and Anna, Dec. 18, 1758.
McConoughey, Mary, d. David Jnr and Anna, Nov. 25, 1765.
McConoughey, Rachel, d. David Jnr and Anna, Dec. 1, 1763.
McConoughey, Samuel, s. David Jnr and Anna, Nov. 2, 1769.
McConoughey, Sarah, d. David Jnr and Anna, Jan. 12, 1761.
Mitchel, Elizebeth, d. William and Isable, Aug. 20, 1766.
Mongumrey, Meary, d. James and Meary, May 18, 1737.
Mongumrey, Robert, s. James and Meary, July 13, 1743.
morey, Cetura (? Cetuen?), child of Jemes and Ledeya, Dec. 14, 1752.
Morton, Alexander, s. mr James and mary, Apr. 27, 1762.

Morton, Ann, d. m*r* James and mary, May 29, 1759.
Morton, James, s. m*r* James and mary, Nov. 30, 1752.
Morton, John, s. ye Rev*d* M*r* James and his wife, Apr. 9, 1750.
Morton, margred, d. m*r* James and mary, Sept. 16, 1755.
Mountgumbry, Kathren, d. James and Kathren, May 24, 1750.

Noble, Bethiah, d. Silas and marry, Apr. 11, 1765.
Noble, Louis, child of John and Louis, July 6, 1774.
Noble, mary, d. Silas and mary, Jan. 11, 1771.
Noble, Silas, Juner, s. Silas and his wife, Mar. 9, 1760.
Noble, Solomon, s. Silas and Mary, Sept. 5, 1768.

osborn, Alexander, s. Alexander and Sarah, Sept. 25, 1772.

Peas, Bethiah, d. Joel and Elizebeth, Apr. 13, 1761.
Pease, Lore, d. Levi and hannah, Oct. 4, 1774.
Pease, Lemuel, s. Levi and hannah, Dec. 16, 1771.
Provan, David, s. Matthew and Mary, June 17, 1746.
Provan, Lidia, d. Matthew and Mary, Sept. 20, 1751.
Proven, Bulehe (Beulah?) d. William and Marcey Provence, Aug. 25, 1748.
Proven, Imm . . ., child of William and Marcey Provence, Aug. 24, 17 . .
    (indecipherable).
Proven, Telethe (?) (Talitha?), child of William and Marcey, Dec. 28, 1753.
Provence, Ireno (?) (Irene?), child of William and Marcey, July 11, 1746.
Provence, Marcey, d. William and Marcey, Sept. 17, 1742.
Provence, Mearaey, d. William and Marcey, Aug. 31, 1740.

Robeson, James, s. James and Martha, Feb. 11, 1754.
Robeson, James, s. James and Martha, Nov. 25, 1761.
Robeson, John, s. James and Martha, Mar. 9, 1759.
Robeson, Nathan, s. James and Martha, Mar. 20 (year not given).
Robinson, Alexander, s. James and Martha, Feb. 12, 1756, in Sheffield.
Robinson, William, s. James and Martha, Feb. 11, 1754.

Scot, David, s. John and Rachel, June 25, 1760.
Scot, John, s. John and Rachel, Sept. 27, 1763.
Scot, Margret, d. John and Rachel, Dec. 23, 1761.
Scot, Stewart, s. John and Rachel, Nov. 1, 1765.
Sinnet, Anne, d. John and Margret, Feb. 24, 1772.
Sinnet, Elizabeth, d. John and Margret, Dec. 30, 1773.
Sinnet, Hipsebah, d. John and Margret, May 12, 1768.
Sinnet, Isaac, s. James and Elizabath, Oct. 16, 1764.
Sinnet, James, s. John and Margret, Dec. 12, 1764.
Sinnet, John, s. John and Margret, Feb. 19, 1770.
Sinnet, mindwell, child of James and Elisebath, Oct. 6, 1769.
Sinnet, Robert, s. child of James and Elisebath, July 19, 1766.
Sloper, Eunice, d. Samuel and Eunice, July 8, 1773.
Sloper, Samuel, s. Samuel and Eunice, Apr. 21, 1775.
Stewart, Calvin, s. Paul and Jerusha, May 20, 1767.

Stewart, Daniel Spenser, s. Paul and Jerusea, Feb. 17, 1755.
Stewart, Elesebath, d. Paul and Jerusea, Sept. 10, 1769.
Stewart, Hanah, d. Solomon and Sarah, Nov. 7, 1762.
Stewart, Jehiel, s. Pawl and Jerusiah, Oct. 22, 1750.
Stewart, Jerusha, d. Paul and Jerusha, Sept. 11, 1764.
Stewart, Lusinah (?—i undotted), child of Pawl and Jerushea, Nov. 22, 1752.
Stewart, Luther, s. Paul and Jerushe, Apr. 2, 1762.
Stewart, Margaret, d. Solomon and Sarah, July 7, 1772.
Stewart, Molley, d. Solomon and Sarah, Oct. 31, 1769.
Stewart, Rhoda, d. Solomon and Sarah, July 9, 1767.
Stewart, Sarah, d. Solomon and Sarah, Feb. 2, 1765.
Stewart, William, s. Solomon and Sarah, June 20, 1760.
Stewart, William, s. Paul and Jerushe, Nov. 3, 1759.

Wheler, Elias, s. Samuel and Bathiah, June 20, 1768.
Wheler, Moses, s. Samuel and Bathiah, Feb. 26, 1766.
Wheler, Samuel Junr s. Samuel and Bathiah, Jan. 16, 1764.
Willson, Agnas, d. John and Elisibath, Mar. 19, 1765 (?).
Willson, John, s. John and Elisibath, Nov. — 1765.
Willson, Mary, d. John and Elisibath, May 4, 1763.
wolson, John, s. John and Sary, Feb. 11, 1774.
Word (Ward? Work or Wark?), Roderack word, s. Stephan and Abigail, Jan. 29, 1773.

Yong, DavidYong, born s. Robert and Griswol, born—(no date).
Yong, Elizabeth, d. Robert and Griswol, Oct. 17, 1740.
Yong, Martha, d. Robert and Griswol, Jan. 18, 1742.

SUPPLEMENT TO BLANDFORD BAPTISMS GLEANED FROM A CHURCH FRAGMENT OF 1757

Anderson, James, s. Samuel.

Black, Elliner, d. David.
Black, Thankful, d. Robert.
Blair, mary, d. Mathew.
Boies, Dan, s. David.
Boies, martha, d. John.
Boies, Samuel, s. Samuel.
Boies, Sarah, d. William.
Bolton, Barnard, s. James.
Bolton, abram, s. David.

"Mrs. Campble a niger Child   Dinah."
Crooks, John, s. John.

Knox, Elisabeth, d. William.
Knox, Eunice, d. Adam.

Knox, James, s. John.
Knox, mary, d. John.
Knox, Sarah, d. John.

MccKinstry, Charles, s. John.
MccKinstry, Sarah, d. John.
Mtgomary, willm, s. James.
Moor, James, s. James.

Robeson, alexander, s. James.

White, Ann, d. Widow Margaret.
White, margret, d. Wido Margaret.
Willson, and.w (meaning Andrew—S. G. W.), s. Samuell.

ADDITIONAL BIRTHS, FROM TOMBSTONES IN OLD BURYING GROUND, BLANDFORD

Barnes, Abigail (wife of Elihu Sperry), 1750.
Blair, Martha, consort of Mr. Adam Blair, Dec. 1, 1755.
Blair, Martha, wife of Jacob Blair, Nov. 1, 1734, in Derry, N. H.

Morton, Rev. James, in Middletown, County of Armagh, Kingdom of Ireland, 1714.
Morton, Mary, relict of Rev. James, in Boston, July 29, 1724.

Sperry, Deac. Elihu, 1747.

Thompson, John, in Dublin, Ireland, St. Nicholas Parish, Aug. 24, 1707.

Wallace, Mrs. Jane, in Belturbet, County of Cavan, Ireland. No date given: died, 1804.

FRAMINGHAM BIRTHS

Blair, Samuel, s. William dec. and Mary, Nov. 20, 1724.

Cook, Jno., s. James and Lydia, Dec. 3, 1738.
Lydia, d. James and Lydia, Jan. 22, 1739.
(Others, of later dates)

Gibbs (in Worcester from 1709,—numerous; impossible for a stranger to give the Blandford lines).

How (in Worcester from 1702).

Rice, Josiah, s. David and Hannah, Aug. 19, 1701.

Stone, Daniel, s. Micha and Abigail, Apr. 11, 1727.
Daniel, s. Daniel and Mary, Oct. 13, 1738.

Wilson (family represented from 1713).

HOPKINTON MARRIAGES

(From published Vital Statistics, and Manuscript records)

Ball, Sarah—John Steward, May 20, 1733 (In church record, Sarah Bell, May 17.).

Beard, Thomas Jr., of Mendon—Susanna Walker, Dec. 28, 1732 (in Mendon).

Black, Robert—Jane Osborn, Mar. 22, 1733. (Jenny Osburn in church record).

Blair, Matthew—Mary Hambleton, Nov. 21, 1727 (Matthew Blare in church record).

Cook, Jane—James Hazzard, of Worcester, Dec. 16, 1735.

Crooks, John—Mary Orsborn, Feb. 22, 1739 (Mary Ozburn in church record).

Crooks, Jane—Garritt Rowen, Aug. 28, 1739. (Garritt Roan in church record).

Freeland, James—Sarah Watson, Jan. 8, 1741.

Freeland, Rachel—John Knox of Blandford, Sept. 28, 1741.

Freeland, Thomas—Mary Nutt, Jan. 27, 1743.

Gibbs, Israel—Mary Hambleton, May 18, 1727.

Henry, Mary—James Montgomery, Jan. 23, 1732.

Hambleton, Armour—Agnis Mongomery, July 9, 1728 (variant spellings: Almor, Almon, Armor; Agnes Montgomery in church record).

Hazzard, James of Worcester—Jane Cook, Dec. 16, 1735.

Hambleton, Elizabeth—John Hog, Nov. 6, 1729.

Hambleton, Mary—Israel Gibbs, May 18, 1727.

Hog, John—Elizabeth Hamilton, Nov. 6, 1729.

How, Mary—John Wood, Apr. 13, 1727.

Hambleton, Mary—Mathew Blair, Nov. 21, 1727.

Knox, John of Blandford—Rachel Freeland, Sept. 28, 1741.

Mongomery, Agnis—Armour Hamilton, July 9, 1728 (Agnes Montgomery in church record; variant spellings: Almor, Almon, Almour).

Montgomery, James—Mary Henry, Jan. 23, 1732.

Nutt, Mary—Thomas Freeland, Jan. 27, 1743.

Osborn, Jane—Robert Black, Mar. 22, 1733. (Jenny Osburn in church record).

Osborn, Elizabeth—James Wark, Apr. 20, 1729.

Osburn, John—Mary Work, Jan., 1730.

Orsborn, Mary—John Crooks, Feb. 22, 1739. (Mary Osburn in church record).

Rowen, Garritt—Jane Crooks, Aug. 28, 1739.

Sennet, Robert S.—Hepsibah Wetherby, Nov. 6, 1727, in Marlboro.

Steward, John—Sarah Ball, May 20, 1733 (Sarah Bell in church record).

Stone, Daniel S.—Mary Wood, May 11, 1736. (In church record, Jan. 11, 1726; otherwise given, 1725, which is probably "old style").

Taylor, Mary—Thomas Wood, June 4, 1740 (in church record, June 12).

Wark, James—Elizabeth Osborn, Apr. 20, 1729. (in church record, Oaburn).

Work, Mary—John Osburn, Jan., 1730.

Walker, Susanna—Thomas Beard Jr., of Mendon, Dec. 28, 1732, in Mendon.

Watson, Sarah—James Freeland, Jan. 8, 1741.

Wetherby, Hepzibah—Robert S. Sennet, Nov. 6, 1727, in Marlboro.

Wood, John—Mary How, Apr. 13, 1727.

Wood, Thomas—Mary Taylor, June 4, 1740 (in church record, June 12).

Wood, Mary—Daniel S. Stone, May 11, 1736 (in church record, Jan. 11, 1726; otherwise given, 1725, which is probably "old style").

HOPKINTON DEATHS

Wood, Capt. John, Aug. 21, 1725.

FRAMINGHAM MARRIAGES

Buckminster, Elizabeth—John Wood, Mar. 3, 1704.

Crooks, John, of Hopkinton—Sarah Gleason, Jan. 4, 1749.

Frost, Mary—Daniel Stone, Mar. 12, 1733-4.

Gleason, Sarah—John Crooks of Hopkinton, Jan. 4, 1749.

Haynes, Ruth of Sudbury—Deacon Daniell Stone, Nov. 18, 1712.

Hood, Elizabeth—Josiah Rice, May 6, 1728 (should be Wood, Eliz. S. G. W.).

Rice, Josiah—Elizabeth Hood, May 6, 1728. (should be Eliz. Wood. S. G. W.).

Stone, Daniel—Mary Frost, Mar. 12, 1733-4.

Stone, Deacon Daniell—Ruth Haynes of Sudbury, Nov. 18, 1712.

Wood, John—Elizabeth Buckminster, Mar. 3, 1704.

BLANDFORD MARRIAGES

Alexander, Jan—David Black, Jan., 1771.

Andeson, Jean,—Solomon Brown, June 18, 1759.

anderson, David—mary Wilson, Feb. 15, 1753.

Ballard, Stephen of Sandisfield—Anne yong, Sept. 24, 1772.

Beard, John—Agns Brown, June 27, 1754.

Beard, Ruth—william Watson, Sept. 23, 1758.

Birchard, James—Abighel King of No. 4, Feb. 3, 1757.

Birchard, Matthew—mary messenger, both of No. 4, Aug., 1758.

Black, David—Jan Alexander, Jan., 1771.
Black, John—Lydia Ward of Springfield, Sept. 17, 1773.
Black, Submite—William Knox 4th, Apr. 20, 1771.
Blair, Dolley—David Boies, Dec. 1 (no year given; follows entry of 1772.)
Blair, Elizabeth—William Mitchal, Dec. 28, 1749.
Boies, Anne—William Scott of Suffield, Nov. 19, 1766.
Boies, David—Dolley Blair, Dec. 1 (no year given).
Boies, David—Rachel Crooks, Feb. 6, 1755.
Brown, Agns—John Beard, June 27, 1754.
Brown, Elizabeth—Israel Carnfield of Granville, Nov. 17, 1768.
Brown, Martha—James Robinson, June 7, 1753.
Brown, Solomon—Jean andeson—June 18, 1759.
Brown, ... —John Davies of No. 4, Feb. 16, 1758.

Caldwell, James—Mary Hambleton, Nov. 14, 1750.
Caldwell, widow mary—Samuel Loughead, May, 175- (probably 1758).
Carnachen, John—Rebacka Gibbs, July 28, 1758.
Carnfield, Israel of Granville—Elisabeth Brown, Nov. 17, 1768.
Clark, Alexander of Coldrein—Elezebeth Danaghy, Apr. 11, 1754.
Clark, Elizabeth—Daniel Meeker of Murrayfield, Nov. 8, 1768.
Cochrain, Susanah—James Nutt of Athol. No date; inserted following
    entry of Aug. 1770).
Crooks, Rachel—David Boies, Feb. 6, 1755.

Davies, John— . . . . . Brown, Feb. 16, 1758.
Delinqut, John—Elizbeth young, June 22, 1758.
Donaghy, Elezebeth—Alexander Clark of Coldrein, Apr. 11, 1754.

Ferguson, Ezabl—William Knox, Dec. 21, 1749.
Ferguson, Samuel—Margret Stewart, Jan. 4, 1753.
Fleming, David of Palmer—Sarah Loughead, May 22, 1755.

Gibbs, Isaac—Agnes Hamilton, Oct. 30, 1768.
Gibbs, Mary—Samuel Watson, May 24, 1750.
Gibbs, Rebacka—John Carnachen, July 28, 1758.

Hambleton, Mary—James Caldwell, Nov. 14, 1750.
Hamilton, Agnes—Isaac Gibbs, Oct. 20, 1768.
Hamilton, David—Mary Knox, Jan. 14, 1768.
Hamilton, Isabel—William marrs of Western, Aug. 15, 1770.
Henry, Jonahs of Murrayfield—Margret Henry, May, 1771.
Henry, Jonathan—Sarah Sitton, Jan. 1 (?), 1771.
Henry, Margret—Jonahs Henry of Murrayfield, May, 1771.
Henry, mary—Henry Steward, June 4, 1761.
Henry, William—Mary Willey, June, 1770.
Hunn, Rev. mr. Zadok of Becket—mrs mary morton, Nov. 18, 1773.

Jonson, Ranald, mary Treadwell, Aug., 1770.

King, Abighel of No. 4—James Birchard, Feb. 3, 1757.

Kingsley, Amose—mary Wadsworth of No. 4, Feb. 3, 1757.
Knox, Mary—David Hamilton, Jan. 14, 1768.
Knox, William—Ezabl Ferguson, Dec. 21, 1749.
Knox, William 4th—Submite Black, Apr. 20, 1771.

Loughead, Sarah—David Fleming of Palmer, May 22, 1755.
Loughead, Samuel—widow Mary Caldwell, May, 175- (probably 1758).

marrs, William of Western—Isabel Hamilton (no date: somewhere between 1770 and 1773).
Mitchal, William—Elizabeth Blair, Dec. 28, 1749.
Meeker, Daniel of Murrayfield—Elisabeth Clark, Nov. 8, 1768.
morton, mrs mary—Rev. mr Zadok Hunn of Becket, Nov. 18, 1773.

Noble, John—Louis Sexton of Sumers, Sept. 21, 1773.
Noble, Silas—Mary Taylor, Aug. 28, 1769.
Nutt, James of Athol—Susannah Cochrain (no date; following entry of Sept. 21, 1773).

Pease, Hannah—David Whelar of Lainsborough, Nov. 19, 1767.

Robinson, James—Martha Brown, June 7, 1753.

Scott, William of Suffield, Ct.—Anne Boies, Nov. 19, 1766.
Sitton, Sarah—Jonathan Henry, Jan. 1 (?) 1771.
Steward, Henry—mary Henry, June 4, 1761.
Stewart, Margret—Samuel Ferguson, Jan. 4, 1753.
Stewart, Solomon—Sarah mcc Conoughey, Apr. 13, 1758.

Taylor, Mary—Siles Noble, Aug. 28, 1769.
Treadwell, mary—Ranald Jonson, Aug., 1770.

Ward, Lydia of Springfield—John Black, Sept. 17, 1773.
Watson, william—Ruth Beard, Sept. 23, 1758.
Willey, Mary—William Henry, June, 1770.
Watson, Samuel—Mary Gibbs, May 24, 1750.
Wilson, mary—David anderson, Feb. 15, 1753.

yong, Anne—Stephen Ballard of Sandisfield, Sept. 24, 1772.
Young, Elezebeth—John Delinqut, June 13, 1758.

BANNS OF MARRIAGE, BLANDFORD

Bagg, Elisebath—Hazakiah Joans of Pittsfield, June 9, 1764.
Bagg, Joseph—Eunas Loomis of Lainsburough, Dec. 29, 1765.
Banjmian, Asha of Granville—Elesebath Black, May 15, 1771.
Barnes, Phineas of Granvelle—marcy Provan, Oct. 13, 1765.
Bement, Judah—Mercy Fowler of Westfield, June 2, 1765.
Black, Elesebath—Asha Banjmian of Granvelle, May 15, 1771.
Black, Elizabeth of murrisfield—Samuel Boys Jur, May 10, 1773.
Black, George, of murrisfield—ann Boise, May 9, 1774.
Black, Robert—Janet Freeland, Feb. 27, 1763.

Blair, Alixander—Elisebeth Marrs, Oct., 1762.
Blair, David—Miriam Boies, Dec. 20, 1771.
Blair, Robert Jur—Hanah Haward of Westorn, Aug. 20, 1770.
Blair, Samuel—Margret Smith of Palmor, May 2, 1774.
Boies, Miriam—David Blair, Dec. 20, 1771.
Boise, ann—George Black of murrisfield, May 9, 1774.
Boys, Samuel Jur—Elizabeth Black of murrisfield, May 10, 1773.

Campbel, Widdow Janet—William Stewart, Oct. —? 1771.
Campbel, Sarah—Alexander osborn of Bolton, Dec. 2, 1754.
Campble, Charls—Widdow Agnes Hamilton, Mar. 6, 1768.
Campble, Jennet—William Knox, Nov. 24, 1765.
Cannen, Elizebeth—Ameci Durham of Lainsburow, Dec. 16, 1766.
Cook, Josiah of No 1 Equivalent—Miriam Sheepeard, May 15, 1771.
Cotheren, John—Rodah ferguson, May 30, 1774.
Cotheren, Robart—Jane freeland, May 30, 1774.
Crook, Jeney—Samuel Henry, Sept. 16, 1764.
Crooks, William—Jan Kanady, Dec. 8, 1765.
Crooks, William—Rachel Freeland, Oct. 24, 1762.

Durham, Ameci of Lainsburow—Elizebeth Cannen, Dec. 16, 1766.

ferguson, Rodah—John Cotheren, May 30, 1774.
freeland, Jane—Robart Cotheren, May 30, 1774.
Freeland, Janet—Robert Black, Feb. 27, 1763.
Freeland, Rachel—William Crooks, Oct. 24, 1762.
freeland, Sarah—Joseph mann of murrisfield, Aug. 28, 1775.
Fowler, Mercy—Judah Bement, June 2. 1765.

Hamilton, Widdow Agnes—Charls Campble, Mar. 6, 1768.
Harris, Elisebath of Windsor—James Sinnet, June 9, 1764.
Haword, Hanah of Westorn—Robert Blair Jur, Aug. 20, 1770.
Henry, James—Sarah Stuart, Apr. 5, 1773.
Henry, Samuel—Jeney Crook, Sept. 16, 1764.
Holcomb, Return of No 1 Equivalent Lands—Hanna Niles, July 28, 1768.

Joans, Hazakiah of Pittsfield—Elisebath Bagg, June 9, 1764.

Kanady, Jan—William Crooks, Dec. 8, 1765.
King, Robert—Rachel Knox, Sept. 30, 1768.
Knox, Elizabeth—Elihue miller, Apr. 14, 1774.
Knox, Elizebeth—John McKintry, Sept. 20, 1766.
Knox, Rachel—Robert King, Sept. 30, 1768.
Knox, William—Jennet Campble, Nov. 24, 1765.

Loomis, Eunas of Lainsburough,—Joseph Bagg, Dec. 29, 1765.
Lothrop, Suchah of Norrig—John Sauey, Jan. 23, 1775.
Lowhead, Robert—Deborah moor, Sept. 26, 1762.

mann, Joseph of murrisfield—Sarah freeland, Aug. 28, 1775.
Marrs, Elisebeth—Alixander Blair, Oct., 1762.

Marrs, William of Western—Isabel Hamilton, Aug. 15, 1770.
MccCreelus, Margret—John Sinnet, Dec. 9, 1763.
McKintry, John—Elizebeth Knox, Sept. 20, 1766.
miller, Elihue—Elizebeth Knox, Apr. 14, 1774.
moor, Beette—John Peebles of Granville, Aug. 22, 1766.
moor, Deborah—Robert Lowhead, Sept. 26, 1762.
Moor, Sarah—Abner Pease, Oct. 24, 1762.
Moor, Thomas—Jean Peopels, Jan. 5, 1772.
Mt Gomary, Robert—Mary White of Sr. . . .trey (undistinguishable; possibly Simsbury, Ct.) Dec. 2, 1764.

Niles, Hanna—Return Holcomb of No 1 Equivalent Lands, July 28, 1768.
Nimock, Elenor—Henry Walker of Backet, Sept. 30, 1768.

osborn, Alexander of Bolton—Sarah Campbel, Dec. 2, 1754.

Parks, Aron of Westfield—mary proven, Jan. 2, 1775.
Pease, Abner—Sarah Moor, Oct. 24, 1762.
Peebles, John of Granville—Beette moor, Aug. 22, 1766.
Peopels, Jean—Thomas Moor, Jan. 5, 1772.
Provan, James—Sarah Shepard of Westfield, Nov. 25, 1771.
Provan, Jemimah—Stephen Stowe of No 1 Equivalant, Oct. 28, 1771.
Provan, marcy—Phineas Barnes of Granville, Oct. 13, 1765.
proven, mary—Aron Parks of Westfield, Jan. 2, 1775.
Proven, talitha—David Simons, May 2, 1774.

Root, David—Jeruchea Wood of windsor, June 12, 1768.

Sauey, John—Suchah Lothrop of Norrig, Jan. 23, 1775.
Saxton, Eunas—Samll Sloper, Jan. 25, 1773.
Sheepeard, Miriam—Josiah Cook of No 1 Equivalent, May 15, 1771.
Shepard, Sarah of Westfield—James Provan, Nov. 25, 1771.
Simons, David—talitha Proven, May 2, 1774.
Sinnet, James—Elisebath Harris of Windsor, June 9, 1764.
Sinnet, John—Margret Mcc Creelus, Dec. 9, 1763.
Sitton, Ledy—Solomon Stuart, the 2, Feb. 8, 1775.
Sloper, Samll—Eunas Saxton, Jan. 25, 1773.
Smith, Margret of Palmor—Samuel Blair, May 2, 1774.
Stewart, William—Widdow Janet Campbel, Oct. . . .? 1771.
Stills, Elezebeth of Westfield—timothy walker of Nbr 4, June 13, 1758.
Stow, Stephen of No 1 Equivalent—Jemimah Provan, Oct. 28, 1771.
Stuart, Sarah—James Henry, Apr. 5, 1773.
Stuart, Solomon the 2—Ledy Sitton, Feb. 8, 1775.

Walker, Henry of Backet—Elenor Nimock, Sept. 30, 1768.
Walker, timothy of Nbr 4—Elezebeth Stills of Westfield, June 13, 1758.
White, Mary of Sr . . trey (?) (Indistinguishable; possibly, Simsbury, Ct.)
    —Robert Mt Gomary, Dec. 2, 1764.
Wood, Jeruchea of windsor—David Root, June 12, 1768.

BLANDFORD TOMBSTONE INSCRIPTIONS

Baird, Grace, w. James, June 1, 1746, 65.
    Thomas, s. James and Patty, 1775, 3.
Blair, Mary, w. Matthew, Mar. 25, 1753, 52.
    Matthew, Elder, Sept. 22, 1770, 66.
Boies, Anna, w. David, Aug. 25, 1766, 83.
    David, Ruling Elder, Dec. 15, 1752, 63.
    David, Junr., Sept. 21, 1757, 31.

Carnahan, Miriam, w. William, Sept. 21, 1758.
Campbell, David, Nov. 11, 1769, 58.
    Margaret, 1759, 17.
    Nancy, Jan. 26, 1759, 14.

Ferguson, Samuel, Sept. 19, 1741, 43.
Freelan, Joseph, June 19, 1767, 58 (?).

Hamilton, Hugh, Feb. 20, 1763, 90.

King, Elenor, w. Adam, Dec. 21, 1760, 21 (died in child-bed).
Ker, William, Aug. 4, 1757, 46 (at Fort George).

Mitchel, Elizabeth, w. William, July 6, 1758, 30.
Morton, John, s. of Rev. James and Mary, Jan. 6, 1759, 8, 9 mos.
    Thomas, s. Rev. James and Mary, July 27, 1766, 22.
    "A still born son lies here."

Pease, Abel, s. of Nathaniel and Miriam, 20.
    Asa, s. of Nathaniel and Miriam, June 17, 1762, 15.

Sinnet, John, April 10, 1775, 39.
    Robert, April 10, 1774, 80.
Stewart, Hannah, w. of Charles, Feb. 14, 1751 (last figure uncertain), 78.
    William, Sept. 16, 1757, 27.

Wilson, James, 1759, 81.
    Robert, Mar. 21, 1768, 30.

Note: These deaths recorded on existing inscribed stones in Blandford comprise all there are, down to and including the year 1775—the first forty years of Blandford's history.

A few inscriptions belonging to Blandford family history of this period might be found in Suffield and other near-by or related towns, representing the most perilous years of the French and Indian wars. I have looked in the old cemetery in Huntington for some, but found none that I could feel certainly belonged in this record. In this old ground are many ancient stones marking graves of early settlers and their children in old Murrayfield, part of which was the northeast corner of Blandford. But they contain no revealing inscriptions; most of them never received the marks of a chisel. The above copied inscriptions are all on stones in the old burying place on Blandford hill. None other date back to this time. In this sacred enclosure of the silent dead there are many unmarked graves. Some of these have been now and then innocently and unintentionally disturbed. There are unmarked stones here. There are stones containing initials, a few carrying a bare family name. The ancient ground was somewhat wider than the present. Margins of it have been obliterated by boundary changes and the lay-out of a street or two. And the past holds its own secrets close.

Some of the above-mentioned stones bearing initials or solitary names are the following:

Mr. D. B.	B. N.
Mr. John Boies	L. N.
Mrs. Mary Boies	R. N.
W. H.	Mr. Jno Thompson
Mrs. A. M.	Thankful Sirton
Miss L. M.	

AUTHORITIES CITED OR CONSULTED

My genuine obligations are gratefully acknowledged. This list relieves the body of the book of much foot-note lumber, inasmuch as usually citations and references are given at the foot of the pages simply by means of the authors' names, with frequent notations of pages. I hereby acknowledge with thanks the courtesies of those whose personal assurances of liberty to quote them have been so freely given.—S. G. W.

Adams, Charles Francis: Three Episodes of Massachusetts History.
Adams, Herbert B.: Germanic Origin of New England Towns (in Johns Hopkins Studies, Vol. I.).
Adams, James Truslow: The Founding of New England.
Atkins, Rev. Dr. Gaius Glenn, in "The Congregationalist."

Bacon, Leonard Woolsey: A History of American Christianity.
Barry, John Stetson: The History of Massachusetts, 3 vols.
Bay Psalm Book.
Berkshire Gleaner: Article by Frank L. Pope, on roads to the westward of the Connecticut river.
Blandford: Original documents, official and unofficial.
Boise, Enos W.: Numerous invaluable data.
Bolton, Charls Knowles: Scotch Irish Pioneers in Ulster and America.
Bowen, Clarence Winthrop: Boundary Disputes of Connecticut.
Butler, Rev. Daniel, D.D.: Manuscript.

Campbell, Douglas: The Puritan in Holland, England and America.
Carlyle, Thomas: Oliver Cromwell's Letters and Speeches, 2 vols.
Connecticut Valley Historical Society Proceedings. It is only just to say that "Irish Pioneers of the Connecticut Valley," in this series of studies, by Edward A. Hall, must be taken with discernment. For example, Mr. Hall says: "Francis Brinley, A. M. Collins, Samuel Knox and Patrick Boies came up from Hartford and purchased land of Christopher Lawton and Francis Wells, to whom the Legislature had conveyed undivided parts of the township." Some of these men were separated from one another by nearly or quite a century.
Copeland, Judge: History of Hampden County, Mass.

Drake, Samuel Adams: The Old Boston Taverns and Tavern Clubs.

Earle, Alice Morse: Home Life In Colonial Days; Customs and Fashions In Old New England.
Eggleston, Melville: Land System of The New England Colonies (in Johns Hopkins Studies, Vol. IV.).
Encyclopaedia Britannica, 9th Edition: Article, Ireland.

Farrand, Max: The Development of The United States.
Fisher, Sydney George: Men, Women and Manners in Colonial Times.

Fiske, John: The Beginnings of New England, or The Puritan Theocracy In Its Relations to Civil and Religious Liberty.

Gibbs, Dr. H. A.: Gibbs Family Bulletins.

Gibbs, William H.: An Address delivered before The Literary Association, Blandford, 1850.

Green, J. R.: A Short History of The English People; also, The Larger History.

Green, Samuel A.: Three Military Diaries.

Green, Samuel Swett: The Scotch-Irish in America.

Hanna, Charles A.: The Scotch-Irish, or The Scot in North Britain, North Ireland and North America.

Hayward, John: The New England Gazeteer, 1839.

Hetherington, W. M.: History of The Church of Scotland, 1844.

Holland, J. G.: The History of Western Massachusetts, 2 vols.

Hopkinton: Original records of Church and Town; Manual of First Congregational Church, 1881; Vital Records; Century Sermon by Rev. Nathaniel Howe, 1815.

Holyoke Folio: U. S. Geological Survey, Charles D. Walcott, Director. 1898. (Now out of print.)

Hume, David A.: History of England.

Jenkins, Stephen: The Old Boston Post Road.

Johnson, Edward: Wonder-working Providence of Zion's Saviour in New England.

Johnston, W. and A. K., Ltd., Edinburgh and London: The Scottish Clans and Their Tartans.

Keep, John: Historical Discourse delivered at Blandford, Mass., March 20, 1821; Manuscript notes on the same.

Larned, J. N.: History for Ready Reference, original edition.

Lincoln, Waldo: Genealogy of The Waldo Family, 2 vols.

Lincoln, William: History of Worcester, Mass.

Linehan, John E.: The Irish Scots and The "Scotch-Irish."

Macaulay, Thomas Babington: History of England.

Mann, Albert W.: Walks and Talks About Historic Boston.

Massachusetts Archives, State House, Boston: Soldiers of The French and Indian Wars.

Massachusetts Bay Province: Acts and Resolves—Provincial Records.

Massachusetts Historical Society: Proceedings.

Mather, Cotton: Magnalia.

McLean, J. P.: An Historical Account of The Scotch Highlanders in America.

Melville, Herman: Moby Dick; quoted in The Foreword.

New England Historical and Genealogical Record.

Old South Leaflets.

Osgood, Herbert L.: The American Colonies in the Seventeenth Century.

Palfrey, John Gorham: Compendious History of New England.

Parker,   History of Londonderry, N. H.

Parmenter, C. O.: History of Pelham, Mass.

Perry, Arthur Latham: The Scotch-Irish in New England (in his Miscellanies). Origins in Williamstown, Mass.

Porter, Noah: The New England Meeting House.

Ramsay, Dean: Reminiscences of Scottish Life and Character.

Rawson, Marion Nicoll: Candle Days.

Reid, James Seaton: History of the Presbyterian Church in Ireland, 3 vols. A monumental work, very scholarly and very minute; long out of print. My best apology for the extensive use I have made of this treatise in the text is (1) its intrinsic value, (2) its inaccessibility, and (3) the fact that the historian Macaulay used it as a valued source.

Registries of Deeds: (1) Suffolk County, Boston; (2) Middlesex County, Cambridge; (3) Old Hampshire County, Springfield; (4) Worcester County, Worcester.

Registry of Probate: Northampton. All wills and inventories of early Blandford citizens were filed and probated here.

Registry of Court of Sessions: Northampton (for county highways, etc. of old Hampshire County).

Shelton, Jane deForest: The Salt-Box House.

Sinnett, C. N.: Sinnett Genealogy.

Sprague's Annals of The American Pulpit, Vol. III.

Stowe, Harriet Beecher: Old Town Folks.

Temple, J. H.: History of the Town of Palmer, Mass.; History of North Brookfield, Mass.

Vital Statistics: Towns of Brookfield, Framingham, Hopkinton, Worcester.

Weeden, William B.: Economic and Social History of New England.

Willis, William: Scotch-Irish Immigrations to Maine, and A Summary History of Presbyterianism (in Collections of The Maine Historical Society, Vol. VI.).

Wood, Sumner Gilbert: The Taverns and Turnpikes of Blandford, 1733-1833; Articles contributed to The Magazine of History.

Wood, William: Description of Massachusetts (in Young's Chronicles of the Colony of Massachusetts Bay).

Wood, William S.: Descendants of The Brothers Jeremiah and John Wood.

Wright, Richardson: Hawkers and Walkers In Early America.

INDEX OF NAMES IN APPENDIX I

(Seven-Years War Soldiers)

Note: Indexes do not include any material from the genealogical tables.

INDEX OF PERSONAL NAMES

INDEX OF PLACES

INDEX OF SUBJECTS

ERRATA

Page 8, footnote: Pen sketches by Mrs. Wood should be Nos. 2, 9, 10, 17, 20.

Page 276, top line: "villages" should be "villagers."